Timing the Market

Timing the Market

*How to Profit in
the Stock Market
Using the Yield Curve,
Technical Analysis, and
Cultural Indicators*

DEBORAH J. WEIR

WILEY

John Wiley & Sons, Inc.

Published by John Wiley & Sons, Inc., Hoboken, New Jersey.
Published simultaneously in Canada.

For general information on our other products and services or for technical support, please contact our Customer Care Department within the United States at (800) 762-2974, outside the United States at (317) 572-3993 or fax (317) 572-4002.

Wiley also publishes its books in a variety of electronic formats. Some content that appears in print may not be available in electronic books. For more information about Wiley products, visit our web site at www.wiley.com.

Library of Congress Cataloging-in-Publication Data:

Weir, Deborah J.
    Timing the market : how to profit in the stock market using the yield curve, technical analysis, and cultural indicators / Deborah J. Weir.
        p.   cm.—(Wiley trading series)
Includes bibliographical references and index.
ISBN-13: 978-0-471-70898-8 (cloth : alk. paper)
ISBN-10: 0-471-70898-4 (cloth : alk. paper)
    1. Investment analysis.   2. Speculation.   3. Stock price forecasting.   I.
Title. II. Series.
HG4529.W454 2005
332.6—dc22

                                                                2005012275

Printed in the United States of America.

10 9 8 7 6 5 4 3 2 1

To my husband, the last Renaissance man, for his loving support

Michael B. Weir, LLB and USMC, Retired

Contents

Acknowledgments   xi

Introduction   xiii

PART I   Yield Curve Analysis   1

CHAPTER 1   Demystifying the Investment World   3

CHAPTER 2   Back of the Envelope Forecast Model   10

CHAPTER 3   Money Markets Matter   32

CHAPTER 4   Long-Term Bonds Give Advance Warning   41

CHAPTER 5   Expected Returns for the Stock Market   51

CHAPTER 6   Bond Quality Spreads   60

CHAPTER 7   Federal Funds Rates   69

CHAPTER 8   Summary of Yield Curve Analysis   84

PART II   Technical Analysis   95

CHAPTER 9   Market Breadth: Advancing Issues
              in the Dow   98

CHAPTER 10   The Volatility Index   107

CHAPTER 11   The Put/Call Ratio   113

CHAPTER 12   Moving Averages   121

CHAPTER 13   Using Moving Averages: The MACD Line   130

CHAPTER 14 **Leverage: Short Positions and Margin Debt** **139**

CHAPTER 15 **Summary of Technical Analysis** **146**

PART III   **Cultural Indicators**   **157**

CHAPTER 16 **Changing Standards of Feminine Beauty** **159**

CHAPTER 17 **Demographics** **169**

CHAPTER 18 **Corporate Spending** **182**

CHAPTER 19 **War and Rumors of War** **197**

CHAPTER 20 **Summary of Cultural Indicators** **217**

PART IV   **Choosing Investments**   **231**

CHAPTER 21 **Asset Classes** **233**

CHAPTER 22 **Mutual Funds** **246**

CHAPTER 23 **Exchange-Traded Funds** **258**

CHAPTER 24 **Security Selection** **265**

CHAPTER 25 **Final Summary** **280**

PART V   **Capitalism at Work**   **293**

CHAPTER 26 **Outrageous Wall Street Stories** **294**

CHAPTER 27 **America! America! God Shed His Grace on Thee** **310**

APPENDIXES   **321**

2.1	Yield Curves and the S&P 500 Index, 1960–2004	322
2.2	Chapter 2 Return Calculations	334
3.1	U.S. Treasury Bill Spreads, 1960–2004	335

3.2	Chapter 3 Return Calculations	347
6.1	Speculative Bond Spreads (Ba1 and Lower Rated), 1991–2003	348
7.1	Federal Funds Rates during 1987, 1998, 2001 Bear Markets	351
7.2	Chapter 7 Return Calculations	353
8.1	Ten-Year Note Total Return Index, 1960–2004	354
9.1	All 30 Dow Industrial Stocks Fell on July 19, 2002	355
9.2	Chapter 9 Return Calculations	356
16.1	Playmate of the Year, S&P 500 Index, and the Russell 2000 Index, 1960–2000	357
16.2	Monthly Playmates and the S&P 500 Index, 1982–2004	358
19.1	Gross Domestic Product and War, 1800–2004	361
19.2	S&P 500 Index and War, 1800–2004	367
19.3	War in Iraq and the S&P 500 Index, 1990–1991	369
19.4	War in Iraq and the S&P 500 Index, 2002–2003	370
19.5	Chapter 19 Return Calculations, 1960–2002	371
20.1	Part Three Return Calculations, 1960–2005	372
21.1	Changes in Housing Prices, 1970–2004	373
21.2	Returns Including Treasury Bills, 1960–2004	374
21.3	Year-End Prices of Gold, 1800–2004	375
21.4	Returns Including Gold, 1974–2004	377
21.5	Euro Exchange Rates and U.S. Business Cycles, 1969–2004	378
23.1	Gold and Nasdaq Return Calculations, 1974–2004	379
23.2	Nasdaq Composite, 1984–2005	380
24.1	Nasdaq and Centex Return Calculations, 1990–2005	382
24.2	Nasdaq and Placer Dome Return Calculations, 1990–2005	389
Sources and Suggested Reading		**397**
Index		**401**
About the Author		**413**

Acknowledgments

With grateful appreciation to Professor of Finance Bernard Schumacher, CFA, Post University, and Professor of Psychology Robert W. Jaynes, Lakeland College for their peer review and excellent suggestions; the credit for this book is theirs . . . any errors are mine.

With special thanks to: Erkin Y. Sahinoz, economic analyst and research team coordinator Federal Reserve Bank of Cleveland; Lyn Harmon, Ph.D.; Ann Caron, Ph.D.; Joyce French, Ph.D.; Miriam Lewin, Ph.D.; Marie Amoruso, Ed.D.; Rev. Anita Keire; Sandra Berris; Joanne Dearcopp; Marie Schwartz; Bette Willis; Isabel Maddux; Jonathan A. Jaynes; Peter H. Jaynes, Ph.D.; Gabriel Baracat, Ph.D.; Richard Fulljames, CFA, FSA; Gregory M. Hryb, CFA; Cynthia Giglio, CFA; Charles Baker, CFA; Morris Markovitz; Merry Sheils; Caitlin H. McConoughey; and Michael Stinchcomb.

Additional thanks to: Kim Witherspoon, partner, InkWell Management; Alexis Hurley, agent, InkWell Management; Kevin Commins, editor, John Wiley & Sons, Inc.

Introduction

The best way to profit in the stock market is to identify its absolute tops and bottoms and then have the courage to trade them. *Timing the Market* shows you how to come very close to accomplishing that goal.

Timing the Market is for investors who want to increase their returns and reduce their stress while making profits in the stock market. Investors of all experience levels can use public information and simple arithmetic to achieve this end. Private investors with very little time to devote to their portfolios will find that this guide simplifies their lives. Active traders with more time to devote to their investments can apply leverage to the concepts in this book. Professional investors can use the principles in the following pages to cut through their information overload and identify the most important issues. *Timing the Market* addresses all investors' needs by starting with the broadest, most critical issues and systematically working down to individual security selection.

If you do not have a large computer filled with scrubbed data and an experienced staff of Ph.D.'s, or if you *do* but would like to speak intelligently in their absence, you will depend on this book. Many of the graphs in *Timing the Market* display two centuries of economic, social, and stock market data, some of which is reprinted in the appendixes together with web sites for the source material.

This compilation of Wall Street practices has never been written before. Professional money managers and street-smart investors around the world pass this intelligence along an underground network of friends, families, and clients. Their insights are too valuable to be handed down like tribal war stories around a campfire; someone had to write them down in an organized manner with illustrations and anecdotes.

That someone had to be one of the few former schoolteachers with experience on Wall Street. Elementary school teachers are used to breaking a process down into simple steps and then explaining it with stories. Teachers who believe a subject is important want to motivate the audience to a better understanding of its critical concepts. We clarify with parables and pictures and then make sure that our listeners have the tools (in your case they will be newspapers, books, and web sites) to accomplish the task. Your task is to improve your investing, and you will succeed because you are more motivated than any classroom of children that I ever taught.

When my family moved from the Midwest to New York City, I went to a different classroom. But this time I sat in the back instead of at the teacher's desk up front.

The siren call of Wall Street enticed me to New York University for a master's degree in business administration, and this is the book that I wish I had in graduate school. I would have read it twice: once at the beginning of the program and again at the end of my study.

At the beginning of the MBA program *Timing the Market* would have given me the background I needed to understand the lectures. It would have provided some terminology, stock market history, and concepts upon which to build financial theory. It would have provided the bridge I needed from my nonbusiness background.

At the end of my graduate work in finance I needed *Timing the Market* to translate Wall Street theory into practice. This book would have prepared me for some of the jargon on the trading floor and in the boardroom. It would have given me simple arithmetic for making investment decisions and meeting with clients. It would have provided some of the benchmarks and signals that allow a professional to find the forest among all those trees. *Timing the Market* would have drawn a map through that forest and made me a much more productive employee.

Timing the Market grew out of a list of investing criteria that I have used over the years. Organizing these ideas for my own use turned into this book. These market timing benchmarks are common Wall Street practices that never made it into a book until now. Here is the conventional wisdom that is exchanged around the watercooler in successful brokerage firms and money management offices around the world.

These investment insights come in three forms, and each one has its own section in *Timing the Market*. There is a summary after each part of the book for experienced investors with sufficient background to skip the explanations and go straight to the conclusions.

Part One is yield curve analysis and is the backbone of this book. The Federal Reserve Bank of Cleveland uses the shape of the Treasury yield curve to help it forecast the economy. Millions of investors use the yield curve to forecast the stock market, and it is one of the most powerful and most widely used indicators in existence.

Part Two, technical analysis, measures the levels of investors' fear and greed. This application of behavioral psychology builds on Freud's observations of crowd mentality. It simplifies technical analysis down to a few benchmarks for assessing the crowd's emotions. We can then profit from the effects of mob psychology.

Part Three, cultural indicators, analyzes the economy and the stock market for people who think with their right brain to avoid math at all costs. The world is full of intuitive investors who know how to read their environment, and economists often include anecdotal evidence in their thinking.

Whether we realize it or not, we probably draw from all three forms of insight when we make major investment decisions.

The first three parts of the book develop the purchase and sale decisions on the graph in Figure I.1 in a manner that enables readers to continue on their own as independent investors.

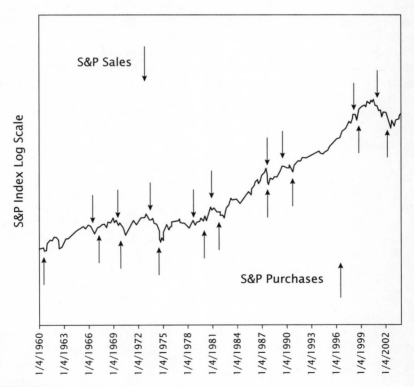

S&P 500 Index: 1960–2005

FIGURE I.1 Final Graph

Part Four applies the stock market timing decisions to specific investments. You can use index mutual funds or separate securities with leverage depending on how much homework you want to do and how aggressive you are.

Leverage, of course, adds risk to markets that are already volatile, and past performance is not necessarily an indication of the future. Every effort has been made to ensure accuracy in this book but there can be no guarantees.

Part Five illustrates capitalism at work. Mankind has tried to improve his financial and social position by trading the markets ever since history has written down stories. Some of these tales tell how people have been seduced by outrageous investments, and some tell of spectacular achievements. The final two chapters present some of the most audacious, as well as some of the most charming, stories of the opportunities available to us who live in a capitalistic economy.

Your financial security requires that you learn how to profit from timing the stock market. You are the only person who can protect your portfolio and make it grow. It is critical that you make the volatility in the market work *for* you. If you lost money when the bubble burst in 2000, you need to get that money back. The only way to recoup your loss is to time the next big market moves correctly. If you have dreams for the future that require a large portfolio, you need to profit from buying and selling at the right time. The next market moves may be extraordinary and could affect the global economy.

You need the ability to build your own fortune and create your own destiny.

PART I

Yield Curve Analysis

Charles got married just as the stock market peaked in 2000. Since Sally owned her own home, he moved in with her and let his house stand vacant. His friends ridiculed him for not selling or even renting the property and investing in growth stocks. His new father-in-law named his house The Escape Hatch.

Charles ignored their teasing for a couple of years. Then he watched his friends try to rebuild their portfolios after the stock market crashed. He watched them take second jobs so they could save. While they moved into small condos to cut their living expenses, his house doubled in value. Charles sold his house near the top of the real estate market and put the proceeds into depressed stocks. The S&P 500 index was still lower than it was the day he got married.

Charles almost seemed to have a road map to the investment world. Most people would like to have such a guide. You need to know whether the economy is expanding or contracting and when the stock market is getting ready for a major change in direction. It would also be valuable to know when to buy or sell real estate, start a new company, or stay in a secure job. All of your major life decisions are easier and more productive if you know where we are in the economic and investment cycles. In particular, you need to know when to buy or sell the stock market.

We will develop a road map with these investment decisions since 1960 (see Figure P.1). We will see why this map, which is based on yield curve analysis, technical analysis, and cultural indicators, works so well. Each chapter is a complete discussion of a separate tool so that you can read as much or as little of this book as you want and still improve your investing skills. The web sites in each chapter enable you to find the

S&P 500 Index: 1960–2005

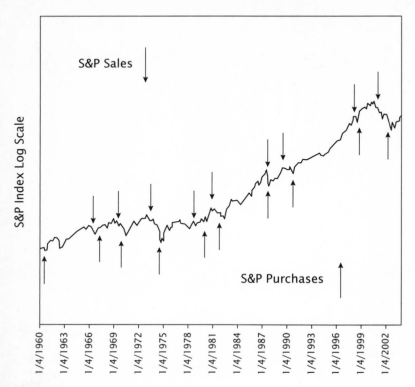

FIGURE P.1   Final Graph

data you need to forecast the economy and the stock market on your own. You will be completely independent when you finish reading *Timing the Market*.

You will acquire such a firm understanding of the markets that you will have the same courage of your convictions as Charles did when he kept his Escape Hatch until it doubled in value.

First, let us demystify the investment world by looking at some curves.

CHAPTER 1

Demystifying the Investment World

The investment map that we will develop in this book works so well because it is rooted in fundamental economics. These fundamentals will be our first screen for identifying the major tops and bottoms in the stock market.

We need to start with two major facets of economics: the supply-demand trade-off, and interest rates. These two subjects come together in that snapshot of U.S. Treasury securities prices called the yield curve. This curve tells us what investors think, and it will demystify the investment world for us.

Fundamental economics, or the study of supply and demand, works because people bid prices up or down according to the supply of goods and services. The inverse relationship between price and supply drives everything from the price of apples to the price of stocks and is particularly important in the bond market.

SUPPLY AND DEMAND

To use a simple example, if people buy a lot of apples, farmers raise their prices to allocate their scarce supply of the fruit. As apple prices increase, so do farmers' profits and earnings. Wall Street likes earnings, so investors bid up the prices of farm stocks. Apple farmers like earnings, too, so they plant apple trees from fence post to fence post.

The following year there are more apples than anyone can eat and they rot on supermarket shelves, which causes apple prices to decline.

Investors translate rotting apples into declining earnings for farmers, so they sell farm stocks. The farmers need fewer bushel baskets, and the basket makers suffer. Soon the whole economy declines into a recession, which causes investors to sell even more stocks.

Apples were expensive when they were scarce; but their price declined when there were too many of them. There is an inverse relationship between price and supply. The other thing that happened when there were too many apples was that we could not use all of them and the apple business slowed down. Investors watching these prices anticipated the recession by selling stocks in apple farms.

Investors buy stocks that they think will have increasing earnings. When investors expect a recession in the near future, they expect earnings to decline and they sell stocks. Conversely, they buy stocks when they expect a strong economy.

Similarly, the price of money, or interest rates, reflects the supply and demand for money. Since everyone uses money, interest rates are important to all of us and can affect the strength of the economy.

IMPORTANCE OF INTEREST RATES

Interest rates determine how much a business can borrow. When rates are low, it can borrow a lot of money and expand its operations. However, when rates are high, it must cut back on production and may even have to fire some of the staff. The economy declines into a recession. Recessions depress the earnings that motivate investors, so they sell stocks when they see an economic slowdown coming.

The level of interest rates affects everyone. Companies borrow money every day to pay salaries, buy supplies for their manufacturing processes, and keep the lights turned on in their stores. If interest rates are low, they can pass these savings on to their customers; otherwise, they have to raise their prices to cover these costs. Not only do we consumers have to pay inflated prices, but the interest rates on our credit cards, student loans, and margin accounts with our stockbrokers also go up.

Mortgage rates are probably the largest influence on our economy. Low mortgage rates allow more people to buy homes and all the furnishings, lawn mowers, and kiddy pools that go with them. New homeowners keep factories humming. Of course, high mortgage rates cause people to keep renting small apartments without room to accumulate manufactured goods. They don't want to paint and repair the landlord's property; and they certainly don't want to upgrade the mechanics or smart-wire for technology. Interest rates, especially mortgages, are one of the major determinants of the strength of our economy.

Because interest rates have such a large impact on the economy, they change direction before the economy does. Investors understand this relationship. They also know the importance of the economy on the stock market, so they use interest rates to forecast major changes in the direction of the stock market.

Interest-bearing loans trade in the marketplace like any other item with economic value. While their prices change according to supply and demand, the underlying contracts continue to specify the required interest rates and payment dates. We use the term *yield* to take all of these variables into consideration and calculate what an investor actually earns given the price he or she paid for the security.

Yields on government securities are particularly important. A graph of them, from the shortest maturity dates to the longest dates, is called the Treasury yield curve. Investors use this yield curve as one of their primary tools for anticipating directional changes in the economy and the stock market.

THE SHAPE OF THE YIELD CURVE IS KEY

The shape of the U.S. Treasury yield curve is the key to our road map because it tells us what investors think will happen to both the economy and the stock market.

As you know, the yield curve is a graph of each Treasury security, from 30-day bills to 30-year bonds, and the return for each investment (see Figure 1.1). You may expect to get an annual rate of 3 percent, for example, if you lend the government your money for 30 days and 6 percent if you lend the money for 30 years. Beyond the intuitive fairness of this arrangement, there are sound economic principles at work.

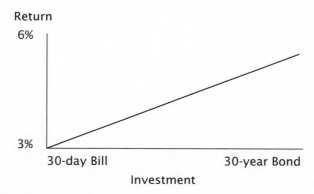

FIGURE 1.1 Basic Yield Curve

Suppose that you want to buy a new Porsche. You can save for it faster by investing in U.S. Treasury securities than you can in your savings account at your local bank. All you have to do is figure out which Treasury security to buy.

You'd like to have your investment earn as much as possible, so you first consider buying a 30-year bond. You will probably reject that option very quickly in favor of alternatives. First of all, you don't want to wait that long to buy your new Porsche. Second, a lot can happen in 30 years. While you expect the U.S. government to be able to repay your loan, the price of your car could go up. If you lend your money for a long period of time, you want to be compensated very well for the risk that prices may increase in the interim.

The other thing that could go up is interest rates. Not only might the price of cars go up, but the price of money may increase. You may prefer to roll over a series of 30-day investments during the time that you save if you think that each one will give you a higher return than the preceding one.

However, if you think that interest rates will *decrease* while you are saving for your car, then you will buy the longer-term security. You will lock in that high interest rate and reinvest those great coupon payments while you save for your car.

How far into the future you lend your money depends on whether you think that interest rates will go up or down during that period of time.

Millions of investors make that decision every day. They decide whether they think interest rates will increase or decrease during the time that they will hold their investment. At the end of the day many newspapers and web sites plot each of those decisions on a graph of the Treasury yield curve.

The yield curve is a picture of all these decisions regarding the future of interest rates. Because these decisions imply a forecast of future interest rates, the yield curve is also a picture of this interest rate forecast. Bond market investors give us a picture of their expectations for future interest rates in a yield curve.

NORMAL YIELD CURVE

For example, the yield curve shown in Figure 1.2 from May 1980 is a typical curve with a normal shape. If you lent your money to the U.S. government for three months, you got a yield of eight percent. You received 10 percent for a 10-year note and 10.5 percent for a 30-year bond. The longer you let the government have your money, the more interest you earned.

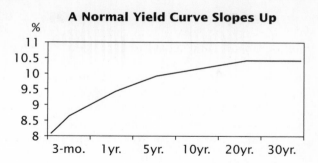

FIGURE 1.2 Normal Yield Curve

There is an inverse relationship between price and yield in the bond market. As with most things we buy, the more you pay for anything, the lower return you can get. You know better than to spend a million dollars on a house in a bad neighborhood because you may lose money on it when you sell it. You understand intuitively that the more you pay for something the less your return will be.

That is most apparent in the bond market because each investment has a stated return, or yield, printed right on the face of the contract. Bond investors are particularly aware of the inverse relationship between price and yield.

On this graph, people preferred to keep their money in short-term investments. They bought so many three-month Treasury bills that the price was high enough to drive the yield down to 8 percent. One reason for their behavior was that they assumed that each time their bills matured, they could buy more bills at a higher rate of return. They expected to be able to replace each maturing bill with another one with a better interest rate. This graph angles upward because investors thought that interest rates would go up in the future.

INVERTED YIELD CURVE

However, sometimes the shape of the yield curve is *not* normal; it's inverted. Figure 1.3 shows that investors had a different view of the market in August 2000. Notice that the highest return was on the shortest investment. Who in his right mind would accept a lower return for 30 years than for 30 days?

Someone who expected interest rates to decline might do so.

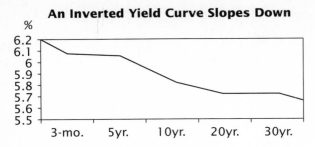

FIGURE 1.3 Inverted Yield Curve

Someone who wanted to lock in what he thought was a good rate on a 30-year bond and who thought that the price of money would decline along with the level of economic activity; someone who saw a recession coming, was selling stocks, and wanted to protect his profits with bonds; someone who thought that money market funds would have a lower return next month and wanted to protect his income stream by owning long-term bonds might accept that lower rate.

Someone who expected bond prices to increase while yields decreased and, therefore, expected bonds to outperform other asset classes.

Who was that "someone" in 2000? One of the biggest players who was driving up the prices of long-term bonds and forcing yields to decline was the U.S. Treasury. The Treasury announced a program to shorten the average maturity of its debt, so it initiated a program to buy back 30-year bonds. It bought so many that the yield dropped below everything else on the curve.

Some people noticed the inverted yield curve and protected themselves from the coming recession and stock market decline. Charles was one of those people.

THE YIELD CURVE PREDICTS

This book has applications beyond Charles and the U.S. Treasury.

Economists consider the yield curve to be a useful tool for predicting the business cycle and the stock market in most industrialized countries. There is a growing body of knowledge, notably the work of Fabio Maneta, suggesting that the yield curve also predicts economic cycles in the euro zone. Investors take his work one step further and use the shape of the yield curve to predict the direction of stock markets in that part of the world. You can download his work from the Social Science Research Network web site at: http://ssrn.com/abstract=487474.

The Chartered Financial Analysts Institute web site at www.cfainstitute .org is an excellent source of scholarly research on all yield curve analysis.

SUMMARY

The investment map that we will develop is based on the fundamental economics of supply and demand. Prices allocate scarce supplies of everything from apples to U.S. Treasury bonds. Higher prices mean lower returns, or yields, on all our purchases whether they are houses, apples, or bonds.

The yields of all Treasury securities from short-term bills to long-term bonds are reflected on the graph called the yield curve. Investors know that the shape of this curve forecasts the direction of both the economy and the stock market in most industrialized nations. A normal, upward-sloping curve suggests a strong economy and stock market, while a negative, downward-sloping curve indicates a coming recession and a bear market.

The shape of the yield curve, or yield curve analysis, and its ability to forecast the stock market is one of the trade secrets that professional money managers discuss around the watercooler.

You deserve to have that secret, too.

CHAPTER 2

Back of the Envelope Forecast Model

Not everyone read the yield curve as well as Charles did during the 2000 stock market peak. Some people rationalized away the bad news in the shape of the curve by saying that there really was no recession coming; it was just the government buying back some of its own bonds.

They were wrong on two counts.

First, the U.S. government is big enough to move markets. Calling the U.S. Treasury "just the government" is really trying to fight city hall. The Treasury may be the largest participant in the bond market aside from those who are laundering money. If anyone this big thinks that interest rates will decline, we would all be well advised to listen.

Second, the government is the ultimate inside trader. They know what is going to happen to the economy because they are making it happen. In the summer of 1999, the central bank announced that it would slow down the economic system; it then proceeded to take the necessary actions, which we will examine in more detail in later chapters, to cause a recession. A year later, at the time of our graph, their actions had changed the shape of the yield curve. They did what they said they would do and we started down the path toward slower economic growth. Their actions showed up in the downward-sloping, inverted yield curve.

ECONOMIC FORECASTING MODEL

The Federal Reserve believes that there is a direct link between interest rates and the economy. It published the following back-of-the-envelope formula in the mid-1990s so the public could forecast the growth of the economy, or gross domestic product (GDP), one year ahead:

Growth of GDP one year ahead = a function of (Ten-year note yield
minus Three-month bill yield)

The difference between the yield on the 10-year note and the yield on three-month bill, or spread, is believed to forecast the growth of the economy one year in the future. When this spread is positive and the yield curve is normal, the economy is expected to expand by the next year. Conversely, a negative spread from an inverted yield curve points to a recession.

Economists at the Federal Reserve Bank of Cleveland plot the yield curve spread and the growth of the economy in their monthly publication *Economic Trends*. This valuable summary, which sometimes has a hilarious introduction, is available on the bank's web site at www.cleveland fed.org/Research/pubs.htm; click on *Economic Trends*. They "lag" the spread one year so that it will line up on the graph with the economy that it forecasts. The yield curve's forecasting ability is excellent. Almost every time the spread is negative we have a recession within six months to a year; conversely, a positive spread usually indicates a growing economy. When the spread line on this graph dips below zero the economy declines and when it moves above zero the economy expands (see Figure 2.1).

The spread between the 10-year and the three-month investments is generally accepted among economists as a strong and reliable indicator of the economy in one year. Since the economy influences the stock market, we can infer that this same spread also forecasts the stock market. Figure 2.2 shows how the same spread line dips into negative territory about the same time that the stock market peaks. It then moves back into positive space near the bottom of the stock market. This relationship is important, so we will examine each critical date separately later on in this chapter.

Many investors watch the shape of the yield curve and adjust their holdings when this curve changes direction. We will use the terms "buy" and "sell" throughout this book in a general sense because few people make such drastic moves in their portfolio on one day. Hedge fund traders, though, may move this decisively and possibly with borrowed money or other leverage as well. You may want to invest more or less aggressively at different stages in your life depending on your risk tolerance, time, and interest in the markets. "Buy" and "sell" are terms of art in this book; "buy" can mean anything from "ease into the market" to "take out a second mortgage on your house to buy the security today."

Appendix 2.1 at the back of the book shows the data that generated

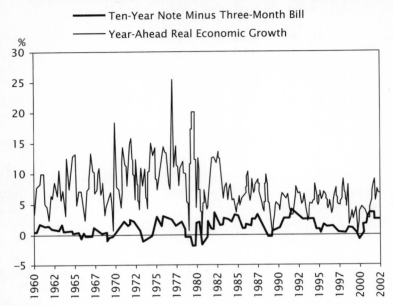

FIGURE 2.1   Economic Growth and Yield Spread

the buy and sell signals in this chapter. The trade dates and related information are in bold type for your convenience.

GRAPH OF TRADES

Before we look at a graph of those trades we need to identify its scale. This graph, and most others in this book, is on a log scale, which illustrates percent changes rather than absolute changes. Using a log scale allows us to see relative changes more easily.

For example, you and your friend are both invested in different stocks. His portfolio is much larger than yours and grew from $1 million to $2 million last year. Your portfolio grew from only $1,000 to $3,000 during that same time. He thinks he is pretty smart until you show him a graph on log scale in which the line depicting your return increases much faster than his.

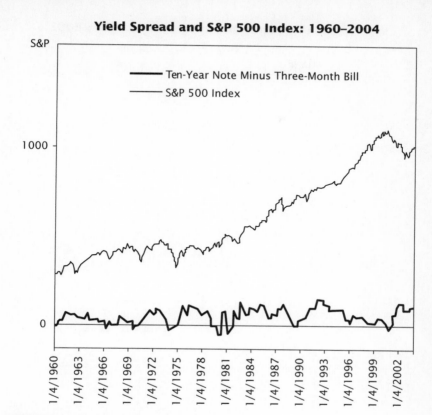

FIGURE 2.2 Yield Spread with S&P 500 Index

Most of the graphs in this book are on a log scale in order to keep size in perspective as our economy grew during the past decades.

Now we can look at a graph of our trades in Figure 2.3.

The dates on the graph are listed in Table 2.1.

You probably noticed that, while each trade was profitable, there is plenty of room for improvement. In some cases, we reentered the market at a higher price than our previous sale, while in others we missed some major moves in the market. Most of our trades will improve with subsequent chapters. The point here is to see if the 10-year, three-month spread forecasts the economy and, therefore, the stock market. By the end of the book we will establish each trade on our graph, which was the "road map" in the Prologue, using various segments of the yield curve as our primary indicators.

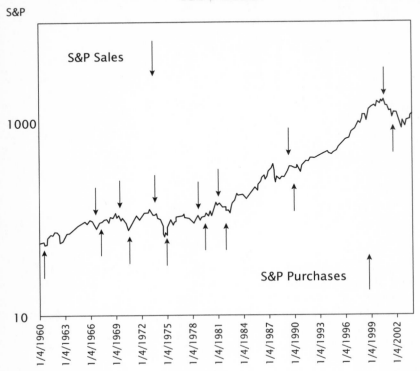

FIGURE 2.3　Trades Indicated by Yield Spreads

WHERE TO FIND DATA

A graph of the Treasury yield curve is available to the general public in many places. You can find it on page C2 in the *Wall Street Journal*. Both of the yields that we use in this chapter, the three-month and the 10-year, are in a box at the bottom of page C1. Be sure to use the column marked "Yield" to get the right number. *Investor's Business Daily* prints the yield curve graph, as does the Bloomberg web site, Bloomberg.com. Although *USA Today* does not print a graph of the yield curve, it does list the yields at the top of page 1. The three-month and 10-year returns that we use in this chapter are easy to find.

StockCharts.com is an entertaining and instructive web site. On the "Dynamic Yield Curves" page (http://stockcharts.com/charts/YieldCurve.html)

TABLE 2.1 Trade Dates

Trade	Date	S&P 500 Index
Buy	January 1960	59
Sell	September 1966	77
Buy	February 1967	86
Sell	July 1969	97
Buy	February 1970	85
Sell	June 1973	105
Buy	October 1974	63
Sell	December 1978	94
Buy	May 1980	106
Sell	November 1980	127
Buy	September 1981	122
Sell	October 1989	340
Buy	January 1990	353
Sell	August 2000	1430
Buy	January 2001	1320

you can find the yield curve that prevailed on any day in the stock market. Ignore StockCharts' definitions of "normal" and "inverted" yield curves. StockCharts does not attach as much importance to the three-month Treasury bill as the Federal Reserve Bank of Cleveland does. The intriguing aspect of this web site is its ability to relate the yield curve to the stock market. If you place the pointer anywhere on the graph of the stock market, it will give you the yield curve on that date.

There is a note under the yield curve that says "Trail Length" and refers to the variation in yields, or price volatility, on that day. Set the "Trail Length" to the extreme left so you will have a thin line that's easy to read. It's fun to set this graph on "Animate" and watch the red indicator move along the stock market graph while the yield curve undulates. You can right click on your mouse and copy these graphs if you want to save them or explore the data. The site gives you detailed instructions for downloading these pictures in different formats.

You can even save these yield curves in a journal you set up on your computer. You can paste in today's yield curve and forecast the economy for the next year and for the S&P in a few days. You may want to revisit your journal when you finish each chapter of this book to see how your projections worked out or to make another forecast.

I constructed most of the following graphs with assistance from Earkin Sahinoz, who is an economic analyst and research team coordinator at the Federal Reserve Bank of Cleveland. He recommended using data from the Federal Reserve's web site. Most of my graphs use monthly averages of "constant maturity" securities that you can download from the Fed's web site: www.federalreserve.gov/releases/h15/data. You will need to click on "All historical data files" to retrieve the historical data on the three-month bill. I used this data just as the site delivers it—on a discount rather than a yield basis—so that you can replicate the results.

Monthly averages, however, fail to capture some vital daily information. The 1990 recession is a prime example of this need to look at daily numbers. An indicator of this recession is noticeably absent from any graph using monthly average yields. Economists have commented on this weakness in the 10-year, three-month spread's forecasting ability since the 1990 recession. Investors, of course, read the daily newspapers and saw the spread turn negative at the end of October 1989. Monthly averages smoothed the data and obscured the fact that the curve was inverted for the rest of that year. The recession started, right on schedule, almost a year later. Daily information provided the detail that investors needed. I used the *Wall Street Journal* to create Figures 2.15 and 2.16 later in the chapter.

BOND RETURNS VARY WIDELY

You may find it interesting to compare the height of various yield curves between 1960 and 2005: they range from over 15 percent down to 4 percent. Consumers, investors, governments, and businesspeople all have found this wide range to be a challenge to their planning efforts.

The longest bond lost half its value and its yield went to 16 percent for a few days in the 1980s. You can imagine the brakes that put on businesspeople trying to borrow to expand their firms! The ensuing double-dip recession, from 1980 to 1981 and again from 1982 to 1984, was the most severe since the Great Depression. Unemployment reached 8 percent and makes subsequent recessions look tame by comparison.

The longest bond became so expensive in 2003 that its yield fell to 4.5 percent, and many interest rates, adjusted for inflation, were negative. Such low rates allowed young people to buy houses but were a disaster for elderly people living on the interest earned by their savings. Young people bought the houses that old people were unable to maintain and were forced to sell.

The other item you will note is the emergence and disappearance of the 30-year bond. The Treasury introduced this bond in the late 1970s because interest rates had fallen and the national debt had mushroomed. The Treasury wanted to borrow as much money as possible at relatively low rates. This was a smart move on the government's part because this particular bond had lost half of its value in the 1980s. The Treasury then retired, or bought back, the bond when its price rose in 2001.

Let us look at what people were thinking at each trade date on our graph. The 1960s saw rapid economic growth, but the 1970s experienced a debilitating combination of inflation and economic stagnation nicknamed "stagflation." Inflation peaked during the 1980s and then almost disappeared in the following decade. The twenty-first century opened with very low rates of inflation. Each scenario influenced our political and social lives as well as our investments.

RAPID GROWTH IN THE SIXTIES

Buy: January 2, 1960

We were facing the second recession in two years; we did not dare hope that we were entering a decade of rapid economic growth . . . but we were.

The 1950s had seen interest rates more than double during the decade. Investors worried that rates would continue to increase during the next 12 months, and their fears show in the shape of the graph (see Figure 2.4); the yield curve goes up from three months to one year. Nevertheless, the 10-year Treasury note has a higher yield than the three-month Treasury bill, so the economy would be ready to start growing again in 12 months. Stock market investors had already discounted the coming recession, so it was time to buy the S&P 500 index again.

Investors had a lot to worry about. Unions were strong enough to impact recessions with their strikes. Fidel Castro brought Communism to our backyard in 1959 when he took over Cuba. Russia had launched the first spacecraft, Sputnik; and we were afraid that our schools were not

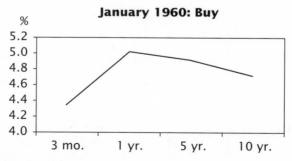

FIGURE 2.4　1960—Buy

producing enough scientists to compete. We had just elected our first Catholic president, John F. Kennedy. We did not know we were headed for Camelot and that interest rates would not be this low again for 45 years.

January 2, 1960: Three-month = 4.35%   Ten-year = 4.72%
Spread = 0.37%   S&P = 59

Sell: September 1, 1966

Investors expected interest rates to rise during the following five years. They were wrong about that; interest rates fell slightly, as Figure 2.5 shows. This graph's negative 10-year, three-month spread does, however, correctly forecast a recession and a bear stock market.

Bigger was better. Conglomerates were the darlings of the stock market as large international companies such as Litton Industries, LTV Corporation, Gulf & Western, and ITT Corporation defined glamour. If they were too complicated to understand, their prices went up even more. As usually happens near the top of the market, investors bought glamour and forgot about earnings. These stocks grew by acquiring other companies, most of which failed to generate any earnings. Someone pointed out that the emperor had no clothes—or rather, earnings—and everything started to unravel.

Mutual funds became popular and bought the conglomerates' stocks. Some of the funds became pyramid schemes that did not have the cash to repay investors who wanted to redeem.

We were in the middle of the go-go era of the 1960s when little white go-go boots dominated women's fashion and named the decade characterized by excess. Excess usually means sell.

September 1, 1966: Three-month = 5.37%   Ten-year = 5.18%
Spread = –0.19%   S&P = 77

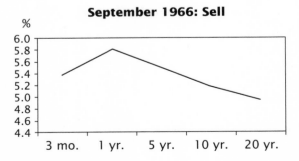

September 1966: Sell

FIGURE 2.5   1966—Sell

Buy: February 1, 1967

A few months later there were bargains in the market. Here is an invitation to buy those bargains if you can see beyond the bump in the five-year area of the graph in Figure 2.6. The 10-year note has a higher yield than the three-month bill, but it's a little hard to see with the five-year in the way. As usual, people expected interest rates to rise for several years, five years in this case, before inflation declined.

Students helped drive stock prices lower as they demonstrated against the establishment. They marched against companies like Dow Chemical for making napalm that was being used to defoliate the jungles in Vietnam. They destroyed automobiles by putting sugar in gas tanks as they carried on their private war against the military-industrial complex.

Sex, drugs, and rock and roll changed our society. It was hard to overcome the gloom and to invest in stocks.

February 1, 1967: Three-month = 4.56%   Ten-year = 4.63%
Spread = 0.07%   S&P = 86

Sell: July 1, 1969

It is easy to see the negative spread between the three-month and the 10-year in Figure 2.7. Clearly, a recession and a poor stock market lay ahead. Notice that interest rates on the one-year Treasury bill are higher than on the three-month bill. This is because investors expected interest rates to rise during the next 12 months and cause the economy to slow even further. The long-term outlook for inflation, however, was good. The low interest rate on the 20-year shows that people expected inflation to decline after the recession.

Once again, glamour replaced earnings as a reason to buy stocks. We bought anything that sounded high-tech such as the soon-to-disappear

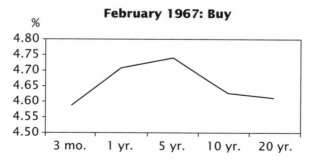

FIGURE 2.6   1967—Buy

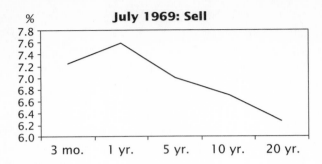

FIGURE 2.7 1969—Sell

Solitron Devices. We bought any stock with an X in it, especially Xerox which used two of them. Digital Equipment went public in 1968 and turned the original investors' 1959 investment of $70,000 into $37 million. This 100 percent annual return inspired a flood of new stocks coming to market. There would not be this many new stock issues for another 30 years.

Mutual funds completed their metamorphosis into Ponzi schemes that could not pay investors who wanted to redeem their shares. Mutual funds were ready to crumble and the stock market was facing 13 years without capital gains.

July 1, 1969: Three-month = 7.20%   Ten-year = 6.72%
Spread = –0.48%   S&P = 97

STAGFLATION IN THE SEVENTIES

Buy: February 1, 1970

The 10-year, three-month spread is normal and predicts an improving economy and stock market. The hump in the middle of the graph reflects investors' expectations that interest rates would increase during the next five years (see Figure 2.8). They were right about that; the 1970s experienced an unpleasant combination of rising prices but little economic growth. The graph dips from the 10-year note to the 20-year bond because investors expected lower inflation in the early 1980s. Investors misjudged the length of time that we would have to endure rapidly increasing inflation.

Penn Central Railroad, lifeblood of the eastern seaboard, filed for bankruptcy. This was the largest bankruptcy the United States had ever

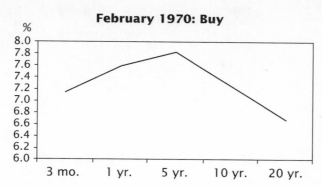

FIGURE 2.8　1970—Buy

seen. Amtrak and Conrail took its place in the transportation network, but nothing could replace the money that investors lost in Penn Central stock.

The mutual fund industry also saw its worst bankruptcy. Bernie Cornfeld, a fund salesman born in Turkey and operating out of Switzerland and Canada, sold worthless mutual fund shares in Investors Overseas Services. The fund's collapse brought down several European and American banks, and stocks of all kinds became bargains.

Investors overcompensated for the fact that our economy was still hamstrung by too many regulated industries (such as trucking, telephone, and electricity); unsustainably high wages for unionized workers; a war; increasing welfare programs; and insufficient research and development for productivity gains.

February 1, 1970: Three-month = 7.13%　Ten-year = 7.24%
Spread = 0.11%　S&P = 85

Sell: June 1, 1973

Figure 2.9 shows another strange shape, yet the 10-year three-month spread is negative. So is the outlook for the economy and the S&P 500 index. Anyone who avoided stocks in 1974 was a hero! Investors expected rates to increase for a year, decrease dramatically in five years, and then go back up again. Investors were right about the last part of that forecast; rates did go up a lot in the late 1970s.

In 1973 we did not know that the Arab countries would punish us for supporting Israel in the Yom Kippur War by withholding their oil from us. Our economy runs on oil from the Middle East, and their embargo would raise our cost of doing business enough to cause a recession in addition to long lines at the gas pumps.

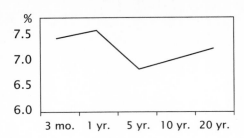

FIGURE 2.9   1973—Sell

Technology stocks, as usual, were glamorous and overpriced. Few people knew what Techtronics made, but we bought the stock anyway.

June 1, 1973: Three-month = 7.19%   Ten-year = 6.90%
Spread = –0.29%   S&P = 105

Buy: October 1, 1974

The three-month, 10-year spread is normal, but the way it wiggles across the page, you wonder if it has any conviction. Traders were scared during the 1974 bear market and thought that rates would increase at the end of the year. The 20-year yield, which angles sharply upward, suggests serious inflation ahead (see Figure 2.10). These inflation expectations were correct, but there was money to be made in the meantime.

The Arab oil embargo drove gasoline prices up 150 percent; the price of a gallon of gas rose to $3.50 in 2005 dollars. Stocks of every company

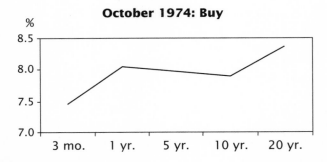

FIGURE 2.10   1974—Buy

that needed oil or gasoline in its business became bargains. Manufacturing and transportation stocks were particularly good values.

Although the Vietnam War ended in 1973, we were left demoralized by its ignoble conclusion. News footage of our poor American troops hanging on the pontoons of helicopters scrambling to escape a country that we had defoliated seared our first military loss into our national consciousness.

Wage and price controls in 1972 had not eased inflation, Richard Nixon left office in disgrace, and the national mood soured. You had to be able to read the yield curve to see any good news.

October 1, 1974: Three-month = 7.46%   Ten-year = 7.90%
Spread = 0.44%   S&P = 63

Sell: December 1, 1978

Do not let the hump in the one-year Treasury bill in Figure 2.11 fool you. The 10-year, three-month spread is negative and so is the outlook for the economy and the stock market. The flat line from the five-year to the end of Figure 2.11 says that investors thought inflation was here to stay. We had given up hope that price increases would return to lower levels and wrote cost of living adjustments (COLAs) into everything from union contracts to alimony payments. The early 1980s saw double-digit interest rates that shaped a whole generation of investors just as surely as the Depression shaped their parents and grandparents.

The three-month Treasury bill paid 9 percent and provided a lucrative alternative to investing in stocks. Sophisticated investors sold stocks and put their money in the bank.

This time the excesses included loans to developing countries such as India and Mexico. Banks would be so embarrassed by these loans that they would create new terminology to erase the experience from their

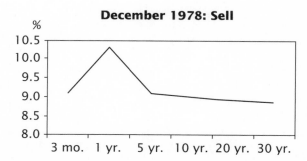

FIGURE 2.11 1978—Sell

books. The next century would call these "emerging markets" and would include Russia and China.

Investors were overly excited by President Jimmy Carter's popular deregulation of energy, transportation, communications, and finance industries that would take many years to bear fruit. Deregulation would lower the cost of making, transporting, and reporting on every product these industries touched. Prices would decline while productivity increased, and there would be more of everything for everyone . . . in a few years. It was too early to celebrate or to buy stocks.

December 1, 1978: Three-month = 9.08%   Ten-year = 9.01%
Spread = –0.07%   S&P = 94

INFLATION IN THE EIGHTIES

Buy: May 1, 1980

Almost every data point on the graph in Figure 2.12 is higher than the previous one, which is as it should be. It is unusual to see interest rates this high, much less this high from three months through 30 years. The tapering off from 20 to 30 years indicates that investors thought that these unusually high interest rates could not go much higher. Once more, they misjudged the seriousness of our inflation that became the hallmark for this decade.

The other unusual development here is, as we will see in later chapters, that investors usually buy bonds rather than stocks when they can get such a high return in the bond market. The only hint that investors had of the strengthening stock market in May 1980 was the shape of the

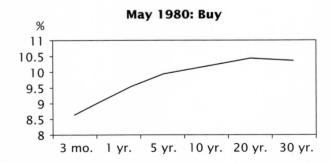

FIGURE 2.12 1980—Buy

yield curve. We still had too many people on welfare, increasing inflation, and too little research and development. President Carter's deregulation, groundbreaking though it was, had not yet changed the
economic landscape.

It was a hard decision to buy stocks unless you knew how to read the
yield curve.

May 1, 1980: Three-month = 8.58%   Ten-year = 10.18%
Spread = 1.60%   S&P = 106

Sell: November 1, 1980

The hump in the one-year Treasury bill in Figure 2.13 indicates that investors expected interest rates to continue to rise during the next year.
People were resigned to inflation in 1980, and the graph says that they
expected bonds to stay at double-digit rates for 20 years. Nevertheless,
people were dismayed to see bonds trading at 16 percent a year later.
Once again, stocks had serious competition from the three-month U.S.
Treasury bill; this time you earned almost 14 percent while you sat out
the stock market in a three-month bill! Mortgages went to 18 percent
and locked a whole generation out of the housing market. Money market mutual funds paid 20 percent and siphoned money out of both
stocks and bonds.

Despite the bad news, investors had faith in our new president, the
Great Communicator. President Ronald Reagan rode into the White House
on a wave of popularity reserved for movie stars. He lived up to our expectations of a hero in a Western by liberating the hostages in Iran. We believed our own PR and it was time to sell.

November 1, 1980: Three-month = 13.73%   Ten-year = 12.68%
Spread = –1.05%   S&P = 127

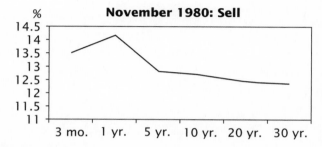

FIGURE 2.13   1980—Sell

Buy: September 1, 1981

Figure 2.14 shows a wildly bullish forecast for the coming year. The 10-year, three-month spread is very wide because investors expected a strong economy and a great stock market in about 12 months. The big bump in the one-year bill and the five-year note suggests that investors feared higher interest rates during that time frame. Their fears soon subsided, as we will see in the next chapter. The lower interest rate on the 30-year bond says that these same investors finally expected inflation to decline over the next few years.

You had been paid handsomely while you sat on the sidelines; the yield on three-month bills had increased to almost 15 percent. Your 11 months in a savings account, money market fund, or Treasury bills gave you an average return of 14 percent during the prior 11 months!

Investors took their money out of the stock market and bought gold and silver. Gold cost $800 an ounce, and the price of silver had risen 400 percent during the previous two years. Almost everything in the stock market was inexpensive and ready to rally. IBM and many other technology stocks were due for a long upswing.

Investors were dizzy from the double-dip recession. Secretive monetary policy confused us to the point that it was hard to make economic or business plans. Many of us thought that double-digit interest rates were permanent. Common advice was to put your money into a loaded gun and a working farm. Seriously. We thought the world as we once knew it had ended. The world did not end.

September 1, 1981: Three-month = 14.70% Ten-year = 15.32%
Spread = 0.62% S&P = 122

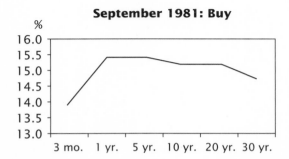

FIGURE 2.14 1981—Buy

Sell: October 31, 1989

Wall Street was in love with itself. This time, glamour was defined by deal makers who were considered kings while anyone who produced real stuff was unimportant. We revered change for its own sake. Conservative savings and loan institutions made high-risk loans that caused about 90 percent of them to disappear.

The Federal Reserve Bank's monthly averages of "constant maturities" failed to predict the 1990 recession because the yield curve inverted too late in October to show up in the monthly average. Investors, however, use daily interest rates and saw graphs similar to the two that follow. The current yield curve is solid while the previous week's line is dashed. Sometimes, as is the case in Figure 2.15, these two lines show a sudden change in outlook on the part of investors.

October 31, 1989: Three-month = 7.99%　Ten-year = 7.90%
Spread = –0.09%　S&P = 340

These curves have strange shapes, but we are looking at just the three-month and the 10-year. The older curve, the dashed line, is normal from three months to 10 years; the later curve, the solid line, shows an 8.05 percent return for three months and just 7.9 percent for 10 years. This inversion clearly forecast the 1990 recession.

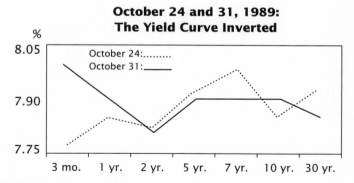

**October 24 and 31, 1989:
The Yield Curve Inverted**

FIGURE 2.15　1989—Sell
Source of data: Wall Street Journal.

DISINFLATION IN THE NINETIES

Buy: January 2, 1990

This time the yield curve changed shape too early in the month to affect the monthly averages provided by the Federal Reserve (see Figure 2.16). The dashed line shows the inverted yield curve on December 26, 1989. The solid line shows a normal yield curve on January 2, 1990.

When the federal government had to buy the foreclosed houses abandoned by the bankrupt savings and loan (S&L) industry, we thought that the housing market would never recover. There were more real estate agents in the country than there were real estate closings, and average prices declined for three years in a row. The housing market did recover, though, as did the stock market. The 1990 recession was fairly short by historical standards; so the yield curve normalized, or sloped upward, just a few months later. The decade of the 1990s broke the back of inflation and produced 10 years of unusual economic expansion.

January 2, 1990: Three-month = 7.63%   Ten-year = 7.93%
Spread = 0.30%   S&P = 353

Once again, the earlier curve is dotted and inverted. The later curve is a solid line and slopes upward. In this case, the change occurred too early in the month to affect the monthly average. You caught this changing shape of the yield curve only by reading the daily newspapers.

Once the excesses in the savings and loan industry were corrected, both the economy and the stock market produced historic growth. It was scary, but it was time to buy stocks.

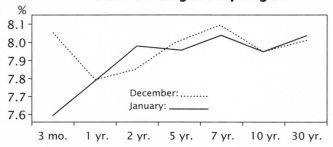

December 26, 1989 – January 2, 1990: The Curve Changed Shape Again

FIGURE 2.16   1990—Buy
Source of data: Wall Street Journal.

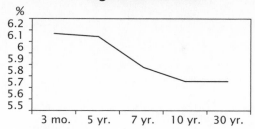

August 2000: Sell

FIGURE 2.17 2000—Sell

DISINFLATION IN THE NEW CENTURY

Sell: August 1, 2000

This downward-sloping curve in Figure 2.17 is a clear signal to sell stocks as a decade of stellar economic growth gave way to disinflation.

Investors thought that the business cycle had been eradicated and that we were in a whole new world. We called it a "paradigm shift" to emphasize the extreme change in the economic environment. We bought stocks in new companies that not only did not have earnings; they did not even have sales! On its first day of trading in 1999, VA Linux Systems' share price increased almost 700 percent even though it had no sales, earnings, or dividends. Investors were dazzled by VA Linux's research on new product development and did not require the company to have actual sales. The S&P declined 40 percent between 2000 and 2002 as investors remembered that old axiom, "Wall Street buys earnings." VA Linux lost its glamour in a few months in 2000 as its price went from $320 to 52 cents.

We had three years of stock market losses in a row. We had not seen a string of losses like that since the 1929 crash.

August 1, 2000: Three-month = 6.09%   Ten-year = 5.83%
Spread = –0.26%   S&P = 1430

Buy: January 1, 2001

The next graph foretells an improving economy and stock market when, in fact, the S&P's losses had just begun. You will not be caught in this situation after you read Chapter 3, which explains the problem with Figure 2.18.

January 1, 2001: Three-month = 5.15%   Ten-year = 5.16%
Spread = 0.01%   S&P = 1320

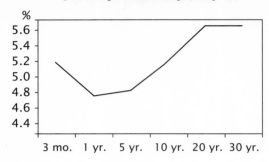

FIGURE 2.18   2001—Buy

SUMMARY

Did our trading improve the traditional method of buying stocks and holding them? Yes, even without counting the double-digit returns in our savings account during the early 1980s or dividends from our stock investments, our active portfolio is almost 25 percent more productive than the passive portfolio. Yield curve analysis added 1.5 percent to the annual returns from 1960 to 2002 (see Figure 2.19).

Improving your portfolio by 1.5 percent may not sound like much, but over the 40 years that people save for retirement it can add almost double your portfolio. We saved ourselves part of the stock market declines associated with each recession; and, more importantly, we avoided buying at the tops and selling at the bottoms of each cycle.

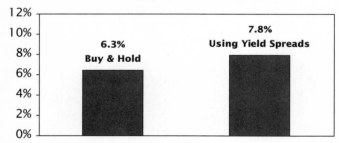

FIGURE 2.19   Return Is 7.8 Percent

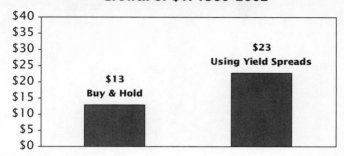

FIGURE 2.20 Portfolio Is $23

Active trading made a big difference to us at the bottom of the stock market because we had protected some of our profits along the way. Figure 2.20 shows how our portfolio looked from January 1, 1960, to the lowest point in the market cycle in October 2002.

Investors who paid attention to short-term securities avoided being sucked back into the stock market too early. The next chapter shows how they accomplished this feat.

CHAPTER 3

Money Markets Matter

" Just tell me whether the market's going up or down!"

It was January 2001, and George had bought technology stocks for his clients in 2000 at the peak of the Internet bubble. He needed those trades to at least break even before his next reporting period ended. He really wanted to hear some good news about the outlook for stocks.

"But the spread between the three-month and the 10-year is positive!" he wailed. He felt entitled to a stock market rally; in fact, his job depended on it. George was looking at our final yield curve graph from the previous chapter (see Figure 3.1):

January 1, 2001: Three-month = 5.15%   Ten-year = 5.16%
Spread = 0.01%   S&P = 1320

January 2001: Buy (Maybe)

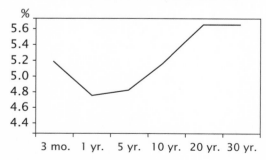

FIGURE 3.1 Too Soon to Buy

The yield curve, however, was *not* normal from three months to one year. Most people do not pay much attention to these very short-term securities because they usually have the smallest return; they do, though, have a large impact on the financial markets, the economy, and your investments. These are money market instruments.

Money market securities mature within one year and include both corporate and government instruments. In fact, every fixed-income security of any length eventually falls into this category as it nears maturity. If you buy a 30-year Treasury bond and sell it after 29 years, your broker executes your trade through the money market rather than the bond-trading desk. We can get useful information about the economy and the stock market from both corporate and government money market instruments.

Some economists pay special attention to yield curves in a segment of the corporate money market, commercial paper.

Commercial paper is an unsecured debt of, or a good-faith loan to, the corporation that matures within 270 days and usually comes in round lots of a million dollars. This paper appeals to large institutions such as mutual funds because, while only the highest-quality firms are able to borrow in this manner, they still must pay more than the U.S. Treasury pays. You probably own more commercial paper than you think because so many banks, insurance companies, and mutual funds buy it for your accounts.

Economists see commercial paper as a window into the issuing firm's order book. The commercial paper yield curve is one place where we may be able to see into the cash flows of the firm.

To oversimplify, let us say that General Electric (GE) does not expect to sell a lot of lightbulbs in the next six months. The company therefore may not pay a high interest rate on short-term commercial paper it issues for fear of attracting money to that part of the yield curve. If the GE treasurer thinks that interest rates will decrease over the next six months, he offers an even lower rate and his yield curve slopes downward even more.

George's problem was that the treasurer at GE saw customers cutting the night shift at their factories and GE's lightbulb order book was drying up. The treasurer thought that interest rates might decline during the next three months as well, so his yield curve sloped steeply downward. GE's yield curve probably inverted like that shown in Figure 3.2, created from historical data on the Federal Reserve Bank of New York's web site at www.federalreserve.gov/releases.

Commercial paper and other money market interest data are in the financial press and on the Internet every day. There is a box entitled "Money Rates" in the *Wall Street Journal* section C, and there is extensive information every day on another page of the Federal Reserve's web site at www.federalreserve.gov/releases/h15/current/.

Cash flow is the lifeblood of any corporation and is one of the few

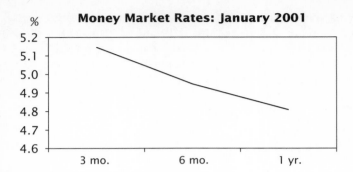

FIGURE 3.2   Inverted Money Market 2001

accounting entries that cannot be manipulated. Here is a chance to take the firm's temperature without the patient biting the thermometer to hide the results.

TREASURY BILLS ARE A BENCHMARK

One of the most important money market securities for our purposes is the U.S. Treasury bill. Bills range in maturity from one day to one year and allow the U.S. Treasury to manage its cash flow. Academics consider the three-month bill to be the risk-free rate because not much can go wrong with the highest-rated borrower, the U.S. Treasury, during the next three months. The Treasury borrows regularly and in significant amounts for three months, thus creating a large pool of bills for academic study.

This risk-free rate is a benchmark for professional money managers as well as academics. For instance, you may have noticed in the previous chapter that when the three-month bill rate went into double digits during the early 1980s, money drained from the stock market. As soon as Treasury bills paid less than 10 percent, managers moved their money back into the stocks and the 1982 bull market began. The three-month Treasury bill is the gold standard for investment returns.

It is critical to let this gold standard and its related money market investments return to normal before buying back into the stock market. Treasury bills are part of the daily interest rate graph on page C2 in the *Wall Street Journal*. You can also find them on the Internet at www .federalreserve.gov/releases/h15/current/, www.econstats.com, and www .bloomberg.com.

Appendix 3.1 for this chapter gives Treasury bill rates with related S&P 500 index prices. You can see that money market yield curves usually assumed a normal, upwardly sloping shape at the same time as the traditional measure: the three-month and the 10-year investments. The decades of the 1960s, 1970s, and 1980s followed this pattern. The following two decades behaved differently and changed the stock market reentry dates to our advantage.

MONEY MARKETS MUST BE NORMAL

Investors with the patience to wait for the Treasury bill yield curve to normalize saved themselves the agony of two long stock market declines during major recessions. In 2001 it took 10 months, during which we had terrorist attacks that shut down the stock market for five days, for the money market curve to normalize. Investors who waited saved themselves about 25 percent when they reentered the stock market. They also had peace of mind as they sat on the sidelines while the September 11 attacks closed the markets. In 1990 it took a solid year for the shortest part of the curve to come into line, and during that year stocks declined in anticipation of the Gulf War.

In 1981 the money market yield curve normalized just two months after the traditional three-year and 10-year spread turned positive. Investors saved only one point in the S&P, so we will ignore 1981 in our analysis.

Here's how our original buy decisions would have changed with the addition of money markets in the graphs.

In 1990, we had a strange-looking graph at the beginning of the year (see Figure 3.3). The relationship between the three-month and the 10-year were normal, but nothing else was. The level of interest rates was rather high for an economic recovery in addition to the unusual shape of

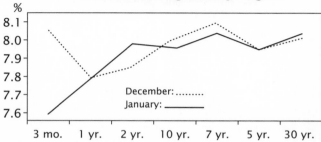

FIGURE 3.3 1990 Too Soon to Buy

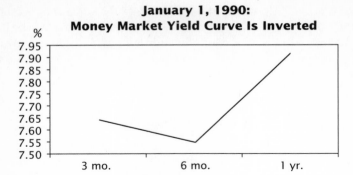

FIGURE 3.4   Inverted Money Market 1990

the curve. Also, as you can see from the Treasury bill rates in Appendix 3.1, the money market was not normal (see Figure 3.4). People expected interest rates and the economy to decline for six more months before returning to normal. That might have happened if the Gulf War hadn't intervened and stimulated the economy.

Buy: January 2, 1991

By the time the money market normalized at the beginning of the next year, the Treasury yield curve, including money market instruments, looked like Figure 3.5.

January 2, 1991: Three-month = 6.22%   Six-month = 6.28%
One-year = 6.64%   S&P = 330

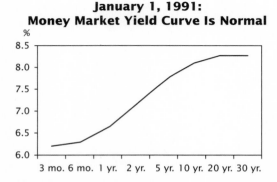

FIGURE 3.5   Normal Money Market 1991

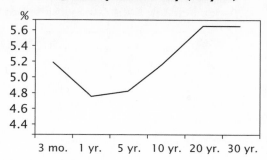

January 2001: Buy (Maybe)

FIGURE 3.6   2000 Too Soon to Buy

The stock market was a little cheaper after the uncertainty surrounding the war lifted, so waiting a year gave us a slightly better price for the S&P 500 index. We earned a 6 percent return on Treasury bills while we waited on the sidelines in the money market.

KEY TO TIMING STOCK PURCHASES

The next recession, in 2001, was very different. The money market yield curve normalized less than a year after the three-month and the 10-year did, and waiting really paid off. Not only did investors buy stocks at a 25 percent lower price, but also they avoided the terrorist attacks on the World Trade Center on September 11 of that year.

Our original graph of 2001 (see Figure 3.6) focused on the three-month and the 10-year rather than the money market; but you probably noticed that it resembled the Little Dipper and had reservations about buying stocks at that time. You were right.

Investors expected the Federal Reserve to reduce interest rates for a year, during which time the economy would gradually position itself for a recovery. Investors became more optimistic about interest rates and the recovery during the next nine months as money market rates gradually normalized, but the terrorist attacks delivered a shock in September. (Economists always qualify their forecasts by saying, "absent any external shocks to the system." Now we know that "external" means someone from another country; "shocks" means that he lands his plane inside a sky-scraper; and "system" means on Wall Street.)

Buy: November 1, 2001

Our financial system proved to be resilient and the entire yield curve was normal by the end of October (see Figure 3.7). At the beginning of November

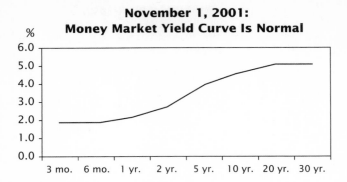

FIGURE 3.7   2001 Better Time to Buy

2001, the yield curve including money market instruments said that investors thought that interest rates had dropped as far as possible. In fact, they anticipated a slight rise each quarter in the future.

November 1, 2001: Three-month = 1.87%   Six-month = 1.88%
One-year = 2.18%   S&P = 1059

It is interesting that the money market curve usually normalizes along with the three-month and the 10-year securities. In the two cases that it did not, however, there was an international incident that led to war while the curve was inverted. It is probably just a coincidence, but it is more than a gentle reminder to investors to watch this curve. If you are journalizing and forecasting as you read this book, this curve is for you.

Our updated road map illustrates how the money market helped us avoid losses while the money market yield curve was inverted (see Figure 3.8).

Buying stocks at lower prices improves our annual return (see Figure 3.9). In fact, the value of our actively managed portfolio is more than double that of the passive portfolio (see Figure 3.10).

SUMMARY

Most people do not pay much attention to the shortest-term securities because they usually have the smallest return. Money market instruments, however, serve two important purposes. They give us a window

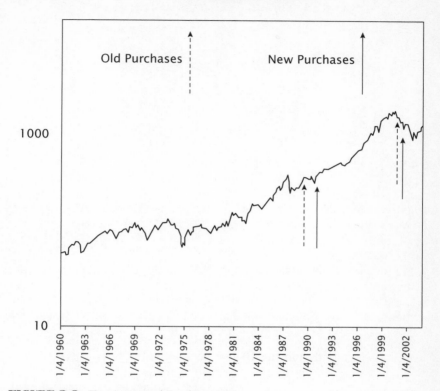

FIGURE 3.8 Two Improved Purchase Dates

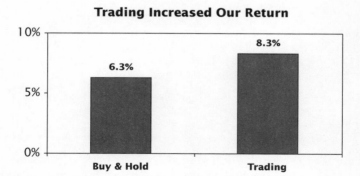

FIGURE 3.9 Return Increased to 8.3 Percent

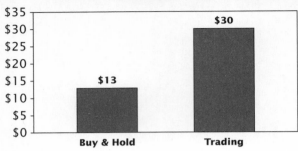

FIGURE 3.10   Portfolio Is $30

into corporate headquarters' order books and provide a benchmark risk-free rate. This benchmark is the gold standard for investment credit: the three-month U.S. Treasury bill. Academicians and investors alike depend on this rate for their analysis.

Money market securities also keep us out of the stock market until it is truly safe to reenter. These interest rates from three months to one year have a large impact on the financial markets, the economy, and your investments. It is not enough to see that the yield curve is normal from three months to 10 years before buying the S&P 500 index; money market interest rates must be normal as well.

Next we will look at long-term interest rates for help in timing the stock market. The bond market, like the military, has a distant early warning (DEW) line. The DEW line in bonds is at the longest end of the yield curve and can help us prepare for the worst kind of market crash.

CHAPTER 4

Long-Term Bonds Give Advance Warning

Margaret Letterman could not pay her mortgage. She did not have anything in her checking account, so she dropped her house key into the payment envelope and mailed *that* in to the bank. The date was August 3, 1987.

Her bank manager knew that he should not have lent money to someone with Margaret's low credit rating, but he was under pressure to play the high-yield game with the big boys. He had joined the thousands of bank and savings and loan managers who lowered their credit standards in the mid-1980s. In addition to lending to people like Margaret, managers were buying so-called junk bonds from Mike Milken so that they, too, could be glamorous deal makers. The price of admission to Mike's annual Predators' Ball was putting his low-quality bonds in their bank or savings and loan portfolios. The party started in 1985 and lasted through the first half of 1987.

The hangover lasted longer than the party.

Some revelers left the party early and got to keep their party favors and goody bags. They also got to keep their reputations, profits, and liberty. How did they know when it was time to go home? Where did they get the courage to withstand being called "chicken" by the cool crowd who partied late into the year?

They had advance warning of trouble in the stock market because they knew how to read the shape of the long-term portion of the Treasury yield curve.

TEN-YEAR NOTE IS PIVOTAL

The spread between the 10-year note and the longest bond is the early warning system in the battle for stock market profits. We will see why this note is critical to our financial system and how to use it to time the stock market.

All Treasury securities—bills (maturing in one year), notes (maturing from one through 10 years), and bonds—reflect investors' expectations for the future of interest rates. The 10-year note is pivotal in these expectations because it separates two very different streams of income that lead to two very different approaches to valuation. Investors understand this intuitively and usually prefer to get their money back sooner rather than later.

The value of maturities shorter than 10 years, the ones we examined in the previous chapters, is primarily determined by the time left to the maturity of these securities. Bills and notes mature so quickly that their value is greatly influenced by the time remaining in their contracts. Securities maturing after 10 years are bonds. Bonds have a different name from the notes and bills we looked at before because their value depends on a different aspect of their contract: their interest payments.

The semiannual interest payments on a 30-year bond are a tidal wave of cash drowning the investor in a reinvestment problem. If interest rates remain high, you amass a very large fortune from reinvesting these interest payments (coupons) by the time you get your principal investment back. If rates decline, you have a painful decision to make every six months *until* you get your principal back. In this case, you have to decide in which low rate you will invest the coupon. Either way, high interest rates or low, coupon payments dominate a bond's cash flow. The reinvestment rate of all these payments, therefore, is more important to long-term investors than to anyone else in the fixed-income market.

Let us say that you bought a long-term bond to save for your child's college education. You chose a bond that would mature while he was in college. You, of course, were smart enough to have a child in November 1981 so you could 20-year buy a U.S. Treasury 15¾ percent bond due on November 15, 2001. You paid $10,000 and you knew that you were going to get your investment back. If you kept this bond until it matured, you would be entitled to 40 semiannual payments of $787.50 each. Those payments would total $31,500 over the 20 years and were more important to you than the $10,000 you would get back when the bond matured.

If you depended on putting those coupon payments in a savings account earning the 15¾ percent that you saw back in 1981, you were sorely disappointed. Interest rates declined immediately after you bought your bond, your savings account grew at an average rate of only 5 percent, and your child went to trade school. (Well, not *your* child. Your child got a scholarship to Yale.) The reinvestment rate is most important to people with the largest income stream from their coupons.

LONG-TERM TREASURY BONDS ARE THE FIRST TO INVERT

As you can see, the longest-maturing bonds have the most at stake in the reinvestment game. Investors in these securities are usually the first to anticipate a decline in reinvestment rates. When they think that current interest rates are unsustainably high, they buy the longest-term bond that they can in order to lock in that high yield. They want to have as much money as possible to invest when the reinvestment rates fall.

The other group that buys long-term bonds when they think that rates are too high is the U.S. Treasury. It does not want to continue to pay those high interest rates, so it "retires" the longest bonds by buying them back. This is a euphemism for saying that they call the bonds, and the first ones they took back were the 15¾ percent bonds that you bought in 1981.

As with any investment, the more that people buy it in the secondary market the more they drive up the price. The yield declines accordingly. The bond market is no different; when prices go up, yields go down.

Just one year after you bought your bond for $10,000 you could have sold it for almost $14,000. So many other people wanted your bond that you had about a 40 percent profit in one year and you made one of the best investments in the history of the bond market. Buyers drove up the price of your bond to $14,000 and caused the return to fall to around 11 percent in just one year. Interest rates in general fell that year and your bond became exceedingly valuable.

Normally, each bond offers a little higher return in exchange for using your money for a longer period of time. When a bond attracts more buyers than normal, its yield becomes lower than normal, and we have the inverted yield curve that we saw in the previous chapters. The yield curve inverts from 10 years to the longest bond when investors anticipate lower interest rates in the distant future. Economists refer to investors' choices along this part of the curve as their long-term outlook for inflation.

Money managers take this analysis one step further and assume that inflation will decrease because of an impending recession that will cause the usual stock market decline.

These managers usually sell stocks soon after the yield curve inverts from the 20-year to the 30-year bond. By the time the inflection point in the yield curve moves in to the 10-year note, money managers have already increased their sales of the S&P 500 index. The stock market decline is often well established by this time. Both of these spreads off the 30-year bond are important signals for professional managers.

The reliability of these two spreads as indicators of the stock market seems to depend on the prevailing level of inflation. During the early 1980s, when inflation was severe, this spread was a poor stock market indicator. Investors expected inflation to fall every year or so, and the inversion in the longer-term Treasuries failed to predict either a recession or a lower stock market.

Again, because there are so many false signals when interest rates are high, we will not add any trades to our graph until later chapters validate this signal with other indicators. For the moment, we will use these two spreads as just a warning to prepare us for the fact that a change may be imminent.

PROBLEM REAL ESTATE LOANS

On August 3, 1987, just as Margaret Letterman mailed her loan officer a house key instead of a check, the yield curve inverted and the stock market decline began three weeks later (see Figure 4.1).

August 3, 1987: Twenty-year = 9.19%   Thirty-year = 9.01%   S&P = 317

By Friday, October 16, even the 10-year was higher than the 30-year bond. The inflection point, at the 20-year, was more pronounced and the stock market was falling fast (see Figure 4.2).

October 16, 1987: Ten-year = 10.24%   Twenty-year = 10.40%
Thirty-year = 10.16%   S&P = 282

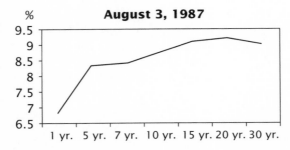

FIGURE 4.1   Margaret Mailed Her Key

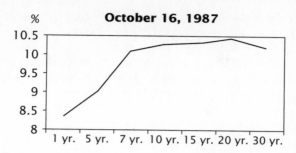

FIGURE 4.2   October 16, 1987

The Dow fell to 2220 and had already lost 17 percent from its August peak; the S&P and the Nasdaq were down almost as much.

Investors watching the fixed-income markets took their chips off the poker table, folded their hands, and left the party that Friday. They left to taunts from the cool guys who stayed through the weekend. Over the weekend a government official hinted that they would change the conditions under which the game is played.

Monday morning, October 19, 1987, was beautiful and sunny but the stock market was neither. It opened lower than the previous close and dropped all day. The Dow lost 500 points for a 25 percent decline in one day; the S&P dropped 20 percent in sympathy.

Stock market investors lost about one-third of their money in the three months from August, when long-term bond yields inverted, to October 19, which became known as Black Monday (see Figure 4.3).

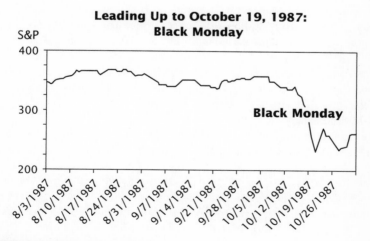

FIGURE 4.3   Black Monday, 1987

Watching the bond market could have prevented that loss. We will re-visit this lead-up to the October crash in later chapters because there were several warning signs from the bond market.

There were two other occasions on which changes in the shape of the long-term part of the yield curve proved significant. One was in 1998 and the other was in 2000, and both were very productive.

INTERNATIONAL PROBLEMS

I was in Japan when the international financial markets started to unravel in 1997. The cold October rain never stopped the whole week I was in Kyoto, and the bad news never stopped, either. Every day I got two newspapers under my hotel room door, and every day another venerable Japanese bank was in the headlines. Each headline screamed the same word, "Failed!"

Japan's trading partners in Southeast Asia soon felt the reverberations. In an area prone to earthquakes, this part of the world experienced an international financial quake. It registered about an 8 out of 10 on the financial Richter scale. Japan had been outsourcing its manufacturing to Taiwan, Korea, and Indonesia, where labor was less expensive. As Japanese banks failed (or as the government propped them up so they wouldn't fail), business slowed. Manufacturers had fewer jobs to export to Southeast Asia, and the recession spread like cleavage in the earth.

European and American investors fled the Pacific economies. In their search for "the next big thing" they descended on Russia.

The Soviet Union abandoned Communism in favor of capitalism in the early 1990s. Americans love change, and this was a big one. Our old nemesis became the new land of opportunity—the new frontier. All we could see were natural resources waiting for extraction and a population waiting for Western goods. We knew that our blue jeans and jazz destroyed Communism as much as their failed five-year plans for the economy. We couldn't wait to feed Russians' desires for our products! It didn't hurt that they had oil that we hoped would liberate us from dependency on the Middle East.

My husband's law firm led the march into Russia as soon as the Berlin Wall came down. It cost the firm "only" a couple of million dollars a year in losses that were projected to extend for "only" a decade or so into the future. (Never mind that Russian currency was worthless and that the Coca-Cola Company had to accept vodka in exchange for Coke.) Americans shared in the pride of this firm's young, photogenic associates featured in the Sunday *New York Times Magazine* while they westernized Moscow.

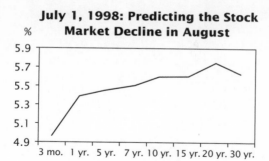

FIGURE 4.4 Predicting the 1998 Decline

Americans threw money at Russia as they bought bonds issued by the new government. One notable investor in these bonds was a hedge fund whose founding partners included two Nobel Prize winners. Long-Term Capital Management (LTCM) not only bought a lot of Russian bonds, but they borrowed so much money to do so that they reportedly had $30 invested for every dollar of their own money. This leverage was fine until the Russian government decided not to pay any more interest on the bonds in the summer of 1998. Long-Term Capital suddenly had a short-term loss that put the fund out of business. The other people who had a problem were those who lent them $30 to invest for each dollar that they actually owned. As usual, the problem spread to investors who were not even connected to the Russian market.

All stock market indexes lost 18 percent between the time of Russia's default in July and LTCM's near failure in August. The other thing that happened on July 1 was that the yield curve inverted and warned us of the coming problem. The curve inverted between the 20-year and the 30-year bonds (see Figure 4.4).

Investors started selling the stock market when they saw that yield curve inversion (see Figure 4.5). Astute investors who watched the yield curve saved themselves about 18 percent of their portfolio along with their pride.

INTERNET PROBLEMS

The 2000 bubble caught many investors by surprise. People thought that the Internet changed the way we live to the extent that there would never be another recession. Naturally, we fell in love with the industry that liberated us, or so we thought, from the business cycle. We judged Internet

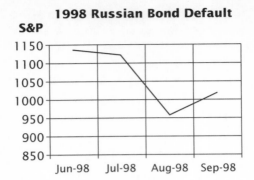

FIGURE 4.5   Default of Russian Bonds, 1998

stocks not by their earnings, because they didn't have any, but by how long people lingered on their web sites. We thought we were entitled to see profits in anything we bought in the stock market.

Friends of mine were having the time of their lives investing in Internet stocks. Every night they counted their profits and dreamed of homes on the Riviera.

They, naturally, wanted to share this excitement with their father, who was in a nursing home, and planned to move his portfolio into the equity market for him (never mind that he was using all of his bond income to pay for this facility). Dad would love to be a multimillionaire and pay his expenses out of capital gains! They were ready to sell Dad's bonds and replace them with stocks in January 2000 when the eldest son noticed that the yield curve had inverted (see Figure 4.6). He got right on the phone and canceled the trades in time to save the family from heartache. The Nasdaq, which is what the family had planned on buying to surprise their father, dropped nearly 80 percent during the next three years (see Figure 4.7).

SUMMARY

The 10-year note is just as important in our financial system as the risk-free investment of three-month Treasury bills.

The 10-year note is pivotal because it separates fixed-income securities into two groups depending on whether they get their return from the passage of time (short-term instruments) or from coupons (long-term in-

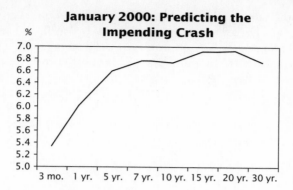

FIGURE 4.6 Prediction in January 2000

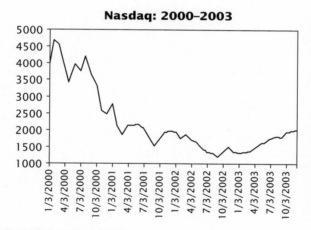

FIGURE 4.7 Nasdaq 2000–2003

vestments). Coupons create so much cash flow for the bondholders that the reinvestment rate is important to them. Bondholders are the first to react to anticipated declines in interest rates, and they protect themselves by locking up the highest yield available. If they have to reinvest at lower rates, they want to do so with the most money possible.

Their purchases depress yields in the longest maturities and cause that part of the curve to invert. The spread between the 10-year note and the longest bond, therefore, may give us an early warning of an impending recession and its accompanying stock market decline.

You may want to include the shape of the yield curve among long-term bonds in your daily analysis and stock market forecasting. These spreads can give you an early warning of major declines in the S&P 500 index.

Combined with the 10 percent rule in the next chapter, these long-term bond yield spreads become absolutely potent.

CHAPTER 5

Expected Returns for the Stock Market

I sat across the desk from one of the largest pension plan managers in New York City as I presented the services of an equity manager. I savored views of the Manhattan skyline through one window of his corner office and watched horse-drawn carriages in Central Park from another.

I had left the Scudder, Stevens & Clark investment counseling firm (now part of Deutsche Bank) and started my own marketing company for specialty, or boutique, investment managers. Eight years of managing institutional fixed-income portfolios had given me the asset allocation skills necessary to select investment managers ahead of changes in the investment cycle. Like any business planner, I had to forecast the economy with enough lead time to develop new products.

So did Bob. He had to make changes in his portfolio before the crowd started buying and removed any chance of a profit. Trading several billion dollars takes lead time, too.

Bob saw dozens of people like me every year because he had a "farm team" that tested new managers before moving them up to a full investment position in the main portfolio. A sliver of Bob's pension trust could turn a fledgling manager into one of the big boys, and this was the first of many due diligence meetings that Bob required to screen new managers.

I was lucky; Bob was in the mood to share his market timing secrets.

Bob exuded the casual charm that comes with money . . . even someone else's money. He rocked back in his thronelike chair as he shared the inside story of how his pension trust had avoided the October 19, 1987, crash known as Black Monday.

"We'd already made 10 percent in the equity portion of our portfolio by the end of March that year; and, since that's all we can expect from the stock market in any one year, we sold some of our stocks. Statistically, we had the whole year's return during those first three months. Of course, we felt a little foolish over the summer when the stock market continued to go up, but by the middle of October we saw a few things that we didn't like so we sold even more.

"As you know, Deb," he continued, using my family's nickname for me to show that he was in a good mood, "the yield curve had been inverted from the 20-year to the 30-year since August. By October, it was inverted from the 10-year note all the way out to the 30-year. Now, we all know that this particular indicator can be a false signal to sell stocks; nevertheless, it always puts me on the alert for trouble."

By this time I was thinking to myself, "You and everybody else who manages money for a living!"

Bob saw my mind wander and jolted me back to attention. "What caused me to pull the trigger in the middle of October was the 10 percent return on the 10-year note. An alarm goes off in my head every time I see that combination."

Now he had my attention; anytime an alarm goes off in a prospect's head, I want to know what makes that clock tick!

Bob proceeded to tell me what makes *him* tick. "If I can get our expected return from the stock market—10 percent—in a nice, safe U.S. Treasury note, that's a no-brainer! Getting our 10 percent expected return on stocks from the safety of a government note suits me just fine!

"And," he added, fairly bursting with enthusiasm for his own portfolio management, "everyone knows that 10 percent interest rates can cause a recession. So we sold on Friday, October 16th, and just missed Black Monday on the 19th!

"Maybe I wasn't the only money manager looking at a 10 percent U.S. government note in an inverted yield curve," he concluded with uncharacteristic modesty.

HOW PROFESSIONALS THINK

Bob knew that most professionals use yield curve analysis and have their "sell" tickets ready when the curve inverts. He also knew that he and his colleagues write large enough tickets to send the stock market into a decline on the day that the 10-year Treasury note reaches 10 percent. While the severity of Black Monday shocked the whole financial community, Bob and his peers were less surprised than most. They knew a lethal combination when they saw one.

That lethal combination included: one U.S. government security at 10 percent, one expected return from the stock market of 10 percent, one recession-inducing interest rate of 10 percent, and institutions' tendency to take profits after the stock market increases 10 percent during the first quarter of any year. Even if Bob had not been astute enough to sell stocks in the spring to protect his stock market gains, his portfolio guidelines might have mandated that he do so.

Bob's counterparts around the country were making similar moves. The state of Maryland's pension plan sold stocks early in October to protect its profits, and the portfolio manager put the proceeds into bonds yielding 10 percent. He was happy to replace stock with bonds at that rate and announced that the fund would use the coupons to pay for their current retirees' benefits. In addition, he needed the fund to cut its stock market exposure back to the level dictated by its guidelines. The New Jersey and Colorado pension trust managers reported similar moves. When that many large institutions need to bring their portfolios back into their required asset allocations, and if they can meet their required portfolio returns with a government-guaranteed note, there is a major impact on both stock and bond markets. We had better learn how these managers meet their required portfolio returns and the benchmarks they use: a 10 percent expected return for stocks, asset allocation guidelines, and the importance of the 10-year note.

PORTFOLIO BENCHMARK RETURN

These managers have a fiduciary responsibility for the assets of their beneficiaries. Pension trusts like Bob's, and also life insurance companies, have a long-term investment horizon. Long-term can mean 10 years to an individual investor, 20 years for a pension plan whose average employee who will work that long, or 30 years for life insurance companies underwriting young families. For example, life insurance companies usually have the longest investment horizon and the most money in our financial system; they are the ones who buy 30-year bonds in sufficient quantities to invert the curve even when there is no recession or stock market decline in the offing. They are just matching their assets to their liabilities when interest rates are higher than normal.

Most pension plans and insurance companies hire actuaries to analyze the demographics of the population covered by the plan and determine the time frame for that particular portfolio. Actuaries then study historical and projected returns on the stock and bond markets to set a required rate of return, or actuarial assumption, for the investments. They start with data such as that represented in Figure 5.1, a graph of the S&P 500 index from 1800 to 2004; the trend line (log scale) illustrates the 5.5

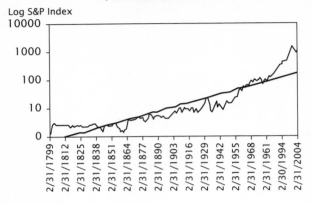

FIGURE 5.1 S&P Returns for 200 Years
Source of data: www.globalfindata.com.

percent growth rate, without dividends, for the period. The data source is Global Financial Data, Inc. at www.globalfindata.com.

Actuaries compare stocks to fixed-income securities for their historical returns. The next graph, Figure 5.2, shows why many portfolios emphasize stocks over bonds or notes. The historical growth of stocks, even without dividends, is superior to that the 10-year note. Again, Global Financial Data at www.globalfindata.com is the source of data for this graph.

You probably noticed that the graph of the stock market shows much

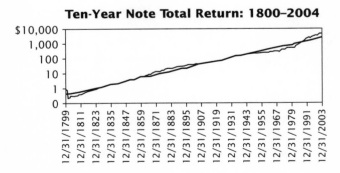

FIGURE 5.2 Ten-Year Note Total Return for 200 Years
Source of data: www.globalfindata.com.

more volatility than that of the 10-year note. Professional managers would prefer to own notes if they could get a competitive return on them.

These managers, however, have another concern. Actuaries give the investment managers a required return for their portfolios. Whenever the managers can buy bonds that yield more than this required return, they can be pretty sure that the retirees will be able to receive their benefits from a portfolio that will suffer less market volatility.

Once in a while there is a sweet spot in the investment environment that allows investment managers to have this best of both worlds.

STOCKS' LONG-TERM EXPECTED RETURN

Professional managers have another benchmark: the expected long-term return for the stock market. Again, if they can exceed this return in the safety of a U.S. Treasury bond, they often do so.

In his landmark book, *Stocks for the Long Run*, Wharton professor Jeremy Siegel found that during nearly two centuries from 1802 to 1998 stocks' average annual returns were a little over 10 percent. His return calculation, unlike ours, includes dividends.

You can make your own estimate of this critical benchmark. You can start with our buy-and-hold return of 6.3 percent for the period from 1960 to 2002 as your benchmark. This return is without dividends. Figure 5.3 uses data from Globalfindata.com and illustrates that the average dividend yield for the 134 years from 1871 to 2004 is just over 4 percent.

For the 42 years that we are looking at, however, the average dividend

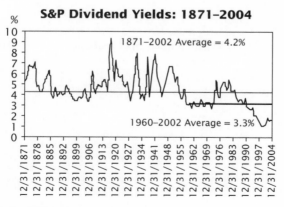

FIGURE 5.3 Dividends for 134 Years
Source of data: www.globalfindata.com.

yield is only 3.3 percent annually. Therefore, adding a dividend yield of 3.3 percent to our buy-and-hold stock return of 6.3 percent gives us an expected return for the stock market of 9.6 percent. You can see why professionals may prefer to get 10 percent from a 10-year government note.

TEN PERCENT RATES RISK RECESSIONS

There are economic as well as portfolio reasons behind their logic. Professionals know that 10 percent on a long-term security, such as the 10-year note, may throw the economy into a recession. Notice how a recession often occurs when this critical investment rises and particularly when it reaches 10 percent; the shaded areas indicate a recession (see Figure 5.4). EconStats provides this information on its excellent web site at www.econstats.com. The National Bureau of Economic Research determines whether the economy is in a recession.

STAYING IN PORTFOLIO GUIDELINES

Professional money managers have portfolio guidelines, typically 60 percent in equities and 40 percent in fixed income, that limit their exposure to each asset class. A rally in the stock market will cause the bonds' value to shrink. The manager is expected to bring the asset allocation back into the guidelines, or rebalance, when market moves disturb the balance.

For example, if the stock market posts a 10 percent profit, the portfo-

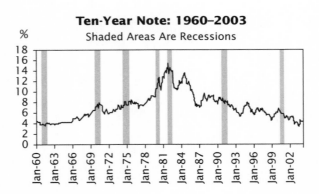

FIGURE 5.4 Recessions
Source of data: www.econstats.com.

TABLE 5.1 Trading the Ten-Year Note

Date	Ten-Year Note	Trade	S&P 500 Index
1979-10-01	10.30	Sell	109.32
1980-06-01	9.78	Buy	111.24
1980-07-01	10.25	Sell	114.24
1987-08-01	8.76	Buy	318.66
1987-10-15	10.19	Sell	298.00
1987-11-01	8.86	Buy	251.79

lio value grows to 66 percent in equities and has only 34 percent in bonds. It is time to take profits in the stock market and rebalance the portfolio regardless of the outlook for investments.

Bob found his portfolio in this situation twice in 1987: in the early spring after the first big increase in stocks and again at the end of the summer after the market continued to climb. After the crash, he had the reverse situation: his bonds had big profits while his remaining stocks fell and he was outside his guidelines again. Continuous rebalancing forced him to take profits on winners and buy underpriced bargains regardless of how he felt about the market. Private investors often use this discipline to great advantage as well.

TRADING THE TEN-YEAR NOTE

If you had done nothing more than sell stocks when the 10-year note reached 10 percent and then bought stocks when the note retreated below that amount, your decisions would have looked like Table 5.1.

Your first trade lost about 6 percent including dividends in the stock market, but you more than made up for it. You held a note with a double-digit coupon, had a capital gain on the note, and came out way ahead of the stock market. Your third trade was a big winner. You avoided a 22 percent loss on Black Monday and also saw a capital gain on the note. While your second trade caused you to miss 200 points in the S&P, you were paid so well in your note that you actually improved your return by 6 percent in each of the seven years that you owned bonds instead of stocks. Table 5.2 shows how the 10-year note index almost tripled in value between 1980 and 1987.

Despite the superior returns of the stock market over the long term, an investor would have been better off in the 10-year note during this particular period. Figure 5.5, originally from page 6 in the third edition of

TABLE 5.2	Ten-Year Note Total Return Index, 1980–1987
Date	**Return**
12/31/1980	$ 517.86
12/31/1981	$ 538.76
12/31/1982	$ 777.33
12/31/1983	$ 787.35
12/31/1984	$ 907.71
12/31/1985	$1,200.62
12/31/1986	$1,469.45
12/31/1987	$1,424.91

Professor Siegel's book, *Stocks for the Long Run*, shows the bond return going almost straight up during the early 1980s. His line depicting stocks' returns rises at a slightly slower rate.

Professional money managers assume that the stock market will provide a total return of about 10 percent each year on average. When they can get that return from a higher-quality investment with a more

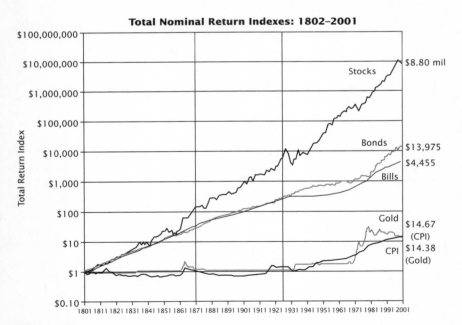

FIGURE 5.5 Total Returns for Each Asset Class
Source: Jeremy J. Siegel, *Stocks for the Long Run*, 3rd ed. (New York: McGraw-Hill, 2002), p. 6.

stable price, such as a U.S. government bond, they often sell stocks and buy bonds.

SUMMARY

Professional money managers have several important benchmarks. The most important one is the actuarial assumption that their portfolios must achieve in order to pay benefits. Second, they know that a 10 percent yield on the 10-year note may cause a recession. Third, they expect a 10 percent average return, including dividends, from the stock market. When the 10-year note satisfies their actuarial return requirement and also meets the expected return from the more volatile stock market, they prefer to own the fixed-income investment.

My friend Bob used these benchmarks to give him the courage of his convictions when he needed to reallocate his portfolio's assets. These reference points enabled him to stay calm while everyone else panicked on Black Monday in 1987. The goal of this book is to give you enough confidence in these benchmarks to have the courage of your convictions when you need to make a change in your portfolio.

But I had a little more experience in the bond market than Bob did, and I had an additional tool that gave me even more confidence to make decisions in the markets. The next chapter describes that tool.

CHAPTER 6

Bond Quality Spreads

I attended both summer sessions at New York University and earned an MBA in 18 months. This off-season schedule meant that I started working on February 1, 1978. Eighteen inches of snow had fallen on Park Avenue the night before, and my new boss came to work on his cross-country skis.

Training started with listening in on bond traders' telephone conversations. Everything was so different that I felt as though someone had dropped me on the moon. The traders spoke a foreign language that combined mathematics and wit. Each security had a nickname; the 30-year bond had a 7 percent coupon and matured in 2007, so it became the "Bond bond." Even our market reports were otherworldly; a toy moose head hanging over the trading desk gave ongoing market reports. Esmerelda, as we called her, sported a fake rose between her teeth when bond prices went up and hid her eyes behind a veil when they fell. Equity portfolio managers saw her on their way to the cafeteria and got their market updates at a glance.

QUALITY SPREADS

I soon learned that there is more to life than U.S. government bonds. Corporate bonds play a major role in our economy and in the market timing model we are developing in this book. I soon learned that the differences in prices between these two kinds of bonds, or quality spreads, give their own market report. The sizes of these price differences measure investor confidence in our financial system. Bond investor confidence soon affects the stock market, so we can use changing bond quality spreads to forecast the S&P 500 index.

You probably behave like a bond market investor when your friends ask to borrow money. You may lend money to your friend the doctor at a lower interest rate than you would to your friend the unemployed actor. When you see a recession coming, you may ask for an even higher interest rate from the actor because you think that it will be even harder for an actor to find work. You prefer to lend to better-quality credit risks, such as doctors, when you are concerned about the economy; and the interest rates you demand reflect your preference. When the recession is over, you may go back to lending money to your indigent actor at lower interest rates. The doctor's services, however, are always in demand, so you are always happy to lend to your physician friend at the same low rate regardless of your outlook for the economy. You can see how the difference in your lending rates, or quality spread, changes as your outlook for the economy changes. Your spread widens when you are fearful of the outlook for the economy and of being repaid; your spread narrows as you regain confidence.

In the bond market, the U.S. government is like your friend the doctor; and low-quality corporations are more like the actor. Price differences between these two groups of bonds change as investors' confidence in the economy changes. An extreme example of the difference in returns on bonds of different quality occurred during the 1991 recession. Investors preferred to own safe U.S. government bonds rather than low-quality bonds such as those issued by nuclear utilities. People remembered the 1980s accidents at some of these utility plants and were afraid to buy their bonds. People bought government bonds even though these risk-free bonds paid only half as much income as nuclear utilities. Government bonds paid only 7 percent, which paled by comparison to the 14 percent paid by nuclear utilities. The 7 percent difference between these two investments was the largest spread on record. By 1994 when the economy improved and the memory of nuclear incidents faded, people became more willing to lend to those power plants. The spread between these two investments fell to their normal rate of 3 percent.

BOND QUALITY SPREADS FORECAST STOCKS

Because the difference in price between bonds of varying quality shows investors' outlook for the economy, the Federal Reserve considers this spread to be an excellent economic forecasting tool. "Rising Junk Bond Yields" by Simon Kwan expands on the Fed's use of bond quality spreads in their economic forecasting efforts. We will take their thinking one step further and look at the stock market. If bond quality spreads forecast the economy, then they should also forecast the stock market and help us know when to buy or sell stock.

We will use an index with a long history of measuring bond quality: Moody's Investors Service's BAA medium-grade quality index. The difference between Moody's BAA bonds and the 10-year Treasury bond changes with investors' confidence. This spread is the dotted line on the next graph (Figure 6.1), while the S&P index is the solid line. Notice how the two move in opposition to each other. The dotted line, the bond quality spread, often moves just a little before the stock market and is a valuable leading indicator of that market.

To see their relationship, you can download bond quality spread and stock market data from the Federal Reserve web site: www.federalreserve.gov/releases/h15/data.htm, and click on: All historical data files for Treasury and Moody's BAA corporate yields. This graph shown in Figure 6.1 is in log scale so that you can focus on the changes rather than on the absolute levels of the data. As you can see, a rapid increase in spread often precedes a stock market decline. The reverse is also true; when the dotted line goes down sharply, investors often expect better market conditions and stocks rise.

There were two periods when bond quality spreads gave us more information about the future of the stock market than most other indicators. One was before the crash of 1987, and the other was before the 1998 failure of the hedge fund Long-Term Capital Management.

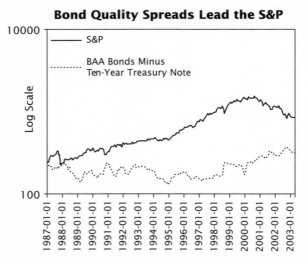

FIGURE 6.1   Quality Spreads Lead the S&P

THE 1987 CRASH

During the 1980s, American businesses restructured both their operations and their financing. Stocks had declined so much and inflation was so high in 1981 that it was cheaper to buy your competitor's factory than to build a new one. Buyout specialists like Ivan Boesky bought companies with underutilized assets and very little debt on their books. Drexel Burnham Lambert then issued high-yield bonds to the public who assumed that Mr. Boesky could turn the company around quickly and repay the lenders.

As so often happens on Wall Street, this good idea attracted too many participants, who bid up the prices of available firms. By 1987, these deal makers were paying inflated prices for companies with less valuable assets to turn around. Investors worried about the fact that some deal makers paid 20 percent for financing. Moody's bond rating service called these bonds high-yield or speculative. Investors called them by a more colorful name, junk bonds. The spread of Treasury bonds over corporate bonds of every quality, BAA as well as junk, widened with historic speed.

Many stock market participants ignored this signal from the bond market and continued to push up stock prices during the 1987 summer months. Bond market specialists also noticed the fact that interest rates were rising enough to create a recession. Some bond traders were not surprised to see the yield curve invert in August, nor were they shocked to see the 10-year Treasury note reach 10 percent in October. Many of them sold stocks before the October 19 crash. Figure 6.2 shows how stocks continued to rally in the face of widening bond quality spreads shown by the dotted line.

Yield spreads were becoming wider every day. The fact that the spread was changing with increasing speed caused us to put another "sell" decision on our graph. The date of our sale is October 15, 1987. Quality spreads were increasing, the yield curve was inverted between the 10-year and the 30-year, and both of these securities' interest rates were over 10 percent. If we had not sold earlier when the curve inverted at 10 percent, the condition of the quality spreads compelled us to make a change in our portfolio.

The S&P 500 index, which closed at 298 that day, had been dropping ominously for two months.

After the 1987 crash, the investment community paid more attention to high-yield bonds and particularly to their spreads over Treasuries. Several bond rating services created indexes of these bonds, one of which appears daily in the *Wall Street Journal* "Credit Markets" column. Most financial Internet sites include such an index. Moody's index

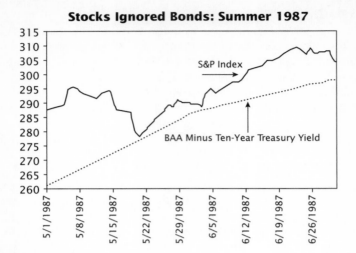

FIGURE 6.2 Quality Spreads' Warning in 1987

of speculative-grade bonds is in Appendix 6.1 at the back of the book along with Treasury notes and their spreads. Despite the short history of this new index, it makes the point vividly. Notice in Figure 6.3 how the junk bond spread widens with increasing speed right before the stock market falls.

This speculative quality spread widened before the stock market declines of 1998, 2000, and 2002. This spread even widened before the 2001 terrorist attacks although the spread reflected fear of increasing bankrupt-

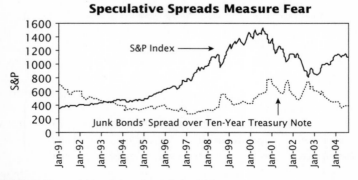

FIGURE 6.3 Speculative Spreads and the S&P

cies rather than terrorism. Speculative-grade companies are the most vulnerable to political and financial risk because of their position at the edge of the financial system. Like the canary that coal miners used to bring into a mine shaft to test for noxious gas, it is their vulnerability that makes them excellent indicators of change.

In fact, the line on this graph goes straight up in 1998 as a reflection of investors' accelerating fears.

THE 1998 MARKET DECLINE

Foreign investments had been a problem for a year. Japanese banks failed in the fall of 1997 because they made too many low-quality loans. Their trading partners in Southeast Asia failed during the following winter because they depended on Japan's business. Investors, looking for yet another foreign country to buy, poured money into Russia. We were so enthusiastic about the fall of Communism and the opening of commerce in the Soviet Union that some investors borrowed money to buy the new Russian government's bonds. A hedge fund whose partners included Nobel Prize winners, Long-Term Capital Management, borrowed heavily to buy these bonds.

Yet many investors had been worried about the safety of putting money into developing countries for several months. Their concerns showed up in the form of wider spreads between speculative bonds and U.S. Treasuries.

When the Russian government announced in June that they could not meet the next interest payment, quality spreads widened even more. Two months later, Long-Term Capital Management's problems surfaced. Several other investment funds, as well as the banks and brokerage firms that lent to them, also got into trouble. For a few weeks it looked as though the entire international financial system was going to fall apart.

One of the advantages of watching high-yield bond indexes is that they capture foreign bonds, such as the Russian bonds, as well as our own. When this spread widens rapidly, you know that there may be trouble somewhere in the financial system worldwide. Figure 6.4, a graph of Moody's speculative-grade bonds, shows how the spread grew almost 10 percent each month during the summer of 1998. Again, the stock market paid no attention . . . at first. Once the margin calls started, the trouble escalated. One financial institution after another found itself in difficulty until the Federal Reserve called an emergency bailout meeting. The bankers patched together a rescue and preserved our financial system until the next melodrama.

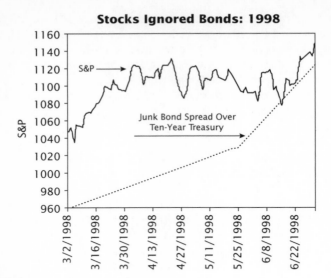

FIGURE 6.4   Increasing Spreads in 1998

APPLICATION TO EMERGING ECONOMIES

The 1998 experience illustrates how global the financial community has become. Now that speculative or high-yield bond indexes include nations with emerging economies, such as Russia, we can see the level of confidence that investors have in those markets. Members of emerging nations can use this spread to help determine when they should buy or sell their own countries' securities.

A friend in China asked how anyone could time *his* stock market and invited me to see the world from his point of view. My response was to watch the spread between the 10-year U.S. Treasury and the high-yield index. When this spread changes direction, so has investor confidence. There is probably a change in the U.S. economic outlook, international politics, or in an emerging country that caused this change in confidence. Now that he has a general framework for his analysis, he can look at his own country's bond spread off the 10-year U.S. Treasury. If that spread has changed, then maybe he should change his portfolio.

It is probably best to own stocks of emerging economies when the high-yield spread is declining and to sell them at the first sign of a widening. Many emerging market securities did well during 2003 when the high-yield spread collapsed from 7 percent to 4 percent. The most dramatic part of that decline occurred between October 2002 and March 2003 in anticipation of improving economic conditions worldwide.

The Federal Reserve uses the speculative bond quality spread to help them forecast the economy, and we can use it to help us forecast the stock market. We will add two sales to our list of trades: October 15, 1987, when the S&P 500 index stood at 298, and July 1, 1998, when the S&P was 1133 (see Figure 6.5).

The Federal Reserve protected us from the two crises in confidence during the 1980s and 1990s. We could have protected ourselves from these crises by looking at bond quality spreads.

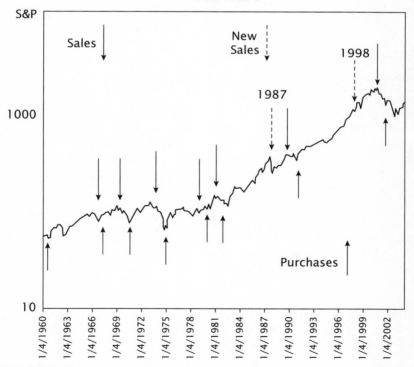

FIGURE 6.5 Quality Spreads Improve Our Graph of Trades

SUMMARY

Investors' confidence in our financial system shows up in quality spreads. The most dramatic example of this is in the lowest-quality corporate bonds nicknamed junk bonds. When these bonds' spread over the 10-year Treasury note widens, there may be trouble ahead in the stock market. If these quality spreads widen with increasing speed, there is almost certainly a serious stock market decline in the next few weeks.

Our next chapter will look at how our central bank operates and a simple method for us to profit from its actions.

CHAPTER 7

Federal Funds Rates

"What! You say we have too many people working and you want to raise the unemployment rate?"

The speaker slammed his hands on his desk and catapulted toward the bureaucrat who threatened his career.

President Bill Clinton, who grew up on the wrong side of the tracks in Little Rock, Arkansas, knew the importance of having a job. He was yelling at the most powerful man in the United States, Alan Greenspan. The Federal Reserve chairman had just suggested that perhaps the economy was growing too fast and that the supply of workers was becoming tight. The chairman's solution was to slow down the economy and raise the unemployment rate to avoid inflation. He had rescued us from double-digit interest rates in the late 1980s and wanted to avoid a repeat of that scenario. President Clinton wanted to be reelected and, apart from his personal experience with poverty, wanted the voters to have jobs. Every president knows that voters with jobs are more likely to reelect the sitting commander-in-chief.

To find out the resolution of this fictional account of the very real conflict between the president and the chairman, read *Maestro: Greenspan's Fed and the American Boom* by Bob Woodward of Watergate fame. It is a delightful book full of social gossip as well as details about running our economy.

Who is this powerhouse, the chairman of the Federal Reserve? Exactly what is the Fed, how does it work, and how can we profit by watching its moves? How did this organization rescue our financial system in 1987 and 1998?

The answers to these questions will add one more weapon to the arsenal we have been building throughout this book. This weapon, the federal funds rate, is often considered to be the most powerful of all because it drives our financial system. Active traders and corporate treasurers use the direction and level of this critical number to make their decisions. We will find out what fed funds are and how we can profit when the rate increases by one-half of 1 percent.

Just as every corporation has an account at a bank, so does every major country; but in this case, the country owns that bank. A country's bank, the central bank, has various duties that protect that nation's financial health. The Federal Reserve is our central bank and literally makes our money. Its job, among others, is to walk a fine line—creating enough money for our economy to grow at a sustainable rate but not so much money that we will have inflation. The Federal Reserve Bank of New York's web site, www.newyorkfed.org, summarizes this mandate as "noninflationary growth."

Once we see how the Fed accomplishes that goal, we can see how to profit from its actions.

HOW THE FEDERAL RESERVE CREATES MONEY

The Federal Reserve's actions that create and destroy money are at the heart of our financial system. The Fed does this through its primary dealers.

Primary Dealers

Primary dealers are large banks and brokerage firms that buy and sell securities at the Federal Reserve's request. When the central bank wants to buy securities, it buys them from the dealers, and when it wants to sell securities, it sells them to these same dealers. These transactions implement the Federal Reserve's policies.

Primary dealers are the subway trains of the financial world. Invisible, powerful, and running all day, they carry money throughout our financial system. The Federal Reserve flips the switch that starts and stops these money trains. That switch is called "open market operations."

Open Market Operations

Open market operations are purchases and sales of government securities by the Federal Reserve. The Fed does these trades with the primary dealers in order to create or destroy money. The purpose of these actions is to change interest rates and, therefore, the direction of the economy.

Dealers must participate in all of the Fed's transactions and with competitive prices. The central bank could just dictate the interest rates that they want, but competitive bidding forces the market to take that responsibility. A less capitalistic economy may allow its central bank to set interest rates, but the United States has found that allowing market forces to determine interest rates has a better impact on the economy.

How the Federal Reserve Creates Money

For example, when the Federal Reserve wants banks and brokerage firms to have more money to lend, it buys securities from the primary dealers. Dealers get money in exchange for the securities that they sell to the Fed. That money goes directly into the dealers' accounts at the Fed. Now that there is more money available, the price of money comes down. Dealers can lend more money to their customers and charge them lower interest rates as well.

These accounting entries are electronic, of course, with no actual cash changing hands.

How the Federal Reserve Destroys Money

Sometimes the central bank takes money out of the system in order to avoid inflation. This time the Federal Reserve *sells* securities to the primary dealers. Dealers must buy whatever the Fed wants to sell, often three-month Treasury bills, and pay for them with cash. Now the dealers' accounts at the Fed are lower and so are their lending abilities. You and I may not get that car loan we had our hearts set on because interest rates just went up.

The central bank decides how much money we need to achieve its goal of sustainable, noninflationary economic growth and then adds or subtracts funds through its primary dealers. These additions (Fed purchases) and subtractions (Fed sales) are open market operations. Financial market participants often refer to Fed purchases as "easing" and to sales as "tightening." You can see today's operations on the Federal Reserve Bank of New York's web site at www.ny.frb.org/markets/omo.

Open market operations change the most basic interest rate in our system, the federal funds rate.

Definition of the Federal Funds Rate

The federal funds rate is the interest rate that banks charge each other for short-term loans. Primary dealers are not the only institutions that must keep an account at the Federal Reserve. Banks, brokerage firms, and all other depository institutions must also have accounts with our central bank. Often a bank has more money in this account than the Federal Reserve requires, so it lends money to other banks. Because these loans are high-quality and for short periods of time, usually just overnight, the fed funds rate should be among the lowest on the yield curve.

The federal funds rate may be low, but it is more important than any other interest rate because it reflects the amount of money in our system. Changes in the amount of money, or money supply, determine the direction of our economy.

MONEY SUPPLY AFFECTS THE ECONOMY

The amount of money available to us directly affects the economy. An abundant supply of money allows us to spend freely and creates jobs. A shortage of cash limits those activities. As wonderful as full employment sounded to President Clinton in 1994, Chairman Greenspan knew that all those jobs depended on an ever-increasing money supply. They both knew that too much of that particular good thing—money supply—causes inflation. Serious inflation can lead to a lack of confidence in our whole financial system.

In previous chapters we saw that the level of interest rates is an important determinant of economic strength. High interest rates tend to slow business activity and cause recessions while low interest rates foster economic growth. Government spending and tax rates also have major impacts on the economy, but the Federal Reserve can influence the direction of the economy by changing the level of interest rates. The Fed makes this change through open market operations, which show up in changes in the federal funds rate.

THE FEDERAL FUNDS RATE PREDICTS

The federal funds rate is one of the most important in our financial system.

Federal Funds Rate Predicts the Economy

Because the fed funds rate results from open market operations, this interest rate says a lot about the central bank's desire for future economic growth.

If Chairman Greenspan won the argument in the Oval Office that we overheard at the beginning of this chapter, and he decided to slow the rate of economic growth, then he would direct the Open Market Trading Desk to sell securities to the dealers. Dealers would have to make competitive bids to buy them even though it meant giving up cash in their reserve accounts at the Fed.

The dealers' reserves at the Fed may then fall below the 10 percent minimum requirement and force them to borrow from another bank. This loan would take place in the federal funds market. Interest rates would go up as the shortage of cash spread. The fed funds rate would be the first interest rate to reflect the change as dealers scrambled to meet their reserve requirements on time.

Banks use the fed funds rate as a benchmark for the rest of their loans, so the rest of the Treasury yield curve would gradually move up in sympathy. High interest rates choke off business activity and are a major factor in starting a recession. Of course, the reverse is true as well; low interest rates encourage businesses to grow.

Figure 7.1 illustrates how the funds rate increases before the shaded areas outlining a recession. The rate then turns around during the worst part of the recession, or inside the shaded area, and declines before a recovery.

We can see these cycles coming if we watch the funds rate, which is available every day in the *Wall Street Journal* section C table entitled "Money Rates." Many Internet sites such as Bloomberg and EconStats include it as well. The best sources are the Federal Reserve's own web sites at www.federalreserve.gov/releases and www.ny.frb.org/markets /omo.

The rate jumps up at the ends of most quarters when many businesses close their books.

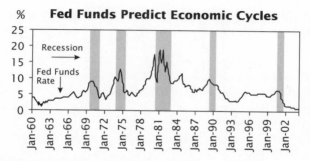

FIGURE 7.1 Fed Funds Rate Rises Before Recessions

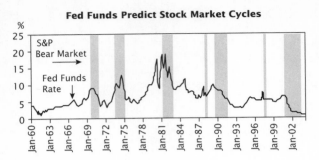

FIGURE 7.2   Fed Funds Rate Rises Before Bear Markets

Federal Funds Predict the Stock Market

If we can use the fed funds rate to anticipate economic cycles, we should be able to use it to predict something that moves in advance of these cycles, the stock market. Figure 7.2 shows how the federal funds rate increases just before we slip into bear markets, which are the shaded areas. The rate then turns around during the bear markets inside the shaded areas. This critical interest rate then declines dramatically before the next bull market begins.

INVESTING WITH THE FEDERAL FUNDS RATE

Rapidly rising fed funds rates warned investors of most major market declines. This same interest rate announced the beginning of each new bull market. A funds rate over 7 percent usually slows both the economy and the stock market, and a rate at or below 4 percent appears to stimulate growth.

Investors need to be wary when the rate is rising rapidly as it did before the 1987 crash and the 1998 decline. They need to be especially concerned when that rate is rising while the yield curve is inverted as it was in 1987 and 2000. By contrast, it is time to put fear aside and buy stocks when the curve has normalized and the fed funds rate is falling rapidly. This is particularly true when the Federal Reserve is bailing us out of a major crisis such as in 1987, 1998 and 2001.

In these three instances, the Federal Reserve used its open market operations to lower the fed funds rate dramatically and preserve the financial system after a disaster.

Size of Federal Funds Rate Changes

The fed funds rate changes constantly throughout the day in a reflection of market conditions. Dealers anticipate their end-of-day cash positions and participate in this highly liquid market all day long. Traders at every major financial institution arbitrage the dealers' needs and profit from the resulting imbalances. The daily fluctuation in the fed funds rate is normally only a few hundredths of a percent or one in ten thousand. You have a better chance of winning the lottery. However, when the Federal Reserve wants to support the financial system after a market crash, it changes the funds rate by a much larger amount. If the Fed wants to protect the international financial system after a crisis, it adjusts the funds rate by more than one-half of 1 percent in a few days.

Examples from three stock market crashes will underscore the importance of buying stocks if the fed funds rate drops at least half a percent immediately after the crisis.

The Federal Reserve Rescue in 1987

The market crashed on Monday, October 19, and the central bank reduced the rate over a full percentage point during the next two days (see Figure 7.3). This rate reduction was 10 times a normal move and designed to send a message to investors. Historical funds rates are available on the Federal Reserve's web site at www.federalreserve.gov/releases/h15/data/d/fedfund.txt.

Investors who realized that the Fed was serious about protecting the financial system bought stocks. They bought the S&P 500 index around 235, and the market never saw a price that low again. There were recessions and crises over the next decade, but the third week in October of 1987 was the investment opportunity of a lifetime.

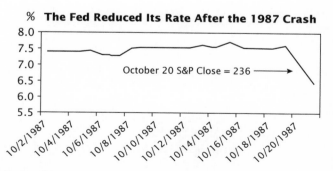

FIGURE 7.3 Fed Funds Rate Fell After 1987 Crash

We were one of those investors who saw that opportunity and will put a new trade on our ongoing list at the end of this chapter.

Buy: October 20, 1987, at 236

We are buying the S&P 500 index at a price that is 20 percent lower than when we sold it in Chapter 6. That sale was on October 15, 1987, at 298; we protected our portfolio from a 20 percent loss during five frightening days.

Another Rescue in 1998

The next crisis was in 1998 and resulted from the Russian government's default on its bonds. More accurately, the crisis came from investors' borrowing so much to buy those bonds. History books will remember the hedge fund Long-Term Capital Management as the trigger for the market decline; but several other hedge funds and major banks copied LTCM's investments and also share the blame.

Once more, the Fed increased its open market operations to flood the system with cash. The funds rate declined half a percent in a few days, and savvy investors bought stocks on or near September 4 of that year (see Figure 7.4).

We were one of those savvy investors and will add this trade to our cumulative record.

Buy: September 4, 1998, at 973

By now you can see the pattern. A crisis occurs and the stock market loses more than usual. (The S&P is a blue-chip index and its daily fluctuations are about 1 or 2 percent.) The Federal Reserve steps in with open

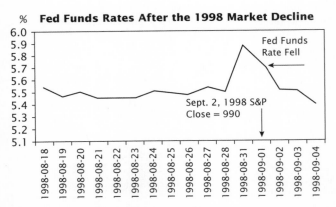

FIGURE 7.4   Fed Funds Rate Fell After 1998 Decline

market operations designed to add large amounts of money to the system. Investors see that the Fed is serious about protecting the markets and they gradually start to buy stocks again.

If the S&P normally fluctuates about 2 percent in a day, you can see why investors panicked on October 19, 1987, when it lost 20 percent and again on September 1, 1998, with a 7 percent loss. Can you imagine how they would feel if the stock market actually shut down for a week?

Terrorist Attacks in 2001

Investors more than panicked while the World Trade Center burned; they were too scared to move at all. People stayed out of the shopping malls and watched television with their families and friends. The economy did not just slow down; it ground to a halt.

This time the Federal Reserve did more than increase our money supply. There was a rumor that it "suggested" to large pension plans that they buy stocks when the market reopened in order to prevent a complete collapse. Of course, the Fed stepped up its open market operations to create massive amounts of money.

Normally, the Fed adds about $3 billion to the money supply every day. Investors who went on the Fed's web site at www.ny.frb.org/markets/omo/dmm/temp.cfm the day before the attacks saw that the central bank added a routine $2 billion. The Fed bought securities to hold for 29 days after which time they would revert to their original owners. This is called a "repurchase agreement," shortened to "repo" by the traders. Table 7.1 is a snapshot from the Fed's web site on September 10, 2001.

TABLE 7.1 September 10, 2001

Temporary Open Market Operations for September 10, 2001
The Desk has entered the market
announcing: **29-day RP**

	Treasury Collateral Operation	Agency Collateral Operation	Mortgage-Backed Collateral Operation
Weighted Average Rate	3.356	3.39	N/A
Stop Out Rate	3.35	3.39	N/A
Highest Rate Submitted	3.39	3.39	3.4
Lowest Rate Submitted	3.25	3.32	3.34
Total Propositions Submitted (in $bil.)	9.95	5.85	6.5
Total Propositions Accepted (in $bil.)	1.54	0.46	0
Total Money Value of Operation (in $bil.)	2		

TABLE 7.2 September 12, 2001

**Temporary Open Market Operations for
September 12, 2001**
The Desk has entered the market
announcing: **O/N RP**

Weighted Average Rate	**3.542**
Stop Out Rate	**3.5**
Highest Rate Submitted	**3.6**
Lowest Rate Submitted	**3.25**
Total Propositions Submitted (in $bil.)	**46.25**
Total Propositions Accepted (in $bil.)	**38.25**

The day after the attacks the same page on the web site showed that
the Fed entered into much larger repurchase agreements with its dealers
for over $38 billion (see Table 7.2); these agreements were just for
overnight. The Fed did not specify what securities it bought; perhaps that
was to protect the privacy of the dealers' inventories.

In case investors had any doubt about the Fed's intentions to preserve
the system, it stepped up its open market operations to $70 billion on the
next day (see Table 7.3). Again, the repurchase agreements were for
overnight.

On September 14, the stock markets were still closed, the World
Trade Center fires were still smoldering beneath the melted and twisted
steel wreckage, and the weekend was approaching. The Fed increased the
size of its over-the-weekend repurchase agreements to a historic $81 bil-
lion (see Table 7.4).

The stock markets reopened on Monday, September 17, and the Fed
added $57 billion in order to create confidence that there would be money

TABLE 7.3 September 13, 2001

**Temporary Open Market Operations for
September 13, 2001**
The Desk has entered the market
announcing: **O/N RP**

Weighted Average Rate	**3.602**
Stop Out Rate	**3.5**
Highest Rate Submitted	**4**
Lowest Rate Submitted	**3.5**
Total Propositions Submitted (in $bil.)	**70.2**
Total Propositions Accepted (in $bil.)	**70.2**

TABLE 7.4 September 14, 2001	
Temporary Open Market Operations for September 14, 2001 The Desk has entered the market announcing: **O/W RP**	
Weighted Average Rate	**3.537**
Stop Out Rate	**3.5**
Highest Rate Submitted	**3.75**
Lowest Rate Submitted	**3.5**
Total Propositions Submitted (in $bil.)	**81.25**
Total Propositions Accepted (in $bil.)	**81.25**

in your local cash machine and your employer's payroll account. Investors were able to watch all of this on the Federal Reserve's web site as if they were bond traders on a government dealer's desk.

The funds rate dropped to a historic low of 1 percent on September 19, and investors tiptoed back into the market. This decline in the funds rate was probably the largest drop ever engineered by the Fed; the rate fell two whole percentage points, or 70 percent, in a few days (see Figure 7.5). For the time being, we will replace our November 1, 2001, purchase with this improved trade, which is based on the powerful Fed action. Later chapters defer to a force superior to the Fed—the investing public.

Buy: September 20, 2001, at 984

Some investors had sold stocks in 2000 and bought them back on September 20 because the funds rate was so low. They protected themselves from

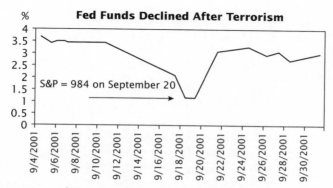

FIGURE 7.5 Fed Funds Rate Fell After 2001 Terrorism

a more than 400-point drop in the S&P 500 index and saved 30 percent of their portfolio. (Smaller stocks that trade on the Nasdaq lost about half their value during this period.) Appendix 7.1 gives the daily funds rates and corresponding stock market prices so you can relive these exciting events. The important funds rates and corresponding S&P values are in bold type so you can identify them easily.

Benchmarks and Trading Results

While the events were exciting, they were also terrifying. Investors saw their savings melt like ice cream in July and were afraid to buy stocks during these crashes. This book hopes to provide a few simple benchmarks that may help us overcome both the fear and the greed that dominate investors at market extremes. The benchmarks so far:

1. The stock market moves before the economy.
2. The federal funds rate reflects the Federal Reserve's desire to expand or contract the economy.
3. Falling federal funds rates expand the economy, and rising rates cause it to contract.
4. Therefore, buy stocks when the federal funds rate is falling and sell stocks when this rate is rising.
5. Especially buy stocks after a crash and the Federal Reserve has lowered the funds rate one-half of 1 percent.

Assuming that we were among the few who mustered up our courage to buy each time that the Federal Reserve lowered the funds rate at least half a percent after a crash, we will add three S&P 500 index purchases to our cumulative trading record:

1. October 20, 1987: Buy the S&P 500 index at 236.
2. September 4, 1998: Buy the S&P 500 index at 973.
3. September 20, 2001: Buy the S&P 500 index at 984.

Our cumulative record is shown in Table 7.5, and our graph shows the results (see Figure 7.6).

Our buy-and-hold return at the lowest point of the recent bear market on October 2002 remains about 6.3 percent. Watching the Federal Reserve's actions in this chapter, quality spreads on speculative bonds in Chapter 6, and the level of the 10-year Treasury note in Chapter 5 in-

TABLE 7.5 Trade Dates

Trade	Date	S&P 500 Index
Buy	January 2, 1960	59
Sell	September 1, 1966	77
Buy	February 1, 1967	86
Sell	July 1, 1969	97
Buy	February 1, 1970	85
Sell	June 1, 1973	105
Buy	October 1, 1974	63
Sell	December 1, 1978	94
Buy	May 1, 1980	106
Sell	November 1, 1980	127
Buy	September 1, 1981	122
Sell	October 15, 1987	298
Buy	October 20, 1987	236
Sell	October 31, 1989	340
Buy	January 2, 1991	330
Sell	July 1, 1998	1133
Buy	September 4, 1998	973
Sell	August 1, 2000	1430
Buy	September 20, 2001	984

creases our trading results to nearly 9.5 percent. (see Figure 7.7). In other words, trading our portfolio provides 50 percent more return than a buy-and-hold strategy. These returns are without the 3.5 percent dividends we calculated in a previous chapter. We were able to multiply the dollar value of our portfolio to almost four times that of a buy-and-hold portfolio (see Figure 7.8).

In addition to increasing our portfolio's rate of return and its dollar amount, we have reduced its volatility along with our blood pressure. We sleep better at night having cash in the bank during stock market declines.

SUMMARY

We have added a powerful weapon to our arsenal. The federal funds rate, or the interbank loan rate, moves the rest of the yield curve and changes the direction of the economy. The funds rate is the magnetic north pole of the financial world. When this magnetic north changes by

S&P 500 Index Trades with Yield Curve Analysis: 1960–2005

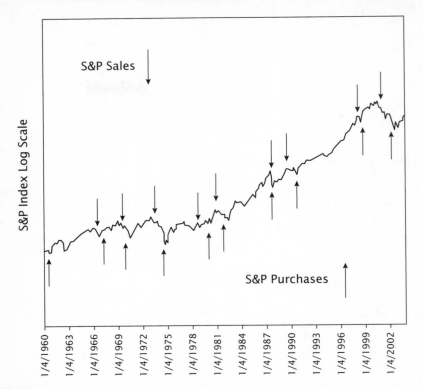

FIGURE 7.6   Part One Graph of Trades with Yield Curve Analysis

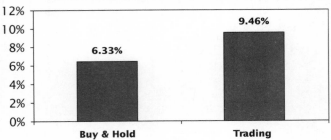

FIGURE 7.7   Part One Return is 9.46 Percent

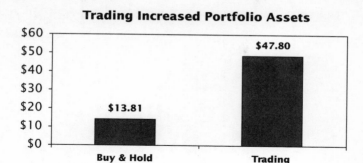

FIGURE 7.8 Part One Portfolio is $47.80

one-half of 1 percent, the whole world shifts from impending financial failure to safety. We can use this compass point to guide us back into the stock market after a crisis. It is no wonder that traders and treasurers use the fed funds rate in their decisions.

Navigating the financial markets is easier with a map and a few landmarks. Now that we have a map, our next chapter will summarize with an overview of where we have been and point out some helpful landmarks. We will then assess the future for investors as we conclude Part One on yield curve analysis.

CHAPTER 8

Summary of Yield Curve Analysis

We have just taken a 40-year trip through the stock market. Along the way we encountered some rough spots, but we had the courage to make the tough decisions because we know the rules of the road. We will summarize those rules, graph their trading history, identify some landmarks, and forecast the next big move in the economy and the stock market.

SUMMARY OF YIELD CURVE ANALYSIS

Buy stocks when:

- The federal funds rate is declining.
- And the money market yield curve is positive.
- And bond quality spreads are shrinking.
- And the 10-year note, three-month bill spread is positive.

Sell stocks when:

- The federal funds rate is rising.
- And the 10-year, three-month spread is negative.
- And bond quality spreads are expanding.
- Or the yield on the 10-year note is greater than 10 percent.

APPLICATION TO A MODEL PORTFOLIO

As we developed these trading guides, we applied them to trading the S&P 500 index between 1960 and 2002. We made the trades shown in Table 8.1.

TABLE 8.1 Part One Trade Dates

Trade	Date	S&P 500 Index
Buy	January 2, 1960	59
Sell	September 1, 1966	77
Buy	February 1, 1967	86
Sell	July 1, 1969	97
Buy	February 1, 1970	85
Sell	June 1, 1973	105
Buy	October 1, 1974	63
Sell	December 1, 1978	94
Buy	May 1, 1980	106
Sell	November 1, 1980	127
Buy	September 1, 1981	122
Sell	October 15, 1987	298
Buy	October 20, 1987	126
Sell	October 31, 1989	340
Buy	January 2, 1991	330
Sell	July 1, 1998	1133
Buy	September 4, 1998	973
Sell	August 1, 2000	1430
Buy	September 20, 2001	984

A graph of these trades suggests that yield curve analysis does a fairly decent job of forecasting the stock market (see Figure 8.1). There is still some work to do, however, in the following chapters on technical analysis and cultural indicators.

The yield curve allowed us to increase the yield on the passive portfolio by half. Without taking dividends into account, we raised the return from 6 percent to 9 percent on an average annual basis (see Figure 8.2). Dividends would have added about 3 percent to each number.

The dollar amount of each portfolio shows an even larger difference; the active portfolio has over three times as much money in it (see Figure 8.3).

Hard to Buy but Easy to Sell

You probably noticed that our trading rules make it is easier to sell stocks than to buy them. The reason is that markets seduce people into them slowly and then crash when the margin calls begin. Let us see this seduction throughout an economic cycle and then we will find an average yield curve so that you will have a benchmark. This benchmark will allow us to evaluate the Federal Reserve's success in meeting its own stated goals and provide us with a glimpse of the future for investors.

S&P 500 Index Trades with Yield Curve Analysis: 1960–2005

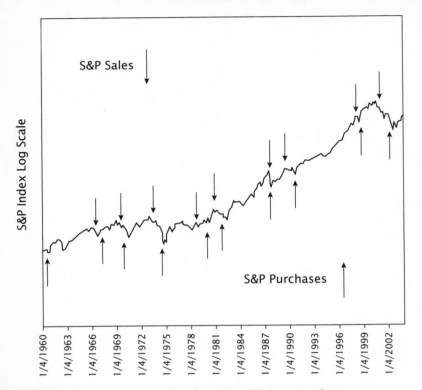

FIGURE 8.1 Part One Graph of Trades with Yield Curve Analysis

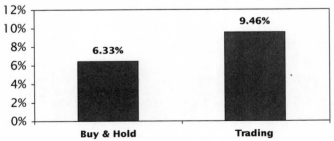

FIGURE 8.2 Part One Return Is 9.46 Percent

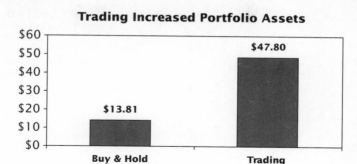

FIGURE 8.3   Part One Portfolio Is $47.80

A MARKET CYCLE

A market cycle has four major stages and the Fed influences each one.

Stage One: Strong Stock Market

As the economy starts to expand, the Federal Reserve adds funds to keep the nascent recovery healthy. The fed funds rate declines, the yield curve is normal, and bond quality spreads are becoming narrower every day. Confidence is coming back into the financial markets after a recession. It is time to buy stocks when the yield curve is normal, interest rates are low, and most investors are still battle-scarred from the recession. Early stock market investors reap the biggest reward; this first stage of the stock market is usually very strong (see Figure 8.4).

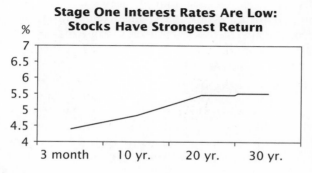

FIGURE 8.4   Stage One

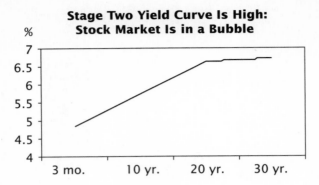

FIGURE 8.5   Stage Two

Stage Two: Overheating

As the economy becomes too strong and the Federal Reserve worries about inflation, the central bank gradually withdraws money from the system. Less money in the system pushes the funds rate up and drags the whole yield curve with it. Interest rates rise enough to slow business, erode investors' confidence, and raise fears of a recession. At this point, sophisticated investors are afraid to hold lower-quality bonds, so quality spreads begin to widen. We may be in a stock market bubble (see Figure 8.5).

Stage Three: Peak

The central bank continues to tighten the money supply, and fed funds rates move up to the level of the rest of the curve, which is now flat. Quality spreads widen more quickly as more sophisticated investors begin to worry that a recession is coming. This is often the peak of the stock market; it may start its decline on the day that the yield curve becomes flat (see Figure 8.6).

Stage Four: Stock Market Decline

The Fed can do fewer reverses now because the flat curve sends a recessionary signal to the financial community, who will then buy bonds and make the curve invert. Popular demand for the long-term bond causes this inversion because more investors sell stocks and buy bonds (see Figure 8.7).

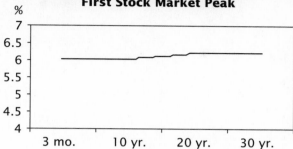

FIGURE 8.6   Stage Three

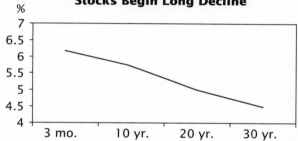

FIGURE 8.7   Stage Four

Investors Buy Bonds

Investors know that the long-term bond is one asset that may actually make money during a normal recession. The 1980 recession was the exception because interest rates rose so high and so quickly. Figure 8.8 shows the total return of interest payments plus the capital gain on the 10-year Treasury note during seven recessions. The line indicating total return goes up in all of the recessions except the one in 1980. The total return index and economic growth rates are annotated for expansions, peaks, and recessions in Appendix 8.1.

The one time that bondholders failed to profit during a recession was in 1980. Investors made 50 percent returns on their long-term bonds when interest rates and inflation finally came down during the 1982 recession

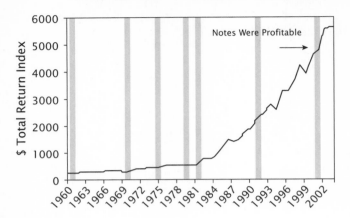

Ten-Year Note Total Return Increased During Most Recessions: 1960–2003

FIGURE 8.8   Ten-Year Note Total Returns

just two years later. They averaged 15 percent returns during each year in that period and outperformed the stock market by a wide margin.

The Cycle Repeats

During a recession, the Federal Reserve starts to create money again as part of the government's economic recovery program. As the Fed eases, the funds rate is the first to fall. Other interest rates follow suit and the yield curve gradually returns to normal. Quality spreads come down from their previous highs, and investor confidence gradually returns.

BENCHMARKS

A few averages for inflation, economic growth, and shape of the yield curve will anchor our yield curve analysis. These benchmark numbers will also allow us to evaluate the Federal Reserve's stated goal of sustainable, noninflationary growth and then project the future of the stock market.

THE FEDERAL RESERVE'S GOALS

We can look into the deliberations of the central bankers and see how they grade themselves on their own work.

Inflation: 1914–2004

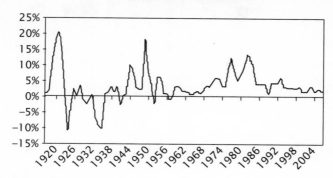

FIGURE 8.9 Inflation
Source of data: Bureau of Labor Statistics, www.econstats.com.

Acceptable Inflation

Well, they certainly subdued inflation since the 1970s. Each decade since then has seen reduced rates of inflation. The average rate between 1914 and 2004 was 3.4 percent. That number ballooned to 6.7 percent during the 1970s and deflated to a mere 2.5 percent during the first four years of this century. The Federal Reserve, under the leadership of Chairmen Paul Volcker and Alan Greenspan, has created the lowest and most stable inflationary environment in decades. Figure 8.9, a 90-year graph of the consumer price index, uses Bureau of Labor Statistics data in 1982 constant dollars as presented on the EconStats web site at www.econstats.com/BLS/blsnaa1.htm.

Economic Growth

Economic growth, unadjusted for inflation, averaged 6.8 percent from 1931 to 2004 (see Figure 8.10). This, too, has become more stable.

The downward trend of economic growth on this graph since 1980, however, is disturbing. How serious is it?

THE FUTURE FOR INVESTORS

In order to answer that question, we need a benchmark from the past to project the future. All we need is an average of historical yield curves and a simple formula to approximate future economic growth.

Smoother Economic Growth: 1931–2004

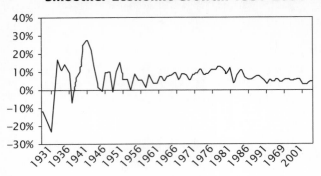

FIGURE 8.10 Change in Economic Growth Rate
Source of data: EconStats at www.econstats.com.

Average Yield Curve since 1952

If you take an average of the past 52 years of interest rates, you can construct and "average" yield curve. This, of course, is fictitious, but it does provide a benchmark. Since 1954, the three-month Treasury bill yield has averaged 5.28 percent. The 10-year Treasury note averaged 6.62 percent; the long-term bond (the 20-year or the 30-year, as available) had an average return of 6.76 percent during this period. Figure 8.11 is a graph of these returns.

Economic Forecast

The Federal Reserve Bank of Cleveland published a simple economic formula in one of its monthly publications available to the public, *Economic Trends*. This oversimplified but handy formula forecasts economic

Average Yield Curve: 1952–2004

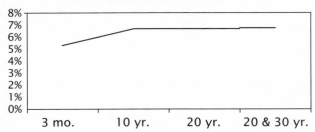

FIGURE 8.11 Average Yield Curve

growth, or gross domestic product (GDP), in one year. This forecast depends on the shape of the yield curve, as you might expect; but in this case the Federal Reserve substituted the 30-year government bond for the 10-year note:

Growth of GDP one year ahead = 1.8 + [0.97 × (Thirty-year bond yield minus Three-month bill yield)]

Simply put, 12 months from now the economy is expected to grow about 1.8 percent plus 97 percent of the difference between the 30-year bond yield and the three-month bill rate. The result will tell us how well the Federal Reserve achieved its goals.

The Federal Reserve Met Its Goals

If we insert the numbers from our "average" yield curve into the formula, we can expect our economy to grow about 3.2 percent in a normal year. That number probably meets the Federal Reserve's goal of sustainable, noninflationary growth and suggests that the recent Fed leaders have tackled a difficult agenda with stunning success.

Their success may allow recent productivity gains to stimulate the economy to grow faster than expected. These gains created unexpectedly strong economic growth during the late 1990s and may well do so again. As usual, we can expect a strong economy to underwrite a great stock market.

We are in a position to exploit that opportunity.

SUMMARY

We have established trading rules based on yield curve analysis. We know how to use maturity spreads and quality spreads to identify market peaks and troughs. We use the 10-year note at 10 percent as a benchmark for holding bonds rather than more volatile stocks. We know how to read the actions of the Federal Reserve to help us move into and out of the stock market. We are well on our way to becoming proficient at timing the market.

PART TWO COVERS TECHNICAL ANALYSIS

Now that we have completed yield curve analysis, perhaps some more tools are in order and we should augment fundamental economics with technical analysis.

Technical analysis looks at stock prices and volume. Some practitioners refer to this powerful theory as price-based analysis in order to differentiate it from fundamental economics. These investors often follow the theories of Charles Dow, who created the Dow Jones Industrial Average in 1896, and believe that the price of a security is the *only* thing that matters. Some of these investors have become quite wealthy as a result of using technical analysis, and we will join them in Part Two.

Technical Analysis

M y graduate school professor of securities analysis said, "Always use fundamental analysis. Stick to the fundamentals. Never stray from fundamental security analysis."

The more he droned on about the subject, the more curious I became about that significant other, *not* fundamental analysis. Of course, he never told us the name of that demon for fear that we would succumb to its seductive powers. Sure, I had heard of chartists who draw pictures of heads and shoulders on stock charts; I just never took them seriously enough to consider them a threat to my professor's beloved fundamental analysis. But other people took chartists very seriously indeed.

CHARTING

My first experience with charting was a fleeting comment by one of the best portfolio managers at Scudder, Stevens & Clark, now Deutsche Bank. He dropped into my office with his usual casual elegance. (All of Scudder's equity managers were casually elegant, in stark contrast to us scruffy fixed-income managers.) Ed wanted some of those terrific Treasury bonds with a 16 percent yield. When I said that the market had moved and that yields had declined, he said,

"That's all right. There's always a second chance to buy," with such conviction in his voice that I knew he had another source of information.

Something clicked in the back of my mind, and I remembered that chartists talk about double tops and bottoms when the market changes direction. Our bond market sure had changed direction; devastatingly high yields were finally coming down and allowing the economy to revive. A few months later, though, we had 16 percent bonds again and Ed was back in my office buying with both hands. I began to suspect that there might be something to this stepchild of finance called technical analysis.

TECHNICAL ANALYSIS

Fast-forward to a Stamford CFA Society meeting at the Greenwich Country Club in Connecticut in 2002 after the stock market bubble burst. People had lost 80 percent of their money in the Nasdaq and were looking for ways to time the stock market. Ralph Acampora, chief technical analyst at Prudential Securities and founder of the Market Technicians Association, gave a lecture on technical analysis. He said that technicians use security prices rather than fundamental economic analysis to make their investment decisions. When an audience member asked if it was time to buy bonds, whose prices had just reached a 45-year high, Ralph stood on a dainty gold painted chair, pointed to the ceiling, and exclaimed,

"Bonds are not cheap!"

The audience roared with delight and invited him back every year. For an introduction to technical analysis with a minimum of math, read Mr. Acampora's charming book, *The Fourth Mega Market*.

If you want to become an expert technician, contact the Market Technicians Association at www.mta.org to find out about their courses and certification.

BEHAVIORAL FINANCE

As technical analysis became more popular, it included some aspects of behavioral finance. In his highly readable Introduction to his book *Behavioural Finance* (notice the British spelling), James Montier presents the psychological link between investing and behaviorism. The basis of his work is that my professor's beloved fundamental economics is dead wrong; Montier says that man is *not* rational and, therefore, none of the tenets of traditional economics hold up under scrutiny. According to Montier and other followers of behavioral finance, man is irrational and overreacts to all of the emotions that drive our financial markets.

Montier may have read that original treatise on emotional overreacting, *Group Psychology and the Analysis of the Ego* by Sigmund Freud. Freud's work is more interesting than the name would imply. This is the same man who wrote "On Cocaine" in 1884, so we should not be surprised to read his description of crowd behavior as "coarse" and that its members exult in their loss of limitations and find the experience "pleasurable." No wonder he describes the relationship between the crowd and its leader in terms that are sexual.

We need to protect ourselves from the effects of mob psychology. Part Two shows you how to take the emotional temperature of the investment crowd so you can protect yourself from that particular mob.

CHAPTER 9

Market Breadth: Advancing Issues in the Dow

Charles Dow created his famous average with 12 major U.S. companies in 1896 so that he could measure the gross movement of these stocks. His work was a breakthrough because using one number at the end of each day made it easier to see whether the market was expanding or contracting than the previous method of looking at each stock individually. It is interesting to note that of the original 12 stocks, only one, General Electric, remains on the list (see Table 9.1).

Industry leadership changes over time, and the index is updated to reflect those changes. Investors cannot assume that they are safe to buy a great company and hold it forever because of the rapid changes in global business. Even the bluest of blue-chip stocks, the Dow industrials, have changed dramatically over time, and the original Dow stocks have been replaced by companies in industries that did not even exist in 1896.

Some critics note a certain irony surrounding the 1999 changes in the Dow. Microsoft moved into the average when its price was near its peak, and International Paper was removed a few years later when its price was near its bottom. Because this index changes so rarely, some analysts think that the stock market in general is overvalued when existing components give way to new names. When the Dow is updated to reflect a popular stock, that stock may be ready to fall and bring others with it. We certainly saw this happen from 2000 to 2002 when technology stocks declined and stock prices of companies making commodities such as paper increased.

More than 100 years after its creation, this index is still the best-known number on Wall Street. According to the Dow Jones web site

TABLE 9.1 Dow Jones Industrial Average Components

1896	2005
American Cotton Oil	Alcoa Inc.
American Sugar	Altria Group Inc.
American Tobacco	American Express Co.
Chicago Gas	American International Group Inc.
Distilling & Cattle Feeding	Boeing Co.
General Electric	Caterpillar Inc.
Laclede Gas	Citigroup Inc.
National Lead	Coca-Cola Co.
North American	Disney
Tennessee Coal & Iron	DuPont de Nemours & Co.
US Leather preferred	ExxonMobil Corp.
US Rubber	General Electric Co.
	General Motors Corp.
	Hewlett-Packard Co.
	Home Depot Inc.
	Honeywell International Inc.
	IBM
	Intel Corp.
	Johnson & Johnson
	JPMorgan Chase & Co.
	McDonald's Corp.
	Merck & Co. Inc.
	Microsoft Corp.
	Pfizer Inc.
	Procter & Gamble Co.
	SBC Communications Inc.
	3M
	United Technologies Corp.
	Verizon Communications Inc.
	Wal-Mart Stores Inc.

www.djindexes.com, at the end of 2003 the Dow represented more than $11 trillion and 25 percent of the U.S. market.

We will see what that number is and how it can help us identify market tops and bottoms. We will see how our usage is different from most other people's and why I find it so powerful.

DOW DEFINED

The Dow Jones Industrial Average is an index of 30 of the largest companies in the United States. It used to be limited to manufacturing firms but now includes a cross section of our economy such as financial services, technology, retail, entertainment, and consumer goods. It is this wide variety of industries that makes the average so useful to us. The Dow tells us what investors are buying today in a diversified portfolio of 30 of the largest stocks in the country. We will use the Dow a little differently than most people do, however, because we will look at each of the 30 components separately rather than at the average.

USING THE DOW

Traditional Usage

Technicians use Dow theory in many ways, and two are the most popular.

The first usage is to compare two indexes. Charles Dow created an index of the major transportation stocks in order to confirm movements in the industrials. His reasoning was that manufactured goods need transportation to a market. The companies in his transportation index move the goods manufactured by the companies in his industrial index to markets where the profit actually is created. He wanted to see the two averages moving together before he bought stocks.

The other major use of Dow theory is to establish an average price range, or trend line, for each stock and each index. These ranges are comfort zones for the investor who owns the security. When prices get outside of these normal ranges, they are too high or too low and present a trading opportunity. Technicians may sell stocks that are higher than this normal range and buy stocks that are cheaper than normal. This commonsense approach to evaluating prices helps us put them in perspective.

Difficulties Using Dow Theory

There are two difficulties in using Dow theory, but one of them will be an advantage for our trading.

The first difficulty is in deciding where to start drawing the trend line for either a stock or one of the averages. You get radically different results if you start on a day when the price was high, say in January 2000, rather than on a poor day such as July 19, 2002. Dow theory depends on this starting point to estimate a normal price range for a benchmark. Investors then use this standard to gauge potential gains and losses, so the starting date affects all of the decisions that depend on it. For example, a major trend reversal usually costs the market one-half of its profits. If we expect the market to give back half its gains, we are even more dependent on that starting price for our calculation. Do we sell in anticipation of a serious loss going back to our price in 1929, or should we ride out a minor loss since the price last week?

The other difficulty is the calculation of the industrial average. Each stock has the same weight regardless of how many shares are outstanding. A stock with a high price, such as Microsoft before the crash, will cause the whole average to move up. One very popular stock can dominate this average and mask the movement of all the others. The Dow can move up because just one stock is popular even if all the others are declining. This is exactly what happened for many months before the crash when Motorola propped up the other 29 stocks that were falling.

Despite the difficulties, many investors look at a chart before making a trade. I consider myself a fundamental rather than a technical analyst, but the first thing I do when evaluating an investment is look at the chart. For one thing, I want to make sure that a major trend is starting to reverse. There is a certain comfort in looking at the historical prices to get a perspective.

Where to Find the Dow

Dow Jones & Company owns the *Wall Street Journal* and reports the industrial average on the first page every day. We, however, are more interested in the list of underlying stocks on page 2 of section C. Here you will find a list of all 30 stocks and the amount by which they increased or decreased the day before.

Our Usage of the Dow

Our analysis looks at the *number* of these stocks that increase in price every day on the assumption that investors will overreact at market extremes. This overreaction will show up in the number of stocks that increase in price each day. A healthy market is broad-based with most of the Dow industrials moving up. If all but one or two stocks decline, something is wrong. Investors are taking the market too far in one direction or the other. Let us see how it works.

Investors' Behavior at Market Tops

The stock market is just like high school; everyone wants to date the prom queen. In this case, everyone wants to buy a few popular stocks.

At the top of a major bull market, investors are caught up in the excitement of new and glamorous stocks. They sell boring old stocks and buy the latest highflier that pays in dreams rather than in dividends. Most of the Dow 30 industrial stocks become wallflowers as a result.

The few popular stocks attract enough money to drive the average to new highs. During the 1999 bubble, people referred to this phenomenon as a "stealth bear market." You might call it "trying to date the prom queen." Investors sold most of the stocks in the Dow during 1999 because they were boring old economy stocks that did not make sexy toys with a large, new market like cell phones. One member of that index, however, was glamorous because it *did* make cell phones, Motorola. This stock doubled during the last quarter of 1999 when it went from $30 to $60 per share. Motorola took the whole Dow Jones Industrial Average to new highs every day during the market peak. The trouble was that all of the money was in this one stock, so when investors sold Motorola down to $8 a share, the whole index fell.

Just a few glamorous stocks advance every day during a bubble because everyone wants to date the prom queen.

Investors' Behavior at Market Bottoms

Nobody wants to date the prom queen or anyone else at the bottom of the market. Prom queens stay home with the rest of the crowd because of mass depression. A clear sign that investors are overly bearish is that all *30* of the Dow industrial stocks decline on the same day.

Because these 30 stocks represent diversified industries, some of them should move in opposition to each other. For example, defensive drug stocks should move differently than aggressive technology stocks; Pfizer and Microsoft should behave differently from each other. When all 30 Dow stocks decline on the same day, the market is close to its absolute bottom.

Examples of Dow as Indicator: Terrorist Attacks

The Dow indicated that the terrorist attacks were *not* the bottom of the market. We did not see all 30 of the Dow stocks decline after the 2001 terrorist attacks. Defensive stocks such as Coca-Cola, Merck, and Procter & Gamble posted gains when the market reopened on September 17. Communications stocks also did well that day: SBC Communications and Motorola. Five of the Dow Jones Industrial Average companies were up that day and suggested that it was not the bottom of the market. The Dow closed at 8920 and the S&P at 1038; these markets would lose another 15 to 25 percent over the next year.

Market Bottoms in 2002

The S&P hit bottom on October 9, 2002, at 773, and you would think that all 30 of the Dow stocks would have declined on that day as part of the general malaise. That was almost the case; Philip Morris was the only Dow stock that posted a gain that day. It is so rare for all 30 stocks to go down at once that we did not see it happen even at the very lowest point.

Did it ever happen?

Yes, on July 19, 2002, each of the Dow industrials posted a loss on the same day. There was a clear signal to astute investors to buy the Dow at 8019 or the S&P at 847. Bloomberg radio announced the news after the market closed because it is so unusual to see this event. Dow Jones & Company, the owner of this index, has daily closing prices of all 30 stocks on its web site at www.djindexes.com, and Appendix 9.1 lists the two days in question. Abacus Analytics in Norwalk, Connecticut, examined the data and confirmed that July 19, 2002, was the only day between 2000 and 2004 on which all 30 Dow industrials fell together.

ADDING A NEW TRADE TO OUR RECORD

We, of course, bought the S&P 500 index that day because the rest of our market requirements were in place:

- The fed funds rate was declining.
- The yield curve was upward-sloping, or normal.
- Bond quality spreads were shrinking as investor confidence improved.
- The 10-year Treasury yield was less than 10 percent.

In fact, interest rates had just hit a 45-year low and the yield on the 10-year note was under 4 percent. Clearly, investors had been selling stocks and buying bonds in record amounts despite the strong fundamental economic conditions. We took advantage of all these conditions and bought the S&P 500 index, so we will add the following trade to our cumulative record:

Buy: July 19, 2002, at 847

Part One provided us with a backdrop, or required conditions from yield curve analysis, for being in the stock market. Part Two refines the analysis by adding technical indicators. The first of these, advancing issues in the Dow, kept us out of the market from the August 2000 peak to the trough in August 2002. Yield curve analysis alone told us to buy stocks too early: right after the 2001 terrorist attacks. Waiting until all 30 of the Dow stocks fell postponed the trade almost a year and protected us from a 14 percent loss in the S&P 500 index during that time.

Table 9.2 is our updated list of trades.

TABLE 9.2 Trade Dates Using Yield Curve and
Technical Analysis

Trade	Date	S&P Index
Buy	January 2, 1960	59
Sell	September 1, 1966	77
Buy	February 1, 1967	86
Sell	July 1, 1969	97
Buy	February 1, 1970	85
Sell	June 1, 1973	105
Buy	October 1, 1974	63
Sell	December 1, 1978	94
Buy	May 1, 1980	106
Sell	November 1, 1980	127
Buy	September 1, 1981	122
Sell	October 15, 1987	298
Buy	October 20, 1987	236
Sell	October 31, 1989	340
Buy	January 2, 1991	330
Sell	July 1, 1998	1133
Buy	September 4, 1998	973
Sell	August 1, 2000	1430
Buy	July 19, 2002	847

The graph of our transactions moves the last arrow to the very bottom of the market decline (see Figure 9.1). Notice that the title of the graph has changed to include technical as well as yield curve analysis.

IMPROVED RETURNS

Our average annual return from January 1960 to July 19, 2002, almost the lowest point in the recent bear market, is about 10 percent in our trading portfolio. This compares favorably with the 6 percent return in the inactive portfolio that bought and held the S&P 500 index (see Figure 9.2). Both returns are without dividends of approximately 3 percent. The calculations are in Appendix 9.2.

Compounding our money at 10 percent made a big difference during the 42 years in question; we have four times more money in our active portfolio than we do in the passive one (see Figure 9.3).

Once again we protected ourselves from stock market volatility in the safety of a bank account during a difficult period. As an added bonus, we felt that we understood both the economy and the markets as we used

S&P Trades Indicated by Yield Curve and Technical Analysis: 1960–2005

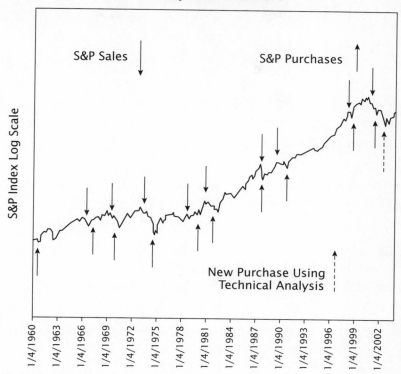

FIGURE 9.1 Yield Curve and Technical Analysis Trades

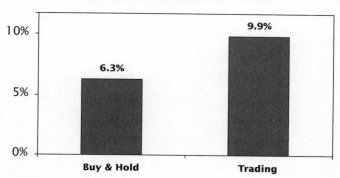

FIGURE 9.2 Return Is 9.9 Percent

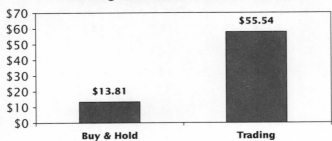

FIGURE 9.3   Portfolio Is $55.54

that knowledge to control our financial security. We met one of man's most basic psychological needs: we were in control of our environment.

SUMMARY

All 30 of the Dow Jones Industrial Average stocks rarely decline on the same day. When they do, and all of our fundamental analytics are in place, we can make a productive purchase of the S&P 500 index. We have come full circle. We look at the 30 Dow stocks individually just as investors did before Charles Dow created his index.

The rest of the chapters in Part Two provide additional specific benchmarks to aid your work in timing the markets.

CHAPTER 10

The Volatility Index

The goal in this book is to come as close as possible to identifying absolute tops and bottoms of the stock market. We are well on our way to accomplishing that goal and will complete the process in Part Three. In the meantime, we have identified one other aspect of the market: the difficulty of trading at such unpopular times. By definition, trading against the crowd at market extremes puts us on the outside of the party looking in. Everyone else is having fun buying stocks when we sell, and they enjoy hating the market when we buy.

It takes extraordinary courage of our convictions to trade the way we do, and we need all the help we can get. The rest of Part Two finds ways to strengthen our resolve with corroborating evidence. These indicators are important if only because they allow us to look at the market from a different perspective. They allow us to see sophisticated traders' short-term views of the market.

The volatility index is one of the most beloved of all the technical indicators. This index, nicknamed the VIX, is one of the most widely quoted numbers on Wall Street. We will define this term, see where to find it in the media and on the Internet, and then find out how technical analysts use the VIX to time the market. You may want to add this index to the list of indicators you watch every day; and, if you are forecasting the stock market as you read this book, the VIX may make a big difference in your results. This chapter will introduce the index and Chapters 12 and 13, on moving averages, will make it easier to read.

DEFINITION OF THE VOLATILITY INDEX

The volatility index is a measure of investors' expectations for stock market volatility.

The securities in the VIX are thought of as insurance policies on the stock market; and when people are afraid, they pay more for this insurance. We can measure investors' level of panic by looking at how much they are willing to pay for insurance.

A more technical explanation boils down to this: just as the body mass index (BMI) compares people's weight regardless of their varying heights, the VIX is a measure of option prices that removes their different time factors. The Chicago Board Options Exchange (CBOE) collects data on eight S&P contracts that are close to the price of the underlying investment. This data is entered into the Black-Scholes option pricing model. Instead of solving for price, which was the original intent for this model, they solve for volatility.

In any case, the VIX measures fear and complacency in the stock market.

The S&P 500 Index

Sophisticated investors have a shortcut for buying and selling the S&P 500 stocks. Rather than buy all 500 stocks individually and write up 500 different order tickets costing millions of dollars, they buy the S&P 500 index (SPX). This index is similar to a mutual fund that holds all 500 of the S&P stocks. There are two important differences between a mutual fund and this particular security.

The first is that the SPX trades all day long. This continuous trading gives people unlimited opportunities to make hasty, ill-considered decisions as they get caught up in crowd psychology. We will rise above the crowd and take advantage of the mob's reduced mental capacity. As usual, we will use this indicator in a contrary manner and trade against the crowd.

The second difference between the SPX and a mutual fund is the exclusive forum in which it trades. Mutual funds are designed for the general public, and the securities in these funds usually trade on the New York Stock Exchange. The SPX is designed for a more limited audience: people who trade on the Chicago Board Options Exchange. This lesser-known but very important exchange caters to sophisticated investors. Freud and other behaviorists believe that everyone, including these investors, is prone to emotional extremes. This is what Freud meant when he said in *Group Psychology and the Analysis of Ego* that crowds exult in their loss of limitations.

We will peek into the trading floor of the CBOE to see what the smart money is doing. Then we will do the opposite.

The SPX combines the two ingredients we need to take advantage of mob psychology.

The first is a security that trades all day. This provides overly emotional people the opportunity to express their fear and greed every minute of the day. On particularly nerve-racking days, people can vacillate between the two emotions several times, and the index allows them to act on each one of them. They can trade 500 different stocks with each mood swing and they can do this without taking much time to think. If they were members of the general public trading mutual funds, they would have to move much more slowly and limit themselves to the closing price at the end of each day.

The second interesting facet of this index is its special audience. Because they are trading a vehicle that is out of reach of the masses, they may become a little arrogant. People who have access to the SPX may think they are smarter than people who are constrained to investing in mutual funds.

Nothing destroys capital more efficiently than arrogance.

HOW VIX MEASURES EMOTIONAL EXTREMES

As the Chicago Board Options Exchange executes SPX trades, it updates its pricing model. It publishes this information, or the volatility index, continuously throughout the trading day. You can actually buy and sell the VIX, but we are just going to use it as a stock market indicator because it tells us what traders are doing. It tells us whether they are on the telephone with their brokers or playing poker on their trading desks.

The volatility index measures investors' fear like a clinical thermometer that ranges from about 10 to 40 degrees.

When the Index Is Low

A patient (or stock market) with a temperature (or volatility index) of only 10 degrees is very relaxed. The patient is resting. When the index is this low, we call the market overly complacent and start looking for signs of trouble. The effects of crowd psychology have lulled this patient into a stupor and we can take advantage of his condition. We will get out of the stock market just before the patient rouses; we will sell stocks when the VIX is low and just starting to rise.

When the Index Is High

A high temperature is the result of the opposite situation. Sometimes our hypothetical patient's temperature goes up to 40 degrees as he joins the hysterical crowd and, again, we can take advantage of crowd's diminished mental capabilities. We can buy stocks right after the fever breaks . . . after the VIX turns around and starts back down. Technicians identify these turning points with simple tools that we will examine in Chapter 13 on moving averages and the MACD line. All we have to do now is become familiar with this popular index.

WHY THE VIX IS IMPORTANT

The VIX measures sophisticated traders' level of anxiety and gives us a ringside seat on the Chicago Board Options Exchange. We can pick off these poor, terrified traders and buy stocks when they are crazed with fear. When the VIX is high, fear rules the market.

Conversely, we can sell stocks when the VIX is low because no one is paying attention to the market. These investors who think they know more than everyone else are resting on their laurels. They are comfortable with their portfolios and think that they do not have to do anything to improve them. They may be a little arrogant. Then we can sell stocks while these poor, unsuspecting traders play poker at their desks.

StockCharts.com has a glossary with a more scientific explanation of the volatility index on its education page: www.stockcharts.com/education /IndicatorAnalysis/indic_VIX.

WHERE TO FIND THE VIX

The VIX trades on the Chicago Board Options Exchange. The CBOE has a great web site that provides both historical and real-time quotes for the index at www.cboe.com/data. The *Wall Street Journal* lists the VIX in a table on the page entitled "Index Options Trading." These trades are usually in section C and include a table called "Underlying Indexes." The VIX is the fifteenth entry on that table. You can find free charts of the VIX at StockCharts.com and BigCharts.com.

USING THE VIX

As with so many other technical indicators, we use the VIX in a contrary manner and we trade against the crowd.

There are two reasons for using the VIX this way. The first is that we want to trade against the majority of investors because the majority, by definition, is large enough to push prices to extremes. Secondly, we want to avoid the effects of crowd psychology on our own behavior. Taken together, the size of the crowd and its diminished mental capacity motivates us to behave in opposition to it.

Extreme Prices

The best way to buy stocks when they are cheap and sell them when they are rich is to identify how these prices reach extreme levels. Very simply, the crowd drives the prices there. All we have to do is figure out when the crowd behaves in an extreme manner so that we can do the reverse. The trick is to know when the crowd's extreme behavior is undergoing a change before we make our play. The way to do this is to wait for the VIX to turn around and move in the opposite direction.

For example, in September 2002 the VIX reached one of its highest points in 10 years; it almost reached 40. Then it turned around and started to decline. This was a signal to buy stocks, and it happened near the very bottom of the bear market. The S&P 500 index traded around 800 and was just a few days away from the absolute nadir of the market.

The graph in Figure 10.1 suggests that the volatility index identifies the crowd's extreme emotions for us. The thin line is the S&P 500 index representing the stock market and the thick line is the volatility index. Obviously, the two indexes are mirror images of each other. The VIX peaks at stock market troughs, and then touches bottom when stocks make their biggest gains. (The dates on the graph may look familiar to you because they are similar to those that we developed previously in this book.)

Crowd Psychology

The other reason we want to trade against the crowd is to avoid getting caught up in the effects of mob psychology. We do not want to pile unthinkingly into the same few stocks as everyone else at the top of the market. Neither do we care to bail out at the bottom with the crazed masses. People tend to put reason aside when they join a crowd, which is why Freud said that we sink to the intellectual level of the lowest person in a crowd.

A simple tool that can help us measure the effects of crowd psychology is invaluable. The VIX fills this need because it is just one readily available number that is easy to read and measures the activity of extreme behavior on the Chicago Board Options Exchange. It gives us the courage of our convictions to think for ourselves when everyone else is caught up in the madness of crowds.

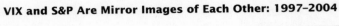

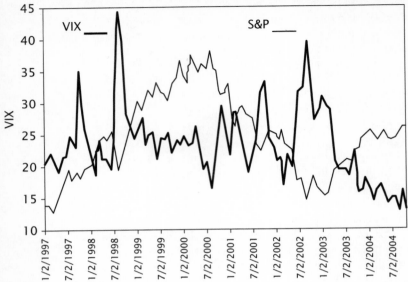

FIGURE 10.1   VIX Mirrors the S&P

SUMMARY

The VIX tells us how much investors are willing to pay for stock market "insurance." It is available in the *Wall Street Journal* and on the Internet. We now understand why behaviorists and other market technicians value this indicator so highly as a measure of extremes in crowd psychology.

When you visited the Chicago Board Options Exchange's web site you probably noticed another number, the put/call ratio. Some traders think that it is a better stock market indicator than the VIX. You can make up your own mind when you read the next chapter.

CHAPTER 11

The Put/Call Ratio

The volatility index (VIX) gave us an idea of what sophisticated traders, who are just as prone to make mistakes as the general public, think the market will do in the near future. Now we will break that number down to see whether there are more buyers or sellers in the market. The put/call ratio will give us one more view onto the trading floor of the Chicago Board Options Exchange. This ratio will allow us to get a second opinion before committing surgery on our portfolio.

There are two reasons for needing second and third opinions before making a new trade. The obvious reason is to make sure that we are right in our proposed action. Less obvious, but equally important, is our need to muster up the courage to implement this action. It is hard to have that courage when everyone else is convinced that we are wrong. No one wants to be the only person in a room who does not go along with the crowd. By definition, the point at which we feel that we should make a major shift in our portfolio is exactly the time when the rest of the world is shouting us down. The louder they shout the more correct we are apt to be in our contrarian opinion.

The best way to have courage when we need it is to have several different indicators to back up our decision. Watching the number of advancing stocks in the Dow Jones Industrial Average gave us a warning to sell as we approached top of each market cycle, and then the number of advancing stocks in the Dow pinpointed the bottom of the market. Noticing changes in the direction of the volatility index added to our confidence to act on all of our signals. Now we will look at another indicator in order to strengthen our resolve: the put/call ratio.

The put/call ratio is popular with technicians because, like the VIX, it measures the emotions of the people who trade the S&P 500 index or SPX. These traders are particularly useful to us because they are a select group of wealthy, sophisticated investors, but these people overreact to their emotions like everyone else. The put/call ratio is based on the SPX that trades on the Chicago Board Options Exchange. It tells us how many sellers there are for each buyer in this part of the market.

If you are going to the CBOE web site at www.cboe.com/data every day to track the volatility index, you may have seen the put/call ratio above it. The first thing we will do is see what people are putting and calling and then look at the ratio's usefulness as an indicator. Then Chapters 12 and 13 will examine an easy way to use both the put/call ratio and the volatility index.

PUT/CALL RATIO DEFINED

The put/call ratio is based on the S&P 500 index. It is the number of S&P put options divided by the number of S&P call options that investors own. Options are a little more abstract than the volatility index in the previous chapter; so let us clarify options with an overly simple example.

Options Are Like Grocery Store Coupons

An option is a chance to buy something at a stated price on or before a stated date. There are two kinds of options: calls and puts.

Your newspaper is full of the first kind of option, calls. Your local grocer gives you call options every time he publishes coupons in the newspaper. These coupons allow you to buy something at the reduced price at your local grocery store. This special price is a limited offer and has an expiration date. You do not have to use your coupons; it is your choice, or option, to use them or not. You can give your coupons to your neighbor; but if the item at the store is particularly valuable, you might prefer to *sell* your coupons. That transaction would make you an options trader. You just sold a call option to your neighbor, who now has the right to call, or take, that item from the local grocer. Your neighbor bought the call option because she expects prices to rise, just as people who buy call options on the S&P 500 index expect stock prices to rise.

The other kind of option, a put, is the reverse transaction. A put option allows you to sell something to someone else at a stated price. You must, of course, do so before the expiration date. If you think that the price of soup will decline, you would buy a put option from your grocer. Of course, you could let your option expire without using it as in the previous case. However, if soup prices decline you would exercise your option to put, or sell, a can of soup to your grocer. You would buy a cheap can of soup and sell it to your grocer at the stated (higher) price. A put option is an inexpensive insurance policy against the possibility that prices may decline, and people who buy puts are bearish on their market.

People trade puts and calls on stocks, bonds, and commodities all day long on the Chicago Board Options Exchange. Active traders like options because they are inexpensive to buy and they are volatile. Volatility is desirable to people who can use it to make money. In this case, however, the trader's decision must prove to be right in a short period of time because options expire. He must accurately forecast both the date and the price of the security before the expiration date. In this chapter we will look at options as an indicator of market sentiment rather than as a potential investment for ourselves. Chapter 24 will expand on options for your personal investments.

The put/call ratio more accurately describes traders' activity than the volatility index does. The VIX tells us how much fear there is among people trading options on the S&P 500 index. The put/call ratio breaks their trading down into the specific options—puts and calls. We hope to gain more insight from this more specific ratio, but it can be harder to read.

Both of these indicators fluctuate so much that it can be difficult to see when they change direction. The fact that they change direction, of course, tells us that the crowd is changing its mind and that it is time for us to make a change in our portfolio. The next chapter will make both of these indicators easier to read.

Put/Call Ratio Is More Volatile than the VIX

The graph in Figure 11.1 shows how much more volatile the put/call ratio is than the VIX. The VIX creates a path in contrast to the ratio that zigzags all over the graph.

WHERE TO FIND THE PUT/CALL RATIO

The put/call ratio, like the VIX, is on the Chicago Board Options Exchange web site and in the *Wall Street Journal*. The CBOE site has a calendar at the top of the page as a link to historical data in case you

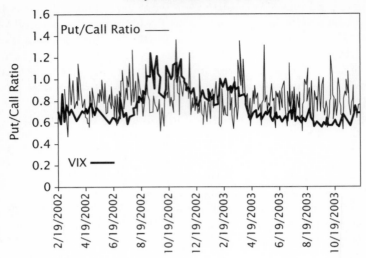

FIGURE 11.1   VIX and Put/Call Ratio

miss a day of tracking your indicators. If you are away from your computer, you can get similar information in the newspaper. *Barron's* prints the ratio, while the *Wall Street Journal* provides the raw data so you can calculate it yourself.

The *Journal* lists the total of all put options and call options on the same page with the VIX ("Index Options Trading") in a table of "Most Active Listed Options." At the bottom of that table is a summary of volume and open interest on several exchanges. All you have to do is find the volume figures for the CBOE and divide the number of put options by the number of call options. Of course, your analysis will be much better if you choose one data source and stay with it.

CRITICAL VALUES FOR THE RATIO

Many stock market technicians buy the S&P when the ratio is at or above 100 percent and sell when it goes down to 60 percent or below (see Figure 11.2).

For example, in March 2003 the ratio was 1.4 and it was a signal to buy. When this ratio is greater than 1.0, then there is more than one op-

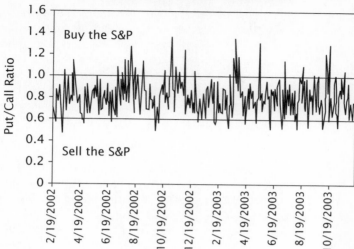

FIGURE 11.2 Sell at 60; Buy at 100

tions trader who wants to sell, or put, stock for each buyer. We would assume that the crowd has gone crazy with fear, as it did that March when we sent troops to Iraq, and we would buy stocks.

Conversely, the year before that date, March 2002, investors were unusually optimistic. The put/call ratio was only 0.45 because there were so *few* traders who wanted to sell, or put, stock. The Federal Reserve had injected new cash into the system after the terrorist attacks, we had not gone to war, and there was no new terrorism, so people thought that all their troubles were behind them. That put/call ratio would have made *us* suspicious of the market because too many people were pushing prices up. We may have sold stock at that point.

Stock market technicians use most of their sentiment indicators in a contrary manner and the put/call ratio is no different. Freud would have loved this ratio; maybe we should call him the father of technical analysis.

PUT/CALL RATIO'S RECORD AS AN INDICATOR

The put/call ratio's record as an indicator may illustrate why it is so popular with investors.

Short-Term Record

If we look at the period just before the 2004 Presidential election, we can see that the ratio produced an excellent buy signal during the summer. The stock market, the thin line on the next graph, declined all summer because of political and international uncertainty (see Figure 11.3). The put/call ratio suddenly spiked on August 6, 2004, and told investors that there was too much fear in the market. The stock market started a strong rally immediately after this signal.

Long-Term Record

The long-term record also looks good. Spikes in the put/call ratio appear to coincide with stock market troughs. The reverse is also true; the ratio was low when the stock market was high. You may recognize some important buy and sell signals that the put/call ratio generated during the difficult years from 1995 through 2003 (see Figure 11.4). Our yield curve analysis gave us the same signals in 1998, 2000, and 2002; we would have been more comfortable making those trades if we had been able to have confirmation from the put/call ratio.

This graph is harder to read because the put/call ratio is so volatile, but you can see some trends in the clusters of data points. We will solve this problem in the next chapter.

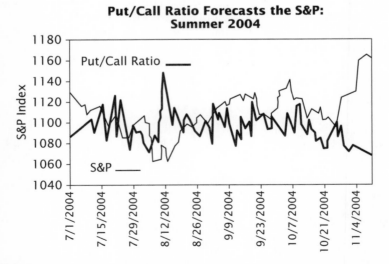

FIGURE 11.3 Put/Call Ratio Said to Buy S&P at 1060, Summer 2004

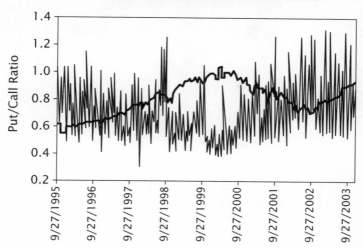

FIGURE 11.4 Put/Call Ratio Mirrors the S&P

You probably noticed the spike in the put/call ratio during the Asian currency crisis in 1997, after the Russian bond default in 1998, after the terrorist attacks in 2001, and as we approached war in Iraq near the end of 2002. In each case the ratio was over 100 percent. Each date appeared in other chapters as major opportunities to buy equities and is highlighted in Appendix 11.1. You probably notice the other extreme as well; the low points in the ratio coincide with stock market peaks.

SUMMARY

The put/call ratio is the number of put options divided by the number of call options on the S&P 500 index as reported daily by the Chicago Board Options Exchange. This ratio is available daily on the exchange's web site, in *Barron's*, and in the *Wall Street Journal*. The put/call ratio and the volatility index are two technical indicators that measure the emotions of a specific group of investors. These wealthy, sophisticated people trade the S&P 500 index options with more speed and money than the general public. Their money and fast trading make them a particularly useful indicator for stock market excess.

For us, the ratio's critical values for the put/call index are 60 percent (a signal to sell stocks) and 100 percent (a signal to buy stocks). We act in a manner that is contrary to the crowd when the ratio touches either of the two critical values. The put/call ratio more accurately reflects traders' activities than the VIX but is almost too volatile to use as a stock market indicator.

Many investors solve this problem by looking at an average of several days' data when they make their decisions. In fact, most data works better when we remove the daily fluctuations from the series. Moving averages smooth daily fluctuations, so we will look at them in the next chapter.

CHAPTER 12

Moving Averages

When Ralph Acampora stepped down off the country club's dainty gold chair, he asked for more questions from the audience at the Stamford CFA Society meeting. He called on a gentleman who asked the question on everyone's mind:

"How do you know when to sell stocks?"

Ralph was generous enough to give his list of 10 criteria and then summed up with one rule for both buying *and* selling:

"When there is a change in the direction of the moving average."

The audience was thrilled to hear him reduce the whole investment process to a dozen words! Perhaps we should find out what these moving averages are, where to find them, and how to use them. We will then test their track record of forecasting the S&P 500 index during the past decade.

DEFINITION OF MOVING AVERAGE

A moving average is similar to the traditional average that you already know, but this one changes over time. An average moves through time by dropping the oldest number and including a new one. The denominator, or number of days during which you are looking at your moving average, stays the same. For instance, if you own a stock that stays at $50 on Monday through Thursday and then doubles to $100 on Friday, your five-day average (which has not moved yet) is $300 divided by five days, or $60. Suppose on the following Monday your stock doubles again to $200. When you calculate your moving average, you drop the previous Monday's price of $50 and add this Monday's new price of $200. Your five-day moving average rises to $90.

At some point your moving average will decline for a few days and you may decide to protect your profits by selling. Moving averages help us identify changes in the marketplace so we can trade our portfolio. If your portfolio has large daily increases and decreases, or wide fluctuations, the moving average helps you see the general trend behind this volatility.

WHERE TO FIND MOVING AVERAGES

Moving averages are the first tool in this book that is not generally available. The more sophisticated our analysis becomes, the more obscure is the information. You will not find these averages in newspapers or magazines, nor are they mentioned regularly on radio and television programs.

Moving averages are, however, available on most web sites designed for investors who use technical analysis. StockCharts.com includes moving averages on most of its prepared graphs and also lets you choose your own parameters on its pages called "SharpCharts." BigCharts.com offers empty charts for you to design any way you want and includes moving averages in several mathematical formats. Yahoo.com gives you several basic tools on each stock's technical analysis page. MarketScreen.com has so many choices that you may linger much longer than you expected to because you enjoy designing your own charts.

IMPORTANCE OF MOVING AVERAGES

We use the moving average to find the underlying trend in a series of numbers with wide swings every day. In the preceding two chapters we looked at two important but volatile indicators, the volatility index and the put/call ratio. The ratio, in particular, is so volatile that it is almost useless; we saw it create a buy signal one day and a sell signal the next, and we do not want to be whipsawed like that. Moving averages help to alleviate the problem by smoothing the data and taking the rough edges off our numbers. It is a little like getting a trim at the barbershop; keep the hair but tame the cowlick.

USING MOVING AVERAGES

Market technicians use these averages to identify major turns in the market. We buy or sell after the moving average changes direction and continues in that new direction for several days. How long is several? Wait just one or two days if you are using a short-term average and about a week or two for longer averages. For example, if you are following a five-day moving average, then you want to trade after a new trend is established for one or two days; a 120-day average would suggest that you wait a couple of weeks for a new trend to develop. Many people use two averages so that they will cross each other and make that decision for them.

Hedge fund managers and commodities traders are some of the best-known market technicians. They trade after their moving averages establish a clear trend. These trend followers are particularly concerned with the question of how many days constitute a moving average.

How Many Days in a Moving Average?

Greg Hryb is president of Darien Capital and was one of the people who developed several Chicago Board Options Exchange products. He uses the number of days by which an indicator leads the S&P 500 Index to select his moving averages. Matching the indicator's lead time to the days in his moving average closes the gap between the trading signal and the expected move in the S&P.

The more days you include in your moving average, the smoother your series of numbers becomes. If you are graphing your data, the line on your graph becomes flatter. The next two graphs of two very different moving averages illustrate that point. These graphs use data that is unusually volatile even for the put/call ratio.

The years 2002 and 2003 were two of the most volatile in stock market history and investors' emotions reflected fear one day (ratio over 1.0) and greed the very next day (ratio less than 0.6). You could have lost a lot of money trading each buy and sell signal; your broker, however, would have loved the commissions. Overlaying a five-day moving average helps put the data in perspective (see Figure 12.1).

Compare that volatile graph to the next one with a smooth line representing a 120-day moving average (see Figure 12.2). This smooth line says that fear crested in October 2002 and declined for the next few months; we know that the stock market improved during those few months. Then you can see a minor bump in the average just before the Iraq war in March 2003. The trend reversed after the war started as fear gave way to greed for the rest of the year; the stock market made about 20 percent during that period.

Suppose that those two graphs were on your desk on October 2, 2002, and you do not know that the next day is the investment opportunity of your lifetime. Which moving average would have helped you forecast the absolute bottom of the stock market on October 3, 2002: the five-day or

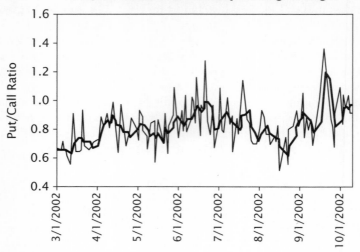

FIGURE 12.1 Five-Day Moving Average

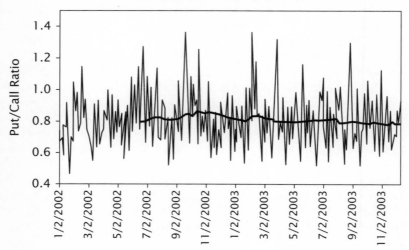

FIGURE 12.2 Longer Moving Average

the 120-day? Would you have seen the opportunity and had the conviction to take advantage of the S&P 500 index at 776, which was the lowest price in six years?

Both moving averages identified the new trend; the shorter one kept you on your toes and probably required other signals to help you read it. The longer moving average was so smooth that it failed to identify a particular trading date. Professionals use both of them together to identify a trade signal when two moving averages cross and then move together in the same direction. Both averages crossed and moved up together several times in Figure 12.3 and created three buy signals. Greed replaced fear in this new trend, and it was time to buy stocks on the days with the arrows.

This graph would have given you some great signals as the stock market bounced along the bottom of the devastating bear market. The first buy signal on this graph is late August (when the S&P was around 900). Another opportunity that this graph identified was in the middle of

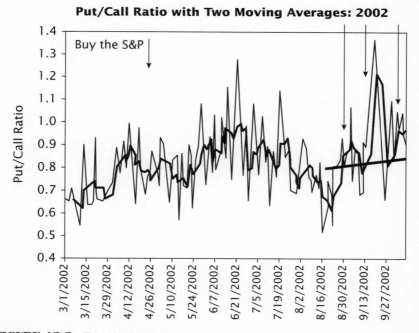

FIGURE 12.3 Two Moving Averages

September. Finally, there was a buy signal on October 3 (when the S&P touched bottom at 776). In addition to the fact that this graph generated these accurate buy signals, there were no misleading sell signals; the long-term moving average kept you in the market at the right time.

If moving averages are so helpful with the put/call ratio, you have to wonder what they can do for the volatility index.

VIX Graph with Moving Averages

The volatility index fluctuates less than the put/call ratio, so the 120-day moving average will not give us any useful information during the summer of 2002. Therefore, we will use two other popular moving averages, the 12-day and the 26-day, which happen to be the building blocks for an analysis in the next chapter. Figure 12.4 shows how they look on the VIX graph for that difficult year of 2002. Again, technicians identify a new trend when the two moving averages cross and move together. Early in June investors shook off their complacency and started to feel nervous, so contrarian technicians sold the S&P 500 index. Fear increased over the summer until that trend reversed itself in early August when it was time to buy the stock market. These two trades saved investors about 15 percent of their portfolios during the two-month span.

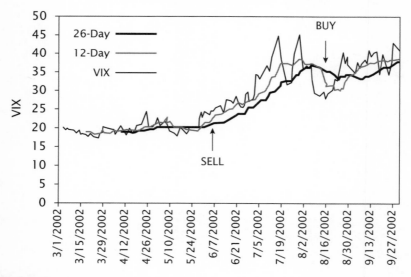

FIGURE 12.4 VIX

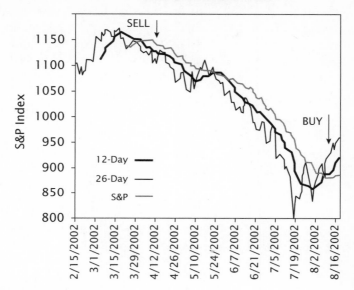

S&P 500 Index with 12-Day and 26-Day Moving Averages: 2002

FIGURE 12.5 S&P with Moving Averages

Moving averages are so helpful with indicators that we have to wonder how they look on a graph of the S&P 500 index itself.

S&P Graph with Moving Averages

We will use the same 12-day and the 26-day moving averages to examine that difficult year of 2002. Again, technicians identify a new trend when the two moving averages cross and move together. Figure 12.5 tells us to sell the S&P in early April at 1130 when the two averages cross and move down together; then it tells us to buy it back in August at 962 because the lines cross and move up together.

Because this graph directed us to sell stocks near the peak of the market and buy them back near the bottom, it protected our portfolio from losing 15 percent of its value in just four months. This is working so well that we should see what moving averages can do for us on a long-term graph of the S&P 500 index.

Figure 12.6 shows the same 12-day and 26-day moving averages plotted against the S&P 500 index for the past decade. As you may expect, these averages captured the major moves but not the short-term ones.

FIGURE 12.6 S&P with Moving Averages over a Decade

There is no way that a moving average of almost one month could have caught the brief currency crisis in 1998, but it was even a little late identifying the major moves.

Many technicians use shorter moving averages to capture more market changes. It just happens that combining a three-day with a six-day moving average gave good results during the past 10 years (see Figure 12.7).

The averages cross and move together in time to catch the major market moves, but it is hard to read a graph with so much information on it. We will address that difficulty in the next chapter.

SUMMARY

Ralph Acampora feels that a change in the direction of a moving average signals a trading opportunity. While it is wonderful to distill the investment process down to its essence, we must choose our averages carefully and know what constitutes a change. Using two of these averages together identifies a point of change.

Moving averages help confirm our trading decisions from previous

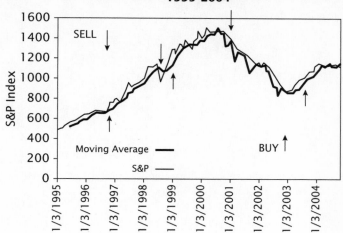

S&P with Three-Day and Six-Day Moving Averages: 1995–2004

FIGURE 12.7 S&P with Shorter Moving Averages

chapters and add to our confidence when we identify a market top or bottom. By definition, these averages will be a little late with their signals, but we can see the lines coming together before they cross. At the very least, moving averages smooth volatile data and identify trends.

Now we need to take the moving averages off the cluttered graphs so we can look at them separately and give them the attention they deserve.

CHAPTER 13

Using Moving Averages: The MACD Line

M oving averages are an important source for the second opinion that we want before we trade. By definition, however, they are a lagging indicator. We can correct part of this weakness by watching each new trade signal as it develops. We may be able to speed up the identification of a new signal by watching its two lines move together or apart from each other. It may help us to know if our two moving averages are converging or diverging and getting ready to generate a new trade signal.

This information is important enough to warrant its own graph.

Stock market technicians have so many tools that sometimes the graphs become hard to read. The solution is to take some lines off the graph and present them in a format that highlights their information. In this case, the information we want to put under the spotlight tells us whether the moving averages are moving toward or away from each other . . . whether they are converging or diverging.

We will diagram their movements in a way that will emphasize the speed with which those changes are taking place. Then we will place these diagrams under the S&P 500 index, the volatility index, and the put/call ratio to make these indexes give us more information and improve our trading. The market lost 30 percent during the first nine months of 2002 and then rallied strongly, so we will test our new tools against this challenging scenario.

MOVING AVERAGE CONVERGENCE/DIVERGENCE LINE

The moving average convergence/divergence (MACD) line tells us whether the moving averages are moving toward or away from each other.

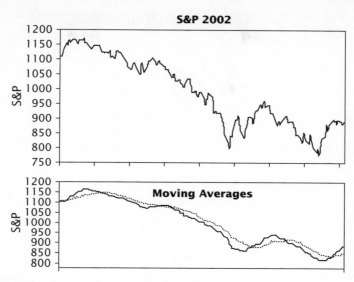

FIGURE 13.1 S&P with Moving Averages Underneath

The idea is to see if these numbers are converging or diverging so we can prepare for a change in the market. Technicians put the two moving averages underneath the graph so they are easier to read.

The specific moving averages that most technicians use are the 12-day and 26-day series that we developed in the previous chapter. However, our new moving averages give extra weight to recent data in order to emphasize its importance. This minor refinement will change the shape of the line that results from the calculation. When the market changes quickly, that difference is magnified. That is the whole point. We give yesterday's price more weight than previous ones to overcome the time lag inherent in technical analysis.

Graphs of these special averages are standard offerings on most web sites such as Yahoo.com, StockCharts.com, and BigCharts.com that cater to stock market technicians. As you can see, it is much easier to read the next graph (see Figure 13.1) than the ones in the previous chapter. In this case, the moving averages are printed separately.

Technicians trade when both of the moving averages cross and move in the same direction together. Because it is not enough for the lines to cross, we add a baseline to show when they move together in a new direction. The next graph (Figure 13.2) draws a baseline through the two moving averages and colors in between the lines to accentuate the comparison. The result looks like mountains of opportunity (buy signals)

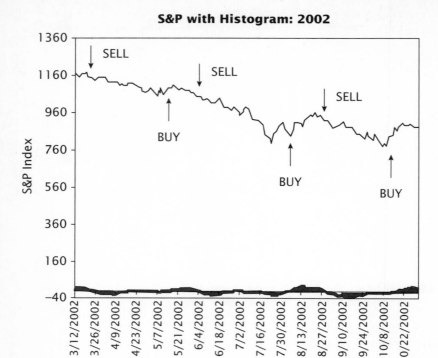

FIGURE 13.2   Market Calls in 2002

and lakes of despair (sell signals). Buy when the line crosses zero and starts climbing the mountain of opportunity; sell when the line crosses zero and dives into the depths of despair.

The technical name for this addition to our graph is a "histogram," or graph of tabulated frequencies. It tells us how many observations there were at each data point. Histograms are so important that we often separate them from the graph and blow them up for legibility. The next section will do exactly that so you can read them more easily. First we will learn how to read a histogram and find what generates a trading signal. The trigger for a trade occurs when the moving average crosses zero: buy when the line crosses zero and moves up, and sell when it crosses zero and descends.

As you can see, moving averages point out some great trades; the active portfolio still lost 5 percent during the six-month period under scrutiny, but the passive portfolio lost 22 percent. More importantly, the active portfolio was out of the stock market during the major decline over the summer (see Table 13.1).

TABLE 13.1 Trading the S&P with the MACD

Action	Date	S&P Index	Active Portfolio Gain/Loss	Passive Portfolio Gain/Loss
Buy	4/22/02	1107.64	$	$
Sell	5/1/02	1086.17	−21.47	0
Buy	5/15/02	1091.07		
Sell	6/5/02	1049.9	−41.17	0
Buy	6/26/02	973.52		
Sell	7/8/02	976.98	3.46	0
Buy	8/1/02	884.66		
Sell	9/3/02	878.02	−6.64	0
Buy	10/11/02	835.32		
End	10/31//02	885.00	49.68	−222
			−$16.14	−$222
			−5%	−22%

Technicians like the MACD line with a benchmark, or histogram, so much that they separate it from the graph and draw it as a bar chart in order to glean even more information from it.

A HISTOGRAM IS A PICTURE

A histogram is a bar chart showing the volume of trades at each price. Technicians use histograms to see how quickly the market is changing so they can forecast the strength of the next trend.

On the assumption that we are creatures of habit, technicians assume that tomorrow will resemble today. Think of how our children resemble us because they share our gene pool; tomorrow's stock market is the child of today's market. If you are a physicist you think in terms of a body in motion staying in motion at the same speed and in the same direction.

Specifically, if the market is starting to strengthen and this change is happening in a big way, investors have a lot of pent-up demand. Money is burning a hole in their pocket and they are buying as fast as they can. Technicians assume that the next trend will be upward and that it will be stronger than average. Conversely, if investors start dumping stocks, panic is taking over and the next move will probably be a serious bear market.

When the change is strong, the next trend up or down may also be strong. Technicians often present the histogram separately and on a large scale in order to get a better look at it. A strong change in direction is easy to spot with a picture like the one in Figure 13.3.

The difference between the two moving averages jumps off the page when a separate histogram appears on a large scale. It illustrates the strength of a change in the market. StockCharts.com explains both the MACD and histograms in its Chart School glossary and tells how to use both of them in trading: www.stockcharts.com/education/Indicator Analysis.

Another way to describe the speed with which the market is changing is "momentum."

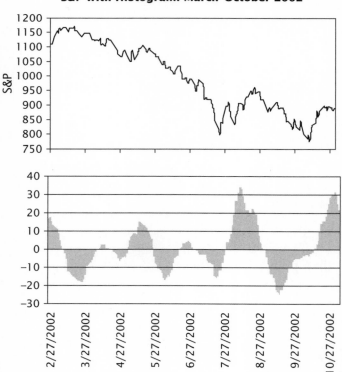

FIGURE 13.3 Separate Histogram 2002

TABLE 13.2 Trade Dates

Trade	Date	S&P 500 Index
Buy	1/2/91	330
Sell	7/1/98	1133
Buy	9/4/98	973
Sell	8/1/00	1430
Buy	7/19/02	847

MOMENTUM

Momentum is so important to investors that we assign our own slant to the definition. To investors, momentum is acceleration, the *change* in the speed at which something is moving. People buy Aston Martins because, in addition to looking sexy, they accelerate from zero to 60 in a few seconds; this car has great momentum compared to a truck.

We used momentum in Part One when we analyzed changing quality spreads in the bond market. We sold stocks because speculative bond returns increased dramatically compared to Treasuries before the 1998 Russian bond default. The line on our graph of these changes, or momentum, went straight up and told us that investors were growing more fearful at an increasing rate. Despite this cautionary signal in the bond market, the stock market continued to set new highs every day. We knew that extreme fear in the bond market would soon translate into a decline in the stock market, so we sold stocks before the crash. A histogram clarifies this concept for us by drawing a picture of acceleration and deceleration.

The histogram identifies all of our trades in 1998, 2000, and 2001 (see Table 13.2 and Figure 13.4).

The most important information gleaned from a histogram is momentum. The sharp upward turns of the histogram at the end of 1998 and in August 2002 accurately forecast the rampant bull markets in the future. On the other hand, the sharp turn down in the middle of 2000 said that the coming bear market would be serious. There were, unfortunately, some false signals right after the terrorist attacks.

HISTOGRAMS WITH THE VIX AND PUT/CALL RATIO

Histograms tell us when and how quickly *any* data is changing. The volatility index, for example, is much easier to read with a histogram

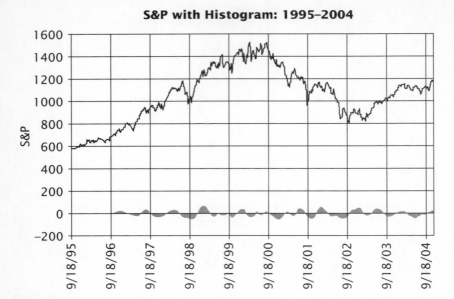

FIGURE 13.4 S&P with Histogram over a Decade

telling us when a change is developing and the strength of that change. This powerful but volatile indicator becomes much more useful when we look at it through the lens of a histogram (see Figure 13.5). Notice how easy it is to identify the coming change in the VIX in August 2002 when the histogram turned at a sharp angle. Many investors bought stocks when they knew that the VIX was ready for a strong move upward.

Even the put/call ratio becomes easier to read with a histogram (see Figure 13.6). You may remember from the preceding chapter that this ratio is bullish for us when it is high because that indicates most people are buying put options to get rid of stock. Even this erratic indicator calms down under the influence of moving averages. The histogram moved up sharply at the end of August and told investors that fear was increasing and that it was time to buy stocks. Then it broke their hearts with a false signal in September.

SUMMARY

The moving average convergence/divergence (MACD) line improves our ability to get that vital second opinion on a trade before we implement it.

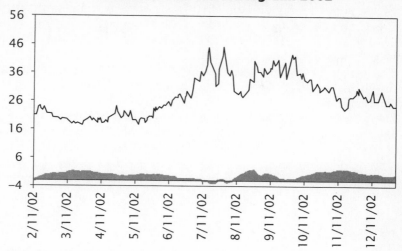

FIGURE 13.5 VIX with Histogram

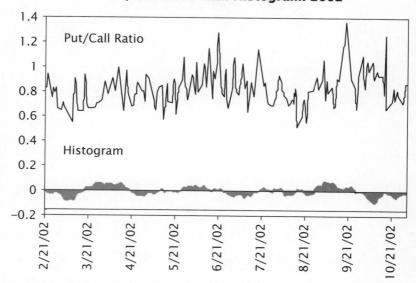

FIGURE 13.6 Put/Call Ratio with Histogram

We have more confidence in our trades if we have confirmation from the VIX or the put/call ratio, and the MACD makes them easier to interpret. An added bonus is the application of the MACD directly to the S&P 500 index as a stand-alone trading tool. Of course, this applies to individual stocks and mutual funds as well.

The histogram that accompanies the MACD line is extremely valuable because it highlights the momentum that may affect the strength of the next market trend.

Many hedge fund managers and commodities traders use moving averages to identify trends. Trend followers expect to capture the center of each market move rather than trade at the absolute tops and bottoms. They make up for missing the very best prices in the market by augmenting their returns with leverage, so we will look at leverage in the next chapter.

CHAPTER 14

Leverage: Short Positions and Margin Debt

L everage in the market deserves special attention as we collect confirming signals to underwrite each new trade decision. Leverage causes stock market bubbles and, when it breaks under its own weight, causes stock market crashes. Leverage is so important and generates such outrageous Wall Street stories that Chapter 26 is so titled and tells the stories. Many investors use leverage, but we will focus on trend followers because they are among the most active practitioners who use this tool.

Trend followers compensate for missing the market's absolute tops and bottoms by using leverage when they *are* in the market. They use three kinds of leverage: margin debt, short positions, and volatile instruments such as options that have leverage built into their discounted prices. We have already explored options in our chapters on the VIX and the put/call ratio. Now we will see how margin debt and short positions can help us as confirming indicators. We will define the two terms and then identify data sources in the media and on the Internet. Finally, we will test this data for usefulness in identifying previous turns in the market.

This discussion of leverage completes our brief overview of technical indicators that many professional money managers combine with yield curve analysis to make their market timing decisions. In Part Three we will add one more tool: cultural indicators.

LEVERAGE CAUSES MARKET EXTREMES

Two variables appear at extreme levels in the stock market: leverage and low-quality investments. These two soul mates find each other at the top of a bubble market and break up at the bottom. When people run out of good investments to buy, they move into low-quality securities such as the speculative bonds we studied in Part One or newly issued stocks with no earnings. Add leverage from margin debt, stir in a little greed, and watch the love match heat up; the affair ends quickly when reality sets in. At the bottom of the market, despair takes over and people practice leverage in the opposite direction by selling short. Margin accounts and short selling are mirror images of each other and provide leverage at each market extreme. Technical analysts watch the levels of margin accounts and short positions like wedding singers and divorce lawyers looking for business.

MARGIN DEBT

Margin debt is the money that people borrow from their brokerage firms. Investors borrow from their brokers through a margin account that they open in order to buy stock with the firm's money. Brokers offer these accounts for three reasons: the high interest rates they pay, the excitement generated by playing with someone else's money, and the ability to lend customers stock for short sales.

Interest on Margin Accounts

The interest rate on margin accounts rises with the general level of interest rates. When the stock market is high, so are interest rates; and brokerage firms can earn additional income from the interest on margin debt. During 1999 and 2000 a well-respected brokerage firm paid its salespeople 10 percent of the interest on their customers' margin accounts as an indication of management's interest in this kind of business.

Excitement in Margin Trading

Good salespeople will create excitement for their firms' products among their customers. Margin accounts fit right into this environment because they heighten the experience of playing the stock market. Not only do customers control larger positions than they otherwise would, but they do so with other people's money. Investing is much more interesting under these conditions.

It is no surprise, then, that margin account debt increases as the stock market goes up. In fact, margin debt and the Nasdaq both peaked in March 2000. Margin debt then fell even faster than the market; by the following September margin accounts fell 48 percent. This game is tame compared to short sales. When you buy stock on margin, your loss is limited to the amount of cash you borrow from your broker. Short sales are subject to unlimited losses.

Short Sales Borrow Stock

Customers borrow stock as well as cash from their brokerage firms in margin accounts. Selling stock you borrowed from your broker is selling short. People borrow stock to sell when they expect the market to decline and they want to sell more than they own. Selling with other people's money is even more exciting than buying with borrowed funds because your potential loss is unlimited. The day you sell the S&P 500 index short could be the day that the stock market actually does grow to the sky, and you must replace the borrowed stock at prices that increase faster than you can place orders. Of course, there are fortunes to be made as well.

Leverage Exaggerates Market Moves

Customers must repay whatever they borrowed in their margin account when the market moves against them. If they borrowed cash to increase their positions at a market peak, then the brokerage firm demands money when the market declines. Investors must come up with cash within 24 hours to meet these margin calls, or the brokers liquidate their holdings.

This forced selling, of course, tends to depress prices that are already dropping and caused the margin calls in the first place. The whole financial system suffers when too many people do this at once.

The same thing happens at the bottom of the market; investors lose money on the stock they borrowed to sell short, so they get another margin call. Again, investors scramble for cash and their actions magnify the move in the market. Margin calls, which are the result of leverage, usually exaggerate each turn in the stock market.

We have seen real examples of margin calls exacerbating each directional change in the stock market. It has been said that the Long-Term Capital Management hedge fund borrowed $30 for each $1 that it owned to buy Russian bonds in 1998, and that its margin calls affected dozens of firms that lent to it. These calls deepened the bear market that followed.

By contrast, overly pessimistic short sellers got caught in the sudden explosion of market optimism in October 2002; margin calls caused them to buy back their borrowed stock at increasingly higher prices. Every time they bought stock to cover their short position they pushed the market higher for the next poor soul who had to meet a margin call. Again, margin calls intensified the market move.

WHERE TO FIND INFORMATION

Margin debt and short sales information is easy to find and requires no calculations to interpret the data. The *Wall Street Journal* publishes both margin debt levels and the size of customers' short positions, called "short interest," in section C ("Money & Investing") once a month. The *Journal* gets raw data from the New York Stock Exchange, which delivers it directly to you on its web site at www.nyse.com. Search for "margin debt" to access the appropriate file, and "factbook" for historical and current short sales. The fact book provided all the data for the graphs in this chapter. The financial press usually has feature articles when either margin debt or short sales reach extreme levels, but balanced reporting obliges the reporters to present both sides of the investment question. You may have to interpret their reports on your own.

USING THE DATA

As usual, we will use this data in a contrarian manner. We will assume that human behavior overdoes everything at the top and bottom of the stock market as fear and greed crowd out common sense. Therefore, we will sell stocks when everyone else is borrowing money from their brokers to buy stock and margin debt is high; and we will buy stocks when everyone else is borrowing stocks to sell short.

Margin Debt Moves with the Stock Market

The graph in Figure 14.1 shows that margin debt moves with the stock market but becomes more exaggerated at the top. Margin debt is a wonderful barometer of greed.

Using margin debt to time the stock market is so productive that it warrants a second look. In order to make it easier to read the data, here is a graph of the difference between margin debt and the S&P 500 index with a trend line to show what is normal (see Figure 14.2).

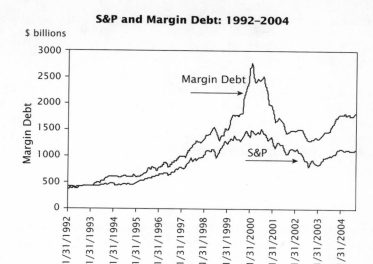

FIGURE 14.1   Margin Debt Magnifies the S&P
Source: New York Stock Exchange report, "NYSE Member Firms Customers' Margin Debt."

Again, there are obvious peaks and valleys around the trend line that identify market excesses. Margin debt peaked right along with the market in 1994, 1998, and 2000. In contrast, margin debt fell below normal during the time that people *should* have added to their stock portfolios during the mid-1990s and in 2003. There is one period when this sentiment indicator led us astray: early in 2002. If you bought stocks during this period you had to wait several months to make money.

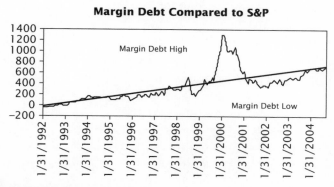

FIGURE 14.2   Margin Debt Trend Line

Short Sales Move Inversely to the S&P Index

The volume of short sales moves in opposition to the stock market. Investors succumb to the pessimism surrounding the worst part of each market cycle and borrow stock from their brokers so that they can sell short. It is fascinating to see how short sales move in mirror images of the stock market. Short sales peaked in 1992 at the beginning of the longest uninterrupted bull market in history; investors sold the most when they should have been buying. Conversely, short sales *declined* in 1969 at the peak of that historic bull market. That is exactly when people should have been selling.

Short Interest

The number of shares sold short has increased along with the size of the stock market in general, so the next graph, Figure 14.3, is in percentage form for easy reading.

Days to Cover

Stock market technicians use the short interest ratio to calculate the number of days it would take for all short sellers to buy back their stock. When it takes more days than usual for them to cover their positions, you can be pretty sure that the market is ready for a rally. One reason for this is that people like to "squeeze the shorts" by driving up the market when short sellers are the most vulnerable. No one said that Wall Street is nice.

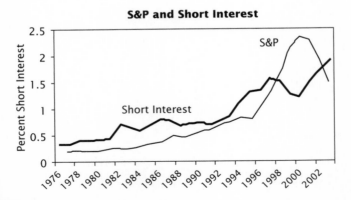

FIGURE 14.3 Short Interest Mirrors the S&P

SUMMARY

Knowing how much leverage is in the market is important to us. Because leverage magnifies important turning points in the market, we need to be aware of how much margin debt is on the books at brokerage firms and how many days it will take to cover short positions. Leverage is more than a coincident indicator that helps us with investment decisions; it causes stock market bubbles to boom and burst.

Because investors express their fear and greed in their leverage, margin accounts may be the best place to see the effects of crowd psychology.

CHAPTER 15

Summary of Technical Analysis

P art Two gave us the tools to measure fear and greed in the market-place so that we could trade against the crowd. We are more able to buy stocks cheaply when everyone else is panic-stricken and wants to sell them to us at any price. However, we like to have a lot of people clamoring for our merchandise when *we* sell, so we are happy to give the optimists a chance to mount a bidding war for our portfolio. It is not our fault that they are making exactly the wrong decision each time. They can not help being victims of the effects of crowd psychology. They do not know that Freud said that the intelligence sinks to the lowest level represented in a crowd. We just measure the crowd's emotions and then trade in the other direction.

We measured the investing masses' fear and greed with tools from technical analysis. One of our tools, the number of advancing stocks in the Dow Jones Industrial Average, became and indicator for us and provided a trade date for the model portfolio. The rest of the tools appear to be a little less reliable in identifying absolute tops and bottoms of the market, so we use them to support our trades. The volatility index, the put/call ratio, moving averages, and the amount of leverage in the market validate our decisions as they strengthen our resolve to defy the crowd.

Technical analysis is a dispassionate observer of behavior. Technical indicators have credibility because they use prices rather than opinions about a company's future earnings or what the Federal Reserve may do. Most investors blend fundamental and technical analysis in an effort to use the best of both worlds.

I think that the best from the world of fundamental analysis is the predictive ability of the yield curve, and I find the number of advancing stocks in the Dow to be the most reliable technical indicator.

Investing in defiance of the crowd is very difficult, however, and we need all the indicators we can get to confirm a proposed change in our portfolio. The volatility index, the put/call ratio, moving averages, and the amount of leverage in the market serve this purpose well.

OUR USE OF THE DOW

Charles Dow revolutionized investing in 1896 when he created the Dow Jones Industrial Average. His benchmark allowed investors to track the whole market easily rather than having to look at each stock separately.

We use his index to isolate 30 of the largest stocks in U.S. business and then we see how many of them advance each day. On those rare days when all 30 of these very different stocks from diverse industries decline, we know that crowd psychology is at work. We know that people are so pessimistic that they are selling stocks from a broad range of industries, including some that often move in opposition to each other. It is time for us to buy the S&P 500 index when pessimism is so widespread.

There was just one instance of all 30 Dow stocks declining at once between 2000 and 2004; on July 19, 2002, all 30 declined and the Dow closed at 847. Not even after the terrorist attacks did we see such pessimism. The market closed for almost a week in September 2001, and when it reopened several telecom stocks in the Dow moved up in price. (People trapped in the burning World Trade Center towers used their cell phones to call for help and dramatized the benefits of this technology.) It was not until July 2002 that investors became so despondent that they failed to see value in any of the Dow industrials.

ADDING A NEW TRADE TO OUR RECORD

Let us summarize the conditions that allowed us to make this new trade:

- The federal funds rate was declining.
- The yield curve was upward-sloping, or normal.
- Bond quality spreads were shrinking as investor confidence improved.
- The 10-year Treasury yield was less than 10 percent.

TABLE 15.1   Part Two Trade Dates

Trade	Date	S&P 500 Index
Buy	January 2, 1960	59
Sell	September 1, 1966	77
Buy	February 1, 1967	86
Sell	July 1, 1969	97
Buy	February 1, 1970	85
Sell	June 1, 1973	105
Buy	October 1, 1974	63
Sell	December 1, 1978	94
Buy	May 1, 1980	106
Sell	November 1, 1980	127
Buy	September 1, 1981	122
Sell	October 15, 1987	298
Buy	October 20, 1987	236
Sell	October 31, 1989	340
Buy	January 2, 1991	330
Sell	July 1, 1998	1133
Buy	September 4, 1998	973
Sell	August 1, 2000	1430
Buy	July 19, 2002	847

The 10-year was well under 10 percent with a yield of 3.80 percent. This was the lowest level in 45 years because investors had been buying bonds in record amounts even though the economy was improving. We bought the S&P 500 index and we will add the following trade to our cumulative record: buy the S&P 500 index on July 19, 2002, at 847. Table 15.1 is our new list of trades.

The graph of our transactions shows our last purchase to be at the very bottom of the market decline (see Figure 15.1). Notice that the title of the graph has changed to include technical as well as yield curve analysis.

Our model portfolio now has a return of 9.9 percent compared to the passive portfolio's 6.3 percent return (see Figure 15.2); both are without dividends, which averaged 3.2 percent during this 45-year period.

The assets in our managed portfolio are now four times larger than the passive portfolio (see Figure 15.3).

Because it is so hard to trade in opposition to the crowd, we like to have confirmation from other indicators. The volatility index (VIX), the put/call ratio, moving averages, and amount of leverage in the system act as second opinions for our trade decisions. The VIX and the put/call ratio

S&P Trades Indicated by Yield Curve and Technical Analysis: 1960–2002

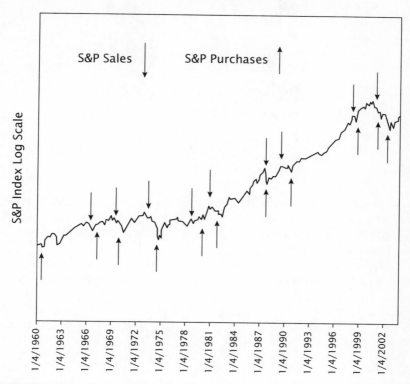

FIGURE 15.1 Part Two Graph of Trades with Yield Curve and Technical Analysis

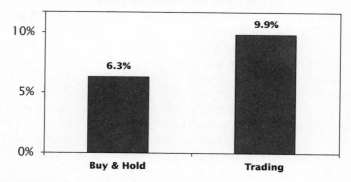

FIGURE 15.2 Part Two Return Is 9.9 Percent

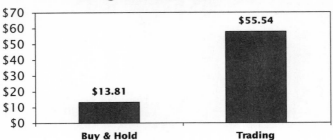

FIGURE 15.3 Portfolio Is $55.54

are so volatile that it is often hard to read their graphs; technicians use moving averages to smooth this kind of data and make it easier to read. Moving averages also identify changes in the direction of the market and can be valuable indicators.

When moving averages are seen as converging or diverging, they give even more information. The moving average convergence/divergence (MACD) line gives advance warning of an impending change and may signal the strength of the developing trend. We like to see support from any one of these technical indicators before making a trade with yield curve analysis.

VOLATILITY INDEX

When investors are in a panic to get out of the market (or into it!), they do not have time to execute 500 separate trades costing millions of dollars. They can have the same effect on their portfolios if they just buy or sell options on the S&P 500 index, and they can do this inexpensively in one quick trade. S&P options trades, therefore, provide an ideal way to measure the emotions of sophisticated, but often fallible, investors who use this vehicle.

Fortunately for us, the Chicago Board Options Exchange measures the implied volatility based on prices of eight near-the-money S&P options and publishes the results every day in the *Wall Street Journal* and on its web site. The volatility index is an excellent indicator of fear and greed, and the rule of thumb is to buy the S&P when the rising VIX changes di-

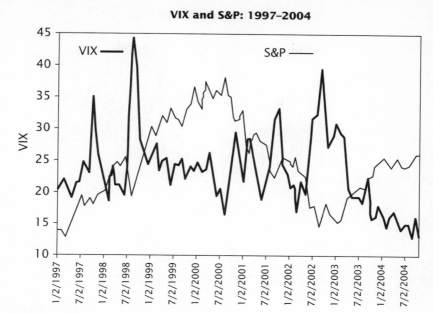

FIGURE 15.4 VIX Moves in Opposition to the S&P

rection. The graph in Figure 15.4 shows the inverse relationship between this indicator and the market.

PUT/CALL RATIO

The put/call ratio breaks the volatility index down into its components. It allows us to see how many sellers (puts) there are for each buyer (calls) of S&P 500 options. The critical values here are 100 percent and 60 percent. Technicians usually buy stocks when the ratio is greater than or equal to 100 percent and sell when it is 60 percent or less. Spikes in the put/call ratio coincide with stock market troughs. The reverse is also true; the ratio is usually low when the stock market is high (see Figure 15.5).

This graph identifies most of the changes in market direction. There was a spike in the put/call ratio during the Asian currency crisis in 1997, the Russian bond default in 1998, the terrorist attacks in 2001, and the

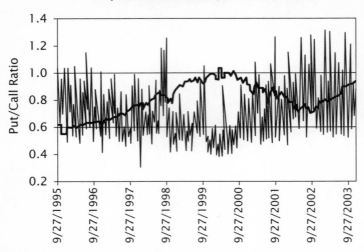

FIGURE 15.5   Put/Call Ratio Moves in Opposition to the S&P

approach to the Iraq war near the end of 2002. In each case the ratio was over 100 percent. Most of these dates are in our model portfolio as major opportunities to buy equities. You probably noticed the other extreme as well; the low points in the ratio coincide with stock market peaks.

MOVING AVERAGES

A moving average drops the oldest number in a series and includes a more recent one. The denominator, or number of days during which you are looking at your moving average, stays the same. A trade signal develops when two moving averages cross and then move together in the same direction. We use 12-day and 26-day moving averages to examine that difficult year of 2002. This graph tells us to sell the S&P in early April at 1130 when the two averages cross and move down together; then it tells us to buy it back in August because the lines cross and move up together (see Figure 15.6).

Because this graph directed us to sell stocks near the peak of the mar-

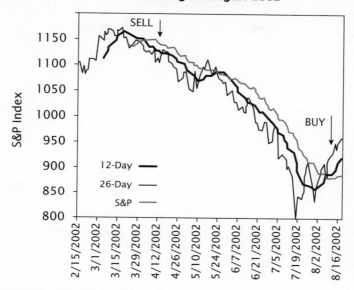

FIGURE 15.6 S&P with Moving Averages

ket and buy them back near the bottom, it protected our portfolio from losing 15 percent of its value in just four months.

The real information, however, is in the averages' movements toward and away from each other as they get ready to generate a new trade signal. The MACD lines illustrate this changing relationship. A histogram shows us two things: we can see a new signal developing and how strong we can expect it to be. The histogram below the graph in Figure 15.7 dramatizes the strength of the developing trends in August and October 2002.

LEVERAGE

Margin accounts and short selling are mirror images of each other. Each is a source of leverage, and each magnifies the market when it reaches an extreme. Margin debt moves in tandem with the market (see Figure 15.8).

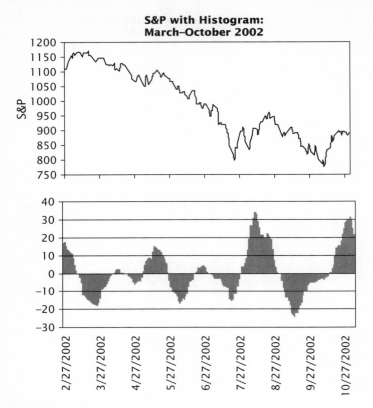

FIGURE 15.7   S&P with Histogram

Short selling tends to move in opposition to the market (see Figure 15.9).

Some analysts think that extreme amounts of leverage have caused every stock market bubble and subsequent crash. It is no wonder that investors keep an eye on these numbers—they are the epitome of the effects of crowd psychology about which Freud warned!

Freud would have loved technical analysis and its ability to measure investors' emotions. Combined with yield curve analysis, these technical indicators help us identify the tops and bottoms of the stock market.

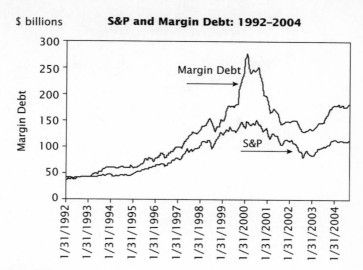

FIGURE 15.8 Margin Debt
Source: New York Stock Exchange report, "NYSE Member Firms Customers' Margin Debt."

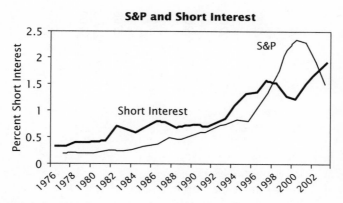

FIGURE 15.9 Short Interest

PART III

Cultural Indicators

The telephone rang in the middle of the night, and I knew it was bad news. No one ever calls after midnight to say they won the lottery and want to share the prize with you. No family member ever calls me on a business trip unless he got fired, and this was no exception.

My niece, who is like a daughter to me, is in one of the most cyclical businesses in our economy: advertising. Because her mother died during childbirth, I have always felt responsible for Elizabeth and I feel like I have been punched in the stomach every time she loses a job at the beginning of a recession. Of course, I am elated when she gets a new job during an economic recovery and we have fun planning her glamorous new career together. Elizabeth is one of my greatest blessings; she is also one of my best economic and stock market indicators. Elizabeth's career epitomizes the cultural signals that grab me and force me to see changes in trends.

Sometimes the yield curve changes shape and technical analysis identifies a new trend in the market, but we just cannot believe what our eyes are seeing. Sometimes we know in our hearts that these indicators are telling us the truth, but we just cannot let go of the dream of making easy money or work up the courage to invest during the depths of a recession. Sometimes we need to get hit over the head by signals from our surrounding culture.

And some of us are poets who use the right side of our brains to uncover truths that evade the bean counters. Many people invest very well without ever reading a yield curve, a moving average convergence/divergence (MACD) line, or a *Wall Street Journal*. I am reminded of a story that one of my graduate school professors told in an economics class to illustrate the point that economic forecasting may be independent of the quantitative approaches we have studied.

157

It seems that the owners of a small bank decided to modernize by installing a computer to forecast the economy, and so they fired their longtime economist. One year later they begged him to return because, while the computer correctly identified changes in the economy, it had the rate of change all wrong. When the computer said that the economy was going to improve, it forecast a straight line of growth that was way out of line with the actual improvement in the economy.

The old economist was so pleased to be invited back to work at the bank that he shared the secret of his success with the bank president. He opened the top drawer of his desk and, to the president's amazement, pulled out one of his wife's dressmaking tools—an S-shaped curve that pattern makers use to design the top of a sleeve where it fits into the armhole! The ruler sloped up gently at the base, angled sharply up the side, and ended with the same gentle curve; the armhole ruler had the same curve as the economy when it changes direction. My professor suggested that we augment computers with artistry when we make economic forecasts.

Some people do not use computers at all. I have a friend who became wealthy by watching his surroundings rather than by using yield curve analysis or technical indicators. Sam manufactures metal identification plates that go on refrigerators, computers, and other finished goods. One of his customers kept increasing its orders for these plates. Sam invested in his customer's stock as soon as it went public in the 1980s and then sold it before the turn of the century when he saw the customer's orders for his plates decline. Sam sold just before the market crashed and his Sun Microsystems stock lost 95 percent of its value.

Some people do very well without ever looking at a number or reading the financial press. Some people, like Sam, know how to read cultural signals when they invest. The best investors may know how to combine yield curve analysis, technical indicators, and cultural signals in order to time the markets.

Part Three will see how the media's ideal of feminine beauty, demographics, corporate spending, and war can help us identify expansions and recessions in the economy and peaks and troughs in the stock market.

CHAPTER 16

Changing Standards of Feminine Beauty

T he old saying that "art reflects life" is useful for an investor who would rather read *Playboy* magazine than a finance textbook. This chapter uses the changing standards of feminine beauty to identify economic and stock market trends.

We will look at beauty through the eyes of Hollywood, the men who vote for *Playboy* magazine's annual Playmate of the Year contest, and the Miss America contest judges to find coincident economic indicators. We will dig deeper into the magazine's monthly data, the bust measurements of the *Playboy* monthly centerfolds, to find a correlation between these measurements and the level of the S&P 500 index.

Sociologists have long suspected that our standards of beauty change with our pocketbooks. They have thought that we seek security when times are bad, and that we look for fun when times are good; this translates into strong, heavier women to take care of us during recessions and curvaceous, childlike objects of desire to play with during economic expansions. Movie stars, *Playboy* magazine, and Miss America seem to substantiate these theories; so these segments of the pop culture serve to underscore the current economic condition. You may not have to read the *Wall Street Journal* to measure the economy or know what the stock market is doing.

MEASURING STANDARDS OF BEAUTY

T. F. Pettijohn II, Abraham Tesser, M. E. Yerkes, and B. Jungberg studied female movie stars, Playmates of the Year, and Miss America contest winners to see if standards of beauty changed with the economy.

We can divide their analysis into two parts because each of these media has a different focus: the movies pay more attention to the face, and the magazine focuses on the body. The authors expected that the Miss America contest would weight both attributes of feminine beauty equally, but it did not. In fact, the pageant results were the most limited of all their studies and identified weight, as measured by the contestants' body mass index, as the best indicator of changing tastes in beauty over an economic cycle. Miss America's face seems to stay the same over time according to the researchers' very specific measurements and criteria. The Playmate of the Year's face changes, but it does so in a random manner that does not appear to coincide with economic cycles. Movie actresses' faces changed the most with economic conditions.

HOLLYWOOD MEASURED FACES

Faces are the most important physical attribute in Hollywood.

Standard of Measure

Pettijohn and Tesser's first paper, "An Investigation of Popularity in Environmental Context: Facial Feature Assessment of American Movie Actresses," assumed that movie stars embody our ideals of beauty. Since the big screen uses many close-up shots of the face, the researchers focused on that part of the anatomy. This paper includes detailed chin, cheek, mouth, and eye measurements, called "facial metric assessment."

They use these standards to describe faces as either childlike or mature. Childlike faces have high foreheads; large, widely spaced eyes; plump cheeks; full lips; and small chins. Mature faces have low, broad foreheads; small, closely set eyes: narrow cheeks and lips; and larger chins. The open face of a child is presumed to be more honest and naive than a mature face, which projects strength and authority. They concluded that the public prefers childlike faces when the economy is good and mature faces during recessions.

Measuring Popularity

The authors rejected the obvious measure of a movie star's popularity, the Academy Awards, to select candidates for this study because the awards reflect talent and charisma along with beauty. A list of Oscar-winning actresses certainly offers some insights into popularity but not necessarily into prevailing standards of beauty as defined by these two authors.

Some of us may disagree. A broader application of their facial metrics may very well validate the Oscar winners as standards of beauty if one includes women of every age in the definition; Jessica Tandy has beautiful bone structure and is lovely to those of us in her fan club. Furthermore, some of us saw through Charlize Theron's heavy makeup, weight gain, and artificial over bite when she portrayed a prostitute turned serial killer in *Monster*; we were able to see past the characterization to the beautiful woman playing the role.

Pettijohn and Tesser used an independent poll that reflects box-office appeal as reported by theater owners in the annual Quigley Publications poll between 1932 and 1995. The actresses at the top of each year's list made up the database. The authors scanned the movie stars' photographs into a computer for careful measurement and then saw how our taste changes with social and economic conditions. For this comparison they needed a measure of hard times.

Measuring Hard Times

They used a broad measure for hard times that included demographics such as the rates of marriage and divorce as well as the traditional benchmarks for personal income and employment. Messrs. Pettijohn and Tesser relied on public information from the U.S. Bureau of Census for most of this data. They later adjusted this "hard times" measure for social and political situations such as President Kennedy's assassination, student protests, and the Vietnam War. Then they plotted the women's facial measurements on a graph of hard times to see if there was any predictability of results. There was.

Standards of Beauty Graphed Against Hard Times

This study focused on the movie stars' faces just as a camera does, and found that the eyes and chin had the most predictable results. The graph in Figure 16.1 summarizes their findings that we prefer small, mature eyes when times are hard and large babyish eyes when times are good.

Chins changed with the economy as well; they get larger and stronger during hard times and smaller and more youthful when we feel better (see Figure 16.2).

Hollywood may have aimed the camera at the star's face, but *Playboy* was looking at something else.

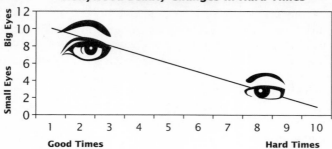

FIGURE 16.1   Eyes

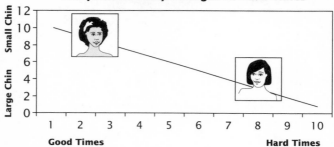

FIGURE 16.2   Chins

PLAYBOY MEASURED BODIES

Facial beauty may be less important in *Playboy* than in Hollywood.

Standard of Measure

Pettijohn and Tesser wanted to expand their study of our changing standards of beauty to include data samples (models) with a broader base of support. The movie theater owners who responded to the Quigley Publications poll were small in number and motivated by ticket sales rather than beauty. The authors decided to go straight to the source: the patrons of *Playboy* magazine. Specifically, they wanted the opinions of the men who voted for the annual Playmate of the Year. This contest would give them one standard of beauty for each year with the validation of millions of readers who participated in the election.

They soon discovered that their investigation would be limited to the torso rather than to the whole woman including her face. Their variables included measures of: facial bones (with no predictable results), age, height, weight, and the traditional waist/bust ratio. Only the last four variables—age, height, weight, and curves—contributed meaningful results in this study.

How the Data Stacks Up

The researchers tabulated their information by year to see how the facial metrics and body measurements reflected the economic times, and the results were amazing.

A Woman's Face Is Not Her Fortune in *Playboy*

The facial measurements, except for the eyes, were so similar that they did not seem to change over time or under different economic conditions. While eyes became predictably larger in good economic times, foreheads, cheeks, lips, and chins had no predicable results. These measurements changed but in what appeared to be a random manner. Faces, which had to be attractive, did not seem to be as important in this test as torsos.

Annual Data from Playmates of the Year

The Playmates' age, height, and weight had important results in this study, but the most powerful economic indicator was their curves.

The interesting fact is that all four of these variables moved together to form the ideal of beauty that one would expect for each economic scenario: curvaceous playthings in good times and sturdy nurturers during hard times. During the good times, men voted for Playmates who were younger and shorter and weighed less than they did during hard times. They also voted for curvier models with higher bust-to-waist ratios when they felt that they could afford them. When they felt poor, they voted for older, taller, heavier women who could take care of them. These nurturing women also had less exaggerated torsos with smaller bust/waist ratios. Figure 16.3 shows how the torsos look on a schematic representation of good times and hard times.

That cheeky British newspaper, the *Sun*, did a corroborating study. Although the page with the results has expired from their web site, a summary is still available on Alphapatriot.com at www.alphapatriot.com/home /archives/2004/06/16/taste_in_women_connected_to_the_economy.php.

I tested the theory against the U.S. stock market with mixed results.

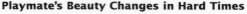

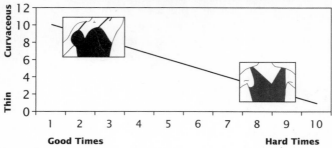

FIGURE 16.3 Torsos

The narrow averages, the S&P 500 index and the Dow Jones Industrial Average, failed to show much correlation with the Playmate of the Year's (POY) bust-to-waist ratio. A broader index of smaller stocks, the Russell 2000 index (symbol RUT) tracked the data a little better, as did the New York Stock Exchange's advance/decline ratio line.

Let us focus on the recent market cycle since 1995. These two broad indexes peaked about 1997 along with the popularity of large-chested women. This was an indication that a stock market bubble began. Then the Playmate of the Year 2000 reflected the stock market decline. She set a record for the lowest bust/waist ratio (139 percent) during the 40-year study with only a nine-inch difference between her bust and waist.

We saw the same phenomenon in the 1960s. The years 1962, 1963, and 1964 saw the most exaggerated feminine graces when Playmates' bosoms measured 38 inches. The bust/waist ratio expanded to 172 percent as the difference between the two numbers grew to 16 inches. About the time that the ideal of beauty changed, so did the broad indexes. The Russell 2000 index and the NYSE advance/decline deflated along with the ladies' proportions during the stock market bubble in the late 1960s. The graph in Figure 16.4 and the supporting data in Appendix 16.1 show the relationship between the broad indexes and the Playmates' measurements. The data is from Playboy, Inc. at Playboy.com and ComStock at Yahoo.com.

Perhaps the lesson here is that we should see what the broader stock market averages are doing when the Playmate of the Year becomes less curvaceous at the same time that the S&P 500 index and the Dow Industrials are setting new highs each year. If the broad averages are declining, as we learned in previous chapters, a few glamour stocks will not be able to prop up the market indefinitely. The annual winner of the Playmate popularity contest may remind us to look at the Russell 2000 and the NYSE advance/decline line.

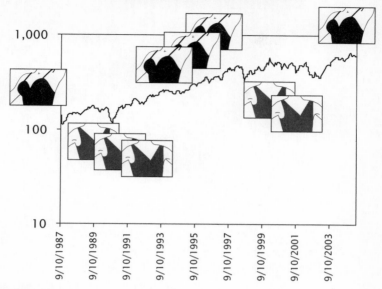

FIGURE 16.4 Torsos with Russell 2000 Index
Sources: Playboy.com, Yahoo.com.

I then looked at the *monthly* centerfold's measurements to see if they tracked the S&P 500 index. While this analysis is designed to entertain more than to forecast—do not take out a second mortgage on your house with these stock market signals—it does highlight the fact that everything in our culture changes, including the stock market.

Monthly Data from Centerfolds

Monthly Playmate data since Marilyn Monroe started the centerfold in 1953 is available on Stephen Schmidt' web site at www.mtsu.edu/~ss-chmidt/methods/project2.html. Figure 16.5 illustrates some similarities between the models and the S&P 500 index during the 1980s and 1990s.

The data for this graph are in Appendix 16.2, and a few of them are worth mentioning. First, the largest model appeared near the start of the bull market. Second, the market declined along with the models' measurements in 1987. Third, the models in general were less curvaceous during the 2000–2002 market decline, with the smallest bust/waist ratio at 125 percent on January 1, 2002. This was the smallest ratio on record and coincided with rumors of a second Iraq war near the bottom of the bear market.

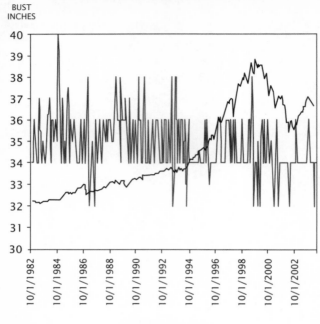

Playmates' Charms and S&P: 1982–2004

FIGURE 16.5 Playmate's Charms and the S&P

Our hardworking sociologists then turned their attention to the Miss America contest in an effort to measure both bodies and faces as our ideals of beauty change with the economy.

MISS AMERICA MEASURED BOTH BODIES AND FACES

This time their experiment had important but even more limited results. Miss America's face does not change over time; she has similar cranial measurements every year regardless of economic conditions. The only things about her that change with the economy are the size of her curves and her body mass. She, too, becomes more of a caretaker and less of a plaything during hard times as her torso straightens from curvy to tubular. During hard times she tends to weigh less for each inch of her height, so she has a smaller body mass index (BMI).

The study concluded that the judges placed more emphasis on talent during the pageant and less on physical attributes. Just a couple of months after they reached this conclusion, however, the contest dropped the talent segment of the program.

Since body mass is important in this study, let us look at some examples. Lillian Russell, who was the queen of the stage and theater in 1900, is said to have weighed 200 pounds. She could not have been tall enough to justify anything near that weight. She may have resembled the first woman in Figure 16.6, who is an example of high BMI during good times. The tall, slim fashion model from the Depression era is off our chart at the other extreme of BMI during hard times.

Your body mass index is calculated by squaring your height (in meters) and dividing that number into your weight in kilograms. Your BMI adjusts your weight for your height so that we can all use the same index to compare our weight. A physician can just look at your BMI and know whether your weight is healthy without having to look you up on a height/weight table.

Miss America and the Stock Market

Her body mass index seems to move with the stock market. Miss America's BMI dropped so much during the late 1990s that the public accused her of setting an impossible standard of thinness for our young women and causing them to starve themselves as anorexics. Miss America's vital statistics disappeared from her web site soon after this bad press.

Perhaps that long decline in her index was a portent of the long bear market that was coming as the century turned. Miss America's BMI reached a historic low around the time of the 2001 pageant. That was the first of several anniversaries of the stock market decline. We also suffered

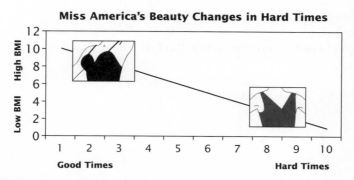

FIGURE 16.6 Body Mass Index

the terrorist attacks that year, and she lived up to our changing ideals of beauty by growing lighter in her height-adjusted weight. The public need not have worried about Miss America becoming too thin, by the way, because she promptly gained weight after the 2001 recession.

MEN'S STANDARDS OF BEAUTY CHANGE WITH THE ECONOMY

One might conclude, based on these and other studies, that men's ideals of feminine beauty coincide with the stock market and the economy.

It is reasonable to assume that this is the case for two reasons. First, people get tired of looking at the same things all the time and need new visual stimulation. The modeling industry says that they need new faces every six months to keep audiences interested. Second, men probably initiate the major changes in visual stimuli. Men control most of the cash in our society and, therefore, shape the economy and the stock market. It is reasonable to assume that changing standards of feminine beauty reflect their preferences.

SUMMARY

It appears that standards of beauty change with the economy or the stock market. Two of our sociological studies coincide with the economy while two others match the stock market. The two that reflect the economy are movie stars' faces and Miss America's weight. The two that move with the stock market are Playmates of the Year and monthly centerfolds. The annual data from the POY match both the Russell 2000 index of small-capitalization stocks and the New York Stock Exchange advance/decline lines, while the latter often coincides with the S&P 500 index.

There is little doubt that our standards of beauty change over time, and in these studies they appear to reflect our current economic environment.

CHAPTER 17

Demographics

My husband and I were walking down our romantic, gaslit street in a Victorian neighborhood in New York City when we saw a couple locked in silence. They did not say a word to each other, but I knew by the stony look on my best friend's face that she was ending her marriage. She had had enough. I had never met her husband even though their brownstone was just a few yards away and our children played together every day. That was the problem—he neglected his family and now she was throwing him out.

Within a year my child's other playmates saw their parents divorce; we were surrounded by couples splitting up as one after another of our friends called it quits. Soon we, too, had made the same decision; the divorce epidemic infected that fragile thing that we had called our marriage. Even Princess Diana filed for divorce before the fever broke.

Was there more going on than met the eye? Were we affected by forces beyond our control, such as the rate of inflation or the strength of the economy? Do some people sense a change in the environment and respond in a rational manner? My personal experience suggests that this may be so. What follows is not a rigorous academic study of sociology or demographics but a look at some data to see if it provides coincidental economic indicators. A lot of people build wealth without Ph.D.'s in economics; perhaps this chapter will shed a light on their street smarts.

Some people seem to be able to measure the economy's strength by reading their local newspaper. They notice whether it is happily full of wedding and birth announcements or depressed with obituaries and divorce proceedings. They see whether the headlines scream murder or extol the virtues of wealthy benefactors donating new wings to the hospital. The economy shapes every aspect of our lives to such an extent that perhaps we do not have to read the financial press to know where we are in the business cycle. In fact, sometimes economists get too close to the forest of data to see the trees, and those of us who look at our culture may have a better idea of how strong the economy really is. This point of view may actually give us a leg up on investing in the stock market if we have the courage to use our soft approach economic analysis in our portfolios.

In this chapter we look at demographic data to see if they have any value as coincidental economic indicators. We will see if the economy coincides with rates of birth, death, marriage, divorce, and crime. Each of these life-shaping milestones may provide us with new vantage points to measure the economy; we may be able to see where we are in the business cycle with our daily experiences as well as with our calculators.

Economists use anecdotal evidence to see where we are in the business cycle when they count the number of cars parked at the mall; our use of demographic data will be similar. You may become one of those people who develops a feel for the business cycle that does not use traditional analysis; you may become street smart.

Once we know where we are in the business cycle, of course, we can apply that information to our investment portfolios.

Let us start with a graph of economic growth and then we will layer demographic data from the U.S. Census Bureau on top of it. Figure 17.1 is the basic graph of the growth of our economy, or gross domestic product, from 1930 to 2003. The shaded areas in the graphs throughout this chapter are recessions or, during the 1930s, the Great Depression.

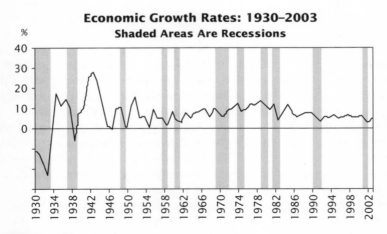

FIGURE 17.1 Basic Graph

The National Bureau of Economic Research (NBER) establishes the dates of our business expansions and recessions. Most people think that a recession is defined as two quarters of slower economic growth, but the bureau has a slightly different approach to the matter. The NBER defines a recession as a broad-based decline in business activity across many economic sectors. This prevents a major decline in one industry from determining the cycle.

There were two such examples during the past 50 years. The most dramatic was the decline in housing during the early 1980s, when 15 percent home mortgages locked most people out of the market. It slowed economic growth for several quarters but did not affect enough business sectors to constitute a recession by the bureau's standards. Similarly, in the early 1950s, there were almost two years of slow growth that the bureau did not call a recession because not enough sectors of the economy felt the decline.

The NBER protects us from reacting to the fortunes of one capital-intensive industry, such as banking or insurance. Wall Street can crash and fire a lot of high-priced brokers without affecting the rest of the country, and the bureau wants to reflect the economy of the whole country rather than just this one street in New York.

BIRTH RATES

"You do not know what happiness is until you have a baby," I heard myself saying to the pretty little blonde in clerical robes.

My minister was expecting her first child and wondered what the experience would be like. Suddenly I forgot the pain of delivery and the six months without sleep. I heard some crazy lady (me) babbling on about how happy new mothers are. The church parlor suddenly became quiet as parishioners glared at me for interrupting their small collation of tea and cookies with my nattering. Enthusiasm crowded out Yankee rectitude as I baptized our minister with a stream of superlatives extolling motherhood.

Parenthood is the biggest step we ever take and it is the only one that cannot be undone. It cannot be divorced, returned with proof of purchase, or traded on the Internet. While many factors enter into creating a child, it takes a large dose of optimism to commit the act of parenthood; you may be able to set your economic clock by the birth rate (not to be confused with each individual's fertility rate) in our country. Just look at the number of people who thought they could gather enough physical, emotional, and financial strength to raise a new baby when the victorious soldiers returned home from World War II.

The year 1947 had the highest birth rate in the postwar era with almost 27 children born to each 1,000 women. We had recently suffered several decades of declining birth rates as a result of industrialism, higher
female literacy rates, two wars, and the Great Depression. Suddenly the
world looked safe enough to bring a child into it, and the soldiers lined up
for fatherhood.

Reality must have set in pretty quickly because you can see in Figure
17.2 how the baby boom promptly burst in 1949 (although it did pick up
again for several years).

The Baby Boom

When we superimpose the graph of birth rates on that of economic
growth, we can see a baby boom that coincided with the 27 percent economic growth after World War II (see Figure 17.3).

In 1947 the birth rate's historic high of 27 per thousand women coincided with double-digit economic growth. The birth rate remained extra-
ordinarily high for an industrialized economy throughout the 1950s and
created the largest demographic cohort in our history: the baby boomers.
The world, and our economy, would feel their presence for many decades
to come.

The Baby Bust

Birth rates tend to decline in industrial societies, and ours was no exception. After the 1947 peak, our birth rate generally declined until 1977
when the baby boomers were old enough to have their own children. It

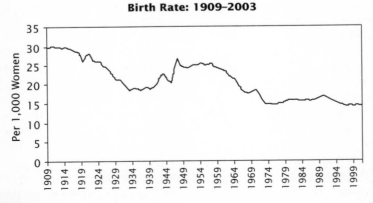

FIGURE 17.2   Rate of Change in Births

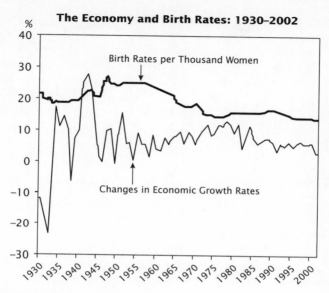

The Economy and Birth Rates: 1930–2002

Birth Rates per Thousand Women

Changes in Economic Growth Rates

FIGURE 17.3 Birth Rate and the Economy

is interesting that this uptick in the birth rate coincided with an economic expansion.

There was one interesting exception.

More War Babies

It is well-known that war stimulates the economy. It appears that the Vietnam War also stimulated baby production until 1970 when there were no new deferments for parenthood. Our birth rate declined after that change in the draft.

The Echo Boom

Boomers started their families in 1977 during a rapidly expanding economy. Baby boomers produced their echo boomers with enough enthusiasm to sustain an elevated birth rate right through the business cycles in the 1980s. The birth rate peaked along with the economy in 1989–1990 and then slowed during the recession that followed. During the rest of the 1990s, the economy grew at modest rates, and the aging boomers had fewer children every year. Both the economy and the birth rate slowed down in the 2001 recession.

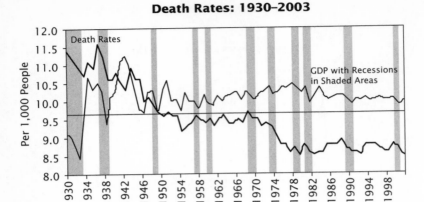

FIGURE 17.4   Death Rate and the Economy

Each population cohort may respond to the emotions surrounding business cycles.

DEATH RATES

The first thing you see on the graph in Figure 17.4 is that the death rate has declined dramatically since 1930 and the Great Depression. You would assume that improved living conditions and modern medicine are responsible for this. You may also assume that we could apply this analysis to the business cycle and see the death rate rise and fall accordingly. However, the data on this graph seems to indicate otherwise. It appears that death rates peak just before, or very early in, a recession. You would think that the reverse would be true. Maybe people lose heart if they cannot keep up with the Joneses during an expansion.

If the death rate increases at the peak of a business cycle, does that mean that money cannot buy happiness?

MARRIAGE RATES

Or can money buy love? Or, more to the point, can it move people toward marriage?

In a word, "No." Figure 17.5 is a graph of the marriage rate from 1950 to 2003, and the decline is steep. Money could not buy marriage af-

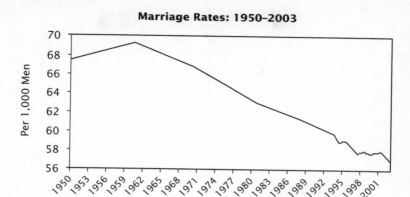

FIGURE 17.5 Rate of Change in Marriage

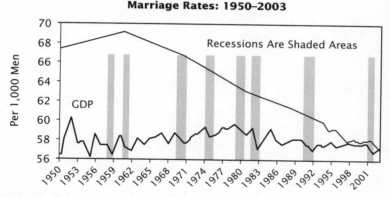

FIGURE 17.6 Marriage Rate and the Economy

ter 1960 when the pill became popular. So much for romance, and so much for someone trying to read the economy in the society pages (see Figure 17.6).

The numbers look even worse if you look at them by decade going back to 1900 (see Table 17.1). It appears that the marriage rate increased with our general well-being as we became an industrialized nation during the first 60 years of the twentieth century. Then something happened in 1960 to change the way we live. Could it have been the pill, which became available for commercial use that year?

A graph of marriage rates at the end of each decade highlights a major

TABLE 17.1	Married Men per Thousand
Decennial	**Married Men per Thousand**
1900	54.6
1910	55.9
1920	59.2
1930	60.0
1940	61.2
1950	68.9
1960	Peak rate 71.1
1970	67.7
1980	62.0
1990	59.3
2000	58.6

change during the 1970s (see Figure 17.7). That decade saw the end of an unpopular war, a president leave office, and increasing rates of inflation. The stagnant economy earned the name "stagflation" and the marriage rate dropped dramatically.

Not even the strong economy in the 1990s convinced couples to marry. In fact, the marriage rate declined with increasing speed between 1993 and 1998 when we had a long stretch of uninterrupted growth (see Figure 17.8). It is interesting to note that, except for 1998, the rate declined with increas-

FIGURE 17.7 Marriage Rates at the End of Each Decade

FIGURE 17.8 Marriage Rates Recently

ing speed during the recessions at each end of the decade. The year 1998 remains a puzzle; surely the Russian bond default and the stock market decline could not have frightened people away from remaining single!

DIVORCE RATES

If marriage is out, is the divorce rate lower as well? Again, the answer is negative. We have been divorcing at an increasing rate for 100 years. Our standard of living may have increased but not our ability to stay married (see Table 17.2).

TABLE 17.2	Divorced Men per Thousand
Decennial	**Divorced Men per Thousand**
1900	0.3
1910	0.5
1920	0.6
1930	1.1
1940	1.3
1950	2.0
1960	2.2
1970	2.8
1980	5.4
1990	7.4
2000	8.6

You probably noticed two dates with major increases in the divorce rates: 1980 and 1990. The first big increase, in 1980, coincides with the twin economic problems of high inflation and recession. Maybe families could not cope with rising prices and fewer jobs at the same time that year.

The divorce rate lost momentum when inflation decreased during the 1980s but picked up speed again in the middle of that decade when interest rates went up for a short time. The graph in Figure 17.9 makes one wonder if inflation causes divorce; the shaded areas are times when both the rate of inflation and the divorce rate increased faster than usual.

It seems that whenever inflation increases rapidly, so does the divorce rate. We saw evidence of this phenomenon in the 1940s, 1970s, and again in the late 1980s. The growth in divorce rates slowed down whenever inflation did.

A wonderful thing happened at the turn of the century; the divorce rate actually declined. The rate went from 8.4 percent in 1999 to 8.1 percent in 2002, holding steady at 8.3 percent during the short 2000–2001 recession. The three difficult years in the stock market from 2000 to 2003 failed to impact the improvement in our divorce rate; the short duration of the recession probably was more important in keeping marriages intact than the value of families' portfolios.

Divorce is not the only thing that may reflect the economy in your local newspaper; how much crime is in your headlines these days?

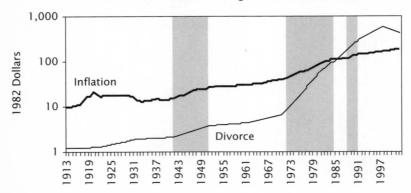

Inflation and Divorce: 1913–2002

Shaded Areas Indicate Rising Rates for Both Variables

FIGURE 17.9   Inflation and Divorce

CRIME RATES

The next graph (see Figure 17.10) makes you wonder if the crime rate is directly correlated to inflation. Do people steal more to cover rising prices?

We had the fastest increases in inflation during the 1970s at the same time that the crime rate tripled. Both crime and the rate of inflation decreased during the next two decades. This graph makes you wonder if the Federal Reserve's influence on inflation is felt on the streets and in deserted parking lots after dark. Perhaps we should check the money supply before we decide how much theft insurance to buy.

Many people think that there is a strong relationship between crime and the strength of the economy, and they could well be right. Table 17.3 shows the rate of all crimes, violent and otherwise, committed per 100,000 people from 1960 through 2002. It is interesting to see the increase in crime during the 1970, 1974, 1980, and 1990–1991 recessions. Crime did not increase during the 2001 recession, but it did stop the steady rate of decline that it had established during the preceding decade.

Perhaps there is a hidden cost in recessions; maybe we lose more than manufactured goods and services when the economy slows down. As to the crime rate's relationship with the economy, see the graph in Figure 17.11; what do you think?

The 1970, 1974, 1980, and the 1990–1991 recessions stick out like sore thumbs at each peak in the crime rate on this graph. This rate declines after recessions when the economy improves. It restores your faith in mankind if you think that someone steals only to put bread on his family's table during a recession.

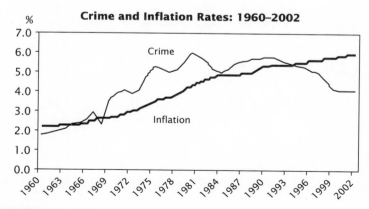

FIGURE 17.10 Crime and Inflation

TABLE 17.3 Crime Rates

Date	Percent	Date	Percent	Date	Percent	Date	Percent
1960	1.8	1971	4.1	1982	5.6	1993	5.5
1961	1.9	1972	3.9	1983	5.1	1994	5.4
1962	2.0	1973	4.1	1984	5.0	1995	5.3
1963	2.1	1974	4.8	1985	5.2	1996	5.1
1964	2.3	1975	5.3	1986	5.5	1997	5.0
1965	2.4	1976	5.2	1987	5.6	1998	4.6
1966	2.6	1977	5.0	1988	5.7	1999	4.2
1967	2.9	1978	5.1	1989	5.7	2000	4.1
1968	2.3	1979	5.5	1990	5.8	2001	4.1
1969	3.6	1980	6.0	1991	5.8	2002	4.1
1970	3.9	1981	5.8	1992	5.6		

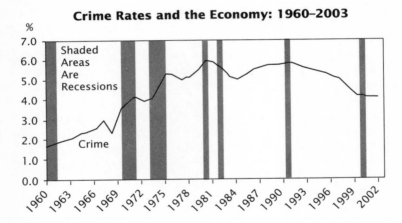

FIGURE 17.11 Crime and the Economy

SUMMARY

There may be some people in our society who sense a change in the strength of the economy and react with a rational decision about marriage, divorce, or childbearing. The rates of crime and death may move with our economic fortunes. These events may act as coincidental indicators for those with the street smarts to identify them.

Many people use nonquantitative means to establish where we are in the business cycle, and most economists use anecdotal evidence in their analysis to validate what the numbers tell them. We all notice when there are more parking spaces available, stores are less crowded, and our jobs feel less secure. Some people can feel a recession in different aspects of their lives and use this information in their investing. They use information that surrounds us every day in our culture to help determine where we are in the business cycle and to protect their assets.

This chapter suggested some coincident economic indicators; the next chapter gives cultural signals that may act as leading indicators.

CHAPTER 18

Corporate Spending

We were walking down Madison Avenue in New York City when Sharon, my fashion-designer friend, delivered the disappointing news.

"We've gone as far as we can with big shoulders; from now on you will see very simple clothes."

Simple clothes! Who wants simple clothes . . . or simple anything for that matter? I was devastated. I had my eye on a red snakeskin suit with broad shoulders and did not want to buy something just as it was going out of style. Sharon's comment saved me from buying one of fashion's classic examples of excess, and I have learned to use the regular reappearance of that suit as an indication of stock market peaks. Red snakeskin seems to show up in the stores about one year before every stock market bubble.

You probably know that my conversation with Sharon took place in 1986 when *Dallas* dominated television and the stock market was getting ready to crash a year later. The bigger Linda Gray's hair and shoulder pads grew on TV's Southfork Ranch, the higher the S&P 500 index climbed. (She probably wore red leather suits on some episodes.) The more outrageous our culture, and especially corporate culture, became, the closer we were to the top of the stock market.

Corporations increase their spending on extreme items about 12 months before the stock market peaks. They spend more than usual on patent defense, advertising pages, and employment costs such as hiring bonuses. We will pay particular attention to the critical relationship between employment rates and the stock market as we explore more nontraditional, nonquantitative ways to measure the economy. Entertainment budgets expand along with competition for customers, and there is a shrinking pool of employees. The products that firms offer to an increasingly jaded public reflect the extreme taste that envelops us; big clothes and big hair merely scratch the surface of the outrageous excess that takes over our culture as the stock market reaches new highs every day. These changes in corporate spending are subtle and addictive; we like to think that they are permanent because we deserve these perquisites, but they are temporary.

However, they are useful to us as leading indicators of the economy, and they give us a chance to prepare to decrease our investment in stocks about a year before the market declines.

RESEARCH AND DEVELOPMENT

Perhaps corporate research and development departments feel like my friend Sharon. Maybe they feel that they have gone as far as they can in a particular field of innovation. Perhaps successful corporations know how to time the markets and adjust their business accordingly. Whatever the reason, some patent attorneys see a cycle similar to the one that Sharon identified. They see a subtle but noticeable increase in the number of patent defense cases six months before each recession.

Senior managers use the yield curve analysis we studied in Part One, among other things, to identify where we are in the business cycle. They switch from spending on research and development to defending existing products through patent litigation when they see a recession coming. Patent defense litigation, which increases about six months before a recession, often coincides with a decline in the stock market. The National Bureau of Economic Research (NBER), the nonprofit organization that determines the dates of our business cycles, has information on patent applications and litigation. You can read about the bureau's work in Professor Bronwyn H. Hall's paper from the University of California, "Current Issues and Trends in the Economics of Patents," or visit the NBER web site at www.nber.org/patents.

One of my neighbors is a patent attorney who has seen litigation increase six months ahead of each recession. He says that he depends on the increase as a leading economic indicator. He probably sells some of his equity portfolio when he sees litigation pick up because he knows that a stock market decline is imminent. I suspect this because of his lifestyle. He and his wife, who is a minister, sail around the world in their yacht. I doubt that she, gifted though she is, paid for it with her salary as a pastor.

ADVERTISING PAGES

Just the weight of your newspaper is a clue to the strength of the economy.

Number of Pages

Corporations increase their spending on advertising pages as the economy expands. This, too, becomes excessive and is easy to identify about a year before the stock market peaks. All of a sudden your daily newspaper is too heavy to carry and has lots of little slippery things falling out of it. Soon you cannot even read your magazines because you cannot turn the pages; there are too many cardboard advertisements glued into the binding. You would be happy to buy the products they tout, but you can't get past the samples that stick your pages together.

You know when advertising becomes excessive, and you should consider selling some stock a year later.

Neiman Marcus Christmas Catalog

The best-known symbol of advertising excess is the Neiman Marcus Christmas catalog. They usually have one outrageous entry designed to shock you with its expense and uselessness. I knew that we were in a recession in 2001 because Neiman's did not send a catalog. Either they dropped it altogether during the recession or they dropped *me* to their B list because I never bought anything from it. Nonetheless, Neiman's usually rates several lines of type in the popular press for their fun, expensive, and totally unnecessary gift suggestions; and if they ever send me another Christmas catalog, I will sell some stock from my portfolio.

Neiman's does not have a monopoly on the market for expensive catalogs. As the stock market increased during the 1990s, so did the luxury advertisements that came under the guise of so-called lifestyle magazines. My favorite was called *Avenue*, which featured photographs from turn-of-the-century New York City. Ostensibly to preserve the colorful past centuries of New York, *Avenue* really sold luxury items. It, too, disappeared from my mailbox during the recession when the publisher had to start charging for subscriptions. When new free magazines take *Avenue*'s place, I will keep an eye out for opportunities to sell stocks.

Sexually Shocking Advertisements

As we become more jaded, it takes more to catch our attention.

Calvin Klein has exploited the concept ever since he paid 15-year-old Brooke Shields half a million dollars for declaring that nothing came between her and her Calvins (jeans, that is) in 1980. The public was appalled and the stock market declined one year later. The next furor erupted over his use of children who seemed to be of elementary school age. These youngsters appeared on a billboard in Times Square playing in suggestive poses and dressed only in his new brand, CK underwear. The public outcry was immediate and the billboard disappeared within 24 hours. One year later the stock market bubble burst and the S&P 500 index began its three-year slide.

Calvin has a gift for identifying when our culture is jaded and then pushing us even further in his commercials. The graph in Figure 18.1 shows how public outrage at his commercials leads the stock market by a year. Even his award marks an important date in the stock market.

There is a good reason for this correlation between the Calvin Klein advertisements and the stock market; both are tied to the economic cycle, which is driven by consumers. If a firm is going to stay in business, it must anticipate both the economy and our consumer spending. In fact, Calvin almost went out of business during the early 1990s, and this experience may have prompted him to take such a big risk when he introduced the new children's line of underwear; he had to make sure that the product got our attention.

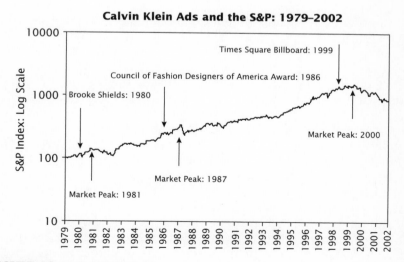

FIGURE 18.1 Calvin Klein Ads

EMPLOYMENT RATES

Nothing attracts our attention as much as a pink slip. Losing one's job is devastating financially and emotionally, and the result shows up in the stock market. When the nation's employment rate is high, so are inflation and the stock market; conversely, when that critical rate is low, so is the market. While it is obvious that we fail to buy goods and services when we have less money, our self-esteem may also be too low to venture out into the competitive world of the shopping mall. Both conditions change dramatically when we have jobs and money to spend and feel proud of ourselves. We spend on toys for ourselves and our loved ones; we donate to charities, and we surround ourselves with status symbols to prove our worth.

I have a friend who literally shopped her way through many years of cancer treatments; she said that shopping reassured her that she was still alive. I guess that as long as clerks accepted her credit card, she knew she still existed. (Now that some hospitals offer nontraditional medicine like acupuncture, maybe health insurers will cover shopping as a form of physical and mental therapy. Right now, we have to be employed to take advantage of the shopping therapy, and the strength of the stock market depends on our employment.)

The next graph (see Figure 18.2) shows the direct relationship between our employment and the stock market. You can translate employment to mean "shopping ability."

In general, unemployment rates have been a mirror image of the stock market.

The 25 percent unemployment rate during the 1930s kept the stock market low. The Great Depression spread from the economy into the S&P 500 index. The economy finally recovered when World War II put people back to work. New paychecks allowed us to spend more, and the stock market improved during the 1940s and 1950s. Unemployment crashed during the war years of the 1940s, and that was one crash that everyone was happy to have. Employment remained fairly steady throughout the decade of the 1950s and underwrote a steady rise in the stock market. Both the stock market and the employment situation took off during the 1960s as we spent a large part of our increasing paychecks.

The exception to the rule occurred during the 1970s. Unemployment rose during the early 1970s and we were lucky that the stock market did as well as it did under those conditions.

The inverse relationship between these two variables became more normal following that decade. As expected, unemployment peaked during the stock market crash of 1987. There was just a mild increase with the market decline in 1990 and even a smaller one during the 2000 to 2002

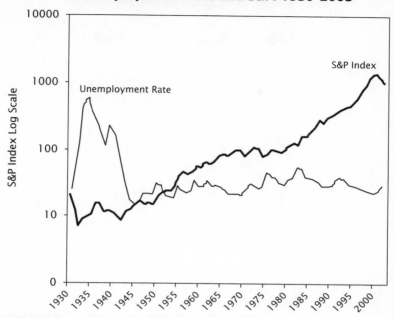

Unemployment Rates and S&P: 1930–2003

FIGURE 18.2 Unemployment Rates and the S&P

bear market. The relationship held even though it was less pronounced. We have been fortunate to have had such low unemployment rates since the early 1980s regardless of some difficult stock markets.

A bar chart for the years from 1980 through 2002 superimposes the two data series on top of each other and may be easier to read (see Figure 18.3).

Changes in the unemployment rate led the S&P by about a year during the early 1980s. The stock market lost 7 percent in 1982 after the previous year's unemployment rate increased to 7.6 percent. Then in 1984 the rate of unemployment dropped substantially, and the following year the S&P gained 16 percent. Joblessness continued to drop right through the 1987 crash and provided investors with knowledge that the crash would not lead to a recession or a continued bear market. The year of the crash, the stock market actually ended higher than it began. The following year, 1988, did suffer a 7 percent market decline; but the next 11 years saw annual gains while more and more people found work.

The only exception was in 1990 when unemployment rose and the market should have declined the following year; instead the S&P rose on

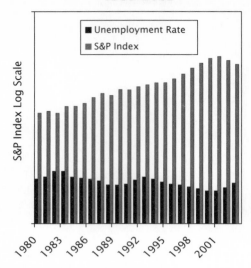

**Unemployment and the S&P:
1980–2002**

FIGURE 18.3 Bar Chart Shows Unemployment

an annual basis right through the ensuing recession. This was our first clue that the decade would see unusual strength in the market. Table 18.1 identifies these trends.

Annual employment data seems to be a good indicator of the stock market, but I promised you some nonstatistical means of forecasting. Here are some ways you can estimate employment numbers while you are out having fun.

CORPORATE LIFESTYLE

Corporations tend to go overboard on lifestyle in order to compete for increasingly scarce workers and customers at the peak of the business cycle.

Expensive Entertaining

The holiday season is a great time to estimate your firm's current and future hiring plans. If your firm is spending a lot on the holidays, it probably is experiencing labor shortages and fighting harder than ever for each in-

TABLE 18.1 Unemployment Rates and the S&P

Year	Unemployment %	S&P Index
1980	7.1	118.78
1981	Unemployment rose 7.6	128.05
1982	9.7	Down 119.71
1983	9.7	160.41
1984	Unemployment dropped 7.5	160.46
1985	7.2	Up 186.84
1986	7.0	236.34
1987	6.2	286.83
1988	5.5	265.79
1989	5.3	322.84
1990	Unemployment rose 5.6	334.59
1991	6.8	Up 376.18
1992	7.5	415.74
1993	6.9	451.41
1994	6.1	460.42
1995	5.6	541.72
1996	5.4	670.50
1997	4.9	873.43
1998	4.5	1,085.50
1999	4.2	1,327.33
2000	**Lowest unemployment rate 4.0**	**Stock market peak 1,427.22**
2001	4.7	1,194.18
2002	5.8	993.94

cremental dollar of revenue. Not only does everyone get carried away with emotional and spending excess, but firms must compete for the attention of customers and new hires. This competition gets tougher at the peak of the business cycle when everyone runs as hard as they can just to stay in place. The taller the gift baskets become, the more likely that our financial system and stock markets will fall in about a year. Expensive champagne and caviar are a good indication that your firm will have to cut back next year, and the stock market will reflect those cuts a few weeks from now.

Do you feel compelled to entertain clients at the most expensive restaurant in town where the menu is so full of adjectives that you can not figure out what the entrée is? Are the prices just as extreme? A friend with a generous expense account took me out for a holiday lunch at a lovely but unusually expensive French restaurant. She said,

"Next year you will not see expensive items like this on the menu. They will have to serve cheaper fare during the recession."

The whole menu had to change, not just the prices on the existing one. Her observation was in December 2000 and the stock market was just a few months into its long decline. She was right about the menu, which did, indeed, change. So did the ownership, the format, and her expense account. At least the restaurant is still there, even though it is now casual Mexican rather than fancy French, but her expense account is gone.

Holiday parties are just the start of year-round entertaining.

Summer interns are courted as heavily as a firm's best clients when the business cycle peaks and labor becomes scarce. When you see that your interns spend all of their time "acquainting themselves with the environment," or going to parties, rather than doing any real work, you can be pretty sure that the situation will change in about a year. Firms may find themselves in this situation at the peak of the cycle, but they really prefer to have their staff deliver a product rather than go to parties. Management resents this activity as much as the colleagues who have to live with it, and so does the public who reads about it in the press.

Staff Parties

If you find yourself circling Manhattan on a private yacht with a full orchestra playing your favorite rock music, write up your resume. Make an extra dozen copies for each celebrity in attendance. The best staff party I ever attended was at the opening of the renovated Rainbow Room at Rockefeller Center. The party featured a famous rock group in black hats and sunglasses. The floor shook with pounding rhythms and frenzied dancing; later that year, 1987, the stock market had its own pounding and the frenzy was not from dancing. The Rainbow Room renovated again in 1999 exactly one year before the next crash.

Is your corporate retreat at a three-star hotel overlooking a tropical beach? You may want to enjoy that beach while you can because next year you could be at Motel 6 overlooking a parking lot.

Games at Work

During the stock market bubble in the late 1990s, technology stocks reigned. Workers with technology expertise were in great demand and were also in short supply. Rather than raise pay scales accordingly, management expanded its use of so-called lifestyle perks to compete for employees.

Suddenly the corporate dress code changed to appeal to these young technicians, and denim replaced pinstripes. Loud printed shirts replaced white button-downs, and ties went out the window. It was cheaper and easier for management to let people come to work in their play clothes than it was to pay them enough for a serious wardrobe, and the young techies loved it.

It was not long before the activities at the office reflected the new dress code, and people putting in long hours to keep up with the demand for new computer code could take a break at the firm's ping-pong table. Some organizations installed basketball hoops, pinball machines, and other grown-up toys for overworked staff members.

It was fun while it lasted, but one day a Wall Street analyst did some basic arithmetic and changed his opinion on the cell phone industry. He said that in order to justify the prevailing prices for telecommunications stocks, every U.S. household with electricity would have to buy a new cell phone during the coming year. His analysis affected not only the purveyors of cell phones, but their suppliers, the media in which they advertised, the stores in which they sold, and the brokers who sold their stock.

When traditional, buttoned-down businessmen start wearing jeans and sandals to the office, we are near the top of the economic and investment cycle. When there is a basketball hoop over your watercooler, you may want to do a jump shot into another, more secure industry . . . and sell your glamour stocks as well.

EMPLOYEE BENEFITS

Management prefers noncash remuneration mentioned earlier for the obvious reasons and because it can be cut off the minute their cash flow declines. There may be other reasons having to do with competing for market share, building a brand image, and just impressing their buddies on the golf course. Noncash remuneration is also popular with management because of its low impact on reportable earnings to investors.

Benefits that cost money, such as health insurance, pensions, and hiring bonuses, are another matter.

Extensive Health Insurance

Along with inexpensive lifestyle changes, management offers more extensive health care benefits to attract workers at the top of the business cycle.

This is a serious expense because it does not disappear as easily as the basketball hoop over the watercooler. Unions negotiate health care benefits with a vengeance and protect them with diligence. These expenses do nothing but go up with new medical discoveries and better treatments. The other side of this double-edged sword is the passage of time and the aging of the workforce; as workers become more experienced and, therefore, more valuable, they also become older and need more of those new medical discoveries. Extensive health insurance is very hard for management to unwind after the business cycle has peaked, and it becomes a larger part of their budget every year.

When your employer offers to put braces on your dog's teeth as well as your own, you may want to simultaneously write up your resume and sell a few of your stocks.

Pension Plans

Pensions are at least as hard for managers to reduce as health benefits. Yet back in the early 1980s pensions were the single largest item on most firms' balance sheets. It took more than a decade for companies to switch their employees over to self-funded pensions with only a portion contributed by the organization. This is one area where decision making is slowed down by legal constraints, regulations, and government lobbying; the firm is stuck with an expensive plan that it cannot afford for years. Firms may try to reduce the cost of funding a pension plan by changing some of the actuarial assumptions that determine their annual contribution, but sooner or later this overhead catches up with them. No wonder so many jobs are outsourced to developing countries where unions have not negotiated large pensions.

When you see that your firm has more invested in its pension plan than in its plant and equipment or research and development, you may want to sell some of your equity portfolio before the general market decline that will start in about a year.

College Tuition Reimbursement

Fortunately, this is one benefit that firms may be able to unwind about every semester. Retraining employees to fit into the firms' business plan makes sense if the associated cost is low enough. When your company offers to send your secretary to Harvard Business School, you might be justified to think that we are nearing the top of a business and investment cycle.

You, of course, will accept all offers for free education, including the Chartered Financial Analyst (CFA) program that is a self-study, inexpensive substitute for a master's degree in business. Many people get the charter after graduate school so that they can have the best of both worlds: business school contacts and membership in a society with ongoing education and ethics oversight.

You could probably time the stock market by your firm's tuition program; buy the S&P when your firm pays for the inexpensive CFA program and sell stocks when it pays for an expensive MBA degree.

Signing Bonuses

Of course you want a signing bonus. They want you so badly that they bribe you to work there; you feel like the most popular kid in high school! Naturally, this is an example of life at the top . . . of the business cycle. Signing bonuses were prevalent in the late 1980s and again in the late 1990s right before each recession and stock market decline. When these bonuses make headlines in the media, you do not have to give up yours; but you may want to lighten your portfolio's exposure to equities.

MANAGEMENT'S BENEFITS

Manager may have benefits of which the public is unaware. The public often objects to these perks when they become outrageous enough to capture the headlines.

Private Clubs

Golf clubs are just the tip of this expensive iceberg. Exclusive health clubs, dining clubs, and university clubs fall into this category. Management needs to entertain prospects and existing clients in an aspirational manner that entices people to join their world by buying their products. As the business cycle peaks, so does this part of the entertainment budget. Here is another financial commitment that can be slow to unwind because some initiation fees are so steep. If you pay $100,000 to join a private golf club, you are stuck with that cost forever. Multiply that price times all of your firm's top management plus the board of directors and the product is another stock market indicator.

Smart managers keep this perquisite quiet; so if you see them featured in *Golf* magazine, you can assume that we are near the peak of a cycle.

Fleets of Private Jets

Fleets of private jets are another perk that managers usually keep under wraps. Business can justify managers using private planes, but sometimes they abuse the privilege. When the press gets wind of that abuse, trouble follows.

Private jets can add to a firm's bottom line in production and in good-will. For instance, private planes are necessary for managers who need to check on isolated production facilities such as Canadian paper mills. These planes may also perform acts of mercy for employees in distress. H. Ross Perot, founder and chairman of Electronic Data Systems (now a division of General Motors) used his private planes in 1980 to rescue kid-napped staff members who were hostages in Iran after a U.S. military attempt failed to get them out. In another case, a friend of mine saw his paper company use a private plane to airlift his child to Texas for surgery after a serious accident in Tokyo.

The press is happy to report these displays of corporate kindness, but it is even happier to tell us when a chief executive officer's wife extends that kindness to her dog's visit to an out-of-town veterinarian.

After such an incident in the exuberant 1980s, the papers ran stories comparing companies' fleets to those of foreign military organizations. It seems that several corporations had more private planes than most developed countries' armed forces. When your boss feels that he has to sneak aboard his private jet and land it out of the sight of the press, you may want to move some assets out of the stock market.

Art Collections

Not all the fine art in the world is in museums or wealthy homes; more than you might think is in corporate offices.

Top management justifies this expense because art is an investment that, at certain times in the cycle, increases in value faster than all other asset classes. The real reason may be the image that such collections project and, therefore, the negotiating edge that they provide. The outside world is intimidated upon entering sumptuous surroundings and feels inferior during discussions with management over issues like labor relations, customer complaints, and suppliers' prices.

There are some good reasons for investing in fine art for the executive suite; but when the public complains, as it did in 1998 when the Sara Lee Corporation donated art by Pierre Bonnard to the Virginia Museum of Fine Art, it may be time to sell some of your equity portfolio.

Sara Lee donated the cream of its collection to museums rather than sell the paintings as other firms did. Management was proud of its gift, but the press wondered why the collection was not sold and the proceeds put into research and development for new products. This was the first time that many members of the investing public heard that corporations have major art collections, and they were not impressed. Sara Lee stock reflected their opinion and the stock dropped

10 percent that month. The stock was on its way down from 30 to 14 dollars a share.

OUTRAGEOUS MERCHANDISE

When there is so much cash in the financial system that corporate life becomes excessive, the consumer demands outrageous merchandise. The Federal Reserve may not pay much attention to the luxury items below, but they scrutinize the money supply that pays for them. Shortly after these outrageous items post strong sales, the Fed reduces the money supply and slows the economy; the stock market, as usual, declines several months before the next recession.

Here is a short list of showstoppers that actually sell well about a year before the stock market declines (see Figure 18.4):

- Diamonds for daily wear, or everyday diamond bracelets, nicknamed "EDDBs" (1990).
- Christmas trees needing cranes to install them in New York City apartments (1990).
- Red snakeskin suits (1980, 1986, 1990, and 1999).

FIGURE 18.4 Merchandise for Jaded Consumers

SUMMARY

Our culture reflects the cyclical nature of both the stock market and corporations.

We can get a sense of where we are in the business cycle, which we know will affect the market, by watching the behavior of corporate America. An increase in patent litigation at the expense of research and development signals that corporations are retrenching. When we see the number of advertising pages increase while the level of good taste printed on them decreases, we know that competition is heating up with the business cycle. Employment rates drive consumer spending and, therefore, the stock market; we can tell when this rate is excessive because benefits, hiring bonuses, and entertainment budgets balloon. Our financial system cannot sustain employee benefits that outweigh productive capacity, and we know that we are near the top of a cycle.

These corporate excesses, caused by jaded consumers like us, usually occur about a year before the stock market declines and about a year to 18 months ahead of a recession. You do not need to read the business press to identify corporate excesses that mark the top of a cycle—all you need to do is look around your environment.

If your environment includes a war, you have a particularly powerful stock market indicator that very few people have the courage to use. The next chapter will give you the courage of your convictions to use this important indicator.

CHAPTER 19

War and
Rumors of War

I always liked Robert even though he was rather effete. Being effete made him wildly *un*popular in our public high school that idolized football players, and the best thing that ever happened to Robert was serving in the 1991 Gulf War. He came home full of manly stories about firing the first Patriot missile, meeting Arabian princes, and outnegotiating Persian carpet dealers. Robert felt so good about himself that he came out of the closet.

War changes our lives.

It changes our social institutions, our economy, and our power structure. War stimulates the economy, creates jobs, and increases inflation. Interest rates usually go up, and the stock market of the country fighting on foreign soil improves. (War on your own homeland, of course, diminishes the means of production and lowers prices on the stock markets that trade them.) Buying stocks when the president or Congress activates troops is one of the hardest investment decisions we ever have to make. We usually have to make this decision when the economy is slow and unemployment is at unacceptable levels. The mood of the nation may be gloomy, but we need the vision to see the stronger economy, lower unemployment, and better stock market that lie ahead.

This chapter will build a case for buying stocks when troops are called up, which usually happens when war is declared, because the onset of war marks the beginning of a new economic cycle. Gross domestic product, employment, inflation, and the stock market all tend to rise in wartime; we will look at the behavior of these components of the economy during every American war for the past two centuries. We will refine one of our previous trades and make a final accounting of our investment process. Later chapters will suggest specific securities in which to invest.

Successful fiscal and monetary policies that moderate business cycles and avoid war are one of our greatest blessings, and we are fortunate to have seen three decades of relative peace since the 1973 end of the Vietnam War. As long as man is predisposed to go to war, however, we must be aware of its influence on the economy and on our portfolios.

Our signal to buy stocks is the declaration of war or its equivalent. Congress has not issued a joint resolution to go to war since Pearl Harbor in 1941; since then, we have gone to war with less formal Congressional backing. We will use the troop call-up date as our signal to buy the S&P for the following conflicts: the Korean police action, Vietnam, the Gulf War, and the war in Iraq. We actually sent soldiers to most of these countries on dates that were quite different from the date when we mobilized troops; but, as the old Wall Street saying goes,

"Buy on the rumor. . . ."

The expression ends with a warning to sell when the news actually materializes, but not in this case. War stimulates the economy and the stock market; so we will buy stocks on the rumor of war, as defined by troop mobilization, and then hold them "for the duration," as World War II soldiers used to say about their term of service.

DIFFICULT CONDITIONS LEAD UP TO WAR

It is hard to invest when troops are called up because of the difficult conditions that lead up to war. People have to overcome their current conditions, often a slow economy and high unemployment, and make the hard choice to believe in the future growth of their nation. This choice is hard to make when the British are blockading our ports, stockbrokers are selling apples on Wall Street, or we are still cleaning up the dust that used to be the World Trade Center. We need to believe in war's ability to stimulate the economy in order to work up the courage to invest under these difficult conditions.

A look at previous wars may help.

WAR STIMULATES THE ECONOMY

Gross Domestic Product Measures Our Economy

The next two graphs illustrate the difficult economic conditions that precede many wars. Investors usually have to overcome the prevailing gloom and buy stocks when the outlook is poor. Those who understand that war stimulates the economy are in a better position to do so.

We measure the strength of our economy by the dollar amount of the goods and services that we produce each year. The proper term is gross domestic product (GDP). It is the *changes* in the growth rate of GDP that make us feel rich or poor rather than the absolute value, because a rapidly growing economy provides jobs while slow growth forces us to cut back on our consumption. The first graph, from 1800 to 1920, shows changes in annual GDP (see Figure 19.1). The second graph, from 1920 to 2005, uses the quarterly numbers that became available with the founding of the National Bureau of Economic Research. The two graphs use the data in Appendix 19.1 and came from a web site that organizes the NBER's data, www.globalfindata.com. The years that the United States was at war are in bold type in Appendix 19.1.

You can see that in almost every case, the economy strengthened during a war. The economic difficulties leading up to most wars, however, made it hard to be optimistic enough to buy stocks.

Nineteenth-Century Wars

The British blockade of our ports early in that century may have caused our economic decline, and many historians think that it contributed to the War of 1812. President Thomas Jefferson countered Great Britain's blockade with his Embargo Act of 1807, which backfired and caused even more economic difficulties for our own merchants here at home. Our economy slowed down 15 percent that year, and Britain continued impressing our citizens into service on their warships against Napoleon. This "second war of independence" was considered to be an economic necessity for the survival of our country. People who understood that war stimulates the economy had the courage to invest at this difficult time, and they reaped the rewards of double-digit economic growth.

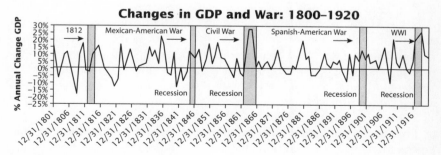

FIGURE 19.1   War and GDP
Source: www.globalfindata.com.

Before the Mexican-American War, we suffered what may have been the worst depression in our history. The economy slowed for seven years leading up to that war. The growth rate of our economy declined more than 20 percent between 1837 and 1844 with just a little improvement as we approached war. This was one time that the economic expansion occurred *after* the conflict and investors had to wait to realize their gains.

The Civil War came at the end of a long and steep economic decline embroiled in political strife. Buying stocks must have been a particularly difficult decision during our transformation into an industrialized nation. People had to make two predictions in this war: which side would win and which land would be spared the destruction of battle. Knowing that war improves the winner's economy gave investors a framework for their decision. The graph shows 25 percent economic growth during the Civil War.

People living through the next war, the Spanish-American War, also had to make hard decisions during economic malaise. They were slowly emerging from a severe recession comparable to the Great Depression of the 1930s. The economy's growth rate had declined about 12 percent during 1893–1894 and made it hard to put money to work in the stock market or anywhere else.

Twentieth-Century Wars

During the twentieth century it continued to be difficult to buy stocks at the beginning of war because the conditions leading up to war were so dismal.

There were a couple of strong economic years before World War I, but the general trend from the beginning of the twentieth century was down. After a strong year in 1909, economic growth slid almost 20 percent over the next two years; growth went from 20 percent in 1909 down to 1 percent in 1911 as business expansion ground to a halt. Cities crumbled under the weight of immigrants moving into them during the industrial revolution. Governments could not, or would not in the case of some European monarchies, meet their needs quickly enough. Investors had to see past the social upheaval that turned their lives upside down; they had to believe in the future even as they sent their children to war. This war produced some of the strongest economic growth in that century.

The second graph (Figure 19.2) covers the period from 1920 to 2005 and has more war years than the first graph. It also has both the shortest and the longest wars that the United States has ever fought; the Vietnam War ran on for nine years while the Gulf War lasted less than two months. War still stimulated our economy although to a lesser degree.

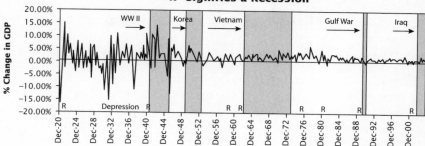

FIGURE 19.2 More War and GDP
Source: www.globalfindata.com.

Investors had every right to be discouraged as we entered World War II. We still suffered the drag of the Great Depression during the preceding decade, and it must have taken great faith to buy stocks while watching newsreels of our fleet on fire at Pearl Harbor. This war, however, stimulated unusually strong economic expansion, with changes in the GDP growth rates up to 15 percent.

World War II's stimulus petered out as we approached the Korean police action five years later. Once again, shell-shocked investors needed courage to buy stocks in the face of a slowing economy. Korea, however, rewarded investors with a 5 percent increase in economic growth.

Our economy avoided serious swings after Korea, and we had a decade of peace. The Vietnam War began after two back-to-back recessions that spanned 1957 to 1961. We fought two wars at once when President Lyndon Johnson declared his War on Poverty the same year that he sent military "advisers" to Vietnam: 1964. We had just seen our president assassinated and the National Guard escort little girls into newly integrated schools. Once again, economic and social upheaval made the investment decision difficult but the economy responded to the stimulus of war. The only good thing about Vietnam was the steady drip of economic growth it injected into our financial system.

The last war during the twentieth century, the Gulf War, also known as Desert Storm, was six weeks long. Again, war coincided with a recession. The 1990–1991 recession may have been mild by some standards, but it decimated our savings and loan institutions that financed the American dream of home ownership. Real estate prices declined in many parts of the country as home sales dried up along with mortgage money. It was the last straw when Iraq invaded Kuwait and confiscated the oil fields that fuel our economy. The conflict lasted 42 days from the January 17 Apache attacks to the February 28 cease-fire. The economic expansion that it triggered lasted a decade.

Twenty-first-Century War

The first, and hopefully the last, twenty-first-century war is still going on in the same part of the world: the Middle East. This second war in Iraq was supposed to have been as short as the Gulf War, but it has dragged on for two years as of this writing. Investors were still reeling from the lingering effects of a recession and terrorist attacks when troops were activated. If they had firm convictions that war stimulates our economy, as long as the war is fought somewhere else, they made a lot of money buying stocks when troops were activated in the summer of 2002.

A second difficult condition often prevails at the beginning of a war: a high rate of unemployment. Investors are already uncomfortable with the social and economic conditions when the country goes to war, and then they have to face the high rate of unemployment. Investors who know that war puts people to work as it stimulates the economy are more likely to overcome their fears and buy stocks when troops put on their uniforms.

UNEMPLOYMENT AND WAR

War transfers wealth from the losers to the winners and those who supply them. It also creates jobs for people on both sides of the conflict. The graph in Figure 19.3 indicates that major wars reduce unemployment while limited engagements have less effect.

In most cases, unemployment declines dramatically when war begins. The first three wars on this graph, World War II, Korea, and Vietnam, had declining unemployment rates even during the preparation phases. The graph suggests that the wars with the widest public participation produced the greatest declines in unemployment. World War II involved almost everyone in the country one way or another. The draft called up most of the qualified men, factories put women to work, and unemployment dropped to almost zero. Korea engaged fewer people and saw a lower reduction in unemployment. Vietnam had even less effect on employment if only because it drew from a larger population cohort, the baby boomers. The Gulf War was so short that its effect on employment during the conflict was minimal. The good news about the Gulf War is that the rate of unemployment declined for the decade afterward. The second war in Iraq is limited in scope but still coincides with reduced unemploy-

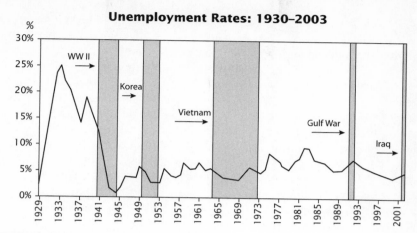

FIGURE 19.3 Unemployment and War

ment. The next graph (Figure 19.4) shows how unemployment rose from 4 percent to 6 percent during the recession that preceded the war and then declined during the conflict.

The bottom line is that one of the very few good things about war is that it provides jobs. It also provides an investment opportunity for those able to see past the bad economic and employment news surrounding the advent of war.

War stimulates economic growth and employment; it also causes inflation.

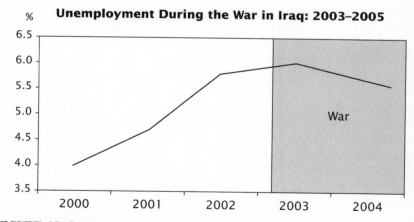

FIGURE 19.4 War in Iraq

INFLATION

The nonscientific definition of inflation is "too much money chasing too few goods." This casual explanation is inelegant but accurate.

War uses up our supply of goods faster than the central bank takes money out of the financial system, so the result is an increase in inflation. Each bomb we detonate uses up raw materials and adds nothing to our productive capacity. In fact, the situation is more serious than that; war takes people out of the labor force and puts them in harm's way; so the cost of labor increases as well as the cost of goods. We train new soldiers in newly built barracks and clothe them in new uniforms. We build new transportation systems to move them abroad and then build new infrastructure once they are deployed. We give them arms, medical supplies, and communication systems that our economy did not need to produce in peacetime. In addition to the armies themselves, we expand our scientific community to address the specific needs of war. Medical scientists investigate new cures for the horrors of each particular war. We hire additional engineers to invent new vehicles to transport our troops and then support them.

It is not surprising that the graph in Figure 19.5, based on the consumer price index from the U.S. Bureau of Labor Statistics, shows an increase in the rate of inflation during each and every war since 1820. This data is available to you at the National Bureau of Economic Research and at www.globalfindata.com.

Every single war on this graph has increasing rates of inflation. Some of them gave us sustained periods of troublesome inflation for many years afterward. Bonds suffer from inflation, so investors probably need to give up the security of fixed-income investments when war breaks out. The last thing we want to do is worry about the effects of increasing rates of inflation on our bond portfolios . . . but investors have to.

The longest and most severe peacetime experience with inflation came after the Vietnam War. The extreme inflation during the late 1970s and early 1980s may have been the legacy of President Johnson's simultaneous War on Poverty and the Vietnam War. This was the ultimate combination of "guns and butter," and it imbedded inflation in our society. Everything from labor contracts to alimony payments included cost of living escalators that matched inflation, and it took a decade to wring inflationary expectations out of our national psyche. We may be able to protect ourselves from moderate inflation by buying stocks at the right time.

The right time to buy stocks is when rumors of war become a mobilization of troops.

FIGURE 19.5 Inflation and War
Source of data: U.S. Bureau of Labor Statistics.

STOCK MARKET

Nothing stimulates business and the stock market so much as the increased federal spending that occurs during wartime. If the Fed increases the money supply the effect is magnified. Except for the War of 1812, the stock market improved during, and usually after, each of our major conflicts. Over the last 100 years, investing at the beginning of a war has been very productive (see Figure 19.6). Appendix 19.2 has the data on this graph from www.globalfindata.com.

The War of 1812

This is the one war that did not see the stock market improve, as Table 19.1 indicates.

This war may be an example of why you do not want to invest in the market of a country on whose territory the war is being fought. This war took place primarily on water. The British barricaded our ports and fought us from the Great Lakes to New Orleans. Along the way, they burned

S&P Index and War: 1800–2005

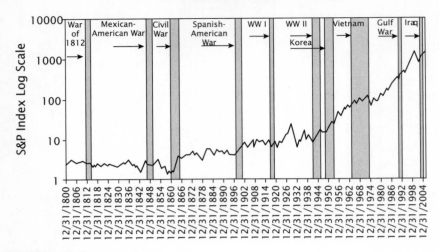

FIGURE 19.6   S&P and War

TABLE 19.1	The War of 1812
Date	**S&P**
12/31/1811	2.6458
12/31/1812	2.7381
12/31/1813	2.7688
12/31/1814	2.3073

down our White House. Perhaps we were lucky that our stock market did not decline more than it did.

Mexican-American War

Depressions plagued the first half of the nineteenth century, and not even the Mexican-American War moved the stock market (see Table 19.2). Continued economic malaise led up to the Civil War in the middle of that century.

Civil War

The Civil War was, among many other things, a battle between the old agrarian economy and the new industrialism. Not only did industrialism

TABLE 19.2	Mexican-American War
Date	**S&P**
12/31/1846	2.4808
12/31/1847	2.5111
12/31/1848	2.4203

win, but it improved the stock market and the economy (see Figure 19.7 and Table 19.3).

A civil war, by definition, is fought on home ground and should have decimated both the economy and the stock market. Our stock market, however, reflects the industrialism of our Northern states on whose land the war was not fought. The South's economy suffered after the war and, if there had been a stock market to reflect its economy, the results would have been poor.

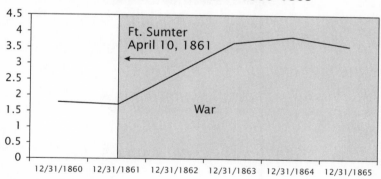

Civil War and the S&P: 1860–1865

FIGURE 19.7 Civil War

TABLE 19.3	The Civil War
Date	**S&P**
12/31/1861	1.6942
12/31/1862	2.6321
12/31/1863	3.6326
12/31/1864	3.8663
12/31/1865	3.5387

TABLE 19.4	The Spanish-American War	
Date		**S&P**
12/31/1897		4.75
12/31/1898		5.65
12/31/1899		6.02
12/31/1900		6.87

Spanish-American War

Investing at the beginning of a war was more productive during the twentieth century than it was during the previous one. The Spanish-American War took place outside our boundaries rather than at home, and the market went up 45 percent (see Table 19.4).

World War I

The First World War also saw a rise in the stock market, and it continued after the Treaty of Versailles ended the hostilities (see Figure 19.8 and Table 19.5).

World War II

Many people feel that the Great Depression did not end until this war stimulated the economy. It certainly stimulated the stock market and en-

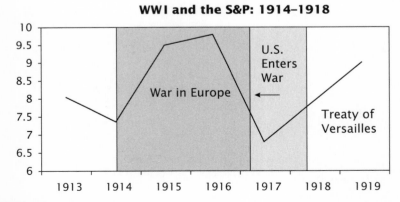

FIGURE 19.8   World War I

TABLE 19.5	World War I
Date	**S&P**
12/31/1913	8.04
12/31/1914	7.35
12/31/1915	9.48
12/31/1916	9.8
12/31/1917	6.8
12/31/1918	7.9176
12/31/1919	9.0235

riched those who bought the S&P 500 index when the war began (see Figure 19.9 and Table 19.6).

Congress' joint declaration of war on Monday, December 8, 1941, marked a good time to buy the stock market, which doubled during the war.

The Korean War

We have not had a formal declaration of war since 1941, so we will use the date on which troops have been called up as our investment date. This is the day that the stock market can put uncertainty behind it and start to rally (see Figure 19.10 and Table 19.7).

The stock market grew about 20 percent despite the fact that this was a limited so-called police action with less economic impact than the two world wars that preceded it.

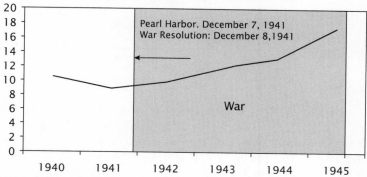

FIGURE 19.9 World War II

TABLE 19.6	World War II
Date	**S&P**
12/31/1941	8.6902
12/31/1942	9.77
12/31/1943	11.67
12/30/1944	13.28
12/31/1945	17.36

Korea and the S&P: 1950–1953

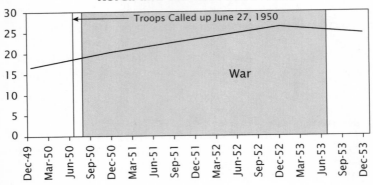

FIGURE 19.10   Korean Conflict

TABLE 19.7	Korean Conflict
Date	**S&P**
12/30/1950	20.41
12/31/1951	23.77
12/31/1952	26.578
12/31/1953	24.814

Vietnam War

The Vietnam War made money for investors who bought the S&P at 83 on August 7, 1964, when the Gulf of Tonkin Resolution called up troops. Investors made almost 20 percent during the next 10 years (see Figure 19.11 and Table 19.8).

Investors suffered two major stock market declines during that war, and we avoided them both with our yield curve analysis in the first part of

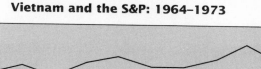

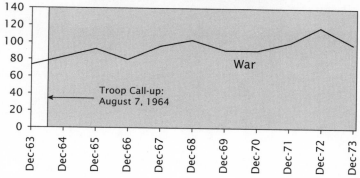

FIGURE 19.11   Vietnam

TABLE 19.8	Vietnam War
Date	**S&P**
12/31/1964	84.75
12/31/1965	92.43
12/30/1966	80.33
12/29/1967	96.47
12/31/1968	103.86
12/31/1969	92.06
12/31/1970	92.15
12/31/1971	102.09
12/29/1972	118.05
12/31/1973	97.55

this book. We were out of the stock market in 1966 but got back in time for the 1967–1968 rally. We avoided 1969 and reentered near the bottom of the market in 1970.

Gulf War

The Gulf War lasted just 42 days and earned the nickname "The Whirlwind War." The stock market went from 307 in August 1990 when troops were called up to 370 the following March when troops withdrew (see Figure 19.12). Daily values of the S&P 500 index during this time are in Appendix 19.3. Investors made 20 percent in six months, and that was just the beginning of the longest and strongest stock market since the Roaring Twenties.

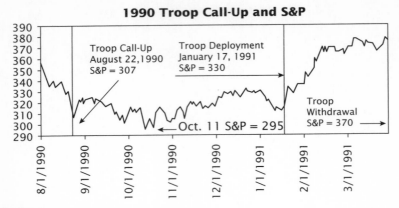

FIGURE 19.12   The First Gulf War

ONE FINAL TRADE: THE GULF WAR

Investors exhibited their usual fear on the day of the troop call-up and they sold the S&P 500 index. We knew that war stimulates the economy, puts people back to work, and improves stock markets; so we will buy the S&P at 307 on August 23, 1990, rather than wait until January 1991 as yield curve analysis dictates. The call-up of troops is the only condition that causes us to invest when the yield curve is negative because we know that war will normalize the curve.

- Old buy: January, 1991 at 330.
- New buy: August 23, 1990 at 307.

Our list of trades is shown in Table 19.9.

It is time for our final accounting. Let us see how we fare by combining yield curve analysis from Part One with technical indicators in Part Two and the cultural signals in this chapter of Part Three.

FINAL PERFORMANCE

Our final graph reflects all of the trades in this book (see Figure 19.13 on p. 214).

In order to look at a worst-case scenario, we will start with one dollar on January 1, 1960, and track its progress to the bottom of the recent bear

TABLE 19.9 Troop Activation Gives New Trade Dates

Trade	Date	S&P 500 Index
Buy	January 2, 1960	59
Sell	September 1, 1966	77
Buy	February 1, 1967	86
Sell	July 1, 1969	97
Buy	February 1, 1970	85
Sell	June 1, 1973	105
Buy	October 1, 1974	63
Sell	December 1, 1978	94
Buy	May 1, 1980	106
Sell	November 1, 1980	127
Buy	September 1, 1981	122
Sell	October 15, 1987	298
Buy	October 20, 1987	236
Sell	October 31, 1989	340
Buy	August 23, 1990	307
Sell	July 1, 1998	1133
Buy	September 4, 1998	973
Sell	August 1, 2000	1430
Buy	July 19, 2002	847

market on October 1, 2002. Trading increased our portfolio's rate of return from the buy-and-hold strategy of 6.33 percent to 9.56 percent; each portfolio is without dividends of approximately 3 percent. Our active portfolio's return is 150 percent of the return on the passive portfolio (see Figure 19.14). In addition, we had the satisfaction of exercising control over our environment by using a few simple tools that are available to the general public for free.

This higher return produced a portfolio over three times as large in dollar value compared to the traditional buy-and-hold portfolio (see Figure 19.15).

We protected ourselves from buying at the top or selling at the bottom of any market cycle. We slept well at night because we had a plan that made sense and were not prey to other people's ideas about where the market might be headed. Most of our capital gains are long-term and benefit from a lower tax rate than short-term gains or ordinary income. Our portfolio had much lower volatility because we were out of the market during the worst periods.

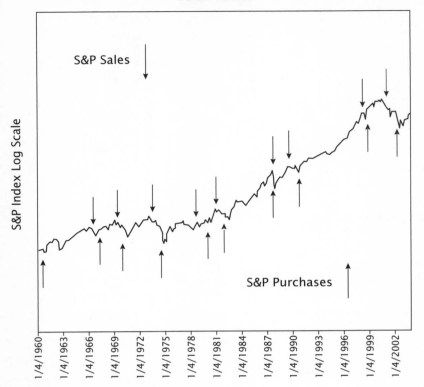

FIGURE 19.13 Graph of Trades Including Cultural Indicators

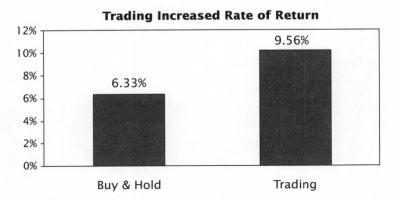

FIGURE 19.14 Return Is 10 Percent

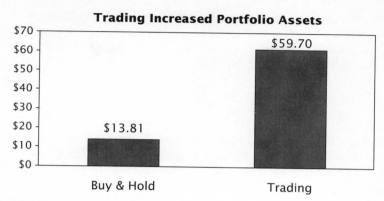

FIGURE 19.15 Portfolio Is $61

SECOND WAR IN IRAQ

We expected the second war in Iraq to be just as short as the Gulf War; but that was not the case. Investors, however, made a lot of money if they bought stocks during the troop call-up on October 10, 2002, which was one day after the bottom of the market (see Figure 19.16). Our model portfolio had already bought stocks three months before and a few points higher, but this was a second chance for anyone who missed the July opportunity. (See Appendix 19.4 for daily data.)

It was clear that we were bouncing along the bottom of the 2000–2002 bear market when troops were called up for Iraq. The S&P touched 819,

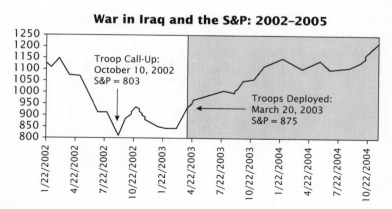

FIGURE 19.16 War in Iraq

776, and 800 as we approached war; and each of those declines offered investors a chance to deploy their own troops—in this case the troops were cash, to fight for their portfolios. Investors using these cultural signals to help manage their money knew that these depressing market levels were just a temporary prelude to a bull market. The S&P ended 2003 about 25 percent higher than it was on the day our troops entered Iraq.

Our model portfolio navigated the recent bear market successfully. We sold the S&P in August 2000 at 1430 because the yield curve inverted. We declined to buy the S&P back a year later when the curve normalized after the terrorist attacks because several of the Dow stocks were up and volume was fairly strong. (Some reports say that the Federal Reserve called a few friends at large pension trusts and asked them to buy stocks when the market reopened after the attacks.)

Instead, we reentered the market on July 19, 2002, at 819 when all 30 of the Dow stocks fell on the same day. The yield curve was still normal and had fallen to historically low levels that promoted business activity. The technical situation was good because light volume, the put/call ratio, and the volatility index (VIX) suggested that people had given up on the stock market.

SUMMARY

We built our case for buying stocks when our troops mobilize because war usually starts a new, stronger economic cycle. We saw how gross domestic product, employment, inflation, and the stock market all tend to rise in wartime; and we looked at their behavior during every American war for the past two centuries. We refined a previous trade and made a final accounting of our investment process. The fun begins in Part Four when we apply this discipline to specific securities and add a little leverage for aggressive investors.

The following chapter reviews the book's investment criteria so that we will know what we are doing when we actually start spending money and select securities for our own portfolios.

CHAPTER 20

Summary of Cultural Indicators

This summary reviews all three parts of this book so we can move on to Part Four with asset allocation, security selection, and leverage. We need to solidify the basic concepts of our discipline before we select specific investments or add leverage. Part One, yield curve analysis, provides us with required conditions to be in the stock market:

- The yield curve is upward-sloping, or normal.
- Bond quality spreads are shrinking as investor confidence improves.
- The federal funds rate is low or declining.
- The 10-year Treasury yield is less than 10 percent, which is the long-term average return for the stock market.

Part Two refines the analysis by adding technical indicators:

- Market breadth.
- Volatility index.
- Put/call ratio.
- Moving averages.

Part Three adds signals from the culture:

- Changing standards of female beauty.
- Demographics.
- Corporate spending.
- War.

Each chapter takes the basic forecasting tool of yield curve analysis and refines it with publicly available information that is easy to use.

PART ONE: YIELD CURVE ANALYSIS

Yield curve analysis is a basic tool on Wall Street.

Basic Forecasting Tool

The premise of this book is that the U.S. Treasury yield curve is the starting point for forecasting both the economy and the stock market. The yield curve contains data from the majority of investors' expectations for interest rates; and, because interest rates help shape the economy and the stock market, we can use this curve to anticipate the S&P 500 index.

The Slope of the Curve

We started with the Federal Reserve's graph of gross domestic product (GDP) and the spread of the 10-year note over the three-month bill (see Figure 20.1).

We took the dates on which the thick line representing the slope of the yield curve dipped below zero and plotted them on a graph of the S&P 500 index to establish our first group of trades. We refined our "buy" trades by making sure that the three-month to one-year interest rates were also positive, because money market rates are critical to an economic recovery.

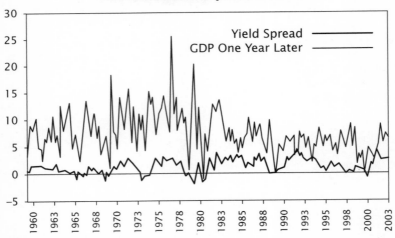

FIGURE 20.1 GDP and Yield Curve Spread

The relationship between the longest bond and the 10-year gave us advance warning of a stock market decline; and the critical importance of a 10-year note yielding 10 percent, which is the long-term return on the stock market, produced an important sell signal before the 1987 crash. We established the value of being in a money market instrument whenever the 10-year note pays the same rate as our long-term expectation for stocks: 10 percent.

The Federal Funds Rate

We then turned our attention to the central bank and the investment opportunities it presents. The Federal Reserve created enough money after the 1987 crash to force the fed funds rate down at an unprecedented rate of speed. As the funds rate collapsed, it dragged the whole yield curve with it and created another buy signal. The Fed intervened in a similar manner in 1988 after the Russian bond default threatened the international financial system, and we bought stocks after this event as well. We refined our yield curve analysis to include a buy signal whenever the Fed reduces the funds rate half a percent after a crisis.

We also learned to keep an eye on this rate every day because this number moves before the rest of the yield curve and is the first responder to the central bank's monetary policy changes that affect economic cycles. The graph in Figure 20.2 illustrates this point.

The Federal Reserve uses bond quality spreads to help them analyze the economy, and we used these same spreads to help us forecast the stock market.

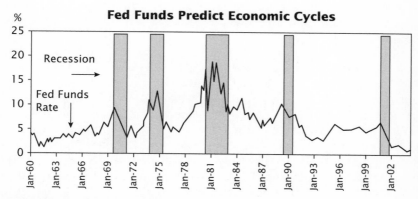

FIGURE 20.2 Business Cycles and Fed Funds Rate

Bond Quality Spreads Forecast Stocks

The Federal Reserve uses the spread of speculative bonds over Treasuries during their deliberations. We used the rate at which this spread increases, an excellent indicator of investors' fear, to forecast trouble in the stock market. When we saw quality spreads widen rapidly before the crashes in 1987 and 1998, we sold stocks and avoided those market declines.

Many professional money managers and economists agree that the shape of the yield curve forecasts the economy about a year before a change takes place. This one-year lead time gives rise to the Wall Street observation that it's easy to predict the stock market in the long run, but no one knows what it will do in the short run.

Since, as Lord John Maynard Keynes said, in the long run we are all dead, investors use technical indicators to try to predict the short-term movements of the stock market.

PART TWO: TECHNICAL INDICATORS

We used technical indicators to help us identify the absolute extreme values of markets. Traditional money managers often combine the fundamental analysis described earlier with a few of their favorite technical indicators such as the market breadth, volatility, and moving averages. We did the same, but we put our own spin on some of these indicators.

Market Breadth

We measured market breadth by looking at the number of stocks in the Dow Jones Industrial Average that advance and decline each day. We used two simple rules.

The first is to prepare to sell stocks when only a few in the Dow stocks rise every day while most of the index declines. Those that do advance are often strong enough to raise the index to new levels every day. Market breadth is poor under these conditions even though the index rises daily as it did in 1999. (When everyone wants to dance with the prom queen, it is time to leave the party.)

Conversely, *our* party is about to begin when no one wants to dance with anyone, and all 30 of the Dow stocks decline on the same day. The only time between 2000 and 2004 that all 30 declined was on July 19, 2002. We bought the S&P 500 index that day at 847 or about 10 percent away from the absolute bottom of the long bear market.

Volatility Index and the Put/Call Ratio

We used the volatility index (VIX) and the put/call ratio to validate our investment decisions indicated by yield curve analysis. These two indicators tell us exactly what sophisticated stock market investors are thinking at any given time and, therefore, should be a gold mine of ongoing information. They did, in fact, support our trading decisions during the Russian bond default in 1998 and the general malaise near the end of 2002.

The VIX and the put/call ratio, like most of our indicators, perform fairly well on their own. Technicians trade the VIX when it changes direction, and they trade the put/call ratio at critical values. The rule is to sell the S&P when this ratio is 60 percent (or less) and to buy the S&P when the ratio is least 100. Both the VIX and the put/call ratio are much easier to use if we overlay a moving average on these volatile indicators.

Moving Averages

A moving average drops the oldest number in a series and includes a new one. The denominator, or number of days during which you are looking at your moving average, stays the same. Market technicians use two moving averages with different time frames, and a trade signal develops when the two moving averages cross and then move together in the same direction. An example from the second half of 2002 shows how productive the put/call ratio is with two moving averages superimposed on it (see Figure 20.3).

The first buy signal on this graph is late August when the S&P was around 900. Another opportunity that this graph identified was in the middle of September. Finally, there was a buy signal on October 3 when the S&P touched bottom at 776. In addition to the fact that this graph generated these accurate buy signals, there were no misleading sell signals; the long-term moving average kept you in the market at the right time.

Many technicians measure how two moving averages come together or move apart; the result is the popular moving average convergence/divergence (MACD) line. The MACD line is easier to read against a baseline, and then it becomes a histogram like the one under the S&P index in Figure 20.4.

A histogram highlights the force with which moving averages approach or move away from each other. More observations of a particular price or the volume of trades, heightens that spot on the histogram.

Momentum Forecasts Strength

Investors use momentum to measure acceleration, or the *change* in the speed at which something is moving. Momentum is important because it

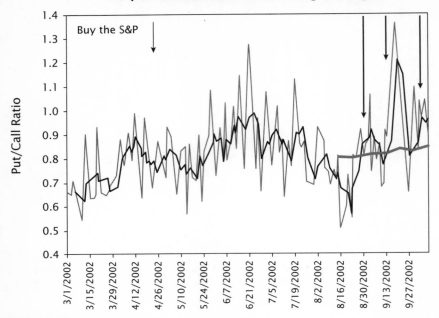

FIGURE 20.3   Put/Call Ratio with Two Moving Averages

suggests the strength of the next trend. You can see that the S&P had strong momentum at the end of July, the end of August, and in the middle of October when the histogram showed steep curves. Indeed, the trends that followed were also strong.

Some hedge fund traders, notably commodities trading advisers, use these tactics to the exclusion of most others. Not surprisingly, they refer to themselves as trend followers. They do not expect to capture the absolute tops and bottoms of each trend as we do, but they make up for it by augmenting their returns with leverage. We use measures of leverage as contrary indicators.

Leverage: Short Positions and Margin Debt

Margin accounts and short selling provide technical analysts with wonderful indicators of extreme market values. Margin debt, or money that investors borrow from their brokers to buy stock, magnifies the movements of the stock market. Debt increased much faster than the S&P during the

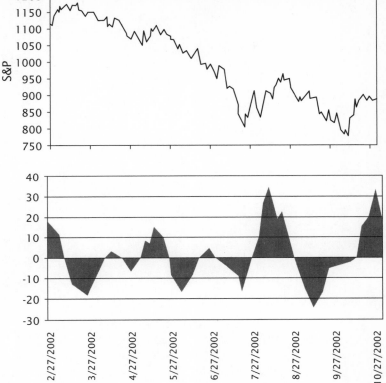

S&P with Histogram: March–November, 2002

FIGURE 20.4 S&P with Histogram

tech bubble and then declined faster than stocks during the subsequent bear market (see Figure 20.5).

Short interest, or stocks that investors borrow from their brokers, has an inverse relationship to the stock market and provides us with another indicator of market extremes (see Figure 20.6). Both measures of investors' borrowings from their brokers give us an idea of when markets are overdone in either direction.

When it takes more days than usual for investors who are short to cover their positions, you can be pretty sure that the market is ready for a strong rally. One reason for this is that traders watch the "days to cover" numbers and then drive up the market when short sellers are the most

FIGURE 20.5 S&P with Margin Debt
Source: New York Stock Exchange report, "NYSE Member Firms Customers' Margin Debt."

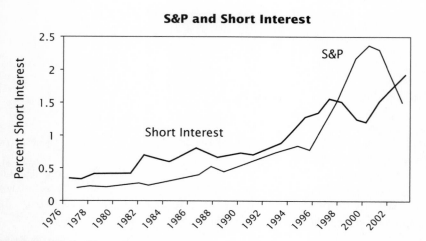

FIGURE 20.6 Short Interest

vulnerable. Desperate short sellers scramble to close their positions, and a normal rally becomes much stronger than usual.

Technical analysis provided us with one additional trade, reentering the market on July 19, 2002, when market breadth was nil. These indicators also verified several others of our trades. We could trade these technical indicators alone if we were willing to spend more time, pay short-term capital gains tax rates, and incur more trading commissions. We would also have to put up with a fair number of false signals. Trend followers attempt to correct this deficiency with stop-loss orders and a low tolerance for losing positions.

PART THREE: CULTURAL SIGNALS

Part Three added cultural signals to our fundamental and technical analysis. These signals were the media's changing standards of feminine beauty, demographics, corporate spending, and war. Our culture has two effects on our trading; it shapes our economy it also forecasts the stock market.

Part Three is important because, in addition to using free and easily accessible information that appeals to nonquantitative investors, our culture is tied to our economy and our stock market. It is my opinion that the economy determines our culture. I have seen standards of beauty and corporate spending change along with the economic cycle; I have seen changes in birth rates that parallel the economy and I have seen nations go to war during recessions. These are the events that shape our lives and our portfolios.

Changing Standards of Beauty

We looked at how our popular culture reflects and forecasts our economy. Standards of female beauty seem to change with the economy because we get bored with current models and move on to new stimulation.

The *Playboy* bust line theory began as a joke but stood up to scrutiny as a coincident indicator of the broad-based Russell 2000 index of stocks. The media's ideal of beauty certainly *does* change over time; models' faces become softer and more babyish as our pockets become fuller. In fact, the fashion modeling industry says that it needs new faces every six months to provide excitement. Everyone knows that the public's taste in entertainment changes; and some of us use that information to confirm our yield curve and technical analysis.

Demographics May Coincide

The economy may coincide with peaks in the rates of birth, death, marriage, divorce, and crime. Perhaps expanding economies fill us with confidence and enable us to have large families, live longer, stay married, and
obey our own laws. Recessions seem to push us toward having fewer children, earlier death, divorce, and crime. In addition to shaping our lives,
these landmarks are visible to us all in our assessment of the economic cycle. You do not have to be a mathematician to know where we are in the
business and stock market cycle; headlines in the local newspaper can
provide coincidental indicators.

Corporate Spending Extremes

Corporations give us, the consumer, what we want; so this chapter held a
mirror up to our own faces. Because firms need some lead time to put new
products on the shelf and make them known to consumers, corporate behavior and products change about six months to a year before the stock
market. Advertising, hiring, and entertaining have approximately a six-
month lead over the stock market, while women's fashions are about a
year early. Calvin Klein has mastered the art of advertising so well that we
could almost time the market around the public's reaction to his most
shocking campaigns.

War Stimulates the Economy

This chapter gave us a stock market indicator with the best track record
in Part Three: the calling up of troops to go to war.

We usually think of war as starting with a joint declaration from Congress, but Congress has not declared war since Pearl Harbor. In the absence of a formal declaration of war, our indicator to buy stocks is the
date on which troops are called up. Gross domestic product, employment,
inflation, and the stock market all tend to expand during wartime, so investors want to be fully invested when we actually deploy our troops; the
day that we activate our troops is the best time to buy stocks. In fact, this
is one time that we could disregard yield curve analysis and invest when
the curve is inverted.

TRADE SUMMARY

It is time to review all of our trades and the rationale for each one (see
Table 20.1). We will have more information, naturally, on the more recent

TABLE 20.1 Trade Rationale

Trade	Date	S&P	Rationale
Buy	January 1960	59	Normal yield curve, quality spreads shrinking, Fed funds rate declining, 10-year Treasury yield less than 10 percent
Sell	September 1966	77	Inverted yield curve
Buy	February 1967	86	Normal yield curve, quality spreads shrinking, fed funds rate declining, 10-year Treasury yield less than 10 percent
Sell	July 1969	97	Inverted yield curve
Buy	February 1970	85	Normal yield curve, quality spreads shrinking, fed funds rate declining, 10-year Treasury yield less than 10 percent
Sell	June 1973	105	Inverted yield curve
Buy	October 1974	63	Normal yield curve, quality spreads shrinking, fed funds rate declining, 10-year Treasury yield less than 10 percent
Sell	December 1978	94	Inverted yield curve
Buy	May 1980	106	Normal yield curve, quality spreads shrinking, fed funds rate declining, 10-year Treasury yield less than 10 percent
Sell	November 1980	127	Inverted yield curve
Buy	September 1981	122	Normal yield curve, quality spreads shrinking, fed funds rate declining
Sell	October 15, 1987	298	Ten-year note = 10%, fed funds and quality spreads rising rapidly, inversion: 30-year bond to 10-year note
Buy	October 20, 1987	236	Normal yield curve, fed funds rate declining, quality spreads shrinking, 10-year Treasury yield less than 10 percent
Sell	October 1989	340	Inverted yield curve
Buy	August 23, 1990	307	Troops activated for Gulf War, quality spreads shrinking, fed funds rate declining, 10-year Treasury yield less than 10 percent
Sell	July 1998	1133	Rapidly rising fed funds rate, rapidly rising quality spreads, VIX = 24 (was 19 in June)

(continues)

TABLE 20.1 *(Continued)*

Trade	Date	S&P	Rationale
Buy	September 4, 1998	973	Normal yield curve, fed funds rate declining, quality spreads shrinking, 10-year Treasury yield less than 10 percent, VIX = 44
Sell	August 2000	1430	Inverted yield curve, VIX = 16
Buy	July 19, 2002	847	All 30 Dow stocks down on one day, normal yield curve, fed funds rate declining, quality spreads shrinking, 10-year Treasury yield less than 10 percent, VIX = 39, P/C ratio = 1.14
End	January 3, 2005	1212	Hold? Normal curve, all yields less than 10%, quality spreads narrowing, fed funds rate rising, VIX = 13, P/C ratio = 0.80

trades because more data is available. Some of our technical analysis techniques are too new for some of our older trades, but yield curve analysis has been money managers' primary tool for generations.

PERFORMANCE SUMMARY

Our trades are on the graph in Figure 20.7 and our portfolio returns follow.

We examined the worst possible case by starting with one dollar on January 1, 1960, and tracking its progress to the bottom of the recent bear market on October 1, 2002. Our trades increased our portfolio's rate of return from the buy-and-hold strategy of 6.33 percent to 9.56 percent and the dollar amount from $13.81 to $59.70.

We can improve our performance if we update those results to January 1, 2005. In this case trading increased our passive portfolio's rate of return from almost 7 percent to about 10.5 percent; our active portfolio performed half again as well as the passive portfolio (see Figure 20.8). Dividends and income may have added about 3 percent to each return. We had less volatility and more control over our portfolio with these simple tools.

This higher return produced a portfolio more than three times as large in dollar value compared to the traditional buy-and-hold portfolio (see Figure 20.9).

S&P 500 Index: 1960–2005

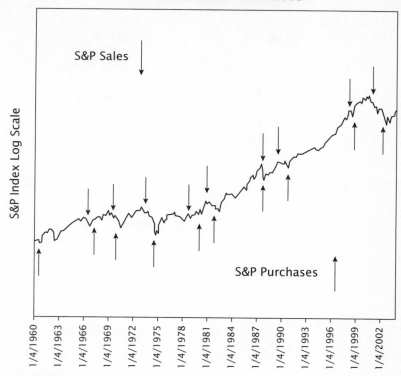

FIGURE 20.7 Final Graph

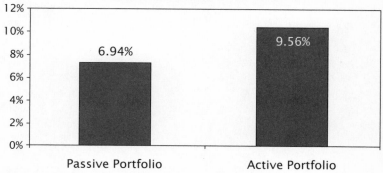

FIGURE 20.8 Return Is 10 Percent

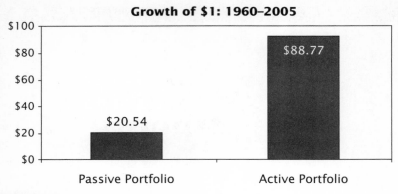

FIGURE 20.9   Portfolio Is $88.77

We protected ourselves from crowd psychology. Most of our capital gains were long-term and taxed at a lower rate than short-term gains or ordinary income. Finally, our portfolio improved its return because we were out of the market during its biggest losses.

SUMMARY

We reviewed all three parts of this book in order to solidify the basic concepts of our investment process before we actually start spending money. Part One gave us the required yield curve conditions for being in the stock market. Part Two added some popular technical analysis tools: breadth, volatility, put/call ratio, and moving averages. Part Three covered cultural indicators that may reflect and forecast the stock market, such as changing tastes in feminine beauty, demographics, corporate spending, and war.

Now we can move on to asset allocation, investment selection, and leverage in Part Four. Now we are talking about *real* money . . . yours.

PART IV

Choosing Investments

Before you start committing funds, you may want to evaluate your investment goals and risk tolerances. Some people set up separate portfolios with descriptive names to keep their different goals in full view.

Part Four continues our top-down approach to portfolio construction. We start with the major asset classes to see how money flows through them during an economic cycle. Then we examine mutual funds, specific securities, and derivatives.

These three investment vehicles are increasingly more risky and appropriate for different kinds of investors at different stages of their lives. You may want to adapt Chapter 22, "Mutual Funds," for your conservative accounts such as college tuition and retirement savings. Chapter 24, "Security Selection," may be more appropriate for your growth portfolio. The last part of that chapter covers the most aggressive of our investments, options and futures. The rule of thumb here is to invest what you can afford to lose because these derivatives can be worthless on their expiration dates. As usual, short sales or their equivalent derivatives can lead to unlimited losses.

You may want to shade the investment allocations in our model portfolio. Dumping one asset class for another may not suit you. You might be more comfortable with a baseline portfolio that holds the S&P 500 index and then makes minor adjustments into cash, bonds, hard assets or foreign currencies throughout the business cycle.

Many professional money managers use this baseline approach. If they manage a pension trust or a college endowment, they probably have a legal responsibility to protect the assets as well as to make them grow. They meet this dual responsibility by adhering to certain percentage allocations for each investment. Profits in one asset class regularly increase the value of their holdings beyond the required allocation. They then sell the profitable asset and buy one in which their allocation is below their requirement. We saw Xerox and several state pension trusts sell stocks late in the summer of 1987 after a rally made their equity portfolios larger than their guidelines allowed. They sold stocks and bought bonds to bring their asset allocations back into their required guidelines. We saw how this rebalancing cut their stock exposure before the crash.

This portfolio rebalancing is easier to do if the yield curve, technical analysis, and cultural signals tell you that a change is coming.

Let us look at the major asset classes and the securities they encompass so that we can improve on our portfolio's returns.

CHAPTER 21

Asset Classes

The financial markets are an ocean of investment opportunities. The tide of asset classes rolls in with regularity. Catch it right and you ride the wave of prosperity; catch it wrong and you drown in the undertow that drags you out to sea.

"Heeeeeelp!" screamed my terrified toddler as she tried to grab me. "I'm afraid of the waves!"

"Don't be such a baby," I said, looking down at the few inches of saltwater on the Cape Cod beach.

The waves barely reached her three-year-old waist, and she was overreacting to a little undertow. I picked her up and carried her to our beach towel so she could dig holes in the sand while I waded in the surf a few yards away. Then a big wave grabbed *me* around the waist as the undertow picked my feet up and threw me face-down in the water. My heart pounded as I scrambled out of the ocean and joined her on the sand. I remembered that scare when I heard the news of the tsunami in Indonesia and Sri Lanka, and I empathized with those who felt an infinitely greater terror as that undertow swallowed everything they held dear.

Investors should have the same fear of the undertow of a retreating asset class.

We learned that lesson the hard way at the beginning of this century when the stock market bubble broke. It was bad enough that the S&P lost almost half its value, but the Nasdaq lost 80 percent as it fell from 5,000 to 1,000 during two years. It will take a long time for people who invested at the top of the Nasdaq market to get their money back; they need to have their portfolios double more than twice just to break even. They need a

400 percent return to dig out of that hole. By the time they do get their portfolios back to where they were in 2000, inflation will have reduced their spending power.

Investors had a similar experience with the stock market in 1972 when the Dow reached 1,000. It took 10 years for these blue-chip stocks to get back to a thousand; and by that time, double-digit inflation had devalued each dollar to 50 cents.

Other assets classes are just as vulnerable.

When money flows out of the bond market and into "the next big thing," principal value washes away like footprints in the sand. Bondholders do not get their principal back until the bond matures, and by that time they, too, suffer a loss of purchasing power through inflation. The summer of 2003 saw the highest bond market prices, and the lowest yields, in 50 years. Anyone who bought a 30-year bond at 4.17 percent on July 1 of that year could see double-digit losses in his portfolio when interest rates go back to normal levels close to 6 percent. By the time that bond matures, inflation will have eroded its purchasing power. Inflation at 3 percent, which is average, will devalue your dollar by half in just 20 years.

At least stocks and bonds are easy to sell if investors want to limit their loss; hard assets, such as gold or real estate, do not trade as easily. Some people who bought houses at the top of the real estate market in 1987 had to hold them for five years to get their investment back, and they had to pay taxes and maintenance during that time. Employees who were transferred or retirees who were unable to meet these costs had to sell under duress to scarce buyers.

When investors flee an asset class, those left holding the bag find their capital sifting out of the hole in the bottom.

FOUR MAJOR ASSET CLASSES

The four major asset classes are: fixed-income (bills, notes, and bonds); equities (stocks); hard assets (gold, commodities, and real estate); and foreign currencies. We may hold more of these classes than we think.

Many investors mistakenly think that they limit themselves to U.S. stocks, bonds, and cash. As all business becomes more global, however, many U.S. companies participate in foreign currencies throughout the economic cycle; and investors may have more international exposure in their portfolios than they realize. The same holds true for commodities; American firms that extract or process basic materials will perform along the lines of hard assets such as oil, paper, and steel. You may think that you do not own real estate, but if you own Wal-Mart or McDonald's you own the land under their many buildings.

Understanding the four major asset classes is imperative for all investors because all four of them show up in the U.S. stock market; you may own them indirectly if not outright.

There is a road map for moving among these asset classes just as there was in Part One for timing the S&P 500 index, and they both use a similar analysis. We will examine each asset class, find out when to buy and sell it, and update our ongoing returns to include some of them.

Interest rates drive the asset allocation process because, as we saw in Part One, they determine the strength of the economy and the stock market.

Each of the four asset classes dominates the economy at a different point in time. For example, firms use raw materials to manufacture a product, deliver a service, or process information. When prices of these hard assets rise, manufacturers' profit margins and earnings decrease and cause the stock market to drop. A recession often results and pushes the Federal Reserve into easing the money supply. Investors prefer to hold a scarce currency, so each central bank's decision to increase or decrease its money supply through interest rate changes determines the value of its currency. Therefore, all four asset classes are interrelated and affect one another. Here is how money flows, with some overlap, through these classes.

The progression starts with fixed-income securities and moves to stocks, then into hard assets, and finally into foreign currencies. The basic dichotomy is paper investments (stocks, bonds, and currencies) versus hard assets (cash, real estate, and gold). Foreign currencies represent paper assets in another country, usually stocks and bonds, and are often a bridge between hard assets and paper investments in our own country. Most investors, of course, use just some of these categories and many prefer to use cash in the bank as their hard asset.

Sophisticated investors are on the leading edge of these moves, while the rest of the world *follows* the money flows through these classes. Now that you are aware of the general order in which a dollar progresses through these assets, you can take advantage of the flow. I will elaborate with more specific criteria to help you identify the tops and bottoms of these markets so that, if you are so inclined, you can augment your portfolio by investing directly in these assets. At the very least, you will avoid buying your next rental property, gold bar, pork belly future, or Eurobond at the top of the market and then selling it at the bottom. You may even book your next vacation in Europe early if you think that the dollar will fall before you go.

PAPER ASSETS

Because interest rates drive the investment process, we can use yield curve analysis to help us through these four major asset classes.

Fixed-Income Securities

Conservative investors prefer to invest in fixed-income securities and accept the erosion from inflation as their trade-off for getting their principal back when their securities mature. If they want a steady stream of income that will not decline during a recession when corporations cut dividends to save cash, they move out of the money market into longer-term securities. However, they know that their bonds and notes may be called away from them and that this will happen at the worst possible time: when interest rates are at their lowest level.

We will start with money market investments. The three-month Treasury bill is an academic's starting point and the place where most people store new money. Your paycheck goes into your bank account, so most investment thinking starts with cash.

Up to now, we have made no assumptions about our model portfolio when it was not in the stock market. We did not give it credit for earning interest in the bank or making money in any other investment. Now we will change that assumption and invest in a three-month Treasury bill while we are out of the stock market.

Model Portfolio with Three-Month Bills

Investing in a Treasury bill makes a big difference in our return. Inflation was high during the 1970s and 1980s and drove up interest rates on this investment. In fact, at one point in the early 1980s, treasury bills went up to 12 percent and money market mutual funds paid 20 percent.

The cumulative result of our cash position adds about 1 percent during the time that we were out of the stock market (see Figure 21.1). The

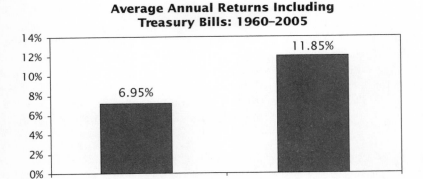

Average Annual Returns Including Treasury Bills: 1960–2005

Passive Portfolio: 6.95%
Active Portfolio: 11.85%

FIGURE 21.1 Return Including Three-Month Bills

trading, or actively managed, portfolio now has almost double the average annual return as the buy-and-hold, or passive portfolio. There are no dividends in either portfolio. There is almost $8 in the active portfolio for each $1 in the passive portfolio (see Figure 21.2).

We could have moved part of our portfolio into the bond market if we were willing to accept the risk of principal fluctuations. When inflation is high, as it was in the early 1980s, long-term Treasuries can lose principal value for months on end if the inverted yield curve moves higher every day. Investors ultimately made money on their bonds during this period, but if they bought when the curve first inverted they had to wait many months to break even.

In contrast, when inflation declines as it did in 2000, buying a long-term bond provides double-digit returns during a poor stock market. From January 2000 to the spring of 2003, the bond total return index grew about 30 percent.

Equities Benefit from Low Interest Rates

When the yield curve is normal and interest rates are low, investors may want to buy stocks. This is the longest part of the investment cycle, but it does not last forever because it depends on a delicate balance of easy money and low inflation. Pretty soon the Federal Reserve prevents serious inflation by taking some of the cash out of the system, and investors must make a difficult decision concerning which asset class to go into next. As our central bank decreases money supply, short-term interest rates rise and the yield curve inverts. We know from Part One that now

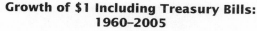

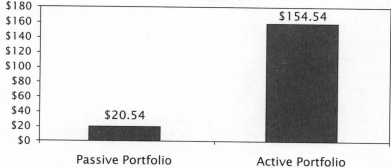

FIGURE 21.2   Portfolio with Three-Month Bills

is the time to sell some stocks and move the proceeds into another asset class.

HARD ASSETS

"They make it on Wall Street and bury it on Main Street."

That old saw refers to people taking profits out of the stock market
to buy real things that they can enjoy, and this advice works best in the
real estate market. Other hard assets often make money a little later in
the cycle.

Real Estate during an Inverted Yield Curve

Investors can expect to profit from a purchase in real estate when the
yield curve inverts because the housing market is often slow at this
point in the economy. You will notice in the graph in Figure 21.3 that
almost every time the change in housing prices hovers around zero,
we are in a recession. While the 2001 recession did not suffer zero
growth in housing prices, it did experience very low growth rates
around 1 percent.

The beginning of a recession is a good time to buy a house if your fi-
nances and your job are secure. Your mortgage rate may be high, but you
can refinance it at a lower rate later in the cycle; you cannot renegotiate
your purchase price. This data is from the Federal Home Loan Mortgage
Corporation at www.freddiemac.com.

Appendix 21.1 gives the prices on this graph and shows how the housing market suffers just before a recession. Interest rates are too high at
this point in the economic cycle, and investors are infatuated with the
stock market. After the stock market peaks, all interest rates including
mortgages decline; the public is disgusted with stocks, and they pour
money into the real estate market.

You can beat the rush into real estate if you swap out of stocks and
into a bigger house when the yield curve inverts. Wait for interest rates, including your mortgage, to fall and then refinance your house even as it ap-
preciates in market value. You may be able to get this best of both worlds
if you are *not* transferred or do *not* lose your job during the recession that
allows you to refinance your mortgage at a lower rate.

What should you do with your stock market profits if you do not want
to buy a house? After all, the upkeep is expensive, taxes tend to increase
over time, the market is less liquid than the one for the S&P 500
index . . . and moving is a lot of work.

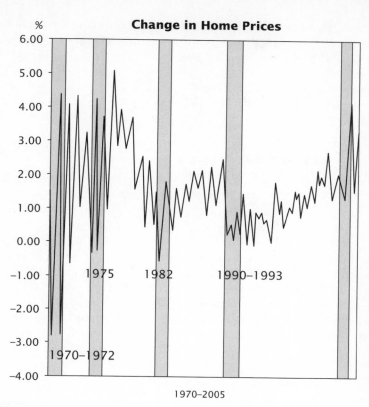

FIGURE 21.3 Home Prices
Source of data: www.freddiemac.com.

Gold and Other Commodities

You can buy other hard assets after interest rates decline. Low interest rates start a whole new cycle because they are the conduit for the central bank's new money into the financial system.

As we saw in Part Three, too many dollars chasing too few goods creates inflation. Gold is the traditional haven from inflation, so gold prices increase after an ease in the money supply causes interest rates to decrease.

As the yield curve sinks back into a normal position, the Federal Reserve's new dollars flow into the banking system in such great volume that investors begin to fear inflation. You will probably get your largest profits from gold when the yield curve is not only normal again but very steep. The average spread between the three-month bill and the 10-year note is a little over 1 percent; when it is more than 3 percent you may want to buy gold. Such a wide spread suggests that the money supply is larger than usual. This wide spread also indicates that investors do not want to hold the 10-year note because they fear that interest rates will increase. Either way you look at it, the outlook is inflationary and the price of gold is likely to go up (see Figure 21.4). The yield curve was exceptionally steep in 1972, 1976, 1982, 1984, 1988, 1992, 1994, 2002, and 2004; and most of those dates preceded a rally in gold (see Figure 21.5).

Historical gold prices from 1800 to 2004 are in Appendix 21.3 and at the web site www.globalfindata.com.

You probably know that the U.S. dollar was convertible into gold at $35 an ounce after the 1944 Bretton Woods Agreement. By 1971 our gold reserves were too small to maintain that exchange, so President Richard Nixon let the dollar float against gold, and that is why you see the spike in its price in the early 1970s. In 1975 the rest of the world followed suit and ended the convertibility of all currencies into gold. That was when the United States allowed its citizens to own the metal for the first time in 41 years, and the price of gold took off to stratospheric heights during the inflationary decade that followed. Gold peaked briefly in 1980 at $800 an ounce, and some people expect a replay of that scenario if China allows her one and a half billion citizens to hold the metal.

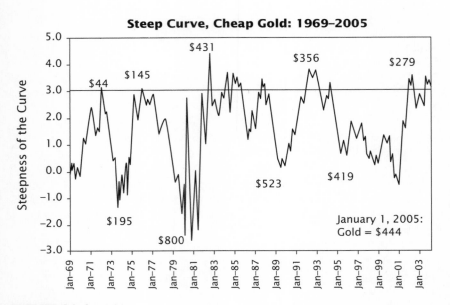

FIGURE 21.4 Gold

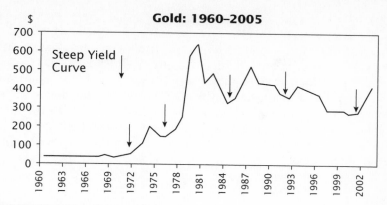

FIGURE 21.5 Another Look at Gold

Inflation was considered to be dead during the 1990s. The public thought that many prices such as those for new technology and some hard assets would continue to decline. This was part of the so-called new paradigm that was going to see the end of the traditional business cycle and the unbroken upward climb of the stock markets. The Nasdaq, in particular, was going to shine, as it was expected to take the leadership position away from the blue-chip stocks in the Dow. When the Nasdaq hit 5,000 and the Dow was backing off from its peak near 12,000, some perpetual bulls expected the Nasdaq average to exceed the Dow.

Gold, of course, was out and even central banks were selling it by the turn of the century. All hard assets, including real estate, were expected to decline in price forever as traditional business moved to the Internet and operated in cyberspace rather than on the ground. Figure 21.6, a graph of

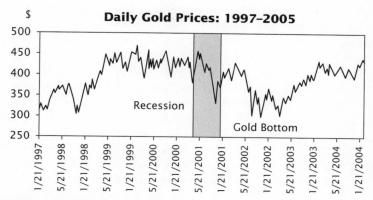

FIGURE 21.6 Daily Gold Prices

gold prices after the 2001 recession, however, suggests that the gold cycle was still alive and well.

Gold prices touched bottom about the same time that the yield curve reached its steepest point in 2002, and a rally in gold began.

One reason for a rally in gold prices is that there are so many additional dollars in the financial system after the Fed eases. Investors fear that our currency will lose value compared to currencies of other countries. They protect their portfolios by selling securities that trade in U.S. dollars, such as Treasuries and the S&P; and they put their money in gold or in other currencies.

Foreign Currencies Hedge Inflation

Investors all over the world fear the devaluation of the U.S. dollar when the Federal Reserve increases our money supply, so people convert our currency into euros, yen, British pounds, and Canadian or Australian dollars. Sometimes they do this by buying foreign products, such as imported luxury goods, and sometimes by buying foreign securities. International stock funds do well when our interest rates decline. In addition to the fact that their economies move in a cycle that is different from ours, their scarce currencies become more valuable when the Fed creates more of ours.

The next graph (Figure 21.7) shows that investors prefer gold and the euro after a recession in the United States. The reasons, as mentioned earlier, are twofold: a different economic cycle abroad and too many dollars in the United States after the Federal Reserve eases our money supply.

Note the time lag between our recessions and the investment opportunities in gold and foreign currencies. During this lag, the Federal Reserve is creating the new money that makes gold and foreign currencies attractive to investors. Appendix 21.5 has this data.

Finally, after our interest rates stop declining, there are so many U.S. dollars sloshing around the world that our manufactured goods become cheap enough to compete with those from foreign countries. Our factories sell more of our own products, their earnings increase, and our stock market can start a sustained rally. The investment cycle can begin again.

Model Portfolio with Gold

The graphs of gold prices indicate extreme interest in this metal during the 1970s and 1980s and again in the early part of this new century. Some people think that gold will outperform most other assets well into the twenty-first century, so we will see how gold looks as our alternative in-

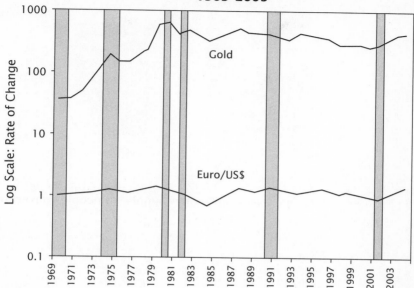

FIGURE 21.7 Euro and Gold

vestment when our model portfolio is out of the stock market. We will use data after gold's price was allowed to fluctuate in the 1970s.

Owning gold while we were out of the stock market made a big difference because gold is such a volatile, emotional asset class. Gold increases our return to more than 16 percent (see Figure 21.8).

The growth of $1 (see Figure 21.9) is so spectacular, in part, because

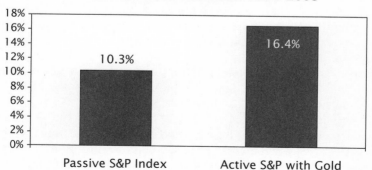

FIGURE 21.8 Return with Gold

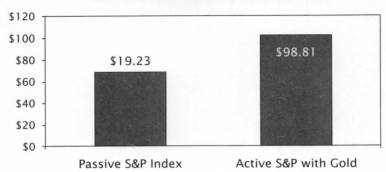

FIGURE 21.9 Portfolio Value with Gold

gold doubled in price in the early 1970s as soon as Americans were allowed to own it. This thinking, of course, is driving current gold bugs who hope that the Chinese will soon be able to own gold as well.

There is a large contingent of investors who think that the current expansion of commodities prices will last as long as the 1982–2000 bull market did in stocks. Eighteen years is a long time for any investment trend to last. I happen to disagree with the optimism of these gold bugs, but I certainly enjoy the passionate arguments on both sides.

SUMMARY

Asset allocation is a passionate topic. For generations we were taught that we had to buy and hold a passive portfolio because no one could time the stock market. Now some people, including behavioral psychologists and stock market technicians, think that we can and *must* time the stock market. Timing the S&P complicates our lives because of all the new decisions we have to make, and the introduction of three other asset classes can be daunting.

Fortunately, there is a road map for these new assets just as there was in Part One for the stock market. Also fortunately, both maps use the same yield curve analysis (see Figure 21.10).

We saw that the best time to buy real estate is when the yield curve inverts, the stock market is at its peak, and a recession is coming. This is the stage in the cycle when investors are so enamored of the stock market, or paper assets, that they forget the value of hard assets such as real estate. Interest rates are high but destined to decline, so you can renegotiate your

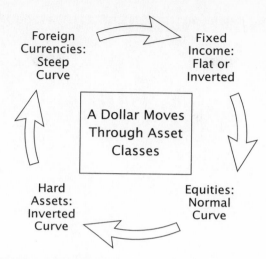

FIGURE 21.10 Flow Chart with Yield Curves

mortgage after the Fed eases. This is also a good time to buy long-term fixed-income securities: before rates decline. A little later in the cycle inflation becomes a worry. When the three-month, 10-year spread exceeds 3 percent, there is an opportunity to buy gold or foreign investments. When this spread returns to normal, just over 1 percent, investors rekindle their love affair with stocks. It is then time to sell gold and foreign investments and to take part in the U.S. stock market until the cycle begins again.

Now it is time to look at specific securities to buy. We will also look at leverage for the most aggressive investors.

CHAPTER 22

Mutual
Funds

U p to this point we have traded with theoretical securities. We have moved among the major asset classes of fixed-income securities, stocks, real estate or gold, and foreign currencies as if they were as liquid and easy to trade as Microsoft or Intel. Real life is not so simple. Real life means calling your broker or going online and trying to find an investment that mirrors the asset classes in our model portfolio.

Each of our asset classes presents its own challenge.

In the case of fixed-income securities, the reality is that small investors rarely get the prices that we have used in this book; usually it is only large institutions that can negotiate those prices and get the yields on which our analysis rests.

Equity investors who want to buy the S&P 500 index would have to buy each stock separately, and buying 500 individual stocks takes so much time that the market would move away from our target price. Commissions would be high, and buying a round lot of 100 shares of each stock would cost over a million dollars.

Hard assets present even more difficult hurdles. Real estate includes more than just your house; it includes shopping malls, hotels, nursing homes, and office buildings; and you probably do not want to own and maintain each one of these in order to hold a diversified portfolio. The price of gold bullion on the exchange in London is unavailable to private individuals; we have to find a local dealer to sell us a gold bar and then rent a safe-deposit box at a bank for storage. Physical commodities are relatively illiquid and difficult to trade.

Exposure to foreign currencies is available to us only when we exchange our dollars at a bank or buy an imported product.

Fortunately, there are mutual funds that allow us to invest in each of these asset classes. Most of the funds that we will look at hold securities in an index, such as the S&P 500, with the objective of matching its return. The only trading it does is to keep the portfolio in line with the index rather than to take advantage of the manager's stock-picking skills. Conservative investors should stay with index funds in the asset classes of their choice. Investing in specific sectors or individual stocks is appropriate for more aggressive investors. The most aggressive investors can follow this analysis to its conclusion in the futures market.

We will follow our usual top-down analysis and move from asset classes to industry sectors. We will find mutual funds for each of our asset classes and then find examples for the industry sectors within them. These sector funds perform two important jobs for us; they increase our returns and allow us to become more knowledgeable in their part of the market. Later, if we want to buy specific securities, we are already experts in that business and have a short list of stocks to research.

In this manner we will be able to sift through the thousands of mutual funds in the marketplace to identify those that suit our model portfolio.

We can get help from a not-for-profit professional association that educates investors about this huge market: the Mutual Fund Education Alliance. This group started helping investors evaluate funds in 1971 after the previous decade's scandals in that industry. Its web site, www.mfea.com, says that their members serve over 80 million shareholders with assets of $3 trillion. Since this is half of the total value of the fund industry, this site may be a good starting place for anyone searching for a fund.

I searched the site for funds that accept investments as small as $50 and found 139 mutual funds, and most of them were names I recognized from mainstream media like the *Wall Street Journal*, *Fortune*, and *Town & Country*. Twenty firms appeared in my next search for mutual funds that offer online trading, and several of these also accept minimum accounts of $50. The next generation of investors grew up computer-literate, and the investment industry is ready for them when they are ready to save. It appears that saving and investing have become available to everyone, and I look forward to the day that mutual funds advertise to young people in *Car & Driver* and *Elle* magazines.

FIXED-INCOME MUTUAL FUNDS

The only difficulty with the Mutual Fund Education Alliance web site is that there is no capability to search for mutual funds in our first asset class, the money market.

Money Market Mutual Funds

Money market mutual funds, most of which invest in U.S. government and corporate securities generally maturing within one year, are the bedrock of the investment world. We have used them in our model portfolio as the safe haven when we are out of the stock market because these funds should have the lowest risk of any of our asset classes. Sometimes they have the highest return as well. During the early 1980s, these funds had double-digit yields when the three-month Treasury bill, academia's risk-free investment, was over 10 percent. The most conservative investors had the best returns during this period.

You can find over a thousand money market mutual fund listings on the web site of one of the oldest publishers of money market newsletters, at www.ibcdata.com. The "Retail Money Funds" link on its home page in turn has a link called "Top Prime Retail MMFs," which will take you to a list of the highest yielding prime-rated money market funds. If you prefer to use a family of funds so that you can change asset classes in your portfolio easily, click on the link to "Largest Retail MMFs."

If you are an income-oriented investor, you may prefer a mutual fund of long-term government bonds when you are out of the stock market.

Long-Term Government Bond Funds

Long-term government bond funds can hold direct U.S. government obligations, such as the 10-year notes and 20-year bonds that we used as benchmarks for our yield curve analysis. Many of these funds also hold bonds in U.S. government agencies. Such bonds are indirect or so-called moral obligations of the U.S. government that created these agencies and we assume that the government will stand behind their ability to repay their principal and interest in a timely manner.

It is important to read the prospectus or annual report of any investment, and this asset class is no exception. Creative Wall Street firms have cut and pasted fixed-income investments to make products that behave very differently from what you might expect. It is common to strip bonds of their coupon payments, rearrange them, and staple them together so they can be sold as a new product.

For example, before people paid bills online every new homeowner received a monthly bill, or a mortgage payment book with receipts to accompany each check. When you sold your house, you did not have to make any more of these payments so you returned the book to the bank. Similarly, if mortgage rates declined, you refinanced at a lower rate and returned your old payment book.

Now, investment and mortgage bankers collect thousands of mortgages and resell them in the fixed-income market. Sometimes they separate the principal and interest payments so that they can sell them separately.

If you buy the interest portion of a mortgage pool, you have no right to the principal repayments when the homeowners sell their houses. Of course, not everyone in your pool will get transferred or buy a larger house on the same day. They may, however, all refinance their mortgages in the same year if interest rates decline. They all, in effect, return their payment books to the bank on the day that they refinance; and investors holding interest-only investments are left with nothing.

Naturally, these interest-only investments in mortgage pools sell with high yields because of this risk. Mutual fund managers sometimes boost their returns by adding a few of these to their portfolios; so read the prospectus of any investment to see what it allows. If any mutual fund, particularly a fixed-income fund that should reflect the yield on a government bond, has unusually high returns, see what is inflating that yield and make sure you understand it before you buy it.

Locating fixed-income mutual funds is easy on the Internet. The Mutual Fund Education Alliance search engine produced 39, and a search of Yahoo.com found 46.

It is also easy to find mutual funds in our next asset class: the stock market. There are thousands of funds in this category, so we will break them down into three groups for easy analysis.

EQUITY MUTUAL FUNDS

Our top-down approach to portfolio management suggests that we start with a large group of stocks, such as the S&P 500, and then look at specific industry sectors such as computers or industrial materials. Style investing gives us another easy way to use our model portfolio. There are index funds in each of these categories.

S&P 500 Index Funds

Our model portfolio needs a way to invest in the S&P 500 index without having to buy all 500 stocks separately. Fortunately, index funds have been available for decades. Vanguard started the trend in 1976 when John Bogle broke the mold for mutual fund firms. He introduced a no-load fund designed to replicate the S&P 500 index, and he priced it to sell. His annual fee of one-half of 1 percent was just a quarter of the normal mutual fund management fee at that time.

Since his iconoclastic move, more than a dozen firms have joined him in his vision of providing investors with this efficient tool. There is a table of about 15 such funds on the Motley Fool web site at www.fool.com, including one with a minimum investment of only $100. You can compare their expense ratios, which range from one-half of 1 percent, or 50 basis points, down to 18 basis points.

John Bogle's concept of a mutual fund that reflects an index rather than a portfolio manager's stock-picking skills is so popular that it has spread. Now there are index funds for every part of the investment world. If there is an index to measure performance, you can probably buy a fund that holds the securities in it. We will look at two kinds that apply to our model portfolio: industry sector funds and style funds.

Industry Sector Funds

Many mutual fund companies sell specialized equity funds that target specific business sectors, such as computers or industrial materials. These funds may not be index funds in the strictest sense of the term. They invest in an industry rather than adhering closely to an index.

Sector funds make it easy to rotate among industries within our asset classes. When the model portfolio indicates that it is time to invest in equities, you can divide the S&P 500 index into industry sectors and rotate among them. Each phase of the economy tends to support a different industry and offers profit opportunities at different times.

Traditional sector rotation breaks the investment world down into two groups: noncyclical (defensive) stocks with fairly constant demand for their products (utilities, consumer staples, and health care) and cyclical stocks that need an expanding economy (industrial materials, consumer discretionary, industrials, telecom services, computer hardware).

Let us look at these sectors in the order that they may go through an *economic*, rather than an investment, cycle. Bear in mind that investors move about three to six months ahead of this economic cycle; but it is easier to picture, so we will start there. This model is built on the fact that some things like toilet paper do not last as long as gold or aluminum siding. Things that wear out quickly tend to be replaced faster than more durable items, and so this model has been popular for generations.

The theory is that as the business cycle peaks, so does our need to buy new computers. This changes as we slip into recession. When business is slow, we buy fewer computers but people still buy staples like soap and food. They continue to need health care and to take medicine during a recession.

After the Federal Reserve creates a lot of new money to pull us out of the recession, mortgage rates decline and people buy new homes that they fill with carpets and refrigerators. As factories expand to meet this demand, they use more industrial materials like aluminum, paper, and glass. Telecom services and computer sales grow with the expanding economy that must transmit and keep track of new orders.

Figure 22.1 offers an example of two sectors that usually outperform at different times in the cycle: computers and industrial materials.

As the economy slowed at the turn of this century, businesses needed fewer computers. When business picked up in 2002, so did the demand for industrial materials, whose stocks saw a sustained rally.

The business cycle supports each industry sector with overlapping waves of strength, and sometimes there is an undertow (such as a terrorist attack on Wall Street or a presidential assassination) that disrupts the flow. In general, however, this is a useful way to visualize the business cycle.

One of the benefits of investing in sector mutual funds is that they are a window into part of the economy. We become experts in this area and can select specific securities easily in this sector if we decide to do so. Most of the stocks in an industry move together, so our choice is very likely to be a profitable one. The most important decision is getting into the right sector; then all we have to do is identify a strong company within that business.

Sector funds also allow us to invest in different styles such as

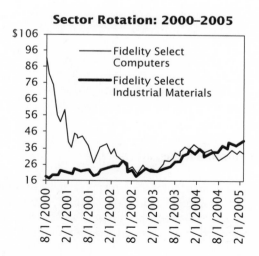

FIGURE 22.1 Sectors

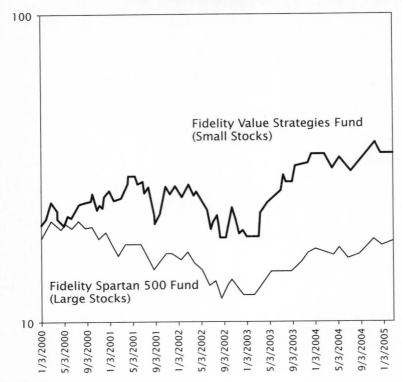

FIGURE 22.2   Style Investing

small-capitalization growth or large-cap value stocks. Style investing is easy to understand because there are only two sizes and two categories.

Style Index Funds

Style investing compares stocks in terms of growth or value and small or large capitalization. Our model portfolio, which draws a sharp line between paper assets and hard assets, translates nicely into style investing. Growth stocks resemble paper assets, while value stocks are more like hard assets.

Growth stocks depend on expectations for future earnings, while value stocks have earnings now and usually pay dividends. Growth stocks tend to be glamorous and popular, while value stocks are pedestrian and out of favor. The rule of thumb is to buy growth stocks when the yield curve steepens and the economy is growing strongly. Then switch into value stocks when the curve narrows and the economy slows. Another way to state this is to suggest buying growth stocks as the money supply expands and buying value stocks as it contracts.

Company size is important. Large, glamorous stocks tend to do well during a bull market such as we had in the 1990s. Small, overlooked stocks outperform when a bubble bursts. In Figure 22.2 two Fidelity funds, Spartan 500 and Value Strategies, show what happened in 2000 when investors tired of large firms with complicated financial statements. They then sold large-capitalization stocks in Fidelity's Spartan 500 Fund and bought the smaller companies in Fidelity's Value Strategies Fund. Investors preferred stocks in simple businesses that are easy to understand.

Most mutual fund companies offer every combination of these styles among their sector index funds.

REAL ESTATE INDEX FUNDS

These funds own real estate investment trusts, (REITs). Once again, we can buy index funds of the whole asset class or sector funds that reflect a slice of that market.

Asset Class REITs

A real estate investment trust is a company that invests in or holds mortgages on real estate and pays out most of its earnings in the form of dividends. Their properties range from luxury apartments to self-storage units and include office buildings, prisons, and shopping malls. Most investments are domestic but some prospectuses allow foreign investments.

Investors buy REITs when the yield curve inverts for two reasons. First, people who need current income see the inverted curve as a signal that interest rates may decline, so they buy REITs in order to get their generous dividends. These trusts often have a current yield that is substantially higher than that of a 10-year Treasury note. Second, investors know that an inverted curve means that paper assets are overvalued and that money will start flowing into hard assets, such as real estate.

The easiest way to invest in this complicated asset class is through an index fund such as the Vanguard REIT Index Fund. Vanguard's index fund tracks most publicly traded real estate investment trusts. The obvious benefit of an index fund is the ease of investing in a lucrative asset class with a minimum of homework.

Industry Sector REITs

Most investment companies that offer sector funds include at least one REIT. As you might expect, their returns vary widely depending on the kind of real estate they buy and where it is located. There is one more consideration: whether the trust is designed to deliver current income or capital appreciation.

There are REITs for both fixed-income and equity investors, and the distinction between the two trusts makes a big difference in your portfolio. For example, Fidelity has two domestic REIT funds; one is of the fixed-income variety and the other is equity. In 2004, the equity fund made three times more money than the fixed-income fund. While both of them had double-digit returns, the difference points out the importance of understanding these two investments.

Yahoo.com lists 200 real estate mutual funds, and you can sort them by assets, ratings, or performance. Performance for the full year 2004 ranged from 40 percent down to 10 percent, and five-year annualized returns went as high as 39 percent. There is no simple way to screen for the lowest five-year performance on this web site.

Diversified mutual funds of REITs helps investors avoid putting all their money in one trust that happens to be in the wrong real estate sector in a part of the world with a declining economy and devaluing currency.

GOLD MINING MUTUAL FUNDS

Nothing captures the imagination like gold. Nothing disappoints more than gold if you buy it at the wrong time. Gold pays no income and plays a small part in our economy; your beautiful bar just sits in your vault gathering dust and expensive storage bills. The American Stock Exchange's Gold Bug index of gold mining companies is one of the oldest and most popular indexes in this asset class, and many of the gold index funds use it as their benchmark. It fell 70 percent during the late 1990s when investors preferred paper assets to hard assets.

These losing streaks are offset by sustained, highly profitable rallies under certain conditions. When the Federal Reserve creates so much new money that the spread between the 10-year note and the three-month bill exceeds 3 percent, gold may be ready to make its largest gains. We saw this situation in January 2002; the yield curve was unusually steep with a spread of 3.5 percent, and gold began its long rally.

Although our model portfolio performed well using gold bullion as a substitute for the stock market when the yield curve inverts, gold mining stocks behave differently. Mining stocks are not the mirror image of the stock market; they are stocks first and commodities second. When investors panic, they sell all stocks—including gold mining—as we saw during the 1987 and 2001 crashes. There is usually a lag between a stock market decline and a rally in gold mining shares. Therefore, you may want to wait after a crash and buy these volatile instruments when the yield curve is steep.

Gold mining mutual funds (there are no gold bullion funds as of this writing) are a convenient way to invest in this asset class; they offer a diversified portfolio of mining stocks that trade on major exchanges. Many investment companies list gold mining mutual funds as an industry sector the way Fidelity does for its Fidelity Select Gold Portfolio (symbol FSAGX).

INTERNATIONAL MUTUAL FUNDS

International index funds give us a way to invest in foreign currencies. Many investors want to hold currencies outside the United States when they think that our rate of inflation may increase *and* they can earn higher bond yields somewhere else. The lure of higher returns combined with less risk of inflation sucks money abroad like a high-powered vacuum cleaner. When the yield curve steepened in 2002, some investors saw the handwriting on the wall and started draining funds out of the U.S. stock market for safer havens. A lot of that money went to European stocks; some went into Canadian gold mining shares; and new capitalist countries like China got their share.

International index funds combine diversification with low management fees. Vanguard has forced the fee schedule down to one-tenth of 1 percent or less among its competitors such as Fidelity. These funds give U.S. investors the opportunity to take advantage of the increasing values of foreign currencies when the dollar declines. International index funds are usually subdivided into each of the four major asset classes, but we will limit our discussion to real estate and gold.

When investors fear inflation in the U.S. dollar, they have two options.

They can buy hard assets or exchange their dollars into foreign currencies. Aggressive investors do both; they buy foreign real estate or gold mining shares in foreign countries.

Foreign Real Estate

A friend of mine bought foreign real estate at the right time. She fell in love with a small apartment in Paris at the beginning of this century when most people were buying stocks on the Nasdaq. She thought that Paris was more fun than numbers in a brokerage account, so she sold stock and bought her dream pied-à-terre near Place de L'Opera. The U.S. dollar was strong and real estate had not become a popular investment in any country. Four years later her apartment had doubled in value. During that time the euro gained 50 percent against the dollar, so she sold her apartment for three times as many dollars as she invested.

She may have had the same return if she had invested in a real estate investment trust (REIT) that owned apartments in Paris. She would have missed the glamour, but not the bureaucratic paperwork, of owning a piece of Paris.

International REIT mutual funds outperformed domestic REIT mutual funds during 2004 for two reasons: both the U.S. currency and U.S. real estate were overvalued compared to that in other countries.

These funds bought relatively inexpensive foreign properties and paid with currencies that were also cheap. The properties *and* the currencies gained in value during the year, so U.S. investors benefited in two ways. The REIT mutual fund with the highest 2004 return on Yahoo.com was Alpine International Real Estate, and it made 40 percent on property it owned in Europe. Alpine's real estate profits grew a second time when they were converted from valuable euros into cheap U.S. dollars. Fidelity also has an international REIT mutual fund. These diversified funds gave investors a chance to participate in two asset classes at once, hard assets and foreign currencies, without having to do much research.

International Gold Funds

International gold funds also combine hard assets with foreign currencies. Although the price of gold that trades on the COMEX division of the New York Mercantile Exchange is standard throughout the world, the currency in which we hold this gold fluctuates. Most gold funds are international because so much gold is mined in Africa and Canada. Several mutual funds, however, specifically limit their investments to foreign companies. Gold funds usually fall into the category of precious metals and include silver and platinum.

SUMMARY

We are fortunate that there are so many investments that make it easy to implement our portfolio strategies. There is a wide variety of new index and sector funds that provide diversification with a minimum of homework. They also give us a chance to become experts in their particular business so that we can select a specific stock if we choose to do so. The only thing missing from this array is a vehicle that allows us to invest in gold bullion, so we will remedy that in the next chapter.

CHAPTER 23

Exchange-Traded Funds

Mutual funds make it easy to invest. They provide diversification, perform record keeping, and do a lot of the research that investors would normally have to do themselves. They have two problems for some investors: capital gains taxes and liquidity.

MUTUAL FUNDS' LIMITATIONS

Every time the fund takes a profit on an investment, everyone in the fund is liable for capital gains taxes. In the year 2000, some investors noticed the inverted yield curve and sold their equity mutual funds. Every time someone left, the fund sold stock at a profit and realized capital gains. All of the investors, those who left the fund and those who remained, had to pay taxes on those gains. Some mutual funds lost a lot of money by the time those taxes were due in April 2001, so the people who stayed in the fund had less money with which to pay their increased tax bills.

The other concern with mutual funds is liquidity. As the public becomes more sophisticated, wired to the Internet, and responsible for its own pension plan, it wants more control over its ability to trade. Mutual funds limit trading to the value of the holdings at the close of the market every day. In particularly volatile markets, people want more flexibility than this; they prefer to trade whenever they wish throughout the day and into the evening.

EXCHANGE-TRADED FUNDS

Exchange-traded funds (ETFs) are like index mutual funds that behave like stocks. They trade all day on recognized stock exchanges such as the American Stock Exchange, and some trade during extended hours. These funds are *not* actively managed; they are like index funds that are passive. They replicate an index, such as the S&P 500 index or a growth stock index, without trying to outperform that index.

The trustee updates the holdings every few seconds to keep the net asset value of the ETF in line with the market. This is a lot of updating, so you obtain better tracking results with a smaller index like the Nasdaq-100 than you do with a large one such as the ONEQ that tracks every Nasdaq stock. As with any trust, there is a custodian who holds the securities that the trustee buys.

There is a lot of free education about ETFs on the Internet now that the public has joined hedge funds in trading these instruments. Nuveen Investments has a web site, ETFConnect, at www.etfconnect.com; and, as usual, Yahoo.com has extensive information on this popular new trading vehicle.

Exchange-traded funds are important to us for two reasons. First, they provide a way for our model portfolio to invest in two potentially lucrative assets: the Nasdaq Composite index and gold bullion. There is no Nasdaq index fund and there is no convenient way to trade gold. Exchange-traded funds are the only way to put these two investments into a real portfolio. Second, they expand our options for sector investing. Both functions are equally important to our model portfolio.

Before we examine the details of ETFs, however, let us inject a little Wall Street wit.

Nicknames for some of the first ETFs reflect this industry's penchant for dry humor. The first ETF appeared in 1993 with the objective of replicating the total return of the S&P 500 index. The name of the trust is Standard & Poor's Depositary Receipts (SPDR). Its stock symbol is SPY, and it quickly earned the nickname "spider." Newspaper advertisements for this fund, or trust, featured a spider building a web of financial security. It is the same with the first ETF for the Dow Jones Industrial Average. The symbol is DIA; the nickname is "diamonds," and the advertisements include gemstones. Vanguard, which started the indexing trend with their family of mutual funds, created a group of ETFs called Vanguard Index Participation Equity Receipts (VIPERs). The Nasdaq-100 ETF has the symbol QQQQ and the nickname "cubes."Wall Street loves nicknames.

EQUITY ETFS

Standard & Poor's Depositary Receipts offer a convenient way to implement the trading decisions generated by our model portfolio. Each SPDR owns all 500 of the stocks in the S&P 500 index in their market capitalization weight. We can trade the SPDR all day and into extended hours; we can buy and sell options on it; and we can leverage it in the futures market. There is a price for all this flexibility; your broker will still charge a commission when you buy any ETF. If you are charged about $30 and you are investing less than $30,000, you are better off in an index fund directly from Vanguard. Larger investments, obviously, benefit from economies of scale in trading commissions.

Vanguard does not, however, offer a mutual fund that replicates the 3,000 stocks in the Nasdaq Composite index. This index is one of the investments that gave us outstanding returns in our model portfolio, but until 2003 there was no way to buy that index. The only way to capture all of the Nasdaq stocks in one trade is to buy the Fidelity Nasdaq index fund called the ONEQ. Its management fee of about one-half of 1 percent causes it to underperform its benchmark a little, but we finally have a way to invest in the Nasdaq Composite index.

Other equity ETFs track a myriad of sector indexes that help us with our sector rotation investing and our selection of individual stocks.

Index ETFs are true index funds as opposed to the sector mutual funds in the previous chapter. Those sector funds may hold only 80 percent of their assets in their sector, but ETF's have as much money as possible invested as a mirror image of their index. Because exchange-traded funds are truly passive, many of them have lower fees and better tracking results than traditional sector mutual funds.

The new exchange-traded funds offer hundreds of ways to track indexes in all of our asset classes. They also include the four styles that we studied in the preceding chapter: large and small capitalization and value or growth stocks. Then, of course, there are ETFs offering indexes of blended styles.

FIXED-INCOME ETFs

Fixed-income ETFs fall into two categories: international and domestic. Barclays Bank is the trustee for a family of foreign fixed-income ETFs that allows investors to choose among several points along the yield curve. Like a traditional bond mutual fund, an ETF will never mature; so investors are just choosing whether they want short-, intermediate-, or long-term investments. In effect, they are buying perpetual bonds of a particular duration. Goldman Sachs acts as trustee for an ETF that mirrors its corporate bond index, and Lehman Brothers is the trustee for several U.S. government security funds. These funds may be one of an investor's better opportunities to get institutional prices for bonds.

REAL ESTATE ETFS

The fund selector on Yahoo.com identified four real estate investment trust ETFs. Each one tracks an index for different parts of the domestic REIT market. The oldest one is the iShares Dow Jones U.S. Real Estate ETF that came out in 2000 when the yield curve inverted. The fund went from $55 per share at inception to $123 per share four and a half years later and earned an average annual return of 20 percent. As you know, the stock market lost 20 percent during those four years. Whoever made *that* new product decision at Dow Jones probably uses the same yield curve analysis that you and I do.

GOLD BULLION ETFS

Gold ETFs are one of the few ways that people can invest in gold bullion near a price that is usually available only on an exchange. These ETFs buy gold bullion and store it in a vault. This is very different from gold mutual funds that own shares in mining companies but do not own the gold itself.

The two investments behave quite differently during a crisis. Mining companies trade like any other stock when investors panic and sell equities indiscriminately. At a time like this, gold stocks decline along with all the others. The physical commodity of gold, however, often provides a safe haven during uncertain times and makes money when stocks crash.

The first gold bullion ETF appeared in November 2004 and attracted a phenomenal $1.3 billion in assets during the first two months. This gold ETF, StreetTracks Gold Shares, uses the symbol GLD. Unlike most ETFs, it trades on the New York rather than the American Stock Exchange.

Yahoo.com shows two performance numbers for each ETF: that of the ETF itself and that of the index it replicates. Investors can see how well their fund is doing its job of tracking its benchmark, and StreetTracks Gold Shares appears to lag the performance of gold by about one-half of 1 percent. This discrepancy is probably due to the cost of storing the gold. Owning an ETF may be the cheapest way to buy and store gold because economies of scale allow the trust to buy gold near the price on a major exchange, such as the COMEX in New York, and spread the storage costs among so many investors.

Now that we have investment vehicles that represent gold on the

TABLE 23.1 Nasdaq and Gold

Stock Trade	Date	S&P	Nasdaq	Gold Trade	Comex Gold Price
Buy	October 1, 1974	63	55.48		
Sell	December 1, 1978	94	116.19	Buy	194.6
Buy	May 1, 1980	106	139.68	Sell	490
Sell	November 1, 1980	127	193.15	Buy	640.5
Buy	September 1, 1981	122	195.17	Sell	421.5
Sell	October 15, 1987	298	422.51	Buy	466.6
Buy	October 20, 1987	236	327.79	Sell	464.3
Sell	October 1, 1989	340	475.19	Buy	366.5
Buy	August 23, 1990	307	360.22	Sell	412.4
Sell	July 1, 1998	1133	1914.46	Buy	296.8
Buy	September 4, 1998	973	1566.52	Sell	285
Sell	August 1, 2000	1430	3685.5	Buy	277.6
Buy	July 18, 2002	819	1356.46	Sell	317.0
End	January 3, 2005	1212	2062.00		420.0

COMEX and the Nasdaq Composite index, we can use them in our model portfolio instead of cash and the S&P 500 index. For the sake of simplicity, however, we will use our usual trade dates rather than buying gold when the 10-year, three-month yield spread exceeds 10 percent. We will start after 1973 when the price of gold was allowed to fluctuate (see Table 23.1).

All of our returns look better with our new starting date; even the S&P 500 index improves a couple of percentage points compared to previous graphs. The more aggressive equity investment, the Nasdaq index, provides one-third more return even without active management; including dividends on the larger index would have closed this gap a little. As Figure 23.1

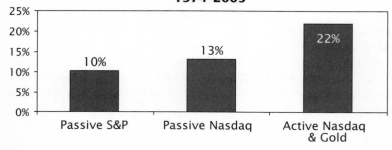

FIGURE 23.1 Return with Nasdaq and Gold

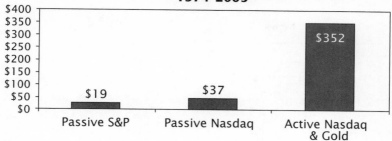

FIGURE 23.2   Portfolio Value with Nasdaq and Gold

shows, trading two aggressive instruments, Nasdaq and gold, more than doubled the return of the unmanaged S&P 500 index.

The dollar amounts of the three portfolios are vastly different because of the impact of annual compounding at different rates (see Figure 23.2). Appendix 23.2 has the Nasdaq's prices beginning in 1984; the historical COMEX prices are privately owned.

The returns might have been even stronger if we had used foreign currencies.

FOREIGN CURRENCY ETFS

Foreign currency ETFs are similar to international equity index funds except that they may own stocks in a global index. There are many global indexes, and the term includes the United States. If your objective is to own nothing but foreign currencies, make sure that your ETF does not include U.S. investments. The web site ETFConnect is one of the few that allow you to search their databases by investment objective, and a search for global investments found 37 funds matching that description.

The difficulty with mutual funds and ETFs is that convenient products like these usually become available a little late in the investment cycle. Cutting-edge investors often have to do their own homework and invest directly in stocks in order to get in at the beginning of each new cycle. Investing directly in stocks provides the opportunity for greater returns than investing in an index fund. Of course, the risks are greater as well, but our market timing model should allow you to focus on the right sector. Once you become familiar with the business and the companies in a sector, you are in a good position to buy a strong security. Sector investing provides the background you need as well as a list of companies from which to select your investment.

SUMMARY

There is a wide variety of new funds that provide inexpensive diversification with a minimum of homework. Exchange-traded funds add to our flexibility for trading throughout the day, and some of them take advantage of extended trading hours. Many of them have lower fees than sector mutual funds that may impose a sales charge or marketing expense. Unlike mutual funds, however, ETFs incur a brokerage fee as if they were a stock.

These funds are important to us because they complete the tools we need to implement our model portfolio. Up to now we have been able to invest in all asset classes except for gold bullion and most equities except for the Nasdaq Composite. Two of these new funds fill those gaps. One fund, StreetTracks Gold Shares with the symbol GLD, gives us a chance to own gold bullion near the price it trades on the COMEX division of the New York Mercantile Exchange. Another ETF, the ONEQ, allows us to own all 3,000 stocks in the Nasdaq.

The rest of the exchange-traded funds offer hundreds of ways to invest in industry sectors and styles with low portfolio management fees. They open a window on a segment of the business world and supply us with a list of companies to study in depth. Once we have mastered an industry, we are ready to choose one of the stocks on this list to buy.

In the next chapter we will select specific stocks and see how options and futures can magnify returns. You will want to keep your investment goals and risk tolerances in mind as we become less diversified and more aggressive in our portfolio management.

CHAPTER 24

Security Selection

There was not a straight wall in the custom-designed house. He said that he had 10,000 square feet under cover and 5,000 more in terraces and porches. His neighbor, a Mr. Harley, was able to put him at the top of the waiting list for the motorcycles his company makes. He invited the whole industry trade association into his new home at the top of the mountain overlooking Phoenix, and we drove past five golf courses inside his gated community on the way to the party. As I admired the city spread out below us, I overheard a conversation about where his money came from. He invested in a small technology stock early in the 1990s.

The best returns come from securities selected from the best industry in the right asset class at the beginning of its expansion.

Each asset class is productive in its own time and there are as many applications to specific securities as there are investors. You may not want to hold a portfolio of mutual funds; you may prefer to select your own stocks. You can own traditional stocks and bonds or the contracts that stand for them called derivatives. If your risk tolerances and income requirements permit, selecting a specific security within your asset class can improve your returns.

We will continue to delve deeper into security selection and increase our risk/return trade-off as we proceed. We will examine each of our four asset classes: fixed-income investments, equities, hard assets, and foreign currencies. Then we will look at derivatives. Derivatives can be almost as staid as a money market fund under the right conditions, but they have the reputation of a cowboy riding down Main Street and shooting out the lights.

FIXED-INCOME SECURITIES: U.S. TREASURIES

There is one asset that does not require much research: U.S. Treasury securities bought directly from the Treasury. You can buy U.S. Treasury bills, notes, and bonds directly from the Treasury Department through a program called TreasuryDirect. You set up a private account online at www.treasurydirect.gov or over the telephone, and you participate in Treasury auctions whenever you like.

You bid in one of two ways: competitive or noncompetitive. If you go into the auction competitively, you bid against the professionals. Your bid may be too low and the Treasury may fill just part of your order. If you submit a noncompetitive bid, your order is filled at the average price in the auction. Either way, your price is similar to, and sometimes better than, the price that government dealers pay on Wall Street. There is no brokerage commission when you buy directly from the Treasury, and this is one of those rare opportunities for an individual to get a price that is normally reserved for large institutions.

Your account reflects your personal investment history with the Treasury and shows you which securities are nearing maturity so you can start planning for the next auction. You can even sign up for a newsletter that reminds you of upcoming auctions.

If you have any financial accounts on the Internet, you probably know to treat your password and user identification as carefully as you do your ATM number and the key to your safe-deposit box. You do not want to have a stranger unlock your account and empty it out or a mischievous teenager play with your asset allocation.

EQUITIES: TOP-DOWN SELECTION

One reason we looked at sector mutual funds and exchange-traded funds in previous chapters was to learn about those parts of the economy. These funds also provided a list of stocks on which to focus our attention. We will want the strongest stock in that sector or subgroup.

We can skip this step and go straight to the equities themselves.

The Standard & Poor's web site, www2.standardandpoors.com, helps us reduce the universe of stocks to a manageable size. This site carves up the stock market into 10 business sectors that are subdivided into 23 industry groups with more than 100 subgroups. Once you have narrowed your search to this level it is time to identify a specific stock. After establishing some guidelines for security analysis, we will look at some specific examples.

There is only one question to ask: "Where will its earnings come from?"

Future Earnings

Your main concern is what will create the firm's future earnings. You are less concerned with where they came from in the past or how fast they grew.

The past is over and only the future matters. If the firm made money selling camera film while digital cameras were coming into the stores, you want to buy computer chips instead of film. If the firm sold a lot of cars while the American dollar was weak, it may not sell as many when it is strong and consumers buy foreign imports. If it sold a lot of houses when interest rates were low, its sales may decline when mortgage rates rise.

You probably have resolved many of these issues already with your top-down approach to security selection, because now you are looking at stocks in the right industry sector.

Product Delivery

Look at the firm's products and make sure that it can increase its sales. See if there is media coverage of new products ready for market. You do not want a long wait for new products, nor do you want to depend on old products with expiring patents. For example, in 2001 some investors were disappointed with their drug stocks, which are a traditional investment during a recession. The usual leaders in this industry, however, had a lot of patents expiring and insufficient new products to replace them. Smaller firms selling generic drugs performed much better than the big pharmaceuticals during that business cycle.

Once you are satisfied with its product, make sure the firm can deliver it to the customer. McDonald's experienced its fastest growth when it built restaurants in neighborhoods where you could see three churches nearby. They knew their customers and sat on their doorstep. Avon ladies rang the doorbell until their customers joined the labor force. Now they sell to them at work.

Profit Margins

Find out about the cost structure of the business. Wal-Mart knew that real estate is an important part of its overhead, so it built outside the city limits where land is less expensive. The company computerized inventory to keep warehousing costs low. They knew that retail is judged by sales per square foot and made sure that they outsold everyone else.

Each industry has a fulcrum for profits. Something causes its margins to expand and contract, whether it is the cost of materials or the cost of money. Sometimes it is intellectual property that is required to drive the business. The industry association may be a good starting place for this critical information. Do the old criteria still hold, or has the environment changed? New government regulations are certainly important in this part of your analysis.

Additional Background Information

Bad press is bad for earnings. A large lawsuit can sink a normally strong stock. Huge settlements impaired the earnings of famous companies like Texaco and Corning. Operating problems can be just as costly, as when a Union Carbide plant in India released toxic gas, killing thousands of people. Overexpansion is deadly, as many real estate developers can tell you. Even Donald Trump fears the vacancy sign and has been in bankruptcy. Investors feed on bad news and depress the stock price even further.

Read everything the firm prints about itself. You may think that you do not understand its financial statements, Securities and Exchange (SEC) filings, and letter to the stockholders in the annual report; but you will understand more than you expect. You may notice that the company's employee benefits are larger than the value of its factory and equipment combined. Or, in contrast, you may see that the company is pouring cash into research and is developing revolutionary products.

Summary Information on the Internet

A great starting point for your research is the business summary for each stock on the Yahoo.com web site. This profile describes the business in simple language and gives the firm's highlights and competitors. You can graph the stock prices of competing firms to compare historical performance, and there is contact information so you can follow up with the corporation's investor relations department.

You will then be able to narrow your search to a few outstanding stocks. Consider a few recent examples from real estate and foreign currencies.

Examples from a Recent Cycle: Real Estate

When the yield curve inverted in the fall of 2000, you knew a recession lay ahead. You knew that interest rates and home mortgages would decline and that real estate would probably benefit. Let us assume that you already had enough gutters to clean and preferred to buy stock in a home builder instead of a vacation home for yourself. You started with the Standard & Poor's web site and drilled down through the S&P 500 index to the sector called "consumer discretionary." (Discretionary items last more than three years, and houses fall into this category.) You found the home builder Centex with its stock trading symbol CTX.

Then you started your traditional analysis as described in *Graham and Dodd's Security Analysis*, Benjamin Graham's famous work. You entered the symbol CTX on the Yahoo! web site to read the company's profile. After reading everything on the Yahoo! and Centex web sites you went to EDGAR Online at www.edgar-online.com to read the recent SEC filing (available to subscribers only). You read the financial statements and computed the ratios in *Graham and Dodd's Security Analysis*.

You did the same for their competitors Pulte Homes, Lennar Corporation, and D. R. Horton.

You completed your research by visiting as many model homes as you could. You noticed that Centex's homes were in locations that you thought would be spared during the upcoming recession. The danger here is that you invested so much time and energy into your study that you were predisposed to like the stock and you were no longer objective.

You could have protected yourself by splitting your investment among all four companies to spread your risk. But since you were comfortable with your selection of this industry subgroup you were pretty sure that most of these four stocks would perform well. In fact, Centex doubled during the following year, and the other stocks almost tripled in value. The critical decision was choosing the industry and its subgroup because the rising market lifted all of the related stocks. Figure 24.1 shows how a

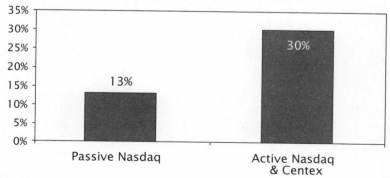

FIGURE 24.1 Return with CTX

combination of the Nasdaq and Centex looks with our trading dates in the model portfolio from 1990 to 2005.

Very few people would hold just one stock, but you can see the impact that Centex had on a portfolio. The actively traded portfolio made an average of 30 percent each year for 15 years, which was more than twice the return on the Nasdaq.

The active portfolio made six times more money than the inactive one (see Figure 24.2). Being out of the volatile Nasdaq at the right time made a big difference; being in a very productive stock while the Nasdaq declined provided a real boost to the portfolio. Appendix 24.1 gives the supporting data for both graphs.

You would have had similar returns from other stocks that fed the housing boom such as Masonite and the toolmaker for the new handyman, Stanley Works. Both stocks doubled during the two-year bear market that followed. The firm that made the housing boom possible, the Federal National Mortgage Association (Fannie Mae), doubled in the six months after the yield curve inverted. Like so many things that are too good to be true, however, this investment stalled when investors changed their minds about the firm's accounting practices.

Examples from a Recent Cycle: Foreign Currencies

When the yield curve became steep in 2002, you wanted to benefit from the changes you expected in foreign currencies (a devaluation of the U.S. dollar) but preferred to own stock in a U.S. firm.

You went back to the Standard & Poor's web site to explore its S&P

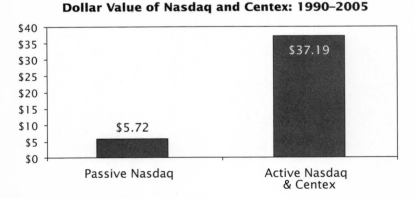

FIGURE 24.2 Portfolio Value with CTX

500 index. You wanted to find domestic firms that would benefit from both our expanding economy and a declining currency exchange rate. A stock in the materials sector, International Paper (IP), fit your specifications. As our economy pulled out of its recession, IP was poised to increase its sales to U.S. businesses and abroad. It would be able to compete with foreign paper companies that had to do business with an expensive currency relative to ours. IP would benefit from our expanding economy and our devalued dollar.

You performed your traditional Graham and Dodd ratio analysis on IP's financial statements, read information from the American Forest & Paper Association (www.afandpa.org), and studied related articles in the media. A year and a half later your IP stock made you 40 percent wealthier.

Our model portfolio's focus on different asset classes helps us identify which U.S. stocks will outperform during each part of the economic cycle. Then we select the strongest contender with the best products, distribution, and industry outlook.

EQUITIES: BOTTOM-UP SELECTION

Every investor's dream is to get in on the ground floor of the next big winner. I do not know how to pick the next Microsoft out of a pile of annual reports, but I do know what the CEOs of most winning start-ups have in common. Certain traits and entrepreneurial visions appear in every outstanding bull market; we saw them in the late 1960s, 1980s, and 1990s. We will probably see them in the last half of this decade as well.

Leadership Character Traits

Leaders with star quality often share certain traits. The public idolizes glamorous leaders during a bull market and they are easy to identify. The next stars will develop new technologies (or services using new technologies) with a large potential market. They will articulate these new products and imbue them with sizzle. They will seek a high profile in the media and project an aura of glamour around themselves and their products. Their products will be in an exciting new field . . . even if it is an old field to which they are adding sizzle.

They will keep their eye on the bottom line of their income statement because they know that Wall Street buys earnings. Their firms will generate strong cash flow for their size because that is the lifeblood of a growing organization. Their staffs will be on a constant lookout for potential problems and prevent them from materializing. Most importantly, they will have good character and will deliver what they promise.

Bill Gates once said that the secret to his success was finding holes in his business plan and plugging them before they became problems; he is too modest to admit to the rest of the attributes on this list. He would be the first to admit the items on the next list.

Leadership Vision

The charismatic entrepreneur's vision will include these words: smaller, faster, cheaper, or global. Technologies and services that develop these themes are worth your attention when you are looking for the next investment star. Part of their appeal will be to offer more choices to increasingly segmented customers. As we move from the Age of Industrialism into the Information Age, we become processors of information. Our businesses are becoming less concrete and more abstract; we have to learn to think like mathematicians—in the second derivative.

Keep in mind that the baby boomers are the largest population cohort in history and that their needs *will* be met. They will vote their needs into reality with their ballots and pocketbooks. Their future is everyone's future as long as their numbers dominate the population. Social Security will find a way to provide for their old age, which will be extended by medical breakthroughs. Housing will adjust to their needs, and so will transportation.

Firms that incorporate these themes will flourish, and Bill Gates would probably be the first to agree.

HARD ASSETS: REAL ESTATE

Our model portfolio uses real estate as an alternative to fixed-income investments or gold when we are out of the stock market. If you do not want to get as detailed in your research as we did in Centex, you can buy a real estate investment trust (REIT) to invest in several builders.

REITs' returns vary widely depending on the kind of real estate they buy and where it is located. The REIT Growth and Income Monitor web site at www.reitmonitor.net tracks the total returns that investors earned in seven of the largest REITs in different market sectors. The returns for 2004 ranged from 10 percent to 40 percent and included double-digit losses for most of the trusts during the summer of that year. Another Internet site, REITNet at www.reitnet.com, is a well-organized starting point to learn about this lucrative but complicated asset class. Here, you can search for real estate investments that trade on exchanges ranging from the New York Stock Exchange to the over-the-counter market and for sectors ranging from golf courses to prisons.

If you buy a REIT when the yield curve inverts as we did in the model portfolio, you may have to decide which geographical areas of the country will be spared during the coming recession. Then decide which sector you want to invest in, such as moderately priced home builders or nursing homes. The right REIT can be very productive in your portfolio.

HARD ASSETS: GOLD MINING STOCKS

Gold mining stocks are more volatile than gold prices. When your business increases its volume and raises its prices at the same time, your profits expand dramatically. If you are able to keep your overhead the same, you and your stockholders benefit even more. This is the description of a gold mining company. Their infrastructure is in place when the price of gold changes, so their net earnings magnify any changes in the commodity. Add foreign currency exchange to the mix and watch the action increase. Foreign gold stocks are available to Americans because many of them are listed on our exchanges.

Gold mining stocks are among the most volatile for their size and they need the benefits of good market timing. You may want to put off investing in these stocks when the yield curve inverts and wait until the curve is very steep. We usually see a *sustained* rally in gold mining shares after the 10-year, three-month spread exceeds 300 percent.

When the curve is this steep there are more dollars than usual in the system. As you know, all this new cash makes investors worry about two things: inflation and the value of the dollar relative to other currencies.

FOREIGN CURRENCIES

As long as you are investing in gold to protect yourself from inflation, you may want to consider foreign gold mining stocks to protect yourself from a falling dollar. You may be like my friend who bought the Parisian apartment that made money on both the real estate and on the exchange rate.

Our next example compares two companies in the same business but in different countries. Placer Dome is a Canadian gold mining company that trades on the New York Stock Exchange; Newmont Mining is a U.S. firm. Both stocks did very well in 2002–2004 when the yield curve was steep. Placer Dome had the advantage of being in the Canadian currency

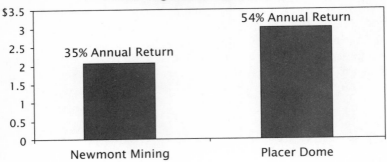

FIGURE 24.3   Newmont and Placer Dome

so it made money two ways: in its gold mining business and in Canada's strengthening currency (see Figure 24.3).

Most people hold more than one stock at a time, but let us put Placer Dome in our model portfolio when we were out of the Nasdaq from 1990 to 2005. Placer Dome doubled the return on the unmanaged portfolio from 13 to 25 percent (see Figure 24.4).

Placer Dome lost a little money for us while we were out of the Nasdaq during the 1998 currency crisis. We would have been better off in cash because gold mining stocks are equities first and inflation hedges second. Mining stocks fall just like other stocks during an international financial crisis. The same thing happened during the 1987 crash; gold stocks fell with the rest of the stock market. Placer Dome *did* reward us, however,

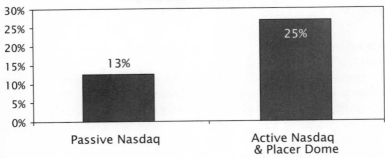

FIGURE 24.4   Return with Placer Dome and Nasdaq

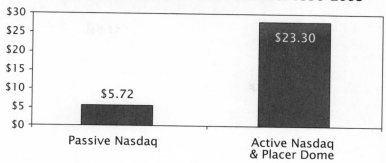

FIGURE 24.5 Portfolio Value with Placer Dome and Nasdaq

after the 2001 recession when investors worried about renewed inflation (see Figure 24.5). The data on both graphs is in Appendix 24.2.

Some of the largest foreign gold mining stocks trade on our exchanges, and if you decide to buy any of these, be sure to read their annual reports to see what you are getting. You may invest in a company headquartered in a chrome-and-glass skyscraper in Toronto, but your gold mine could be shut down or confiscated in another part of the world that is politically unstable.

Gold prices may give leverage to mining stocks, but options and futures apply leverage to everything they touch. Options and futures are called derivatives because they derive their value from the underlying investment. Derivatives cost a fraction of the value of the underlying security such as foreign or domestic Treasury bills, notes, bonds, stocks and currencies, as well as commodities like gold or pork bellies.

DERIVATIVES: OPTIONS AND FUTURES

The value of a derivative comes from its underlying asset. For example, rather than swap frozen pork bellies across the exchange floor, people trade contracts to own these bellies. The contracts' values depend on the value of the item described in the contract.

Two common derivatives are options and futures, and they reside in two entirely different worlds. They trade on separate exchanges and have different regulating bodies. Some large brokerage firms and banks have dual registrations to sell both, but you may need separate brokers if you trade options or futures.

For decades, people have traded options on stocks in order to magnify their price movements. Now they trade futures on individual stocks as well. Futures can be the most highly leveraged instruments in all of our financial markets, and they can make investment portfolios extremely volatile.

There are two kinds of options: puts and calls. We will start with call options because they are the easiest to visualize.

CALL OPTIONS

Buying a call option is like buying a stock; you just write a check for it and do not need a margin account. Call options give an investor the right, but not the obligation, to buy a security at a specified price on or before the specified expiration date. (Think: You *call* your broker and buy a *call*.)

Investors like options because they can be an inexpensive way to participate in the stock market, but you can lose a lot of money as well. Note that there is an expiration date on an option. If the investment fails to produce its intended result by that date, the option becomes worthless, and you lose all of your investment. An option is a legal contract that becomes null and void on the expiration date. Like a coupon that entitles you to a discount on orange juice at the grocery store, it is worth nothing after the expiration date.

For example, on February 1, 2005, the S&P 500 index was at 1181 when I started a paper portfolio to use as an example for this book. I thought that the S&P might go to 1210 within seven weeks, so I "bought" a call option on the S&P 500 index with a strike price of 1210. This option was selling for $690. If I was wrong, I would lose all of my simulated investment. If I was right, my option would be worth $1,210 on the expiration date of March 19 and I would have a profit of 75 percent in seven weeks.

The stock market went up faster than expected. A week later it had increased 22 points and the public changed its mind about the value of options.

I "made" $530, or 77 percent, on the simulated investment during that one week. The leverage came from the inexpensive purchase price in a volatile market (see Table 24.1).

Options have leverage built into them because they cost so little compared to their underlying security. The reason for this low price is that the option expires; you can hold a stock, however, as long as you hope it will make money.

TABLE 24.1 Options

February 1, 2005: SPX Mar 1210 calls = $	690 (S&P 500 Index @ 1181)	
February 7, 2005: SPX Mar 1210 calls =	1,220 (S&P 500 Index @ 1203)	
Change:	$ 530	22
Percent Profit:	Option: 77%	S&P 500 Index: 2%

This leverage works in both directions. Anything that can make money this quickly can lose it just as quickly.

Until recently, the only way to own the S&P 500 index (SPX) was to buy options on it. Now we have the exchange-traded fund described in Chapter 23, the SPDR, so you can own the index itself. There are options on the SPDR as well.

PUT OPTIONS

Puts are options to sell (or put) something to someone else. For instance, if I buy a put option on the SPDR, I can sell you the underlying security at the stated, or strike, price anytime before the expiration date. I would probably buy a put option only when I thought that the market was going to decline.

To complete the discussion, you may be interested in the fact that investors can also sell put and call options. These positions are similar to selling stock short.

FUTURES CONTRACTS

Futures can be the most highly leveraged of all investments and can create large swings in the value of an account.

Futures are contracts that obligate the owner to perform. Your account is priced daily, or marked to the market, to ensure this performance. The brokerage firm makes margin calls as needed when your account falls below its required level. S&P 500 index futures traders are very likely to get margin calls if they deposit the minimum of 5 percent of the contract value with their brokers.

I almost had that experience when I opened a simulated futures account online. The Refco brokerage firm has an education page on their web site at www.refco.com (click on "simulated trading"), which allows you to manage a paper portfolio. They "give" you $50,000 to invest. I

TABLE 24.2 Futures

February 1, 2005: Mar S&P 500 futures profit = $	0 (S&P 500 Index @ 1188.0)	
February 7, 2005: Mar S&P 500 futures profit =	3,850 (S&P 500 Index @ 1203.4)	
Change:	$3,850	15.4
Value of my simulated brokerage account:	$53,850	

"bought" one March S&P 500 index futures contract at 1188, and the computer put $19,688 on deposit in my imaginary margin account. My contract controlled almost $300,000 of stock (contract price of 1188 points × $250 per point), so my deposit was only 6.5 percent of the underlying security.

On February 1, 2005, one futures contract for the March S&P 500 index traded at 1188 and required a deposit of $19,688 in a margin account. February 1 was volatile and the S&P 500 index moved up 7 points between the time I bought options and the time I bought futures. The trading profits are different as a result. One week later the stock market went up 15 points, and my account had a profit of $3,850 (see Table 24.2).

On February 10 the profit rose to $6,000 before the meltdown began. By February 17, the profit was back to $3,225 and dropping by the minute. In 14 trading days my profit went from zero to $6,000 and down to $3,000. It looked as though the profit might disappear in a few more days, so I closed the paper portfolio.

My simulated portfolio would have been more stable if the computer had let me make a larger deposit on my contract, but you can see how volatile the balance can be.

People trade futures contracts on everything that our model portfolio uses: Treasury bills, notes, and bonds; S&P and Nasdaq indexes; mortgage-backed securities; gold; and foreign currencies. There is a growing market for single-stock futures ranging from Newmont Mining to Krispy Kreme donuts. You can even trade options on futures, but these instruments combine the complexities of the underlying security, the options market, and the futures market.

With so many vehicles to trade and with so much volatility attached to each one, some people defer to a professional.

PROFESSIONAL MANAGERS

Professional derivatives managers often run hedge funds or commodities pools for wealthy individuals and institutions.

A hedge fund or commodities pool is a limited partnership for accredited investors with certain net worth requirements established by regulatory bodies. Because there are thousands of private funds with complicated techniques, there are consultants who specialize in creating synergistic portfolios of these managers. Academics have found that diversifying investment styles can smooth returns. Smoothing returns helps to reduce portfolio losses that are so difficult to rebuild; you need to double your money to make up for a 50-cent loss on each dollar. Consultants expect to increase returns by mitigating losses in their fund of hedge funds portfolios. *Managing Hedge Fund Risk* by Virginia Reynolds Parker explores this issue from the point of view of the hedge fund manager as well as the investor.

SUMMARY

We have finished our top-down security selection in each asset class and have increased our risk/return trade-off in the process.

We started with bonds and set up our own TreasuryDirect accounts so we can go into the next auction. We completed our top-down stock selection by finding the stock with the best earnings potential in an industry sector. We looked for the next Microsoft, our one foray into bottom-up investing, by analyzing the market and the entrepreneur's character. We saw how the very small down payment on a derivatives contract makes options and futures portfolios increase their volatility.

Security selection is the essence of investing. You enter into a partnership with the organization whose security you buy, whether it is the U.S. government or an exchange-listed company. You place your financial future in its hands and hope that it will take good care of you. You increase your probability of buying the right security when you select from the right industry in the right asset class.

The rewards can be substantial.

CHAPTER 25

Final Summary

The first three parts of this book establish dates on which a model portfolio trades. We find these dates with the yield curve, technical analysis, and cultural indicators.

Part Four applies this timing to selecting securities in a top-down manner. We start with four broad asset classes, move through sector mutual funds, and then into specific securities. We increase our risk/reward profile as we move from index mutual funds through industry sector funds to individual stocks, bonds, and derivatives.

PARTS ONE THROUGH THREE: TRADE DATES

The yield curve gives us the basic structure for our analysis.

We use the U.S. Treasury curve because the data set is large, liquid, and available every day. Most importantly, the yield curve expresses investors' expectations for the future of interest rates and the economy. Unlike a firm's financial statements, which reflect historical data, the yield curve is forward looking. The yield curve forecasts the economy about one year in the future, and the S&P 500 index usually responds to this forecast within a few days. The yield curve is one of the few tools in financial analysis that looks to the future rather than reflecting the past.

Part One: Yield Curve Analysis

The slope, or shape, of the yield curve gives us our basic trading signals. We use the date that the curve inverts as a signal to sell stocks and the date that the curve normalizes as a signal to buy stocks.

We start our analysis in 1960 when interest rates were low. Rates tripled during the intervening decades and finally, in 2002, returned to the levels of the early 1960s. We use interest rates from the Federal Reserve's web site because they are available to the public. These yields are presented in the form of monthly averages.

We refine our trade dates with three critical values: quality spreads, the level of the 10-year note, and the rate of change in the federal funds rate. These aspects of the yield curve identify two serious, short-term corrections: the 1987 crash and the 1998 international currency devaluation. It is interesting to note that the slope of the yield curve forecasts each long stock market decline, but that these secondary indicators forecast the short, severe corrections. The rate of change in the fed funds rate helps identify these corrections and also tells us when to get back into the market.

Part Two: Technical Analysis

Technical analysis, which we use as a contrary indicator, helps us see what investors expect from the stock market in the short term. The volatility index (VIX) and the put/call ratio are specific indicators that show us what sophisticated investors are doing in the options market. This highly emotional market registers daily swings that may mask a useful trend. Moving averages smooth this volatile data and make it easier to identify an underlying trend. We trade in opposition to these moves because even sophisticated investors can take a market trend beyond its normal range.

One of our best technical indicators is market breadth as it is measured by the number of advancing issues in the Dow Jones Industrial Average. The Dow gives us a powerful measure of a broad base of investor sentiment. Unlike the put/call ratio and the VIX, movements in the Dow tell us what a *large* portion of the investing public thinks. Market breadth, as measured by the number of advancing issues in the 30 Dow industrials every day, helps us identify major market bottoms. When all 30 of these diversified stocks decline on the same day, millions of investors are overreacting to gloom, and it is time for us to buy equities.

Part Three: Cultural Indicators

Cultural signals humanize the market the way that anecdotal evidence does for an economist.

Investors usually sell stocks when war is declared or troops are deployed because they do not realize that war, unfortunately, is good for our economy. The country that is not the battleground usually sees its stock market and business activity increase during wartime. War is the most valuable of our cultural indicators and tells us to buy stocks before going to battle. War is a terrible event. It is also inflationary, and we need to protect our portfolios from the ravages of inflation as well as from the ravages of war.

The graph in Figure 25.1 summarizes the trade dates that we develop using the yield curve, technical analysis, and cultural indicators for 45 years.

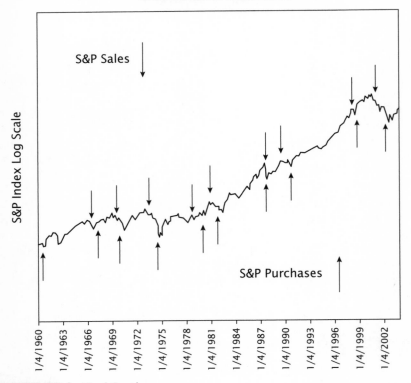

S&P 500 Index: 1960–2005
Trading with the Yield Curve, Technical Analysis, and Cultural Indicators

FIGURE 25.1 Final Graph

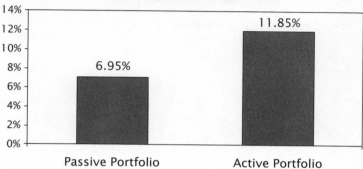

FIGURE 25.2 Return with Treasury Bills

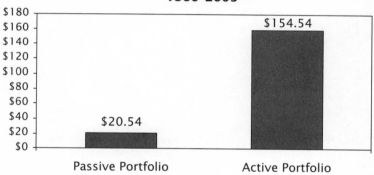

FIGURE 25.3 Portfolio Value with Treasury Bills

A conservative investor may invest in Treasury bills when our model portfolio is out of the stock market. The almost 12 percent return compares favorably to the passive portfolio's 7 percent. Both are without dividends of about 3 percent annually (see Figure 25.2). The incremental return makes a big difference in the dollar value of the active, but conservative, portfolio (see Figure 25.3). Compounding over such a long time makes the active portfolio seven and a half times larger than the inactive S&P 500 index.

Table 25.1 gives the rationale for each trade and the prevailing price of the S&P 500 index.

TABLE 25.1 Trade Rationale

Trade	Date	S&P	Rationale
Buy	January 1960	59	Normal yield curve, quality spreads shrinking, fed funds rate declining, 10-year Treasury yield less than 10 percent
Sell	September 1966	77	Inverted yield curve
Buy	February 1967	86	Normal yield curve, quality spreads shrinking, fed funds rate declining, 10-year Treasury yield less than 10 percent
Sell	July 1969	97	Inverted yield curve
Buy	February 1970	85	Normal yield curve, quality spreads shrinking, fed funds rate declining, 10-year Treasury yield less than 10 percent
Sell	June 1973	105	Inverted yield curve
Buy	October 1974	63	Normal yield curve, quality spreads shrinking, fed funds rate declining, 10-year Treasury yield less than 10 percent
Sell	December 1978	94	Inverted yield curve
Buy	May 1980	106	Normal yield curve, quality spreads shrinking, fed funds rate declining, 10-year Treasury yield less than 10 percent
Sell	November 1980	127	Inverted yield curve
Buy	September 1981	122	Normal yield curve, quality spreads shrinking, fed funds rate declining
Sell	October 15, 1987	298	Ten-year note = 10%, fed funds and quality spreads rising rapidly, inversion: 30-year bond to 10-year note
Buy	October 20, 1987	236	Normal yield curve, fed funds rate declining, quality spreads shrinking, 10-year Treasury yield less than 10 percent
Sell	October 1989	340	Inverted yield curve
Buy	August 23, 1990	307	Troops activated for Gulf War, quality spreads shrinking, fed funds rate declining, 10-year Treasury yield less than 10 percent
Sell	July 1998	1133	Rapidly rising fed funds rate, rapidly rising quality spreads, VIX = 24 (was 19 in June)

TABLE 25.1 *(Continued)*

Trade	Date	S&P	Rationale
Buy	September 4, 1998	973	Normal yield curve, fed funds rate declining, quality spreads shrinking, 10-year Treasury yield less than 10 percent, VIX = 44
Sell	August 2000	1430	Inverted yield curve, VIX = 16
Buy	July 19, 2002	84	All 30 Dow stocks down on one day, normal yield curve, fed funds rate declining, quality spreads shrinking, 10-year Treasury yield less than 10 percent, VIX = 39, P/C ratio = 1.14
End	January 3, 2005	1212	Hold? Normal curve, all yields less than 10%, quality spreads narrowing, fed funds rate rising, VIX = 13, P/C ratio = 0.80

PART FOUR: CHOOSING INVESTMENTS

We follow a top-down analysis that starts with major asset classes. We then examine industry sectors and finally make the security selection. Derivatives magnify portfolio returns, whether they are positive or negative. Top-down security selection allows investors to stop at any level of the analysis to accommodate their risk/return preferences. The most conservative investors may limit themselves to fixed-income securities and use our market timing signals to increase or decrease their portfolios' duration. They would increase the duration, or extend maturities, when the curve inverts and then shorten maturities, and take profits, when the curve normalizes.

ASSET CLASSES

Investors tend to move between paper and hard assets. Each of our trade dates represents a time when investors alternated between paper assets, such as U.S. currency, bonds or stocks, and hard assets, such as cash, real estate, and precious metals. Foreign currencies act as a bridge between paper and hard assets.

Each investor tailors these classes to his or her risk/return parameters and income needs, and many people limit themselves to just the most

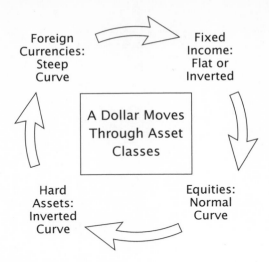

FIGURE 25.4   Asset Class Flows

liquid: cash, the S&P 500 index, and Treasury bonds. Many investors will merely adjust their asset allocations rather than eliminate one class altogether. Professional trustees usually rebalance around their *required* asset allocation; they often find this necessary about the same time that our model portfolio gets a signal to trade.

The shape of the yield curve provides the signal to change asset classes. An inverted yield curve tells us that investors are ready to shift from paper assets (U.S. dollar denominated investments in general and growth stocks in particular) into hard assets such as real estate. When the curve assumes a sharp slope, 3 percent from three months to 10 years, it implies that the U.S. dollar will decline. Gold and foreign currencies often dominate the market until the curve returns to its normal slope of about 1.3 percent, at which time equities regain their popularity.

The pictogram in Figure 25.4 illustrates the flow of money through the basic asset classes.

Investors' preference for either hard or paper assets is so important that it warrants its own graph (see Figure 25.5).

We move from diversified index and sector mutual funds to single stocks and, finally, to derivatives.

MUTUAL FUNDS

We start with index mutual funds in each asset class because they are an inexpensive way to apply our strategy while holding a diversified group of

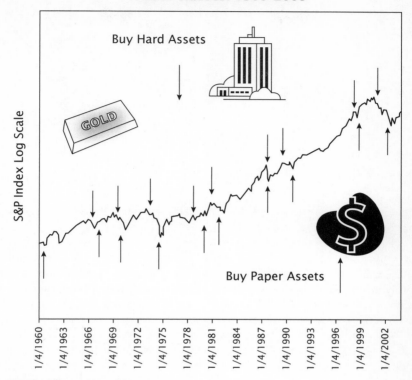

FIGURE 25.5 Hard and Paper Assets

securities. We then look at sector funds because they increase our profits if they are timed accurately.

Traditional sector rotation often follows this path. Starting at the top of an economic cycle, computer hardware often leads the market. During a recession, consumer staples, utilities, and health care often outperform. As the economy starts to recover, finance and technology tend to do well. Finally, basic materials and industrials improve when manufacturing picks up. At the peak of the cycle, computer hardware regains its dominance.

This is just a bare-bones summary to illustrate a point. Each phase of the business cycle tends to support a different sector of the economy, and investors can capitalize on this support.

Sector mutual funds and exchange-traded funds offer hundreds of vehicles to implement sector rotational investing. The ETFs also provide the missing securities for those who want access to all of the sectors including

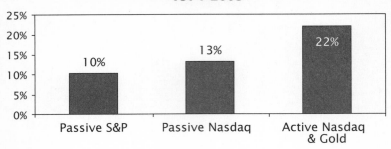

FIGURE 25.6   Returns with Nasdaq and Gold

gold bullion and the Nasdaq. StreetTracks Gold Shares is an ETF that owns gold bullion, and ONEQ is an ETF that owns all 3,000 stocks in the Nasdaq.

If these two funds had been available in 1974 when gold prices were allowed to fluctuate, Figure 25.6 shows how they would have compared to the S&P 500 index in one of the most aggressive versions of our model portfolio. In this example, we use gold prices on the COMEX division of the New York Mercantile Exchange as our alternative to the stock market in the actively traded portfolio.

These returns are without dividends, which would have narrowed the gap between the passive S&P and Nasdaq portfolios shown in Figure 25.7. Trading out of the Nasdaq near the top of its bubble in 2000 made a big difference in the value of the active portfolio. Owning gold when we were out of the stock market helped make the active portfolio almost 10 times larger than the inactive Nasdaq and almost 20 times larger than the passive S&P 500 index.

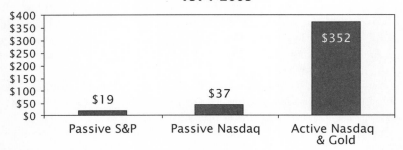

FIGURE 25.7   Portfolio value with Nasdaq and Gold

SECURITY SELECTION

All of the stocks in our top-down examples are screened by sector funds. These funds introduce us to a business that we must study independently to understand the earnings' drivers and current conditions. The stocks in a sector fund become a focus list, which we then augment with traditional ratio analysis.

Our limited discussion of bottom-up analysis emphasizes the vision and personal magnetism of the entrepreneur. Strong stock markets lionize glamorous leaders building new companies in innovative markets. These are often the stars that lift the market to outrageous heights in a bubble; investors who want to be a part of that excess assume that they will sell stock when the yield curve inverts.

Investing in individual securities allows us to combine asset classes in a particularly powerful manner. We saw some of our strongest returns in Canadian gold stocks because both the asset and the currency made money.

Some investors always hold stocks rather than bonds or hard assets. Many of these people prefer to limit their portfolios to stocks that trade on U.S. exchanges. They are still able to move among asset classes throughout the business cycle. For example, Placer Dome is a Canadian gold mining stock that trades on the New York Stock Exchange. American investors in this stock are in two asset classes at once: hard assets and foreign currency. When the U.S. Treasury yield curve is unusually steep, Placer Dome and the Canadian dollar may increase together.

Once again, let us look at our model portfolio using Placer Dome as an alternative to the U.S. stock market in the form of the Nasdaq over the past 15 years (see Figure 25.8). The resulting performance is an average annual return of 25 percent during the 15-year period.

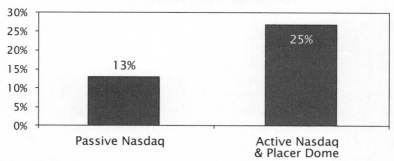

FIGURE 25.8 Return with Nasdaq and Placer Dome

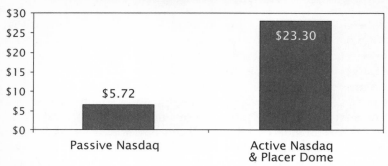

FIGURE 25.9   Portfolio Value with Nasdaq and Placer Dome

Trading between the Nasdaq and Placer Dome increased the value of the portfolio by a factor of four (see Figure 25.9).

DERIVATIVES

Derivatives obtain their value from the underlying security, whether it is a futures contract on a U.S. Treasury bill or an option on a futures contract for stock in Krispy Kreme donuts.

Derivatives—options and futures—can have extreme price variations because they are inexpensive to buy. Their low price reflects the fact that they have an expiration date after which they become worthless. Hedge funds and commodities pools are among the investors who use derivatives, and many of them do so in order to magnify a portfolio's returns.

Options and Futures

Two traditional forms of derivatives are options and futures.

Options are contracts that give the owner the right, but not the obligation, to buy or sell something at a specific price on or before a specified expiration date. Options cost less than the underlying stock for two reasons. First, you do not own the stock; you just have the chance to own it if you exercise your option. Second, the investment must reach a target price in a short period of time before it expires worthless. Because options are so much cheaper than the primary security, their prices are more volatile than that of the primary security.

Futures are contracts that may require performance on or before the expiration date, after which the contract becomes null and void. Futures investors may need to put as little as 5 to 10 percent of their investment on deposit with their broker when they buy a contract. Their contract is marked to the market daily, and they get a margin call if their deposit becomes deficient.

We happened to earn 77 percent during one week in one of our simulated derivative portfolios. This volatility cuts both ways and could have given us large losses as well. For this reason, a profession has grown up around the selection of hedge fund managers and the creation of synergistic pools called funds of hedge funds.

Our top-down security selection moved from well-diversified index funds of broad asset classes through focused sector funds to discrete stocks and derivatives. Each step increased our chances for profit but increased the risk that comes with specialization. Options and futures provided the most risk and reward because of their small cost for an asset that must reach an investment goal in a short period of time.

CONCLUSION

We are indeed fortunate to have the opportunity to invest in so many efficient markets. These markets can enrich us and give us a sense of control over our financial lives. We can improve our standard of living and our status; we can provide for our children and great-grandchildren. We can endow university chairs and build wings on hospitals.

We can drive a status symbol with the top down.

PART V

Capitalism at Work

Finance becomes romance when applied to real life. The financial markets give us the chance to realize our wildest dreams . . . or make complete fools of ourselves.

People have been trading the markets to improve their financial and social condition ever since history has written the tale.

In the process, they have created some outrageously overpriced markets for unusual stocks and commodities. Excessive markets collapse amid social upheaval and the search for a scapegoat. Out of the ashes rises the phoenix of optimism for the next market cycle. Investors who know the old stories and how the system works are the survivors.

Some of these tales tell of spectacular achievements. The opportunity for the largest number of law-abiding citizens to increase their wealth (and status) occurs in a capitalistic economy. The United States has, at this time, the purist form of capitalism; so we will look at the keys to its success. In the process, we will look at the future of investment for ideas that we can put into our portfolios now.

The final two chapters present some of the most audacious, as well as some of the most charming, stories of the opportunities available to us who live in a capitalistic economy.

CHAPTER 26

Outrageous Wall Street Stories

Wall Street loves a good story. It is a good thing, too, because Wall Street and its predecessors provide the subject matter for so many of them. You may notice a certain similarity among these stories because, as David Hume said in the eighteenth century, "Avarice . . . is a universal passion which operates at all times in all places and upon all persons."

The common thread among these tales of avarice is the excitement surrounding a new financial concept or industrial technology. Investors are able to see the value in each new concept, but they underestimate the length of time that it will take to realize its economic gains. The future is telescoped from decades into days. Prices inflate to embrace 10 years' economic benefit into one day's profit. This excitement encourages low-quality investments to enter the market and leverage to multiply every-one's profits. Highly leveraged, low-quality investments are the hallmarks of a mania. Then the wind changes direction, the crowd stampedes to the door amid a panic of margin calls, and a scapegoat is sacrificed to pay for the sins of the people.

These stories go back as far as the second century B.C. during the Roman Republic, and each one includes leverage on low-quality investments.

ROMAN REPUBLIC

The Romans developed a fairly sophisticated banking system that included foreign currency exchange, property insurance, and common

294

stock. Among the crowds of people trading stock in the Forum were *quaestors*, or financial speculators, who had no fundamental economic interest in the companies they traded. The exciting financial development of the day was government contracts for public works such as building temples, maintaining gardens, and collecting taxes. The general population was involved in these projects as construction workers, administrators, or beneficiaries enjoying the use of these beautiful projects. Everyone was aware of these new municipal buildings and profited from them in some manner.

Soon they became aware of the profits in the stocks of the companies that built them. Groups of capitalists similar to our corporations got the government contracts for these projects, and the shares of their stock rose accordingly. Professional stock traders started making fortunes and flaunted their new wealth. People left their old jobs of producing material things in order to follow the new professions of trading and speculating. Physical labor fell into disrepute as this new profession attracted new members. People scorned work, and speculating dominated the economy.

This easy money attracted investors from all levels of society, but the less wealthy were unable to afford the large, established companies' inflated shares. These new investors bought small, unregistered shares in second-rate companies that traded informally, or over the counter, off the regular exchange. People all over Italy traded these shares despite Cicero's contemptuous description of the activity as gambling. They could not help themselves because, as Petronius Arbiter said, "Filthy usury . . . spread through their limbs . . . like some disease."

History tells us that these shares declined in value during the Roman Empire; we do not have a record of who was the designated scapegoat.

DARK AGES

People embraced entirely different values during the Dark Ages. Usury was frowned upon, as was profit of any kind. Trade had to be for something of the same value and devoid of profit. In his delightful book, *Devil Take the Hindmost*, Edward Chancellor notes that St. Augustine listed the three most dangerous sins: a lust for profit, a desire for power, and an unconstrained sexual appetite.

Gradually, mores changed and profits became respectable again.

Laws on the books in Venice suggest that the city must have revived the art of trading. These laws, against insider trading and spreading rumors, suggest that Venice must have had experience with speculation.

There were even laws against something that sounds like the futures contracts that we trade today.

MEDIEVAL FAIRS

Medieval fairs replaced the Roman bacchanalia, and the spirit of exuberant
overindulgence flourished. The city of Leipzig had one of the most famous
fairs during the fifteenth century, and it soon developed into a trading
arena. The most popular stocks at the Leipzig fair were those of German
mining companies. Another fair, St. Germain outside of Paris, specialized
in municipal bonds and lottery tickets. Antwerp's fair ran all year long, and
Bruges' fair became the first organized stock exchange since Rome.

No one seemed to mind trading stocks, municipal bonds, and lottery
tickets in the middle of a carnival.

RENAISSANCE: FIRST JUNK BONDS

The first junk bonds appeared in Lyons and in Antwerp in the middle of
the sixteenth century at their respective fairs. They did not call them junk
bonds for another 300 years, but that is what they turned out to be. The
loyal subjects of King Henry II of France lent money to the government,
and everyone from aristocrats to servants got in on the game. Women sold
their jewels to raise cash to buy bonds. When investors came from as far
away as Turkey, optimists thought that foreigners would come from every
capital in the world to buy their bonds. Expectations continued to rise
right along with prices.

Lower-quality bonds became available as demand increased. As the
market rose, widows sold their deceased husbands' insurance policies to
buy the bonds. When King Henry II defaulted on his bonds in 1557, however, expectations crashed. He suspended payment on all bonds, and their
prices fell 85 percent.

Lyons lost its position as a financial center and Antwerp fell to the
Spanish a few years later. The Antwerp bourse closed and its financial
community fled to Amsterdam. They took with them many of the tools of
modern finance: double-entry bookkeeping, bills of exchange, and stock
markets. Once there, they developed derivatives: options and futures on
stocks. Soon afterward, they invented margin loans and small stocks for
small investors.

They had all the tools they needed for the most spectacular market
boom and crash in history: the tulip mania.

THE MOST FAMOUS MANIA: TULIPS

Tulips came to Holland gradually during the late sixteenth century. The flamboyant varieties of these flowers became popular as the economy improved and morals relaxed. The austere ethics of Calvinism gave way to consumerism as the Dutch learned to enjoy their new prosperity.

Tulips came to the right country; there was not much land in Holland and every bloom had to be showy enough to justify its space in a small garden. Tulips were easy to grow, and some of them had exotic shapes with variegated shots of vibrant color. Horticulturists later learned that it took a virus to turn a bland bulb into an exotic one and that the variation failed to pass the necessary gene for color to the next generation. This uncertainty added to their allure. Tulip bulbs were like small companies with no guarantee of the future of their production. As the Dutch economy improved and conspicuous consumption replaced austerity, tulips became a status symbol of the rich.

Artists loved to paint this colorful symbol of power and wealth, and books of tulip drawings are still popular today. Just after the turn of the next century, two of these flowers appeared in a book with a prophetic motto under them: "A fool and his money are soon parted." The artist could not have known how right he was.

Tulips came from Turkey, where *tulipan* means turban. Wealthy families were the only ones who could afford them, and they added to the flowers' allure by giving them names filled with power and romance. Each variety received a military name that reflected its value. The most important bulb, Semper Augustus, dominated this class because its streaks had the royal color of purple. The rest of the military parade followed: viceroys, admirals, and generals.

As you may expect, their prices reflected their position in this parade, and Semper Augustus commanded a value equal to that of a townhouse in Amsterdam. And this was just the beginning. Tulips' turbanesque shapes, regal colors, and aristocratic association attracted a growing audience.

Around 1635 the general public started buying tulips. These new buyers drove up prices to heights that still dazzle the imagination. Prices multiplied 10 times in a few months. Some bulbs sold for 60 times their previous year's value. At the height of the mania, as Charles Mackay wrote in his 1841 masterpiece, *Extraordinary Popular Delusions and the Madness of Crowds*, a single Semper Augustus bulb traded for 12 acres of center-city land. The new, small investors could not afford these prices, so lower-quality bulbs came to market to meet their demand. Still smaller investors who could not afford any bulbs at all resorted to gambling on bulbs they did not even own.

These gamblers were not the only ones who wrote worthless

promissory notes for future payment on the bulbs. By 1636 it was common practice to promise delivery the next spring when new bulbs would become available. The fact that some sellers promised more bulbs than they had access to and received payment in worthless credit notes created perfect symmetry, and both sides of the bargain got what they deserved. Few people held the bulbs to cultivate them anyway; there was no flower business yet and, therefore, no expectation of income from tulip growing. People just bought the bulbs with the expectation of reselling them quickly for a profit.

Some of the original investors, the wealthy horticulturalists, refused to pay these inflated prices. They kept their possessions diversified among land and productive businesses. They maintained their tulip collections for their own gardens rather than for profit. These value investors, as Benjamin Graham would have called them, were in a position to buy bulbs at bargain prices the next spring when the market unraveled.

On February 3, 1637, according to Mackay's history, there was a rumor that there were no buyers of tulip bulbs in the Haarlem market. The next day, of course, there really were no buyers. One by one, the worthless promissory notes for immature bulbs became as dust in the street. Mortgaged property collapsed with the rest of the leveraged business world. Tulip prices fell and took everything else with them. New princes became paupers, and old dynasties joined them.

Some speculators had a moment in the sun when fleeting profits turned cobblers into worldly merchants. Most of these newly rich, however, lost everything and returned to obscurity and bitterness.

The few who managed to keep their new wealth kept their heads down during the recriminations that followed. They did not want to be accused of reaping a reward with no effort in flagrant disregard of the Calvinist work ethic. They did not want to be seen as the reason for their neighbors' poverty or for the social upheaval that the mania created. They certainly did not want to be blamed for the economic depression that followed.

The original tulip collectors bought Semper Augustus and the rest of the military parade for three and a half cents on the dollar after a year of litigation set their rate at that level. Prices of the most precious bulbs eventually returned to their premania levels, but the inferior goods developed for the masses never recovered their value.

Tulips became the symbol of wickedness like a skull and crossbones on a pirate ship.

While the staid Dutch may surprise us with a colorful story, we expect it from the French. The French, surprisingly, were led astray by a Scotsman. His name was John Law, and his mania featured America.

MISSISSIPPI COMPANY

Born in 1671 to a goldsmith in Scotland, John Law found gambling more interesting than his family's business. Goldsmiths in those days also lent money, and John was destined to combine gambling and money lending into a scheme that would lay the French low. John would sell shares in a French corporation that thought there might be gold along the Mississippi River in America. The precise location of these hoped-for mines was where New Orleans stands today.

John misspent his youth in London learning the business of gambling and extravagant living. One of his adventures led to a duel that would haunt him the rest of his life. A lovely lady who fell for his rugged good looks put him in the position of needing to defend someone's honor on the dueling grounds.

He defended the honor too well and inadvertently killed his fellow duelist. This misstep landed him in jail for manslaughter. He escaped from prison and fled to the Continent, where he continued his education in gambling and extravagant living.

One of his haunts was Amsterdam, which had begun to recover from the tulip mania. He saw that the good Dutchmen were printing government notes (similar to our modern currency). The Dutch notes, however, were convertible into land. Land is a little awkward to divide up into pennies when someone exchanges his currency for the commodity that backs it, but the Dutch government overlooked that detail, as did the populace.

Issuing notes with nothing useful to back them up appealed to this gambler who had written similar ones himself. John returned home to persuade the English government to imitate the Dutch, but he was rebuffed. He also failed to have his murder charge dismissed, so he returned to the Continent where morals were more lenient.

For the next 14 years he gambled his way through the major European cities and honed his theories of economics as he traveled. (His travels expanded each time he was invited to leave a city for moral, if not legal, reasons.) He saw that the countries using paper currency flourished, and he came to believe that such currency was essential for economic success. Soon he had his chance to test his theory.

The Sun King of France, the opulent Louis XIV, passed away and left the country bankrupt from his extravagant living. The country had a large debt but no cash with which to honor it . . . until John Law came along.

John cultivated the regent, the Duke of Orleans, who ran the country for the little boy who would eventually become Louis XV. The first thing John did was flatter the Duke by naming a city after him in the exciting new republic of America. The second thing he did was convince the Duke to pay the interest on France's debt with paper currency. This was easy because the people were on the verge of a revolution over the country's financial mess, and any change was acceptable.

The first printing of paper money was well-received because it was immediately exchangeable into gold at the bank, Law and Company. The new currency revived commerce throughout France. Law and Company was so successful that the Duke took it over and gave it a new name, Banque Royale. This new government-owned bank, however, printed money for which there was no gold backing.

The French did not have gold, but they did have faith in the man who saved their economy. That man, of course, was John Law. John convinced the Duke of Orleans that there was gold in America next to the city called New Orleans on the Mississippi River. All they had to do was to form a company to mine this gold, and they knew that the French people would want to invest in shares of that company: the Mississippi Company. The French were easy to convince by the man who saved them all from financial ruin and who held out the promise of instant riches; Mississippi Company shares would have a *guaranteed* annual dividend of 100 percent of the original purchase price.

The frenzied public oversubscribed to the offering by six to one. Aristocrats bought townhouses next to the distribution center in order to avoid the mobs in the street. Prices increased daily, and the crowd's enthusiasm reached a fever pitch. Lower-class people could not afford the high-priced stock, so the company issued new shares to meet their demand.

Even these watered-down shares showed an immediate profit. No wonder there was a profit; the Banque Royale was printing new money even faster than the company could issue new shares, and the new cash went right into the stock market. Aristocrats and commoners alike bought this inferior stock with leverage and continued the game.

Then, early in 1720, a little trouble developed. Prince de Conti was unable to buy as much stock as he wanted, so he took his government-issued currency to the Banque Royale and asked for the gold that backed his paper money. By this time, the government had printed so much paper money that there was just a little gold dust backing each note. The Prince received his full value of gold in public but was required to return it in private.

Legend has it that the government felt a need to restore confidence in its gold-based currency; so it hired thousands of beggars to parade through Paris with picks and shovels as if they were headed for Mississippi to mine gold. This charming story, from John Kenneth Galbraith's book *A Short History of Financial Euphoria*, ends with the note that the ruse failed to convince those people who recognized the beggars back on the streets of Paris a few days later when they should have been digging for gold in America. Mackay's version of this story says that the beggars sold their tools, and I wonder if they invested the proceeds in Mississippi stock!

Regardless of whether some Parisians saw through the trick, some investors doubted that the madness could last. Their city was uninhabitable at the height of the bubble as thieves committed murder in broad daylight for a few shares of stock. John Law had to have an armed escort to protect him from the mob of would-be investors.

The Duke of Orleans used the public treasury to acquire the infamous 140-carat diamond that he named after himself, the Regent diamond. Too expensive for any private person to buy, it is flawless and plum-sized; it later decorated the crown of France and then Napoleon's sword. Even the conservative middle class spent wildly on jewels, art, and carriages as the influx of hundreds of thousands of foreigners stimulated trade throughout Paris. Stock prices increased 10 and 20 percent in a few hours and enriched commoners in a few days.

As always, a few investors sold their shares early, quietly bought things with real value, and moved their new holdings out of the country.

One stockbroker, so the story goes, traded his Mississippi Company stock for gold, hid the gold under a layer of manure on a farm cart, dressed like a peasant, and drove to Belgium. Others followed suit until the government severely restricted the ownership of gold, including that in jewels and dinnerware. The population hated this new law that diminished the value of their currency, which was supposed to be convertible into gold. Civil unrest grew as quickly as the value of Mississippi stock and government currency fell. The government responded by printing more worthless money and refusing to exchange it for gold at the Banque.

The end of the mania was swift and violent. On July 15, 1720, 15 people were trampled to death during a run on the Banque Royale, and by November stockbrokers were fleeing the country to avoid execution. John Law escaped to Venice, where he spent the rest of his years in prayer and poverty.

This time, history remembers the name of the scapegoat.

SOUTH SEA COMPANY

The lust for profits spread across the channel to England and its South Sea Company.

The British saw the French attract money from all over the Continent and feared that their ancient rival would again present a threat. As more and more investment money moved from London to Paris, the British knew that they had to protect themselves from their old military adversary. They decided to copy John Law's business model of selling stock . . . but with a twist.

This story has a different man named John. John Blunt was an avaricious clerk with a powerful employer and a knack for sales. In 1711 his employer, the Earl of Oxford, convinced Parliament to solve the government's large debt problem in the same manner as John Law: create a public corporation to take over the obligation. Like the French scheme, this corporation would have a romantic name, conduct business in the colonies, and sell shares to the public. John Blunt was delighted with his employer's project, which he planned to escalate into an investment bubble. John knew that he could puff up the price of the shares and get himself out before the public caught onto the scam.

The South Sea Company announced that it would trade in America on the west side of the Mississippi River and in South America. The charter conveniently overlooked the fact that some of this land overlapped Spain's claims to the New World. Again, the lure was the promise of gold in America.

The British added leverage to the French scheme. The South Sea Company offered its stock at a fraction of its cost and let investors pay in equal installments over a period of several months. This may have been the first margin account, and a few astute investors saw the risk; but their warnings went unheeded amid the desire for easy money.

As usual, there were two classes of stock for the two classes of people: high quality and low. Both classes of stock sold at an 80 percent discount with the balance repaid over time. Like the French scheme, each successful stock offering led to another; and each new offering was larger and had more leverage. By 1720, the third subscription came without a limit and the discount was 90 percent. Investors had four years to pay their debt to the company.

The South Sea Company was so popular that dozens of imitators sprang up. There were companies attempting to turn lead into gold, create perpetual motion, and make machine guns. Some of these deals implied that profits would be 800 percent during the first year. Newspapers ran notices of these new subscriptions and gave the name of the coffeehouse that would be the distribution site. Staid Londoners rushed to their corner coffeehouse to buy stock in companies that promised to settle a new land called Australia, and no one cared that the country had not yet been discovered. Investors even bought stock in companies promising to gather saltpeter from the deposits in outhouses.

No investment was beyond belief.

The stock market, as is often the case, raised the prices of all these stocks together. Very little attention was paid to the value of any of these ventures, and everyone prospered. Legend has it that the stock market grew by a factor of 100 between 1695 and 1720. England had never been so rich, and even King George I bought shares in each subscription.

New money brought the classes together in a celebration of wealth. Nobility and commoners danced together and feasted on 200 dishes at a three-day wedding of a couple who had just become rich in the stock market. The South Sea Company dominated every conversation in London at the height of the mania in 1720, and productive business gave way to stock speculation. Daytraders proliferate at the height of every stock market bubble.

This speculation, however, depended on John Blunt's sales skills. He understood that the company could not possibly earn enough to justify the stock prices and that investors would sell as soon as the momentum slowed.

He tried to sustain this momentum in two ways. First he encouraged Parliament to pass a law that would limit his competition from other companies. As these firms began to fail, though, the investment pyramid crumbled. Leveraged investors in one company sold stock in another to raise cash, and the South Sea Company suffered along with the rest of the market. As a final act of desperation, John offered a 30 percent cash dividend payment in the summer of 1720 with the promise of more to come. Some merchants with experience in trade realized that the South Sea Company could never deliver on this promise and they, along with John Blunt himself, sold their stock. Momentum investors had driven the price from about £140 to £1,050; interest rates reached 20 percent; and the bubonic plague reappeared in Marseilles.

Smart investors sold their stock before the fourth and final offering. A few months later, South Sea stock fell 85 percent, Blunt saved his skin by testifying against his own company's directors, and the Tower of London became full.

England outlawed short sales, options, and futures until the middle of the nineteenth century, but it could not outlaw foolishness.

TWENTIETH-CENTURY BUBBLES

America was founded in a tradition of speculation. Only the most optimistic, or the most desperate, pioneers would trade the familiarity of home for the unknown risks of a new country.

We have had bubbles around each advance in technology. Starting in the nineteenth century, we saw excessive investments in canals, railroads, automobiles, television, and computers. Some of these precipitated bubbles in real estate as far-flung as Florida and California. Some Americans even managed to participate in the excessive real estate market in Japanese golf courses during the 1980s.

ROARING TWENTIES

A new era dawned in 1920. This time it would be different. This time Prohibition outlawed alcohol and would make us more productive workers who would spend money on useful things like automobiles rather than on liquor. This time was not different, however, because dreamers and schemers married leverage to flimsy investments, and only a few people sold at the top.

Leverage came from two directions: consumer credit and margin loans. As people charged their daily purchases at the store and borrowed money for stocks, they piled debt on top of debt in their own private pyramid schemes. A public pyramid scheme, in the form of margin debt, was developing at the same time. There were three sources of margin loans: brokerage firms, foreign banks who lent internationally to anyone who wanted to invest in American stocks, and U.S. manufacturing companies. These last two were not under the control of our central bank and were particularly intractable.

Manufacturing companies issuing stock created leverage in the following manner. They would issue stock that paid a 4 percent dividend and then lend the proceeds to the investing public at 15 percent. The difference in these yields, of course, added to their corporate earnings and helped inflate the stock price. This recycling of dollars depended on an increasing stock market to keep the business, and share prices, growing.

Part of the dollar recycling included investment trusts. These trusts held stocks for investors who wanted professional portfolio management, just like our mutual funds today. Investment trusts were so popular in the late 1920s that on average a new one came to the market during each business day in 1929 until the October crash. The public bought these trusts because the advertisements promised to take some of the volatility out of a portfolio; they would buy and sell at the right times and protect the public from market extremes.

The professional managers, however, became victims of the prevailing greed and leveraged their holdings. Time after time they found a new way to add leverage; the national pyramid scheme added another course of bricks to its financial structure. Once again, the most leverage was applied to the lowest-quality stocks and appeared near the top of the market just in time to entice the general public.

Who could resist the excitement of an expanding economy with new toys for grown-ups? There was a little F. Scott and Zelda Fitzgerald in everyone, and everyone wanted to drive with the top down. Women were liberated politically by the vote and domestically by the refrigerator. Men flew across the ocean in airplanes, and stockbrokers read the tape on a "wireless" on ocean liners. Technology made the market seem different this time.

Technology did make it different; it sped up the demise. News of a corporate bankruptcy in London came over the wires in the middle of September and the crash occurred six weeks later. When the Bank of England raised its interest rates in response to the bankruptcy, British investors had to sell stock, and some of it was American. We had so many layers of leverage in our economy that the national pyramid crashed very quickly. Telephone and telegraph wires spread the bad news along with the margin calls.

Glamour stocks fared the worst, and the most famous, RCA, fell from $114 to $2.50. The RCA specialist on the floor of the New York Stock Exchange spent the rest of his life in an insane asylum.

Joseph Kennedy sold early, and his son spent the rest of his life in the White House.

SIXTIES GO-GO YEARS

President John F. Kennedy lived in the White House during the early go-go years. He and his photogenic family symbolized the best in America, and we fell for our own PR. In fact, we threw money at it in the form of mutual funds that sounded more like life insurance policies. These funds often paid generous dividends, and some of them even had the cash to do so. Bernie Cornfeld's fund, Investors Overseas Services, was not one of these.

Mr. Cornfeld, a Turkish social worker living in Geneva, invented a perpetual motion machine . . . for money. He could spin a dollar faster than a pinwheel. He created a family of mutual funds that invested in each other and sold it through six layers of commission-based salespeople. By the time an investor's dollar worked its way through all of the commissions, there were just pennies left to go into the fund. These pennies chased each other around the family of funds and propped up each income statement along the way.

Mr. Cornfeld enjoyed the profits from his perpetual money machine. He posed on magazine covers with live cheetahs, produced movies in Hollywood, and acquired a girlfriend named Heidi Fleiss. Heidi must have had some lively girlfriends to bring to the party because in 1995 she went to prison as the "Hollywood Madam." (She served her time for pandering and then used that legal term as the title for her 2003 book, *Panderings*.) Bernie's party lasted as long as investors paid several hundred times earnings for new stocks at the party on Wall Street.

Then someone had the nerve to take a profit.

Soon there was not enough cash to pay dividends, and Mr. Cornfeld sold his tangle of mutual funds to Robert Vesco. Mr. Vesco had his own financial problems, unfortunately, so he used what money was left in Investors Overseas Services to repay his own debts.

Both men fled the country, but Heidi was recently on U.S. television in a reality show. She was on a blind date with a man too young to recognize her.

EXCESSIVE EIGHTIES

The 1980s saw a long, strong stock market leveraged by junk bonds. These bonds supported stocks in new telecom industries such as MCI that opened up new opportunities to investors and new entrepreneurs alike. They grew amid the wildest party in decades. Heidi Fleiss may have brought her girlfriends to Mike Milken's annual Predators' Ball where Drexel Burnham entertained bored Midwestern bankers in the California sun.

These bankers might have been suspicious when Mike's 20 percent bonds had a clause allowing them to "pay in kind" if necessary to meet the interest obligation. In 1987 the stock market changed its mind about its own future and on October 19 the stock market fell faster than at any time since the Depression. The new technologies that spread the greed shifted gears and spread the fear. Telecoms spread the bad news and computers executed trades automatically without benefit of human controls.

Mike went to jail, and Heidi moved up from employee to management.

JAPANESE GOLF COURSES

Meanwhile, the Japanese had their own party during the 1980s. They bought real estate in the form of houses and golf courses.

Land may have been scarce in Japan, but money was not. Ordinary workers called salarymen took on so much debt to get into the housing market that it would take them 50 years to pay their mortgages. After the crash, householders were paying for homes whose value had dropped by half but whose mortgages would accrue to the next generation.

Housing was just the beginning of the real estate bubble in Japan.

Japanese golfers built some of the largest and most expensive courses in the world on one of the smallest and most heavily populated islands in the world. The Nikkei Golf Membership Index of average membership prices went from $100 to $1,000 from 1982 to 1990, with one club commanding the equivalent of $3 million.

Members received certificates for this illiquid asset and then used them as collateral for loans to buy stock. A secondary market developed for membership certificates complete with commission-earning brokers. At the height of the mania, a Japanese company, Cosmo World, bought the crown jewel of American golf courses, Pebble Beach in California, for $840 million.

Two years later Cosmo World sold Pebble Beach at a 40 percent loss, and two Americans ultimately bought the property: Arnold Palmer and Clint Eastwood.

THE NINETIES TELECOM BUBBLE

Money that fled from real estate in Japan seems to have gone to Internet stocks in the States. The Internet fed on itself as it created new investments and the technology to hype them. Investors bought stocks in the gadgets they owned, and then used the gadgets to make trades in the stock market.

Everyone bought a cell phone, and then everyone placed orders to brokers over the cell phones. Many of these orders were for Motorola because it makes cell phones. Millions of otherwise conservative citizens became day traders working at home on their own computers. They traded online because it was faster and cheaper than calling their broker on a cell phone. Online traders created 10 times the volume of regular brokerage customers, and most of these trades were in technology stocks.

Many of these new, at-home traders bought newly issued stocks without realizing that they come in two kinds. The first is a real investment in an ongoing firm that is gathering new money for future operations. The second is an exit plan for entrepreneurs who want to get out of the business. They want their original investment back plus enough profit to fund their retirement—not future business operations. They are more concerned with their own cash flow than that of the business. When these stocks fall during a general market decline, they often fail to participate in any future recovery of the rest of the market. Many of them go bankrupt.

When one courageous analyst said that every house in America would have to buy a new cell phone in 2000 in order to justify prevailing stock prices, the market started to crumble.

This time the scapegoat was a homemaker who owned stock in a company that was looking for a cure for cancer. Martha Stewart went to jail for an e-mail she sent to her broker about ImClone.

The telecom stock analyst who told customers to buy stocks at the peak of the mania while he sold them short did not have to go to jail. He settled with the SEC for a fine and exclusion from the industry. Jack Grubman paid his $15 million fine out of the $67 million that he had earned during the previous three years.

SUMMARY

We enjoy tales of unbridled greed and its predictable downfall. We have seen leverage applied to everything from tulip bulbs to golf courses and can laugh at other people's mistakes. Perhaps we will recognize some of the signs of the next investment mania and avoid buying low-quality stocks at inflated prices.

We certainly do not want to be the scapegoat for the next investment excess!

CHAPTER 27

America! America! God Shed His Grace on Thee

The world joined us in singing that song on September 11th after the terrorist attacks. Our national character united as we raised our flag and sang our song. We tied yellow ribbons, counted our blessings, and were grateful for the heritage that made us strong.

Explorers came to America looking for gold and the fountain of youth, and the dream lives on. We are fortunate to have become the wealthiest nation in the world with a life full of riches that money cannot buy. We have a democracy with a Bill of Rights, separation of church and state, and an open society. We have an individualistic culture built on the optimism of explorers and immigrants. Our public education provides the tools that our growing, vigorous population will use to keep the American dream alive. We have natural resources and peaceful boundaries with our neighbors. We have a rich investment outlook for those with foresight.

God did indeed shed his grace on us.

DEMOCRACY

Our democracy provides more human rights than most countries and it protects these rights with the most zeal.

Bill of Rights

We are all equal in the eyes of the law. Not many people in many countries can say that. In most countries there are some people who are "more equal" than others, and the difference is that of life or death. Our rights are secured by the Bill of Rights, which guarantees us such things as a speedy trial by a jury of our peers. Even the Magna Charta, the forerunner of the Bill, limited personal freedom to the aristocrats. We are one of the few countries in the world with three centuries of human rights written into law, and people risk their lives coming here for its protection—people like Josephine Hrabak, who boarded a ship to America in 1900 to build a better life than the one she had on a farm in Bohemia. She came alone with no English at her command and no one to meet her in America. She was only 16 years old but she understood the protection offered by a country that guarantees political rights to each citizen.

Josephine also came to practice her religious faith. Although she was Roman Catholic like her countrymen, she hated the pogroms that routinely deprived her of her Jewish neighbors. She knew that her right to practice Catholicism was only as secure as her neighbors' right to practice their religion.

Separation of Church and State

I realized the importance of the separation of church and state when I visited China in 2004. China tries to eliminate religion from its society and replace it with the Communist Party as the ideological focus. This is like substituting the Party for religion because anyone who joins a church is excluded from secure government jobs with generous benefits. The few churches we did see had been turned into T-shirt shops for tourists. There seems to be an irresistible pull on mankind to believe in something mystical beyond themselves, and most of the Chinese I met seemed to embrace the ancient superstitions. If China fails to become a financial success, part of the problem may be its refusal to acknowledge people's need for religion.

The theocracies in the Middle East have not only acknowledged the need for religion, they have forced it on their people. This is the classic form of uneven application of human rights when one group is favored over another. While a theocracy may provide a semblance of civil order, it excludes talented outsiders from contributing to society and everyone loses. Our Bill of Rights applies to individuals rather than to groups, and the separation of church and state ensures the equality of each person under the law.

Josephine understood this even though she was just a teenage girl from the country. She also knew that her humble background and lack of pedigree would not matter in America.

Open Society

Josephine knew that in Europe she would be cast irrevocably into her family's place in society. No amount of work on her part could change that. She loved her family and appreciated all they had done for her, but she wanted more. She wanted the thrill of writing her own life story. She wanted to bounce out of bed every morning anticipating a day full of work that could be rewarded with entry into a higher social class. She wanted an incentive for hard work that transcended money.

She knew that there was only one country in the world where that could happen.

Josephine did not realize that her dream of moving up in society is the key to America's economic world leadership. Our citizens throw themselves into their work like no others in the world. You cannot buy the kind of enthusiasm displayed every day in American business; you have to motivate it with social mobility. People will work harder for the dream of getting ahead than they will for a system that keeps them in their place.

Employers know that they need to whisper the word "partnership" only once to create a worker who will sacrifice everything for the firm. No one ever had to ask such an employee to stay late or work on a holiday. Vacations feel like a speed bump on their drive to the corner office.

NATIONAL CHARACTER

Our open society is at the heart of our national character, which stresses individualism.

Individualism

The outstanding trait of our national character is our individualism. While this can be criticized as self-centered and intractable, it can also benefit the economy. Fortunately, our legal and ethical constraints channel this individualism into creative thinking and economic risk taking.

The importance of individualism to our economy cannot be underestimated. This selfish drive looks inward for validation and the reward of self-actualization. It uses internal resources to glorify that which is special in each citizen. It ignores external values and controls as it exercises the muscle of independent thought. That independent thought leads to innovations that contribute to the welfare of mankind all over the world.

Individualism is the key to America's economic success.

Capital Markets

Combine individualism with effective capital markets and you have a magnet for international talent.

Europe produces at least as many knowledge workers as the United States does, but fails to keep them. Leaders of the European Union are concerned about their brain drain, and they know exactly what causes it; but they have not yet found the solution. Their brightest stars come to America so they can take their ideas mainstream; they want their research to spring to life in the real world; they want to start their own businesses in America.

Knowledge workers all over the world migrate to the American incubator of innovation. Here is where research becomes reality. Here is where thought leaders can assemble a team that shares a vision and then find seed money to create a product. Venture capitalists build on the best products and launch them in the financial markets.

Only in America could an immigrant from India like Vinod Khosla become a billionaire and the most powerful financier in Silicon Valley. This son of an army officer wanted to break out of his prescribed role and build new companies like Sun Microsystems and Juniper Networks. He wanted to sit on their boards and act as their chief operating officer; he wanted to raise companies like mothers raise children. He wanted to be part of the "next big thing," and knew where that thing usually happens: in America.

Spillover Effect

Financial and social success is available to outsiders in other areas of endeavor. The governor of California speaks with the heavy Austrian accent that Arnold Schwarzenegger acquired as a child in Europe. Oprah Winfrey proves that a woman of color can build an entertainment empire. Ray Charles broke barriers to people with physical handicaps. Hillary Clinton rewrote the role of the First Lady.

Everyone is richer in a culture that nurtures individuality in the crucible of effective capital markets. Melding individuality with innovation and providing both support and discipline from financial markets creates a virtuous cycle.

Willingness to Use Technology

Our willingness to incorporate new technology into our lives speeds up this cycle. New inventions do not gather dust; we put them to use. We put new tools to work in a society that values work. We do not substitute inefficient labor for new, productive tools as some countries do. We do not guarantee everyone a job, nor do we mothball new technology in order to create jobs.

Technology gives us productivity gains that are the envy of the world. Our productivity has grown three times as fast as it has in Europe. Between 1996 and 2000, the European Union saw productivity in its high-tech industry grow at less than 4 percent, while that rate exceeded 11 percent in the United States. It is no wonder that knowledge workers prefer to work in the States, where we show our appreciation by using their contributions.

Work Ethic

The hallmark of our national character is our appreciation of physical and mental labor. Many societies scorn productive labor and consider it demeaning. In some parts of the world the ideal is an indolent life of ease. There are stories from Asia about people who think that work is beneath them and that petty thievery is a better lifestyle. We are fortunate to have a culture that attracts and rewards people who contribute to society rather than those who think that there is more status in breaking the law.

Our national character sets us apart from the rest of the world. It consists of cherished ideals inculcated over the centuries. It brings out the best in people and nurtures us all. It cannot be replicated by an economic competitor anytime soon.

We pass these values on at mothers' knees and in public schools.

EDUCATION

We hand down our culture in the world's most effective institutions for teaching creative thinking. We do this with commitment and make it available to people of all ages.

Commitment to Education

We spend more money on each child (almost $11,000 in 2001 compared to $3,000 in central Europe) and require children to spend more time in the classroom than any nation in the world. While they are there, we endeavor to teach them the art of independent, creative thinking. No other school system in the world teaches creativity with as much force and conviction as we do. We know that we will lose our competitive edge if we lose our educational edge.

We understand that critical thinking cannot happen in a vacuum. We are aware that time and money alone do not educate a child. We know that creative thinking needs to work with factual material and that it is dangerous to allow students the luxury of the former without a basis in the latter.

We also realize the dangers of complacency and hubris in our national mentality. The French aristocrat who traveled our country in 1830 and wrote about our culture, Alexis de Tocqueville, cautioned that arrogance could bring us down. We try to heed his warning.

Education Is Available to All

We make education available to more of our citizens than any other country in the world. In addition to free, mandatory education, we have a network of community colleges that reaches adults.

These institutions offer traditional arts and sciences and, importantly, the hands-on technical training that goes to the heart of our economy. Here are the real-life skills of computer science, medical technology, and business communication that make our world work. Here is where teenagers prepare for their first job and adults retrain for the next one. Here is where the average citizen can upgrade his skills and take the next step up the social and economic ladder.

Our people value education because it is the key to our social mobility. In this country we look at a high school diploma to see the name of the school and the name of the graduate. We do not, as they did in some places in Europe during the last century, look at the diploma to see the name of the graduate's father and the father's occupation.

Our schools are ready for the growing and diverse population that will fill them in the future. This population is also young for an industrialized country.

POPULATION

A population's growth, diversity, and age are important to its economic strength.

Growing Population

Our population grew faster in the 1990s than in any other decade since we started keeping records under President Thomas Jefferson. We added almost 33 million people and outnumbered the huge baby boom in the 1950s. This growth came from increased fertility rates and immigration.

Two groups are swelling our ranks: the baby boomers' children (the echo boomers) and immigrants. We need them both. They will feed our intellectual lives and pass on our national character to their children. They will provide workers for our businesses and consumers for our products. They will fill our research laboratories and our government. We hope they will find a cure for cancer and spread peace and democracy around the world.

The population in the United States is growing faster than in any other developed country. The most recent census concluded that we grew 13 percent during the 1990s while the other developed countries—Canada, Japan, Australia, New Zealand, and the European nations—grew less than 3 percent. Their oldest age group is increasing much faster than the workers who will support them. Their dependency ratio is growing much faster than ours is in the United States.

Their growing dependency ratio is serious because they have large financial obligations to their retirees. Add that to the benefits for current workers, such as health care, vacation time, and child care, in a society that resists layoffs, and you have an economy operating with a very large overhead. Europe has some of the highest tax rates in the world to support all these benefits.

No wonder young people with a bright future often move to the United States. About one-third of our growth came from immigration, while some parts of Eastern Europe and Russia lost population during the last decade.

Diverse Population

James Michener, in his book *Hawaii*, tells how the islands became isolated from the rest of the world a hundred years ago. The inhabitants wisely encouraged Chinese immigrants in order to strengthen the population. (They also provided cheap labor, which may have been the real reason for their warm welcome. These cheap laborers, by the way, saved their money and became the islands' businessmen.) Nevertheless, Michener says that the Chinese were necessary in order to provide what biologists call "genetic vigor." This vigor revitalizes the gene pool by adding new genetic material for subsequent generations.

Genetic vigor prevents inbreeding and protects a community from inherited conditions such as hemophilia and mental retardation. Tsarevich Alexei of Russia inherited hemophilia from his relatives who had intermarried for generations. The European aristocracy thought that they had to marry someone in their own class in order to protect their bloodlines. What they did, however, was to increase their children's chances to develop hemophilia.

Any closed society that limits marriage runs the risk of passing on defective genes. Isolated tribes are forced into this situation, but aristocrats sometimes choose to damage their gene pool in this manner. America's immigrants, combined with an open society that allows intermarriage among social classes, ensures that we have a strong, healthy gene pool.

Immigration also helps to keep us young as a nation.

Young Population

While most developed countries have a problem with insufficient young people to support their oldsters, the United States is better off than most for two reasons. First, the 2000 census revealed that the U.S. fertility rate was 1.9 compared to Western Europe's rate of just 1.35. Secondly, our immigration rate was more than double that of Western Europe's. These two forces may allow us to have fewer retirees depending on our workforce per capita in the future.

This difference in demograhics rated a humorous cover on the *Economist* magazine several years ago. A map of the two continents had cartoons representing the demographics of Europe and America. The European was a withered old white man while the American was an energetic caramel-colored baby. The article inside sang the praises of the American demographics that support a strong economy.

The final support of our economy is our geography. We have abundant and accessible natural resources and peaceful boundaries with our neighbors.

NATURAL RESOURCES

We have rich, flat farmland that is the envy of Europe. Broad expanses broken only by rivers that provide transportation and irrigation are easy to farm. This land is in the temperate zone, which is ideal for agriculture. The growing season is long enough, wet enough, and of the right temperature to grow grain in abundance. Our naturally fertile soil, chernozem, is the variety required for growing wheat and corn.

There are just four areas in the world—Russia, India, Australasia, and the United States—with the right conditions for bumper crops. The two largest of these areas, Russia and the United States, require the least irrigation. No wonder we sing of "amber waves of grain"!

We have the minerals and energy necessary to build the transportation system that moves our farm products to our people. Coal in Pennsylvania joins iron ore in Minnesota to make steel for railroads and aircraft. Oil and natural gas fuel the system. Solar power and wind power provide sustainable sources of energy. Meanwhile, our scientists are improving the power of fuel cells.

We are one of the few nations with sufficient potable water. As he traveled around the world in his yellow Mercedes convertible, author/investor Jim Rogers found water shortages almost everywhere he went. He thinks that the fortunes will be made by those who solve the world's chronic shortage of drinkable water. He feels that the "next big thing" will be finding, cleaning, and moving water to places where it is needed.

We are fortunate to be graced with so many natural resources in a world of shortages. We are particularly blessed to have peaceful relationships with our neighbors on each of our long, open borders. Many places in the world have constant and debilitating border disputes that lower everyone's standard of living. Instead, we trade with our neighbors like housewives swapping recipes over the back fence.

Our heritage and our natural resources position us to make money in the stock market if we target the right themes. The "next big thing" usually starts here, so let us take a look at a few contenders.

INVESTMENT THEMES FOR THE FUTURE

The key to successful investing has been in the following adjectives: smaller, faster, cheaper, and global.

Nanotechnology looks at our world in its smallest forms. As nanotechnology moves into manufacturing we may see products that are lighter and stronger. These more efficient products may deliver more precise results for the intended job and may be available at a lower cost than traditional materials. Certainly, the medical world hopes that miniaturization will continue to improve its service. It hopes to continue to provide less invasive and more precise treatments for our baby boomers as they age.

Nanotechnology will make things move faster. The pace of living picks up every time a computer chip gets smaller and more powerful. Smart chips imbedded in products we use every day will deliver information faster. Doctors in our local hospital are wearing name badges with chips inside that replace their beepers and cell phones. These hands-free devices weigh just a couple of ounces and are nonmetallic so they can go into the operating room. Communication just became easier and faster in a place where we need it most—in the hospital.

Our doctors' smart badges save money for our townspeople. They are less expensive than the multipurpose BlackBerry that the doctors used to carry. The badges are limited to conversation and do not have applications that are unnecessary in today's operating room. We may need to e-mail our surgeons in the future, but right now we prefer not to burden their in-boxes with the joke of the day. Their less expensive badges are all they need and all their patients want to pay for.

Soon there will be similar badges on many doctors all over the world as our business becomes even more global.

The Federal Reserve Bank of Cleveland's Economic Commentary dated January 15, 2005, carries the title, "This Is Bangalore Calling: Hang Up or Speed Dial?" This clever title, which is on the Internet at www.clevelandfed.org, crystallizes our mixed feelings about outsourcing. Not only does the author, Catherine L. Mann, come out in favor of outsourcing, but she says it has the potential for major benefits to investors and workers alike.

Ms. Mann points out that technology will have a growing impact on the service sector as in the case of doctors' improved communication devices. In the past, technological gains have applied to our manufacturing sector, but they are now starting to improve our service sector as well. The potential for productivity gains (read: stock market gains) could be enormous.

The author points to the synergy between technology and trade in the global arena. Apply that synergy to our service sector and watch productivity gains go off the charts. When your doctor's name badge has a smart chip that was made in China, the lower cost and faster, clearer communication may get you onto the operating table in time to save your life.

You will be even more grateful if you were smart enough to invest in one of the companies that made your doctor's telephone/badge possible.

As we move from the Industrial Age into the Information Age, the world will get smaller and life will move faster. We can only hope that our policy makers minimize the dislocations, job losses, and lifestyle changes that may accompany this economic change. In the meantime, we can protect ourselves and our families by investing with, rather than against, this rising tide.

If the next wave of technological advance includes the service sector as well as manufacturing, the productivity gains and economic advances will be even larger than before. Productivity gains usually translate into stock market gains, so the best may be yet to come.

The rest of the world would love to be in our shoes. They would love to live in a land graced with natural resources, peaceful boundaries, and an innovative culture. The rest of the world may wish that they had come to America when they were 16 the way Josephine Hrabak did.

What happened to her?

She met a young German engineer who worked for an ice cream company. He learned her language and asked permission to court her. Albert took her to amusement parks and for walks by the lake and made sure that she had all the ice cream she wanted. He fell in love with this Gibson

Girl in her puffed sleeves and tiny waist. She admired his wavy blond hair and hearty laugh and knew they could make a good life together.

Now Josephine's descendants look like a meeting of the United Nations when they gather for yet another Muslim-Sikh-Jewish-Rastafarian-Protestant wedding. They have married, adopted, and otherwise embraced the Scottish, Irish, Indian, Bolivian, and Kenyan cultures to make a fine pot-au-feu. Their kitchens carry the aroma of curry and the stink of sauerkraut. They revel in their genetic vigor that produces healthy, vibrant children.

Only in America could Josephine's great-grandchildren have become research scientists developing alternative energy sources, international educators, psychiatric social workers, and public relations specialists in the new technology of the Information Age.

Appendixes

Date	Three-Month Bill	Ten-Year Note	Ten-Year Minus Three-Month	Trade	S&P 500 Index
1960-01-01	**4.35**	**4.72**	**0.37**	**Buy**	**59.89**
1960-02-01	3.96	4.49	0.53		55.61
1960-03-01	3.31	4.25	0.94		56.12
1960-04-01	3.23	4.28	1.05		55.34
1960-05-01	3.29	4.35	1.06		54.37
1960-06-01	2.46	4.15	1.69		55.83
1960-07-01	2.30	3.90	1.6		56.92
1960-08-01	2.30	3.80	1.5		55.51
1960-09-01	2.48	3.80	1.32		56.96
1960-10-01	2.30	3.89	1.59		53.52
1960-11-01	2.37	3.93	1.56		53.39
1960-12-01	2.25	3.84	1.59		55.54
1961-01-01	2.24	3.84	1.6		58.11
1961-02-01	2.42	3.78	1.36		61.78
1961-03-01	2.39	3.74	1.35		63.44
1961-04-01	2.29	3.78	1.49		65.06
1961-05-01	2.29	3.71	1.42		65.31
1961-06-01	2.33	3.88	1.55		66.56
1961-07-01	2.24	3.92	1.68		64.64
1961-08-01	2.39	4.04	1.65		66.76
1961-09-01	2.28	3.98	1.7		68.07
1961-10-01	2.30	3.92	1.62		66.73
1961-11-01	2.48	3.94	1.46		68.62
1961-12-01	2.60	4.06	1.46		71.32
1962-01-01	2.72	4.08	1.36		71.55
1962-02-01	2.73	4.04	1.31		68.84
1962-03-01	2.72	3.93	1.21		69.96
1962-04-01	2.73	3.84	1.11		69.55
1962-05-01	2.69	3.87	1.18		65.24
1962-06-01	2.73	3.91	1.18		59.63
1962-07-01	2.92	4.01	1.09		54.75
1962-08-01	2.82	3.98	1.16		58.23
1962-09-01	2.78	3.98	1.2		59.12
1962-10-01	2.74	3.93	1.19		56.27
1962-11-01	2.83	3.92	1.09		56.52
1962-12-01	2.87	3.86	0.99		62.26
1963-01-01	2.91	3.83	0.92		63.1
1963-02-01	2.92	3.92	1		66.2
1963-03-01	2.89	3.93	1.04		64.29
1963-04-01	2.90	3.97	1.07		66.57

Note: Bill returns are discounts annualized on a 360-day year. Trade dates are in bold type.

Sources: http://research.stlouisfed.org/fred2 and ComStock, Inc. (Yahoo.com).

Date	Three-Month Bill	Ten-Year Note	Ten-Year Minus Three-Month	Trade	S&P 500 Index
1963-05-01	2.93	3.93	1		69.8
1963-06-01	2.99	3.99	1		70.8
1963-07-01	3.18	4.02	0.84		69.37
1963-08-01	3.32	4.00	0.68		69.13
1963-09-01	3.38	4.08	0.7		72.5
1963-10-01	3.45	4.11	0.66		71.7
1963-11-01	3.52	4.12	0.6		74.01
1963-12-01	3.52	4.13	0.61		73.23
1964-01-01	3.52	4.17	0.65		75.02
1964-02-01	3.53	4.15	0.62		77.04
1964-03-01	3.54	4.22	0.68		77.8
1964-04-01	3.47	4.23	0.76		78.98
1964-05-01	3.48	4.20	0.72		79.46
1964-06-01	3.48	4.17	0.69		80.37
1964-07-01	3.46	4.19	0.73		81.69
1964-08-01	3.50	4.19	0.69		83.18
1964-09-01	3.53	4.20	0.67		81.83
1964-10-01	3.57	4.19	0.62		84.18
1964-11-01	3.64	4.15	0.51		84.86
1964-12-01	3.84	4.18	0.34		84.42
1965-01-01	3.81	4.19	0.38		84.75
1965-02-01	3.93	4.21	0.28		87.56
1965-03-01	3.93	4.21	0.28		87.43
1965-04-01	3.93	4.20	0.27		86.16
1965-05-01	3.89	4.21	0.32		89.11
1965-06-01	3.80	4.21	0.41		88.42
1965-07-01	3.84	4.20	0.36		84.12
1965-08-01	3.84	4.25	0.41		85.25
1965-09-01	3.92	4.29	0.37		87.17
1965-10-01	4.03	4.35	0.32		89.96
1965-11-01	4.09	4.45	0.36		92.42
1965-12-01	4.38	4.62	0.24		91.61
1966-01-01	4.59	4.61	0.02		92.43
1966-02-01	4.65	4.83	0.18		92.88
1966-03-01	4.59	4.87	0.28		91.22
1966-04-01	4.62	4.75	0.13		89.23
1966-05-01	4.64	4.78	0.14		91.06
1966-06-01	4.50	4.81	0.31		86.13
1966-07-01	4.80	5.02	0.22		84.74
1966-08-01	4.96	5.22	0.26		83.6
1966-09-01	**5.37**	**5.18**	**−0.19**	**Sell**	**77.1**
1966-10-01	5.35	5.01	-0.34		76.56
1966-11-01	5.32	5.16	-0.16		80.2
1966-12-01	4.96	4.84	-0.12		80.45

(continues)

Date	Three-Month Bill	Ten-Year Note	Ten-Year Minus Three-Month	Trade	S&P 500 Index
1967-01-01	4.72	4.58	-0.14		80.33
1967-02-01	**4.56**	**4.63**	**0.07**	**Buy**	**86.61**
1967-03-01	4.26	4.54	0.28		86.78
1967-04-01	3.84	4.59	0.75		90.2
1967-05-01	3.60	4.85	1.25		94.01
1967-06-01	3.54	5.02	1.48		89.08
1967-07-01	4.21	5.16	0.95		90.64
1967-08-01	4.27	5.28	1.01		94.75
1967-09-01	4.42	5.30	0.88		93.64
1967-10-01	4.56	5.48	0.92		96.71
1967-11-01	4.73	5.75	1.02		93.3
1967-12-01	4.97	5.70	0.73		94
1968-01-01	5.00	5.53	0.53		96.47
1968-02-01	4.98	5.56	0.58		92.24
1968-03-01	5.17	5.74	0.57		89.36
1968-04-01	5.38	5.64	0.26		90.2
1968-05-01	5.66	5.87	0.21		97.46
1968-06-01	5.52	5.72	0.2		98.68
1968-07-01	5.31	5.50	0.19		99.58
1968-08-01	5.09	5.42	0.33		97.74
1968-09-01	5.19	5.46	0.27		98.86
1968-10-01	5.35	5.58	0.23		102.6
1968-11-01	5.45	5.70	0.25		103.4
1968-12-01	5.96	6.03	0.07		108.3
1969-01-01	6.14	6.04	−0.1		103.8
1969-02-01	6.12	6.19	0.07		103
1969-03-01	6.02	6.30	0.28		98.13
1969-04-01	6.11	6.17	0.06		101.5
1969-05-01	6.04	6.32	0.28		103.6
1969-06-01	6.44	6.57	0.13		103.4
1969-07-01	**7.20**	**6.72**	**−0.48**	**Sell**	**97.71**
1969-08-01	6.98	6.69	−0.29		91.83
1969-09-01	7.09	7.16	0.07		95.51
1969-10-01	7.00	7.10	0.1		93.12
1969-11-01	7.24	7.14	−0.1		97.12
1969-12-01	7.82	7.65	−0.17		93.81
1970-01-01	7.87	7.79	−0.08		92.06
1970-02-01	**7.13**	**7.24**	**0.11**	**Buy**	**85.02**
1970-03-01	6.63	7.07	0.44		89.5
1970-04-01	6.51	7.39	0.88		89.63
1970-05-01	6.84	7.91	1.07		81.52
1970-06-01	6.68	7.84	1.16		76.55
1970-07-01	6.45	7.46	1.01		72.72
1970-08-01	6.41	7.53	1.12		78.05
1970-09-01	6.12	7.39	1.27		81.52

Date	Three-Month Bill	Ten-Year Note	Ten-Year Minus Three-Month	Trade	S&P 500 Index
1970-10-01	5.91	7.33	1.42		84.3
1970-11-01	5.28	6.84	1.56		83.25
1970-12-01	4.87	6.39	1.52		87.2
1971-01-01	4.44	6.24	1.8		92.15
1971-02-01	3.70	6.11	2.41		95.88
1971-03-01	3.38	5.70	2.32		96.75
1971-04-01	3.86	5.83	1.97		100.3
1971-05-01	4.14	6.39	2.25		103.9
1971-06-01	4.75	6.52	1.77		99.63
1971-07-01	5.40	6.73	1.33		98.7
1971-08-01	4.94	6.58	1.64		95.58
1971-09-01	4.69	6.14	1.45		99.03
1971-10-01	4.46	5.93	1.47		98.34
1971-11-01	4.22	5.81	1.59		94.23
1971-12-01	4.01	5.93	1.92		93.99
1972-01-01	3.38	5.95	2.57		102
1972-02-01	3.20	6.08	2.88		103.9
1972-03-01	3.73	6.07	2.34		106.5
1972-04-01	3.71	6.19	2.48		107.2
1972-05-01	3.69	6.13	2.44		107.6
1972-06-01	3.91	6.11	2.2		109.5
1972-07-01	3.98	6.11	2.13		107.1
1972-08-01	4.02	6.21	2.19		107.3
1972-09-01	4.66	6.55	1.89		111
1972-10-01	4.74	6.48	1.74		110.5
1972-11-01	4.78	6.28	1.5		111.5
1972-12-01	5.07	6.36	1.29		116.6
1973-01-01	5.41	6.46	1.05		118
1973-02-01	5.60	6.64	1.04		116
1973-03-01	6.09	6.71	0.62		111.6
1973-04-01	6.26	6.67	0.41		111.5
1973-05-01	6.36	6.85	0.49		106.9
1973-06-01	**7.19**	**6.90**	**−0.29**	**Sell**	**104.9**
1973-07-01	8.01	7.13	−0.88		104.2
1973-08-01	8.67	7.40	−1.27		108.2
1973-09-01	8.29	7.09	−1.2		104.2
1973-10-01	7.22	6.79	−0.43		108.4
1973-11-01	7.83	6.73	−1.1		108.2
1973-12-01	7.45	6.74	−0.71		95.96
1974-01-01	7.77	6.99	−0.78		97.55
1974-02-01	7.12	6.96	−0.16		96.57
1974-03-01	7.96	7.21	−0.75		96.22
1974-04-01	8.33	7.51	−0.82		93.98
1974-05-01	8.23	7.58	−0.65		90.31

(continues)

Date	Three-Month Bill	Ten-Year Note	Ten-Year Minus Three-Month	Trade	S&P 500 Index
1974-06-01	7.90	7.54	−0.36		87.28
1974-07-01	7.85	7.81	−0.04		86
1974-08-01	8.96	8.04	−0.92		79.31
1974-09-01	8.06	8.04	−0.02		72.15
1974-10-01	**7.46**	**7.90**	**0.44**	**Buy**	**63.54**
1974-11-01	7.47	7.68	0.21		73.9
1974-12-01	7.15	7.43	0.28		69.97
1975-01-01	6.26	7.50	1.24		68.56
1975-02-01	5.50	7.39	1.89		76.98
1975-03-01	5.49	7.73	2.24		81.59
1975-04-01	5.61	8.23	2.62		83.36
1975-05-01	5.23	8.06	2.83		87.3
1975-06-01	5.34	7.86	2.52		91.15
1975-07-01	6.13	8.06	1.93		95.19
1975-08-01	6.44	8.40	1.96		88.75
1975-09-01	6.42	8.43	2.01		86.88
1975-10-01	5.96	8.14	2.18		83.87
1975-11-01	5.48	8.05	2.57		89.04
1975-12-01	5.44	8.00	2.56		91.24
1976-01-01	4.87	7.74	2.87		90.19
1976-02-01	4.88	7.79	2.91		100.8
1976-03-01	5.00	7.73	2.73		99.71
1976-04-01	4.86	7.56	2.7		102.7
1976-05-01	5.20	7.90	2.7		101.6
1976-06-01	5.41	7.86	2.45		100.1
1976-07-01	5.23	7.83	2.6		104.2
1976-08-01	5.14	7.77	2.63		103.4
1976-09-01	5.08	7.59	2.51		102.9
1976-10-01	4.92	7.41	2.49		105.2
1976-11-01	4.75	7.29	2.54		102.9
1976-12-01	4.35	6.87	2.52		102.1
1977-01-01	4.62	7.21	2.59		107.4
1977-02-01	4.67	7.39	2.72		102
1977-03-01	4.60	7.46	2.86		99.82
1977-04-01	4.54	7.37	2.83		98.42
1977-05-01	4.96	7.46	2.5		98.44
1977-06-01	5.02	7.28	2.26		96.12
1977-07-01	5.19	7.33	2.14		100.4
1977-08-01	5.49	7.40	1.91		98.85
1977-09-01	5.81	7.34	1.53		96.77
1977-10-01	6.16	7.52	1.36		96.53
1977-11-01	6.10	7.58	1.48		92.34
1977-12-01	6.07	7.69	1.62		94.83
1978-01-01	6.44	7.96	1.52		95.1
1978-02-01	6.45	8.03	1.58		89.25

Date	Three-Month Bill	Ten-Year Note	Ten-Year Minus Three-Month	Trade	S&P 500 Index
1978-03-01	6.29	8.04	1.75		87.04
1978-04-01	6.29	8.15	1.86		89.21
1978-05-01	6.41	8.35	1.94		96.83
1978-06-01	6.73	8.46	1.73		97.24
1978-07-01	7.01	8.64	1.63		95.53
1978-08-01	7.08	8.41	1.33		100.6
1978-09-01	7.85	8.42	0.57		103.2
1978-10-01	7.99	8.64	0.65		102.5
1978-11-01	8.64	8.81	0.17		93.15
1978-12-01	**9.08**	**9.01**	**−0.07**	**Sell**	**94.7**
1979-01-01	9.35	9.10	−0.25		96.11
1979-02-01	9.32	9.10	−0.22		99.93
1979-03-01	9.48	9.12	−0.36		96.28
1979-04-01	9.46	9.18	−0.28		101.5
1979-05-01	9.61	9.25	−0.36		101.7
1979-06-01	9.06	8.91	−0.15		99.08
1979-07-01	9.24	8.95	−0.29		102.9
1979-08-01	9.52	9.03	−0.49		103.8
1979-09-01	10.26	9.33	−0.93		109.3
1979-10-01	11.70	10.30	−1.4		109.3
1979-11-01	11.79	10.65	−1.14		101.8
1979-12-01	12.04	10.39	−1.65		106.1
1980-01-01	12.00	10.80	−1.2		107.9
1980-02-01	12.86	12.41	−0.45		114.1
1980-03-01	15.20	12.75	−2.45		113.6
1980-04-01	13.20	11.47	−1.73		102
1980-05-01	**8.58**	**10.18**	**1.6**	**Buy**	**106.2**
1980-06-01	7.07	9.78	2.71		111.2
1980-07-01	8.06	10.25	2.19		114.2
1980-08-01	9.13	11.10	1.97		121.6
1980-09-01	10.27	11.51	1.24		122.3
1980-10-01	11.62	11.75	0.13		125.4
1980-11-01	**13.73**	**12.68**	**−1.05**	**Sell**	**127.4**
1980-12-01	15.49	12.84	−2.65		140.5
1981-01-01	15.02	12.57	−2.45		135.7
1981-02-01	14.79	13.19	−1.6		129.5
1981-03-01	13.36	13.12	−0.24		131.2
1981-04-01	13.69	13.68	−0.01		136
1981-05-01	16.30	14.10	−2.2		132.8
1981-06-01	14.73	13.47	−1.26		132.5
1981-07-01	14.95	14.28	−0.67		131.2
1981-08-01	15.51	14.94	−0.57		130.9
1981-09-01	**14.70**	**15.32**	**0.62**	**Buy**	**122.7**
1981-10-01	13.54	15.15	1.61		116.1

(continues)

Date	Three-Month Bill	Ten-Year Note	Ten-Year Minus Three-Month	Trade	S&P 500 Index
1981-11-01	10.86	13.39	2.53		121.8
1981-12-01	10.85	13.72	2.87		126.3
1982-01-01	12.28	14.59	2.31		122.5
1982-02-01	13.48	14.43	0.95		120.4
1982-03-01	12.68	13.86	1.18		113.1
1982-04-01	12.70	13.87	1.17		111.9
1982-05-01	12.09	13.62	1.53		116.4
1982-06-01	12.47	14.30	1.83		111.8
1982-07-01	11.35	13.95	2.6		109.6
1982-08-01	8.68	13.06	4.38		107
1982-09-01	7.92	12.34	4.42		119.5
1982-10-01	7.71	10.91	3.2		120.4
1982-11-01	8.07	10.55	2.48		133.7
1982-12-01	7.94	10.54	2.6		138.5
1983-01-01	7.86	10.46	2.6		140.6
1983-02-01	8.11	10.72	2.61		145.3
1983-03-01	8.35	10.51	2.16		148
1983-04-01	8.21	10.40	2.19		152.9
1983-05-01	8.19	10.38	2.19		164.4
1983-06-01	8.79	10.85	2.06		162.3
1983-07-01	9.08	11.38	2.3		167.6
1983-08-01	9.34	11.85	2.51		162.5
1983-09-01	9.00	11.65	2.65		164.4
1983-10-01	8.64	11.54	2.9		166
1983-11-01	8.76	11.69	2.93		163.5
1983-12-01	9.00	11.83	2.83		166.4
1984-01-01	8.90	11.67	2.77		164.9
1984-02-01	9.09	11.84	2.75		163.4
1984-03-01	9.52	12.32	2.8		157
1984-04-01	9.69	12.63	2.94		159.1
1984-05-01	9.83	13.41	3.58		160
1984-06-01	9.87	13.56	3.69		150.5
1984-07-01	10.12	13.36	3.24		153.1
1984-08-01	10.47	12.72	2.25		150.6
1984-09-01	10.37	12.52	2.15		166.6
1984-10-01	9.74	12.16	2.42		166.1
1984-11-01	8.61	11.57	2.96		166
1984-12-01	8.06	11.50	3.44		163.5
1985-01-01	7.76	11.38	3.62		167.2
1985-02-01	8.27	11.51	3.24		179.6
1985-03-01	8.52	11.86	3.34		181.1
1985-04-01	7.95	11.43	3.48		180.6
1985-05-01	7.48	10.85	3.37		179.8
1985-06-01	6.95	10.16	3.21		189.5
1985-07-01	7.08	10.31	3.23		191.8

Date	Three-Month Bill	Ten-Year Note	Ten-Year Minus Three-Month	Trade	S&P 500 Index
1985-08-01	7.14	10.33	3.19		190.9
1985-09-01	7.10	10.37	3.27		188.6
1985-10-01	7.16	10.24	3.08		182
1985-11-01	7.24	9.78	2.54		189.8
1985-12-01	7.10	9.26	2.16		202.1
1986-01-01	7.07	9.19	2.12		211.2
1986-02-01	7.06	8.70	1.64		211.7
1986-03-01	6.56	7.78	1.22		226.9
1986-04-01	6.06	7.30	1.24		238.9
1986-05-01	6.15	7.71	1.56		235.5
1986-06-01	6.21	7.80	1.59		247.3
1986-07-01	5.83	7.30	1.47		250.8
1986-08-01	5.53	7.17	1.64		236.1
1986-09-01	5.21	7.45	2.24		252.9
1986-10-01	5.18	7.43	2.25		231.3
1986-11-01	5.35	7.25	1.9		243.9
1986-12-01	5.53	7.11	1.58		249.2
1987-01-01	5.43	7.08	1.65		242.1
1987-02-01	5.59	7.25	1.66		274
1987-03-01	5.59	7.25	1.66		284.2
1987-04-01	5.64	8.02	2.38		291.7
1987-05-01	5.66	8.61	2.95		288.3
1987-06-01	5.67	8.40	2.73		290.1
1987-07-01	5.69	8.45	2.76		304
1987-08-01	6.04	8.76	2.72		318.6
1987-09-01	6.40	9.42	3.02		329.8
1987-10-01	6.13	9.52	3.39		321.8
1987-11-01	5.69	8.86	3.17		251.7
1987-12-01	5.77	8.99	3.22		230.3
1988-01-01	5.81	8.67	2.86		247
1988-02-01	5.66	8.21	2.55		257
1988-03-01	5.70	8.37	2.67		267.8
1988-04-01	5.91	8.72	2.81		258.8
1988-05-01	6.26	9.09	2.83		261.3
1988-06-01	6.46	8.92	2.46		262.1
1988-07-01	6.73	9.06	2.33		273.5
1988-08-01	7.06	9.26	2.2		272
1988-09-01	7.24	8.98	1.74		261.5
1988-10-01	7.35	8.80	1.45		271.9
1988-11-01	7.76	8.96	1.2		278.9
1988-12-01	8.07	9.11	1.04		273.7
1989-01-01	8.27	9.09	0.82		277.7
1989-02-01	8.53	9.17	0.64		297.4
1989-03-01	8.82	9.36	0.54		288.8

(continues)

Date	Three-Month Bill	Ten-Year Note	Ten-Year Minus Three-Month	Trade	S&P 500 Index
1989-04-01	8.65	9.18	0.53		294.8
1989-05-01	8.43	8.86	0.43		309.6
1989-06-01	8.15	8.28	0.13		320.5
1989-07-01	7.88	8.02	0.14		317.9
1989-08-01	7.90	8.11	0.21		346
1989-09-01	7.75	8.19	0.44		351.4
1989-10-01	7.64	8.01	0.37		349.1
1989-11-01	**7.69**	**7.87**	**0.18**		**340.3**
1989-12-01	7.63	7.84	0.21		345.9
1990-01-01	**7.64**	**8.21**	**0.57**		**353.4**
1990-02-01	7.74	8.47	0.73		329
1990-03-01	7.90	8.59	0.69		331.8
1990-04-01	7.77	8.79	1.02		339.9
1990-05-01	7.74	8.76	1.02		330.8
1990-06-01	7.73	8.48	0.75		361.2
1990-07-01	7.62	8.47	0.85		358
1990-08-01	7.45	8.75	1.3		356.1
1990-09-01	7.36	8.89	1.53		322.5
1990-10-01	7.17	8.72	1.55		306
1990-11-01	7.06	8.39	1.33		304
1990-12-01	6.74	8.08	1.34		322.2
1991-01-01	6.22	8.09	1.87		330.2
1991-02-01	5.94	7.85	1.91		343.9
1991-03-01	5.91	8.11	2.2		367
1991-04-01	5.65	8.04	2.39		375.2
1991-05-01	5.46	8.07	2.61		375.3
1991-06-01	5.57	8.28	2.71		389.8
1991-07-01	5.58	8.27	2.69		371.1
1991-08-01	5.33	7.90	2.57		387.8
1991-09-01	5.22	7.65	2.43		395.4
1991-10-01	4.99	7.53	2.54		387.8
1991-11-01	4.56	7.42	2.86		392.4
1991-12-01	4.07	7.09	3.02		375.2
1992-01-01	3.80	7.03	3.23		417
1992-02-01	3.84	7.34	3.5		408.7
1992-03-01	4.04	7.54	3.5		412.7
1992-04-01	3.75	7.48	3.73		403.6
1992-05-01	3.63	7.39	3.76		414.9
1992-06-01	3.66	7.26	3.6		415.3
1992-07-01	3.21	6.84	3.63		408.1
1992-08-01	3.13	6.59	3.46		424.2
1992-09-01	2.91	6.42	3.51		414
1992-10-01	2.86	6.59	3.73		417.8
1992-11-01	3.13	6.87	3.74		418.6
1992-12-01	3.22	6.77	3.55		431.3

Date	Three-Month Bill	Ten-Year Note	Ten-Year Minus Three-Month	Trade	S&P 500 Index
1993-01-01	3.00	6.60	3.6		435.7
1993-02-01	2.93	6.26	3.33		438.7
1993-03-01	2.95	5.98	3.03		443.3
1993-04-01	2.87	5.97	3.1		451.6
1993-05-01	2.96	6.04	3.08		440.1
1993-06-01	3.07	5.96	2.89		450.1
1993-07-01	3.04	5.81	2.77		450.5
1993-08-01	3.02	5.68	2.66		448.1
1993-09-01	2.95	5.36	2.41		463.5
1993-10-01	3.02	5.33	2.31		458.9
1993-11-01	3.10	5.72	2.62		467.8
1993-12-01	3.06	5.77	2.71		461.7
1994-01-01	2.98	5.75	2.77		466.4
1994-02-01	3.25	5.97	2.72		481.6
1994-03-01	3.50	6.48	2.98		467.1
1994-04-01	3.68	6.97	3.29		445.7
1994-05-01	4.14	7.18	3.04		450.9
1994-06-01	4.14	7.10	2.96		456.5
1994-07-01	4.33	7.30	2.97		444.2
1994-08-01	4.48	7.24	2.76		458.2
1994-09-01	4.62	7.46	2.84		475.4
1994-10-01	4.95	7.74	2.79		462.7
1994-11-01	5.29	7.96	2.67		472.3
1994-12-01	5.60	7.81	2.21		453.6
1995-01-01	5.71	7.78	2.07		459.2
1995-02-01	5.77	7.47	1.7		470.4
1995-03-01	5.73	7.20	1.47		487.3
1995-04-01	5.65	7.06	1.41		500.7
1995-05-01	5.67	6.63	0.96		514.7
1995-06-01	5.47	6.17	0.7		533.4
1995-07-01	5.42	6.28	0.86		544.7
1995-08-01	5.40	6.49	1.09		562
1995-09-01	5.28	6.20	0.92		561.8
1995-10-01	5.28	6.04	0.76		584.4
1995-11-01	5.36	5.93	0.57		581.5
1995-12-01	5.14	5.71	0.57		605.3
1996-01-01	5.00	5.65	0.65		615.9
1996-02-01	4.83	5.81	0.98		636
1996-03-01	4.96	6.27	1.31		640.4
1996-04-01	4.95	6.51	1.56		645.5
1996-05-01	5.02	6.74	1.72		654.1
1996-06-01	5.09	6.91	1.82		669.1
1996-07-01	5.15	6.87	1.72		670.6
1996-08-01	5.05	6.64	1.59		639.9

(continues)

Date	Three-Month Bill	Ten-Year Note	Ten-Year Minus Three-Month	Trade	S&P 500 Index
1996-09-01	5.09	6.83	1.74		651.9
1996-10-01	4.99	6.53	1.54		687.3
1996-11-01	5.03	6.20	1.17		705.2
1996-12-01	4.91	6.30	1.39		757
1997-01-01	5.03	6.58	1.55		740.7
1997-02-01	5.01	6.42	1.41		786.1
1997-03-01	5.14	6.69	1.55		790.8
1997-04-01	5.16	6.89	1.73		757.1
1997-05-01	5.05	6.71	1.66		801.3
1997-06-01	4.93	6.49	1.56		848.2
1997-07-01	5.05	6.22	1.17		885.1
1997-08-01	5.14	6.30	1.16		954.3
1997-09-01	4.95	6.21	1.26		899.4
1997-10-01	4.97	6.03	1.06		947.2
1997-11-01	5.14	5.88	0.74		914.6
1997-12-01	5.16	5.81	0.65		955.4
1998-01-01	5.04	5.54	0.5		970.4
1998-02-01	5.09	5.57	0.48		980.2
1998-03-01	5.03	5.65	0.62		1049
1998-04-01	4.95	5.64	0.69		1101
1998-05-01	5.00	5.65	0.65		1111
1998-06-01	4.98	5.50	0.52		1090
1998-07-01	4.96	5.46	0.5		1133
1998-08-01	4.90	5.34	0.44		1120
1998-09-01	4.61	4.81	0.2		957.2
1998-10-01	3.96	4.53	0.57		1017
1998-11-01	4.41	4.83	0.42		1098
1998-12-01	4.39	4.65	0.26		1163
1999-01-01	4.34	4.72	0.38		1229
1999-02-01	4.44	5.00	0.56		1279
1999-03-01	4.44	5.23	0.79		1238
1999-04-01	4.29	5.18	0.89		1286
1999-05-01	4.50	5.54	1.04		1335
1999-06-01	4.57	5.90	1.33		1301
1999-07-01	4.55	5.79	1.24		1372
1999-08-01	4.72	5.94	1.22		1328
1999-09-01	4.68	5.92	1.24		1320
1999-10-01	4.86	6.11	1.25		1282
1999-11-01	5.07	6.03	0.96		1362
1999-12-01	5.20	6.28	1.08		1389
2000-01-01	5.32	6.66	1.34		1469
2000-02-01	5.55	6.52	0.97		1394
2000-03-01	5.69	6.26	0.57		1366
2000-04-01	5.66	5.99	0.33		1498
2000-05-01	5.79	6.44	0.65		1452

Date	Three-Month Bill	Ten-Year Note	Ten-Year Minus Three-Month	Trade	S&P 500 Index
2000-06-01	5.69	6.10	0.41		1420
2000-07-01	5.96	6.05	0.09		1454
2000-08-01	**6.09**	**5.83**	**–0.26**	**Sell**	**1430**
2000-09-01	6.00	5.80	–0.2		1517
2000-10-01	6.11	5.74	–0.37		1436
2000-11-01	6.17	5.72	–0.45		1429
2000-12-01	5.77	5.24	–0.53		1314
2001-01-01	**5.15**	**5.16**	**0.01**	**Buy**	**1320**
2001-02-01	4.88	5.10	0.22		1367
2001-03-01	4.42	4.89	0.47		1239
2001-04-01	3.87	5.14	1.27		1160
2001-05-01	3.62	5.39	1.77		1249
2001-06-01	3.49	5.28	1.79		1255
2001-07-01	3.51	5.24	1.73		1226
2001-08-01	3.36	4.97	1.61		1211
2001-09-01	2.64	4.73	2.09		1133
2001-10-01	2.16	4.57	2.41		1040
2001-11-01	1.87	4.65	2.78		1059
2001-12-01	1.69	5.09	3.4		1139
2002-01-01	1.65	5.04	3.39		1148
2002-02-01	1.73	4.91	3.18		1130
2002-03-01	1.79	5.28	3.49		1106
2002-04-01	1.72	5.21	3.49		1147
2002-05-01	1.73	5.16	3.43		1086
2002-06-01	1.70	4.93	3.23		1067
2002-07-01	1.68	4.65	2.97		989.8
2002-08-01	1.62	4.26	2.64		911.6
2002-09-01	1.63	3.87	2.24		916
2002-10-01	1.58	3.94	2.36		815.2
2002-11-01	1.23	4.05	2.82		885.7
2002-12-01	1.19	4.03	2.84		936.3
2003-01-01	1.17	4.05	2.88		879.8
2003-02-01	1.17	3.90	2.73		855.7
2003-03-01	1.13	3.81	2.68		841.1
2003-04-01	1.13	3.96	2.83		848.1
2003-05-01	1.07	3.57	2.5		916.92
2003-06-01	0.92	3.33	2.41		963.59
2003-07-01	0.90	3.98	3.08		974.5
2003-08-01	0.95	4.45	3.5		990.31
2003-09-01	0.94	4.27	3.33		1008.01
2003-10-01	0.92	4.29	3.37		995.97
2003-11-01	0.93	4.30	3.37		1050.71
2003-12-01	0.90	4.27	3.37		1058.2
2004-01-01	0.88	4.15	3.27		1111.92

Date	S&P 500 Index	One + % Gain/Loss	Old Index	× Change	New Index
1/1/1960	59	1 + (77 − 59/59)	1.00	1.035	1.305
9/1/66	77				
2/1/67	86	1 + (97 − 86/86)	1.305	1.1279	1.4719
7/1/69	97				
2/1/70	85	1 + (105 − 85/85)	1.4719	1.235	1.8182
6/1/73	105				
10/1/74	63	1 + (94 − 63/63)	1.8182	1.49206	2.71286
12/1/78	94				
5/1/80	106	1 + (127 − 106/106)	2.71286	1.1981	3.2503
11/1/80	127				
9/1/81	122	1 + (340 − 122/122)	3.2503	2.7868	9.0582
10/31/89	340				
1/2/1990	353	1 + (1430 − 353/353)	9.0582	4.05099	36.6946
8/1/00	1430				
1/1/01	1320	1 − (1320 − 815/1320)	36.6946	−0.61742	22.65613
10/1/02	815	Market Low			

Returns	Annualized Returns		Value Added by Trading	
Buy and Hold: 815 − 59/59 = 12.81355				
Return = 41.75th root of index:	*Buy & Hold*	*Trade*		
12.81355 = 1.06299				
Or 6.30%	6.30%			
Trading: 41.75th root of index:				
22.65613 = 1.0776048				
Or 7.76%		7.76%	1.46% (23% more return)	

	Value of $1		
	Buy & Hold	*Trade*	
Buy and Hold Index: 12.81355	$12.81		
Trading Index: 22.65613		$22.66	$9.85 (77% more return)

Date	3 mo.	6 mo.	1 yr.	3–6 mo.	3 mo.– 1 yr.	6 mo.– 1 yr.	OK to Buy?	S&P 500 Index
1960-01-01	3.96	4.30	4.66	0.34	0.70	0.36	OK to buy	59.89
1960-02-01	3.31	3.61	4.02	0.30	0.71	0.41		55.61
1960-03-01	3.31	3.61	4.02	0.30	0.71	0.41		56.12
1960-04-01	3.23	3.55	4.04	0.32	0.81	0.49		55.34
1960-05-01	3.29	3.58	4.21	0.29	0.92	0.63		54.37
1960-06-01	2.46	2.74	3.36	0.28	0.90	0.62		55.83
1960-07-01	2.30	2.71	3.20	0.41	0.90	0.49		56.92
1960-08-01	2.30	2.59	2.95	0.29	0.65	0.36		55.51
1960-09-01	2.48	2.83	3.07	0.35	0.59	0.24		56.96
1960-10-01	2.30	2.73	3.04	0.43	0.74	0.31		53.52
1960-11-01	2.37	2.66	3.08	0.29	0.71	0.42		53.39
1960-12-01	2.25	2.50	2.86	0.25	0.61	0.36		55.54
1961-01-01	2.24	2.47	2.81	0.23	0.57	0.34		58.11
1961-02-01	2.42	2.60	2.93	0.18	0.51	0.33		61.78
1961-03-01	2.39	2.54	2.88	0.15	0.49	0.34		63.44
1961-04-01	2.29	2.47	2.88	0.18	0.59	0.41		65.06
1961-05-01	2.29	2.45	2.87	0.16	0.58	0.42		65.31
1961-06-01	2.33	2.54	3.06	0.21	0.73	0.52		66.56
1961-07-01	2.24	2.45	2.92	0.21	0.68	0.47		64.64
1961-08-01	2.39	2.66	3.06	0.27	0.67	0.40		66.76
1961-09-01	2.28	2.68	3.06	0.40	0.78	0.38		68.07
1961-10-01	2.30	2.66	3.05	0.36	0.75	0.39		66.73
1961-11-01	2.48	2.70	3.07	0.22	0.59	0.37		68.62
1961-12-01	2.60	2.88	3.18	0.28	0.58	0.30		71.32
1962-01-01	2.72	2.94	3.28	0.22	0.56	0.34		71.55
1962-02-01	2.73	2.93	3.28	0.20	0.55	0.35		68.84
1962-03-01	2.72	2.87	3.06	0.15	0.34	0.19		69.96
1962-04-01	2.73	2.83	2.99	0.10	0.26	0.16		69.55
1962-05-01	2.69	2.78	3.03	0.09	0.34	0.25		65.24
1962-06-01	2.73	2.80	3.03	0.07	0.30	0.23		59.63
1962-07-01	2.92	3.08	3.29	0.16	0.37	0.21		54.75
1962-08-01	2.82	2.99	3.20	0.17	0.38	0.21		58.23
1962-09-01	2.78	2.93	3.06	0.15	0.28	0.13		59.12
1962-10-01	2.74	2.84	2.98	0.10	0.24	0.14		56.27
1962-11-01	2.83	2.89	3.00	0.06	0.17	0.11		56.52
1962-12-01	2.87	2.91	3.01	0.04	0.14	0.10		62.26
1963-01-01	2.91	2.96	3.04	0.05	0.13	0.08		63.1
1963-02-01	2.92	2.98	3.01	0.06	0.09	0.03		66.2
1963-03-01	2.89	2.95	3.03	0.06	0.14	0.08		64.29
1963-04-01	2.90	2.98	3.11	0.08	0.21	0.13		66.57

Note: Yields are secondary market discounts annualized to a 360-day year.

Source: www.federalreserve.gov/releases/h15/data; click on: All historical data files.

(continues)

Date	3 mo.	6 mo.	1 yr.	3–6 mo.	3 mo.– 1 yr.	6 mo.– 1 yr.	OK to Buy?	S&P 500 Index
1963-05-01	2.93	3.01	3.12	0.08	0.19	0.11		69.8
1963-06-01	2.99	3.08	3.20	0.09	0.21	0.12		70.8
1963-07-01	3.18	3.31	3.48	0.13	0.30	0.17		69.37
1963-08-01	3.32	3.44	3.53	0.12	0.21	0.09		69.13
1963-09-01	3.38	3.50	3.57	0.12	0.19	0.07		72.5
1963-10-01	3.45	3.58	3.64	0.13	0.19	0.06		71.7
1963-11-01	3.52	3.65	3.74	0.13	0.22	0.09		74.01
1963-12-01	3.52	3.66	3.81	0.14	0.29	0.15		73.23
1964-01-01	3.52	3.64	3.79	0.12	0.27	0.15		75.02
1964-02-01	3.53	3.67	3.78	0.14	0.25	0.11		77.04
1964-03-01	3.54	3.72	3.91	0.18	0.37	0.19		77.8
1964-04-01	3.47	3.66	3.91	0.19	0.44	0.25		78.98
1964-05-01	3.48	3.60	3.84	0.12	0.36	0.24		79.46
1964-06-01	3.48	3.56	3.83	0.08	0.35	0.27		80.37
1964-07-01	3.46	3.56	3.72	0.10	0.26	0.16		81.69
1964-08-01	3.50	3.61	3.74	0.11	0.24	0.13		83.18
1964-09-01	3.53	3.68	3.84	0.15	0.31	0.16		81.83
1964-10-01	3.57	3.72	3.86	0.15	0.29	0.14		84.18
1964-11-01	3.64	3.81	3.91	0.17	0.27	0.10		84.86
1964-12-01	3.84	3.95	4.02	0.11	0.18	0.07		84.42
1965-01-01	3.81	3.94	3.94	0.13	0.13	0.00		84.75
1965-02-01	3.93	4.00	4.03	0.07	0.10	0.03		87.56
1965-03-01	3.93	4.00	4.06	0.07	0.13	0.06		87.43
1965-04-01	3.93	3.99	4.04	0.06	0.11	0.05		86.16
1965-05-01	3.89	3.95	4.03	0.06	0.14	0.08		89.11
1965-06-01	3.80	3.86	3.99	0.06	0.19	0.13		88.42
1965-07-01	3.84	3.90	3.98	0.06	0.14	0.08		84.12
1965-08-01	3.84	3.95	4.07	0.11	0.23	0.12		85.25
1965-09-01	3.92	4.07	4.20	0.15	0.28	0.13		87.17
1965-10-01	4.03	4.19	4.30	0.16	0.27	0.11		89.96
1965-11-01	4.09	4.24	4.37	0.15	0.28	0.13		92.42
1965-12-01	4.38	4.55	4.72	0.17	0.34	0.17		91.61
1966-01-01	4.59	4.71	4.88	0.12	0.29	0.17		92.43
1966-02-01	4.65	4.82	4.94	0.17	0.29	0.12		92.88
1966-03-01	4.59	4.78	4.97	0.19	0.38	0.19		91.22
1966-04-01	4.62	4.74	4.90	0.12	0.28	0.16		89.23
1966-05-01	4.64	4.81	4.93	0.17	0.29	0.12		91.06
1966-06-01	4.50	4.65	4.97	0.15	0.47	0.32		86.13
1966-07-01	4.80	4.93	5.17	0.13	0.37	0.24		84.74
1966-08-01	4.96	5.27	5.54	0.31	0.58	0.27		83.6
1966-09-01	5.37	5.79	5.82	0.42	0.45	0.03		77.1
1966-10-01	5.35	5.62	5.58	0.27	0.23	-0.04		76.56
1966-11-01	5.32	5.54	5.54	0.22	0.22	0.00		80.2
1966-12-01	4.96	5.07	5.20	0.11	0.24	0.13		80.45
1967-01-01	4.72	4.74	4.75	0.02	0.03	0.01		80.33

Date	3 mo.	6 mo.	1 yr.	3–6 mo.	3 mo.–1 yr.	6 mo.–1 yr.	OK to Buy?	S&P 500 Index
1967-02-01	4.56	4.59	4.71	0.03	0.15	0.12	OK to buy	86.61
1967-03-01	4.26	4.22	4.35	-0.04	0.09	0.13		86.78
1967-04-01	3.84	3.89	4.11	0.05	0.27	0.22		90.2
1967-05-01	3.60	3.80	4.15	0.20	0.55	0.35		94.01
1967-06-01	3.54	3.89	4.48	0.35	0.94	0.59		89.08
1967-07-01	4.21	4.72	5.01	0.51	0.80	0.29		90.64
1967-08-01	4.27	4.83	5.13	0.56	0.86	0.30		94.75
1967-09-01	4.42	4.96	5.24	0.54	0.82	0.28		93.64
1967-10-01	4.56	5.07	5.37	0.51	0.81	0.30		96.71
1967-11-01	4.73	5.25	5.61	0.52	0.88	0.36		93.3
1967-12-01	4.97	5.49	5.71	0.52	0.74	0.22		94
1968-01-01	5.00	5.24	5.43	0.24	0.43	0.19		96.47
1968-02-01	4.98	5.17	5.41	0.19	0.43	0.24		92.24
1968-03-01	5.17	5.33	5.58	0.16	0.41	0.25		89.36
1968-04-01	5.38	5.49	5.71	0.11	0.33	0.22		90.2
1968-05-01	5.66	5.83	6.14	0.17	0.48	0.31		97.46
1968-06-01	5.52	5.64	5.98	0.12	0.46	0.34		98.68
1968-07-01	5.31	5.41	5.65	0.10	0.34	0.24		99.58
1968-08-01	5.09	5.23	5.43	0.14	0.34	0.20		97.74
1968-09-01	5.19	5.25	5.45	0.06	0.26	0.20		98.86
1968-10-01	5.35	5.41	5.57	0.06	0.22	0.16		102.6
1968-11-01	5.45	5.60	5.75	0.15	0.30	0.15		103.4
1968-12-01	5.96	6.06	6.19	0.10	0.23	0.13		108.3
1969-01-01	6.14	6.28	6.34	0.14	0.20	0.06		103.8
1969-02-01	6.12	6.30	6.41	0.18	0.29	0.11		103
1969-03-01	6.02	6.16	6.34	0.14	0.32	0.18		98.13
1969-04-01	6.11	6.13	6.26	0.02	0.15	0.13		101.5
1969-05-01	6.04	6.15	6.42	0.11	0.38	0.27		103.6
1969-06-01	6.44	6.75	7.04	0.31	0.60	0.29		103.4
1969-07-01	7.00	7.24	7.60	0.24	0.60	0.36		97.71
1969-08-01	6.98	7.19	7.54	0.21	0.56	0.35		91.83
1969-09-01	7.09	7.32	7.82	0.23	0.73	0.50		95.51
1969-10-01	7.00	7.29	7.64	0.29	0.64	0.35		93.12
1969-11-01	7.24	7.62	7.89	0.38	0.65	0.27		97.12
1969-12-01	7.82	7.90	8.17	0.08	0.35	0.27		93.81
1970-01-01	7.87	7.78	8.10	-0.09	0.23	0.32		92.06
1970-02-01	7.13	7.22	7.59	0.09	0.46	0.37	OK to buy	85.02
1970-03-01	6.63	6.58	6.97	-0.05	0.34	0.39		89.5
1970-04-01	6.51	6.60	7.06	0.09	0.55	0.46		89.63
1970-05-01	6.84	7.02	7.75	0.18	0.91	0.73		81.52
1970-06-01	6.68	6.86	7.55	0.18	0.87	0.69		76.55
1970-07-01	6.45	6.51	7.10	0.06	0.65	0.59		72.72
1970-08-01	6.41	6.55	6.98	0.14	0.57	0.43		78.05
1970-09-01	6.12	6.46	6.73	0.34	0.61	0.27		81.52

(continues)

Date	3 mo.	6 mo.	1 yr.	3–6 mo.	3 mo.–1 yr.	6 mo.–1 yr.	OK to Buy?	S&P 500 Index
1970-10-01	5.91	6.21	6.43	0.30	0.52	0.22		84.3
1970-11-01	5.28	5.42	5.51	0.14	0.23	0.09		83.25
1970-12-01	4.87	4.89	5.00	0.02	0.13	0.11		87.2
1971-01-01	4.44	4.47	4.57	0.03	0.13	0.10		92.15
1971-02-01	3.70	3.78	3.89	0.08	0.19	0.11		95.88
1971-03-01	3.38	3.50	3.69	0.12	0.31	0.19		96.75
1971-04-01	3.86	4.03	4.30	0.17	0.44	0.27		100.3
1971-05-01	4.14	4.36	5.04	0.22	0.90	0.68		103.9
1971-06-01	4.75	4.97	5.64	0.22	0.89	0.67		99.63
1971-07-01	5.40	5.63	6.04	0.23	0.64	0.41		98.7
1971-08-01	4.94	5.22	5.80	0.28	0.86	0.58		95.58
1971-09-01	4.69	4.97	5.41	0.28	0.72	0.44		99.03
1971-10-01	4.46	4.60	4.91	0.14	0.45	0.31		98.34
1971-11-01	4.22	4.38	4.67	0.16	0.45	0.29		94.23
1971-12-01	4.01	4.23	4.60	0.22	0.59	0.37		93.99
1972-01-01	3.38	3.66	4.28	0.28	0.90	0.62		102
1972-02-01	3.20	3.63	4.27	0.43	1.07	0.64		103.9
1972-03-01	3.73	4.12	4.67	0.39	0.94	0.55		106.5
1972-04-01	3.71	4.23	4.96	0.52	1.25	0.73		107.2
1972-05-01	3.69	4.12	4.64	0.43	0.95	0.52		107.6
1972-06-01	3.91	4.35	4.93	0.44	1.02	0.58		109.5
1972-07-01	3.98	4.50	4.96	0.52	0.98	0.46		107.1
1972-08-01	4.02	4.55	4.98	0.53	0.96	0.43		107.3
1972-09-01	4.66	5.13	5.52	0.47	0.86	0.39		111
1972-10-01	4.74	5.13	5.52	0.39	0.78	0.39		110.5
1972-11-01	4.78	5.09	5.27	0.31	0.49	0.18		111.5
1972-12-01	5.07	5.30	5.52	0.23	0.45	0.22		116.6
1973-01-01	5.41	5.62	5.89	0.21	0.48	0.27		118
1973-02-01	5.60	5.83	6.19	0.23	0.59	0.36		116
1973-03-01	6.09	6.51	6.85	0.42	0.76	0.34		111.6
1973-04-01	6.26	6.52	6.85	0.26	0.59	0.33		111.5
1973-05-01	6.36	6.62	6.89	0.26	0.53	0.27		106.9
1973-06-01	7.19	7.23	7.31	0.04	0.12	0.08		104.9
1973-07-01	8.01	8.12	8.39	0.11	0.38	0.27		104.2
1973-08-01	8.67	8.65	8.82	−0.02	0.15	0.17		108.2
1973-09-01	8.29	8.45	8.31	0.16	0.02	−0.14		104.2
1973-10-01	7.22	7.32	7.40	0.10	0.18	0.08		108.4
1973-11-01	7.83	7.96	7.57	0.13	−0.26	−0.39		108.2
1973-12-01	7.45	7.56	7.27	0.11	−0.18	−0.29		95.96
1974-01-01	7.77	7.65	7.42	−0.12	−0.35	−0.23		97.55
1974-02-01	7.12	6.96	6.88	−0.16	−0.24	−0.08		96.57
1974-03-01	7.96	7.83	7.76	−0.13	−0.20	−0.07		96.22
1974-04-01	8.33	8.32	8.62	−0.01	0.29	0.30		93.98
1974-05-01	8.23	8.40	8.78	0.17	0.55	0.38		90.31
1974-06-01	7.90	8.12	8.67	0.22	0.77	0.55		87.28

Date	3 mo.	6 mo.	1 yr.	3–6 mo.	3 mo.– 1 yr.	6 mo.– 1 yr.	OK to Buy?	S&P 500 Index
1974-07-01	7.55	7.94	8.80	0.39	1.25	0.86		86
1974-08-01	8.96	9.11	9.36	0.15	0.40	0.25		79.31
1974-09-01	8.06	8.53	8.87	0.47	0.81	0.34		72.15
1974-10-01	7.46	7.74	8.05	0.28	0.59	0.31	OK to buy	63.54
1974-11-01	7.47	7.52	7.66	0.05	0.19	0.14		73.9
1974-12-01	7.15	7.11	7.31	−0.04	0.16	0.20		69.97
1975-01-01	6.26	6.36	6.83	0.10	0.57	0.47		68.56
1975-02-01	5.50	5.62	5.98	0.12	0.48	0.36		76.98
1975-03-01	5.49	5.62	6.11	0.13	0.62	0.49		81.59
1975-04-01	5.61	6.00	6.90	0.39	1.29	0.90		83.36
1975-05-01	5.23	5.59	6.39	0.36	1.16	0.80		87.3
1975-06-01	5.34	5.61	6.29	0.27	0.95	0.68		91.15
1975-07-01	6.13	6.50	7.11	0.37	0.98	0.61		95.19
1975-08-01	6.44	6.94	7.70	0.50	1.26	0.76		88.75
1975-09-01	6.42	6.92	7.75	0.50	1.33	0.83		86.88
1975-10-01	5.96	6.25	6.95	0.29	0.99	0.70		83.87
1975-11-01	5.48	5.80	6.49	0.32	1.01	0.69		89.04
1975-12-01	5.44	5.85	6.60	0.41	1.16	0.75		91.24
1976-01-01	4.87	5.14	5.81	0.27	0.94	0.67		90.19
1976-02-01	4.88	5.20	5.91	0.32	1.03	0.71		100.8
1976-03-01	5.00	5.44	6.21	0.44	1.21	0.77		99.71
1976-04-01	4.86	5.18	5.92	0.32	1.06	0.74		102.7
1976-05-01	5.20	5.62	6.40	0.42	1.20	0.78		101.6
1976-06-01	5.41	5.77	6.52	0.36	1.11	0.75		100.1
1976-07-01	5.23	5.53	6.20	0.30	0.97	0.67		104.2
1976-08-01	5.14	5.40	6.00	0.26	0.86	0.60		103.4
1976-09-01	5.08	5.30	5.84	0.22	0.76	0.54		102.9
1976-10-01	4.92	5.06	5.50	0.14	0.58	0.44		105.2
1976-11-01	4.75	4.88	5.29	0.13	0.54	0.41		102.9
1976-12-01	4.35	4.51	4.89	0.16	0.54	0.38		102.1
1977-01-01	4.62	4.83	5.29	0.21	0.67	0.46		107.4
1977-02-01	4.67	4.90	5.47	0.23	0.80	0.57		102
1977-03-01	4.60	4.88	5.50	0.28	0.90	0.62		99.82
1977-04-01	4.54	4.80	5.44	0.26	0.90	0.64		98.42
1977-05-01	4.96	5.20	5.84	0.24	0.88	0.64		98.44
1977-06-01	5.02	5.21	5.80	0.19	0.78	0.59		96.12
1977-07-01	5.19	5.40	5.94	0.21	0.75	0.54		100.4
1977-08-01	5.49	5.83	6.37	0.34	0.88	0.54		98.85
1977-09-01	5.81	6.04	6.53	0.23	0.72	0.49		96.77
1977-10-01	6.16	6.43	6.97	0.27	0.81	0.54		96.53
1977-11-01	6.10	6.41	6.95	0.31	0.85	0.54		92.34
1977-12-01	6.07	6.40	6.96	0.33	0.89	0.56		94.83
1978-01-01	6.44	6.70	7.28	0.26	0.84	0.58		95.1
1978-02-01	6.45	6.74	7.34	0.29	0.89	0.60		89.25

(continues)

Date	3 mo.	6 mo.	1 yr.	3–6 mo.	3 mo.– 1 yr.	6 mo.– 1 yr.	OK to Buy?	S&P 500 Index
1978-03-01	6.29	6.63	7.31	0.34	1.02	0.68		87.04
1978-04-01	6.29	6.73	7.45	0.44	1.16	0.72		89.21
1978-05-01	6.41	7.02	7.82	0.61	1.41	0.80		96.83
1978-06-01	6.73	7.23	8.09	0.50	1.36	0.86		97.24
1978-07-01	7.01	7.44	8.39	0.43	1.38	0.95		95.53
1978-08-01	7.08	7.37	8.31	0.29	1.23	0.94		100.6
1978-09-01	7.85	7.99	8.64	0.14	0.79	0.65		103.2
1978-10-01	7.99	8.55	9.14	0.56	1.15	0.59		102.5
1978-11-01	8.64	9.24	10.01	0.60	1.37	0.77		93.15
1978-12-01	9.08	9.36	10.30	0.28	1.22	0.94		94.7
1979-01-01	9.35	9.47	10.41	0.12	1.06	0.94		96.11
1979-02-01	9.32	9.41	10.24	0.09	0.92	0.83		99.93
1979-03-01	9.48	9.47	10.25	−0.01	0.77	0.78		96.28
1979-04-01	9.46	9.49	10.12	0.03	0.66	0.63		101.5
1979-05-01	9.61	9.54	10.12	−0.07	0.51	0.58		101.7
1979-06-01	9.06	9.06	9.57	0.00	0.51	0.51		99.08
1979-07-01	9.24	9.24	9.64	0.00	0.40	0.40		102.9
1979-08-01	9.52	9.49	9.98	−0.03	0.46	0.49		103.8
1979-09-01	10.26	10.20	10.84	−0.06	0.58	0.64		109.3
1979-10-01	11.70	11.66	12.44	−0.04	0.74	0.78		109.3
1979-11-01	11.79	11.82	12.39	0.03	0.60	0.57		101.8
1979-12-01	12.04	11.84	11.98	−0.20	−0.06	0.14		106.1
1980-01-01	12.00	11.84	12.06	−0.16	0.06	0.22		107.9
1980-02-01	12.86	12.86	13.92	0.00	1.06	1.06		114.1
1980-03-01	15.20	15.03	15.82	−0.17	0.62	0.79		113.6
1980-04-01	13.20	12.88	13.30	−0.32	0.10	0.42		102
1980-05-01	8.58	8.65	9.39	0.07	0.81	0.74	OK to buy	106.2
1980-06-01	7.07	7.30	8.16	0.23	1.09	0.86		111.2
1980-07-01	8.06	8.06	8.65	0.00	0.59	0.59		114.2
1980-08-01	9.13	9.41	10.24	0.28	1.11	0.83		121.6
1980-09-01	10.27	10.57	11.52	0.30	1.25	0.95		122.3
1980-10-01	11.62	11.63	12.49	0.01	0.87	0.86		125.4
1980-11-01	13.73	13.50	14.15	−0.23	0.42	0.65		127.4
1980-12-01	15.49	14.64	14.88	−0.85	−0.61	0.24		140.5
1981-01-01	15.02	14.08	14.08	−0.94	−0.94	0.00		135.7
1981-02-01	14.79	14.05	14.57	−0.74	−0.22	0.52		129.5
1981-03-01	13.36	12.81	13.71	−0.55	0.35	0.90		131.2
1981-04-01	13.69	13.45	14.32	−0.24	0.63	0.87		136
1981-05-01	16.30	15.29	16.20	−1.01	−0.10	0.91		132.8
1981-06-01	14.73	14.09	14.86	−0.64	0.13	0.77		132.5
1981-07-01	14.95	14.74	15.72	−0.21	0.77	0.98		131.2
1981-08-01	15.51	15.52	16.72	0.01	1.21	1.20		130.9
1981-09-01	14.70	14.92	16.52	0.22	1.82	1.60	OK to buy	122.7
1981-10-01	13.54	13.82	15.38	0.28	1.84	1.56		116.1
1981-11-01	10.86	11.30	12.41	0.44	1.55	1.11		121.8

Date	3 mo.	6 mo.	1 yr.	3–6 mo.	3 mo.– 1 yr.	6 mo.– 1 yr.	OK to Buy?	S&P 500 Index
1981-12-01	10.85	11.52	12.85	0.67	2.00	1.33		126.3
1982-01-01	12.28	12.83	14.32	0.55	2.04	1.49		122.5
1982-02-01	13.48	13.61	14.73	0.13	1.25	1.12		120.4
1982-03-01	12.68	12.77	13.95	0.09	1.27	1.18		113.1
1982-04-01	12.70	12.80	13.98	0.10	1.28	1.18		111.9
1982-05-01	12.09	12.16	13.34	0.07	1.25	1.18		116.4
1982-06-01	12.47	12.70	14.07	0.23	1.60	1.37		111.8
1982-07-01	11.35	11.88	13.24	0.53	1.89	1.36		109.6
1982-08-01	8.68	9.88	11.43	1.20	2.75	1.55		107
1982-09-01	7.92	9.37	10.85	1.45	2.93	1.48		119.5
1982-10-01	7.71	8.29	9.32	0.58	1.61	1.03		120.4
1982-11-01	8.07	8.34	9.16	0.27	1.09	0.82		133.7
1982-12-01	7.94	8.16	8.91	0.22	0.97	0.75		138.5
1983-01-01	7.86	7.93	8.62	0.07	0.76	0.69		140.6
1983-02-01	8.11	8.23	8.92	0.12	0.81	0.69		145.3
1983-03-01	8.35	8.37	9.04	0.02	0.69	0.67		148
1983-04-01	8.21	8.30	8.98	0.09	0.77	0.68		152.9
1983-05-01	8.19	8.22	8.90	0.03	0.71	0.68		164.4
1983-06-01	8.79	8.89	9.66	0.10	0.87	0.77		162.3
1983-07-01	9.08	9.26	10.20	0.18	1.12	0.94		167.6
1983-08-01	9.34	9.51	10.53	0.17	1.19	1.02		162.5
1983-09-01	9.00	9.15	10.16	0.15	1.16	1.01		164.4
1983-10-01	8.64	8.83	9.81	0.19	1.17	0.98		166
1983-11-01	8.76	8.93	9.94	0.17	1.18	1.01		163.5
1983-12-01	9.00	9.17	10.11	0.17	1.11	0.94		166.4
1984-01-01	8.90	9.01	9.90	0.11	1.00	0.89		164.9
1984-02-01	9.09	9.18	10.04	0.09	0.95	0.86		163.4
1984-03-01	9.52	9.66	10.59	0.14	1.07	0.93		157
1984-04-01	9.69	9.84	10.90	0.15	1.21	1.06		159.1
1984-05-01	9.83	10.31	11.66	0.48	1.83	1.35		160
1984-06-01	9.87	10.51	12.08	0.64	2.21	1.57		150.5
1984-07-01	10.12	10.52	12.03	0.40	1.91	1.51		153.1
1984-08-01	10.47	10.61	11.82	0.14	1.35	1.21		150.6
1984-09-01	10.37	10.47	11.58	0.10	1.21	1.11		166.6
1984-10-01	9.74	9.87	10.90	0.13	1.16	1.03		166.1
1984-11-01	8.61	8.81	9.82	0.20	1.21	1.01		166
1984-12-01	8.06	8.28	9.33	0.22	1.27	1.05		163.5
1985-01-01	7.76	8.00	9.02	0.24	1.26	1.02		167.2
1985-02-01	8.27	8.39	9.29	0.12	1.02	0.90		179.6
1985-03-01	8.52	8.90	9.86	0.38	1.34	0.96		181.1
1985-04-01	7.95	8.23	9.14	0.28	1.19	0.91		180.6
1985-05-01	7.48	7.65	8.46	0.17	0.98	0.81		179.8
1985-06-01	6.95	7.09	7.80	0.14	0.85	0.71		189.5
1985-07-01	7.08	7.20	7.86	0.12	0.78	0.66		191.8

(continues)

341

Date	3 mo.	6 mo.	1 yr.	3–6 mo.	3 mo.– 1 yr.	6 mo.– 1 yr.	OK to Buy?	S&P 500 Index
1985-08-01	7.14	7.32	8.05	0.18	0.91	0.73		190.9
1985-09-01	7.10	7.27	8.07	0.17	0.97	0.80		188.6
1985-10-01	7.16	7.33	8.01	0.17	0.85	0.68		182
1985-11-01	7.24	7.30	7.88	0.06	0.64	0.58		189.8
1985-12-01	7.10	7.14	7.67	0.04	0.57	0.53		202.1
1986-01-01	7.07	7.16	7.73	0.09	0.66	0.57		211.2
1986-02-01	7.06	7.11	7.61	0.05	0.55	0.50		211.7
1986-03-01	6.56	6.57	7.03	0.01	0.47	0.46		226.9
1986-04-01	6.06	6.08	6.44	0.02	0.38	0.36		238.9
1986-05-01	6.15	6.19	6.65	0.04	0.50	0.46		235.5
1986-06-01	6.21	6.27	6.73	0.06	0.52	0.46		247.3
1986-07-01	5.83	5.86	6.27	0.03	0.44	0.41		250.8
1986-08-01	5.53	5.55	5.93	0.02	0.40	0.38		236.1
1986-09-01	5.21	5.35	5.77	0.14	0.56	0.42		252.9
1986-10-01	5.18	5.26	5.72	0.08	0.54	0.46		231.3
1986-11-01	5.35	5.41	5.80	0.06	0.45	0.39		243.9
1986-12-01	5.53	5.55	5.87	0.02	0.34	0.32		249.2
1987-01-01	5.43	5.44	5.78	0.01	0.35	0.34		242.1
1987-02-01	5.59	5.59	5.96	0.00	0.37	0.37		274
1987-03-01	5.59	5.60	6.03	0.01	0.44	0.43		284.2
1987-04-01	5.64	5.90	6.50	0.26	0.86	0.60		291.7
1987-05-01	5.66	6.05	7.00	0.39	1.34	0.95		288.3
1987-06-01	5.67	5.99	6.80	0.32	1.13	0.81		290.1
1987-07-01	5.69	5.76	6.68	0.07	0.99	0.92		304
1987-08-01	6.04	6.15	7.03	0.11	0.99	0.88		318.6
1987-09-01	6.40	6.64	7.67	0.24	1.27	1.03		329.8
1987-10-01	6.13	6.69	7.59	0.56	1.46	0.90		321.8
1987-11-01	5.69	6.19	6.96	0.50	1.27	0.77		251.7
1987-12-01	5.77	6.36	7.17	0.59	1.40	0.81		230.3
1988-01-01	5.81	6.25	6.99	0.44	1.18	0.74		247
1988-02-01	5.66	5.93	6.64	0.27	0.98	0.71		257
1988-03-01	5.70	5.91	6.71	0.21	1.01	0.80		267.8
1988-04-01	5.91	6.21	7.01	0.30	1.10	0.80		258.8
1988-05-01	6.26	6.56	7.40	0.30	1.14	0.84		261.3
1988-06-01	6.46	6.71	7.49	0.25	1.03	0.78		262.1
1988-07-01	6.73	6.99	7.75	0.26	1.02	0.76		273.5
1988-08-01	7.06	7.39	8.17	0.33	1.11	0.78		272
1988-09-01	7.24	7.43	8.09	0.19	0.85	0.66		261.5
1988-10-01	7.35	7.50	8.11	0.15	0.76	0.61		271.9
1988-11-01	7.76	7.86	8.48	0.10	0.72	0.62		278.9
1988-12-01	8.07	8.22	8.99	0.15	0.92	0.77		273.7
1989-01-01	8.27	8.36	9.05	0.09	0.78	0.69		277.7
1989-02-01	8.53	8.55	9.25	0.02	0.72	0.70		297.4
1989-03-01	8.82	8.85	9.57	0.03	0.75	0.72		288.8
1989-04-01	8.65	8.65	9.36	0.00	0.71	0.71		294.8

Date	3 mo.	6 mo.	1 yr.	3–6 mo.	3 mo.– 1 yr.	6 mo.– 1 yr.	OK to Buy?	S&P 500 Index
1989-05-01	8.43	8.41	8.98	−0.02	0.55	0.57		309.6
1989-06-01	8.15	7.93	8.44	−0.22	0.29	0.51		320.5
1989-07-01	7.88	7.61	7.89	−0.27	0.01	0.28		317.9
1989-08-01	7.90	7.74	8.18	−0.16	0.28	0.44		346
1989-09-01	7.75	7.74	8.22	−0.01	0.47	0.48		351.4
1989-10-01	7.64	7.62	7.99	−0.02	0.35	0.37		349.1
1989-11-01	7.69	7.49	7.77	−0.20	0.08	0.28		340.3
1989-12-01	7.63	7.42	7.72	−0.21	0.09	0.30		345.9
1990-01-01	7.64	7.55	7.92	−0.09	0.28	0.37	Old buy	353.4
1990-02-01	7.74	7.70	8.11	−0.04	0.37	0.41		329
1990-03-01	7.90	7.85	8.35	−0.05	0.45	0.50		331.8
1990-04-01	7.77	7.84	8.40	0.07	0.63	0.56		339.9
1990-05-01	7.74	7.76	8.32	0.02	0.58	0.56		330.8
1990-06-01	7.73	7.63	8.10	−0.10	0.37	0.47		361.2
1990-07-01	7.62	7.52	7.94	−0.10	0.32	0.42		358
1990-08-01	7.45	7.38	7.78	−0.07	0.33	0.40		356.1
1990-09-01	7.36	7.32	7.76	−0.04	0.40	0.44		322.5
1990-10-01	7.17	7.16	7.55	−0.01	0.38	0.39		306
1990-11-01	7.06	7.03	7.31	−0.03	0.25	0.28		304
1990-12-01	6.74	6.70	7.05	−0.04	0.31	0.35		322.2
1991-01-01	6.22	6.28	6.64	0.06	0.42	0.36	New buy	330.2
1991-02-01	5.94	5.93	6.27	−0.01	0.33	0.34		343.9
1991-03-01	5.91	5.92	6.40	0.01	0.49	0.48		367
1991-04-01	5.65	5.71	6.24	0.06	0.59	0.53		375.2
1991-05-01	5.46	5.61	6.13	0.15	0.67	0.52		375.3
1991-06-01	5.57	5.75	6.36	0.18	0.79	0.61		389.8
1991-07-01	5.58	5.70	6.31	0.12	0.73	0.61		371.1
1991-08-01	5.33	5.39	5.78	0.06	0.45	0.39		387.8
1991-09-01	5.22	5.25	5.57	0.03	0.35	0.32		395.4
1991-10-01	4.99	5.04	5.33	0.05	0.34	0.29		387.8
1991-11-01	4.56	4.61	4.89	0.05	0.33	0.28		392.4
1991-12-01	4.07	4.10	4.38	0.03	0.31	0.28		375.2
1992-01-01	3.80	3.87	4.15	0.07	0.35	0.28		417
1992-02-01	3.84	3.93	4.29	0.09	0.45	0.36		408.7
1992-03-01	4.04	4.18	4.63	0.14	0.59	0.45		412.7
1992-04-01	3.75	3.87	4.30	0.12	0.55	0.43		403.6
1992-05-01	3.63	3.75	4.19	0.12	0.56	0.44		414.9
1992-06-01	3.66	3.77	4.17	0.11	0.51	0.40		415.3
1992-07-01	3.21	3.28	3.60	0.07	0.39	0.32		408.1
1992-08-01	3.13	3.21	3.47	0.08	0.34	0.26		424.2
1992-09-01	2.91	2.96	3.18	0.05	0.27	0.22		414
1992-10-01	2.86	3.04	3.30	0.18	0.44	0.26		417.8
1992-11-01	3.13	3.34	3.68	0.21	0.55	0.34		418.6
1992-12-01	3.22	3.36	3.71	0.14	0.49	0.35		431.3

(continues)

Date	3 mo.	6 mo.	1 yr.	3–6 mo.	3 mo.– 1 yr.	6 mo.– 1 yr.	OK to Buy?	S&P 500 Index
1993-01-01	3.00	3.14	3.50	0.14	0.50	0.36		435.7
1993-02-01	2.93	3.07	3.39	0.14	0.46	0.32		438.7
1993-03-01	2.95	3.05	3.33	0.10	0.38	0.28		443.3
1993-04-01	2.87	2.97	3.24	0.10	0.37	0.27		451.6
1993-05-01	2.96	3.07	3.36	0.11	0.40	0.29		440.1
1993-06-01	3.07	3.20	3.54	0.13	0.47	0.34		450.1
1993-07-01	3.04	3.16	3.47	0.12	0.43	0.31		450.5
1993-08-01	3.02	3.14	3.44	0.12	0.42	0.30		448.1
1993-09-01	2.95	3.06	3.36	0.11	0.41	0.30		463.5
1993-10-01	3.02	3.12	3.39	0.10	0.37	0.27		458.9
1993-11-01	3.10	3.26	3.58	0.16	0.48	0.32		467.8
1993-12-01	3.06	3.23	3.61	0.17	0.55	0.38		461.7
1994-01-01	2.98	3.15	3.54	0.17	0.56	0.39		466.4
1994-02-01	3.25	3.43	3.87	0.18	0.62	0.44		481.6
1994-03-01	3.50	3.78	4.32	0.28	0.82	0.54		467.1
1994-04-01	3.68	4.09	4.82	0.41	1.14	0.73		445.7
1994-05-01	4.14	4.60	5.31	0.46	1.17	0.71		450.9
1994-06-01	4.14	4.55	5.27	0.41	1.13	0.72		456.5
1994-07-01	4.33	4.75	5.48	0.42	1.15	0.73		444.2
1994-08-01	4.48	4.88	5.56	0.40	1.08	0.68		458.2
1994-09-01	4.62	5.04	5.76	0.42	1.14	0.72		475.4
1994-10-01	4.95	5.39	6.11	0.44	1.16	0.72		462.7
1994-11-01	5.29	5.72	6.54	0.43	1.25	0.82		472.3
1994-12-01	5.60	6.21	7.14	0.61	1.54	0.93		453.6
1995-01-01	5.71	6.21	7.05	0.50	1.34	0.84		459.2
1995-02-01	5.77	6.03	6.70	0.26	0.93	0.67		470.4
1995-03-01	5.73	5.89	6.43	0.16	0.70	0.54		487.3
1995-04-01	5.65	5.77	6.27	0.12	0.62	0.50		500.7
1995-05-01	5.67	5.67	6.00	0.00	0.33	0.33		514.7
1995-06-01	5.47	5.42	5.64	−0.05	0.17	0.22		533.4
1995-07-01	5.42	5.37	5.59	−0.05	0.17	0.22		544.7
1995-08-01	5.40	5.41	5.75	0.01	0.35	0.34		562
1995-09-01	5.28	5.30	5.62	0.02	0.34	0.32		561.8
1995-10-01	5.28	5.32	5.59	0.04	0.31	0.27		584.4
1995-11-01	5.36	5.27	5.43	−0.09	0.07	0.16		581.5
1995-12-01	5.14	5.13	5.31	−0.01	0.17	0.18		605.3
1996-01-01	5.00	4.92	5.09	−0.08	0.09	0.17		615.9
1996-02-01	4.83	4.77	4.94	−0.06	0.11	0.17		636
1996-03-01	4.96	4.96	5.34	0.00	0.38	0.38		640.4
1996-04-01	4.95	5.06	5.54	0.11	0.59	0.48		645.5
1996-05-01	5.02	5.12	5.64	0.10	0.62	0.52		654.1
1996-06-01	5.09	5.25	5.81	0.16	0.72	0.56		669.1
1996-07-01	5.15	5.30	5.85	0.15	0.70	0.55		670.6
1996-08-01	5.05	5.13	5.67	0.08	0.62	0.54		639.9
1996-09-01	5.09	5.24	5.83	0.15	0.74	0.59		651.9

Date	3 mo.	6 mo.	1 yr.	3–6 mo.	3 mo.– 1 yr.	6 mo.– 1 yr.	OK to Buy?	S&P 500 Index
1996-10-01	4.99	5.11	5.55	0.12	0.56	0.44		687.3
1996-11-01	5.03	5.07	5.42	0.04	0.39	0.35		705.2
1996-12-01	4.91	5.04	5.47	0.13	0.56	0.43		757
1997-01-01	5.03	5.10	5.61	0.07	0.58	0.51		740.7
1997-02-01	5.01	5.06	5.53	0.05	0.52	0.47		786.1
1997-03-01	5.14	5.26	5.80	0.12	0.66	0.54		790.8
1997-04-01	5.16	5.37	5.99	0.21	0.83	0.62		757.1
1997-05-01	5.05	5.30	5.87	0.25	0.82	0.57		801.3
1997-06-01	4.93	5.13	5.69	0.20	0.76	0.56		848.2
1997-07-01	5.05	5.12	5.54	0.07	0.49	0.42		885.1
1997-08-01	5.14	5.19	5.56	0.05	0.42	0.37		954.3
1997-09-01	4.95	5.09	5.52	0.14	0.57	0.43		899.4
1997-10-01	4.97	5.09	5.46	0.12	0.49	0.37		947.2
1997-11-01	5.14	5.17	5.46	0.03	0.32	0.29		914.6
1997-12-01	5.16	5.24	5.53	0.08	0.37	0.29		955.4
1998-01-01	5.04	5.03	5.24	−0.01	0.20	0.21		970.4
1998-02-01	5.09	5.07	5.31	−0.02	0.22	0.24		980.2
1998-03-01	5.03	5.04	5.39	0.01	0.36	0.35		1049
1998-04-01	4.95	5.06	5.38	0.11	0.43	0.32		1101
1998-05-01	5.00	5.14	5.44	0.14	0.44	0.30		1111
1998-06-01	4.98	5.12	5.41	0.14	0.43	0.29		1090
1998-07-01	4.96	5.03	5.36	0.07	0.40	0.33		1133
1998-08-01	4.90	4.95	5.21	0.05	0.31	0.26		1120
1998-09-01	4.61	4.63	4.71	0.02	0.10	0.08		957.2
1998-10-01	3.96	4.05	4.12	0.09	0.16	0.07		1017
1998-11-01	4.41	4.42	4.53	0.01	0.12	0.11		1098
1998-12-01	4.39	4.40	4.52	0.01	0.13	0.12		1163
1999-01-01	4.34	4.33	4.51	−0.01	0.17	0.18		1229
1999-02-01	4.44	4.44	4.70	0.00	0.26	0.26		1279
1999-03-01	4.44	4.47	4.78	0.03	0.34	0.31		1238
1999-04-01	4.29	4.37	4.69	0.08	0.40	0.32		1286
1999-05-01	4.50	4.56	4.85	0.06	0.35	0.29		1335
1999-06-01	4.57	4.82	5.10	0.25	0.53	0.28		1301
1999-07-01	4.55	4.58	5.03	0.03	0.48	0.45		1372
1999-08-01	4.72	4.87	5.20	0.15	0.48	0.33		1328
1999-09-01	4.68	4.88	5.25	0.20	0.57	0.37		1320
1999-10-01	4.86	4.98	5.43	0.12	0.57	0.45		1282
1999-11-01	5.07	5.20	5.55	0.13	0.48	0.35		1362
1999-12-01	5.20	5.44	5.84	0.24	0.64	0.40		1389
2000-01-01	5.32	5.50	6.12	0.18	0.80	0.62		1469
2000-02-01	5.55	5.72	6.22	0.17	0.67	0.50		1394
2000-03-01	5.69	5.85	6.22	0.16	0.53	0.37		1366
2000-04-01	5.66	5.81	6.15	0.15	0.49	0.34		1498
2000-05-01	5.79	6.10	6.33	0.31	0.54	0.23		1452

(continues)

Date	3 mo.	6 mo.	1 yr.	3–6 mo.	3 mo.–1 yr.	6 mo.–1 yr.	OK to Buy?	S&P 500 Index
2000-06-01	5.69	5.97	6.17	0.28	0.48	0.20		1420
2000-07-01	5.96	6.00	6.08	0.04	0.12	0.08		1454
2000-08-01	6.09	6.07	6.18	−0.02	0.09	0.11		1430
2000-09-01	6.00	5.98	6.13	−0.02	0.13	0.15		1517
2000-10-01	6.11	6.04	6.01	−0.07	−0.10	−0.03		1436
2000-11-01	6.17	6.06	6.09	−0.11	−0.08	0.03		1429
2000-12-01	5.77	5.68	5.60	−0.09	−0.17	−0.08		1314
2001-01-01	5.15	4.95	4.81	−0.20	−0.34	−0.14	Old buy	1320
2001-02-01	4.88	4.71	4.68	−0.17	−0.20	−0.03		1367
2001-03-01	4.42	4.28	4.30	−0.14	−0.12	0.02		1239
2001-04-01	3.87	3.85	3.98	−0.02	0.11	0.13		1160
2001-05-01	3.62	3.62	3.78	0.00	0.16	0.16		1249
2001-06-01	3.49	3.45	3.58	−0.04	0.09	0.13		1255
2001-07-01	3.51	3.45	3.62	−0.06	0.11	0.17		1226
2001-08-01	3.36	3.29	3.47	−0.07	0.11	0.18		1211
2001-09-01	2.64	2.63	2.82	−0.01	0.18	0.19		1133
2001-10-01	2.16	2.12	2.33	−0.04	0.17	0.21		1040
2001-11-01	1.87	1.88	2.18	0.01	0.31	0.30	New buy	1059
2001-12-01	1.69	1.78	2.22	0.09	0.53	0.44		1139
2002-01-01	1.65	1.73	2.16	0.08	0.51	0.43		1148
2002-02-01	1.73	1.82	2.23	0.09	0.50	0.41		1130
2002-03-01	1.79	2.01	2.57	0.22	0.78	0.56		1106
2002-04-01	1.72	1.93	2.48	0.21	0.76	0.55		1147
2002-05-01	1.73	1.86	2.35	0.13	0.62	0.49		1086
2002-06-01	1.70	1.79	2.20	0.09	0.50	0.41		1067
2002-07-01	1.68	1.70	1.96	0.02	0.28	0.26		989.8
2002-08-01	1.62	1.60	1.76	−0.02	0.14	0.16		911.6
2002-09-01	1.63	1.60	1.72	−0.03	0.09	0.12		916
2002-10-01	1.58	1.56	1.65	−0.02	0.07	0.09		815.2
2002-11-01	1.23	1.27	1.49	0.04	0.26	0.22		885.7
2002-12-01	1.19	1.24	1.45	0.05	0.26	0.21		936.3
2003-01-01	1.17	1.20	1.36	0.03	0.19	0.16		879.8
2003-02-01	1.17	1.18	1.30	0.01	0.13	0.12		855.7
2003-03-01	1.13	1.13	1.24	0.00	0.11	0.11		841.1
2003-04-01	1.13	1.14	1.27	0.01	0.14	0.13		848.1
2003-05-01	1.07	1.08	1.18	0.01	0.11	0.10		916.92
2003-06-01	0.92	0.92	1.01	0.00	0.09	0.09		963.59
2003-07-01	0.90	0.95	1.12	0.05	0.22	0.17		974.5
2003-08-01	0.95	1.03	1.31	0.08	0.36	0.28		990.31
2003-09-01	0.94	1.01	1.24	0.07	0.30	0.23		1008.01
2003-10-01	0.92	1.00	1.25	0.08	0.33	0.25		995.97
2003-11-01	0.93	1.02	1.34	0.09	0.41	0.32		1050.71
2003-12-01	0.90	0.99	1.31	0.09	0.41	0.32		1058.2
2004-01-01	0.88	0.97	1.24	0.09	0.36	0.27		1111.92

Date	S&P 500 Index	One + % Gain/Loss	Old Index	× Gain/ Loss	Equals Cumulative Index
9/1/66	77	1 + (77 − 59/59)	1.00	1.035	1.305
2/1/67 7/1/69	86 97	1 + (97 − 86/86)	1.305	1.1279	1.4719
2/1/70 6/1/73	85 105	1 + (105-85/85)	1.4719	1.235	1.8182
10/1/74 12/1/78	63 94	1 + (94 − 63/63)	1.8182	1.49206	2.71286
5/1/80 11/1/80	106 127	1 + (127 − 106/106)	2.71286	1.1981	3.2503
9/1/81 10/31/89	122 340	1 + (340 − 122/122)	3.2503	2.7868	9.0582
1/1/1991 8/1/00	330 1430	1 + (1430 − 330/330) = 4.333	9.0582	4.333	39.2522
11/1/01 10/1/02	1059 815	1 − (1059 − 815/1059) = .76959 Market Low	39.2522	0.76959	30.20825

Returns	Annualized Returns	Value Added by Trading	
Buy and Hold: 815 − 59/59 = 12.81355 Return = 41.75th root of index: 12.81355 = 1.06299 Or 6.30%	*Buy & Hold* 6.30%	*Trade*	
Trading: 41.75th root of index: 30.20825 = 1.0850 Or 8.5%	8.5%	2.20% (34% more return)	

	Value of $1		
	Buy & Hold	*Trade*	
Buy and Hold Index: 12.81355	$12.81		
Trading Index: 30.20825		$30.21	$17.40 (135% more return)

Speculative Bond Spreads (Ba1 and Lower Rated), 1991–2003

Date	Speculative	7-Year USTN	Spread	S&P
2/28/1991	14.89	7.70	719	367.07
3/31/1991	14.22	7.79	642	375.22
4/30/1991	13.81	7.55	626	375.34
5/31/1991	13.85	7.53	632	389.83
6/30/1991	13.54	7.87	568	371.16
7/31/1991	13.26	7.72	554	387.81
8/31/1991	13.06	7.28	578	395.43
9/30/1991	13.08	6.98	610	387.86
10/31/1991	12.62	6.90	573	392.45
11/30/1991	12.61	6.77	584	375.22
12/31/1991	12.63	6.23	640	417.09
1/31/1992	12.21	6.61	560	408.78
2/29/1992	11.74	6.71	504	412.7
3/31/1992	11.56	6.85	471	403.69
4/30/1992	11.61	6.89	472	414.95
5/31/1992	11.31	6.69	462	415.35
6/30/1992	11.38	6.46	492	408.14
7/31/1992	11.10	5.95	515	424.21
8/31/1992	11.00	6.13	487	414.03
9/30/1992	10.85	5.99	486	417.8
10/31/1992	11.38	6.24	514	418.68
11/30/1992	11.01	6.43	458	431.35
12/31/1992	10.93	6.31	462	435.71
1/31/1993	10.51	5.99	452	438.78
2/28/1993	10.09	5.65	444	443.38
3/31/1993	9.83	5.65	418	451.67
4/30/1993	9.76	5.55	421	440.19
5/31/1993	9.67	5.75	392	450.19
6/30/1993	9.37	5.49	388	450.53
7/31/1993	9.35	5.41	394	448.13
8/31/1993	9.31	5.02	429	463.56
9/30/1993	9.48	4.98	450	458.93
10/31/1993	9.30	5.41	389	467.83
11/30/1993	9.17	5.33	384	461.79
12/31/1993	9.07	5.23	384	466.45
1/31/1994	8.86	5.16	370	481.61
2/28/1994	8.85	5.80	305	467.14
3/31/1994	9.88	6.14	374	445.77
4/30/1994	10.21	6.66	355	450.91
5/31/1994	10.24	6.72	352	456.5
6/30/1994	10.23	7.06	317	444.27
7/31/1994	10.38	6.89	349	458.26
8/31/1994	10.29	7.00	329	475.49
9/30/1994	10.48	7.44	303	462.71
10/31/1994	10.65	7.63	301	472.35
11/30/1994	10.93	7.83	310	453.69
12/31/1994	10.89	7.83	306	459.27
1/31/1995	10.86	7.54	332	470.42

Source: Reprinted with permission from Moody's Investors Service, Inc.

Date	Speculative	7-Year USTN	Spread	S&P
2/28/1995	10.44	7.12	332	487.39
3/31/1995	10.40	7.13	327	500.71
4/30/1995	10.14	6.93	320	514.71
5/31/1995	9.85	6.14	372	533.4
6/30/1995	9.86	6.14	372	544.75
7/31/1995	9.77	6.32	345	562.06
8/31/1995	9.84	6.20	364	561.88
9/30/1995	9.76	6.10	366	584.41
10/31/1995	9.63	5.91	373	581.5
11/30/1995	9.63	5.67	397	605.37
12/31/1995	9.48	5.49	399	615.93
1/31/1996	9.41	5.43	397	636.02
2/29/1996	9.44	5.95	349	640.43
3/31/1996	9.66	6.28	338	645.5
4/30/1996	9.84	6.58	325	654.17
5/31/1996	9.83	6.78	305	669.12
6/30/1996	9.95	6.58	337	670.63
7/31/1996	9.94	6.67	327	639.95
8/31/1996	9.84	6.85	300	651.99
9/30/1996	9.69	6.58	311	687.33
10/31/1996	9.69	6.19	350	705.27
11/30/1996	9.42	5.95	347	757.02
12/31/1996	9.40	6.33	307	740.74
1/31/1997	9.27	6.39	288	786.16
2/28/1997	9.12	6.49	264	790.82
3/31/1997	9.51	6.85	267	757.12
4/30/1997	9.51	6.66	285	801.34
5/31/1997	9.21	6.58	263	848.28
6/30/1997	9.28	6.46	282	885.14
7/31/1997	9.00	5.97	303	954.31
8/31/1997	9.09	6.32	277	899.47
9/30/1997	8.93	6.08	284	947.28
10/31/1997	9.09	5.86	323	914.62
11/30/1997	9.13	5.89	324	955.4
12/31/1997	9.04	5.65	340	970.43
1/31/1998	8.76	5.48	329	980.28
2/28/1998	8.78	5.67	311	1049.34
3/31/1998	8.77	5.70	307	1101.75
4/30/1998	8.91	5.73	319	1111.75
5/31/1998	9.00	5.63	338	1090.82
6/30/1998	9.07	5.52	355	1133.84
7/31/1998	9.06	5.57	349	1120.67
8/31/1998	9.96	4.94	502	957.28
9/30/1998	9.98	4.33	564	1017.01
10/31/1998	10.36	4.47	588	1098.67
11/30/1998	9.66	4.66	500	1163.63
12/31/1998	9.71	4.71	500	1229.23
1/31/1999	9.57	4.73	485	1279.64
2/28/1999	9.70	5.39	431	1238.33

(continues)

Date	Speculative	7-Year USTN	Spread	S&P
3/31/1999	9.32	5.37	396	1286.37
4/30/1999	9.43	5.37	406	1335.18
5/31/1999	9.99	5.66	433	1301.84
6/30/1999	10.05	5.90	415	1372.71
7/31/1999	10.13	6.04	409	1328.72
8/31/1999	10.32	6.12	420	1320.41
9/30/1999	10.40	6.04	436	1282.71
10/31/1999	10.52	6.16	436	1362.93
11/30/1999	10.45	6.27	418	1389.07
12/31/1999	10.64	6.53	411	1469.25
1/31/2000	10.88	6.72	416	1394.46
2/29/2000	10.94	6.65	429	1366.42
3/31/2000	11.25	6.26	499	1498.58
4/30/2000	11.54	6.49	505	1452.43
5/31/2000	11.76	6.48	528	1420.6
6/30/2000	11.81	6.23	559	1454.6
7/31/2000	11.68	6.17	551	1430.83
8/31/2000	11.43	5.96	547	1517.68
9/30/2000	11.70	5.93	577	1436.51
10/31/2000	12.61	5.85	676	1429.39
11/30/2000	13.21	5.50	771	1314.95
12/31/2000	13.14	5.16	798	1320.28
1/31/2001	11.92	5.01	691	1367.11
2/28/2001	11.34	4.86	648	1239.94
3/30/2001	11.50	4.79	671	1160.33
4/30/2001	11.27	5.14	613	1249.46
5/30/2001	10.82	5.15	567	1255.82
6/30/2001	10.68	5.18	550	1226.33
7/31/2001	10.70	5.10	560	1211.23
8/31/2001	10.60	4.75	585	1133.58
9/30/2001	11.74	4.37	737	1040.94
10/31/2001	11.51	4.01	750	1059.78
11/30/2001	10.35	4.53	582	1139.45
12/31/2001	10.30	4.80	550	1148.08
1/31/2002	10.15	4.80	535	1130.2
2/28/2002	10.05	4.64	541	1106.73
3/31/2002	9.70	5.28	442	1147.69
4/30/2002	9.49	4.88	461	1086.17
5/31/2002	9.46	4.75	471	1067.14
6/28/2002	9.82	4.49	533	989.82
7/31/2002	10.36	4.01	635	911.62
8/30/2002	10.48	3.77	671	916.07
9/30/2002	10.66	3.22	744	815.28
10/31/2002	10.93	3.39	754	885.76
11/29/2002	10.04	3.78	626	936.31
12/31/2002	9.89	3.20	669	879.82
1/31/2003	9.60	3.55	605	855.7
2/28/2003	9.40	3.22	618	841.15
3/31/2003	9.13	3.32	581	848.18

1987 Crash

Date	Federal Funds Rates	S&P Index
1987-10-01	7.710	327.34
1987-10-02	7.420	328.07
1987-10-05	7.450	328.09
1987-10-06	7.320	319.22
1987-10-07	7.300	318.52
1987-10-08	7.550	314.17
1987-10-09	7.580	311.05
1987-10-12	7.580	309.39
1987-10-13	7.650	314.52
1987-10-14	7.590	305.23
1987-10-15	**7.760**	**298.08**
1987-10-16	7.550	282.94
1987-10-19	7.610	225.06
1987-10-20	**7.070**	**236.84**
1987-10-21	6.470	258.39
1987-10-22	7.140	248.25
1987-10-23	7.000	248.22
1987-10-26	7.240	227.67
1987-10-27	7.140	233.19
1987-10-28	6.720	233.28
1987-10-29	6.760	244.76
1987-10-30	6.620	251.79

1998 Long-Term Capital Management Failure

Date	Federal Funds Rates	S&P Index
1998-08-18	5.540	1,101.20
1998-08-19	5.480	1,098.06
1998-08-20	5.510	1,091.60
1998-08-21	5.460	1,081.24
1998-08-24	5.510	1,088.14
1998-08-25	5.500	1,092.85
1998-08-26	5.490	1,084.19
1998-08-27	5.550	1,042.59
1998-08-28	5.510	1,027.14
1998-08-31	**5.890**	**957.28**
1998-09-01	5.750	994.26
1998-09-02	5.530	990.47
1998-09-03	5.520	982.26
1998-09-04	**5.410**	**973.89**

Source: www.Econostats.com

(continues)

Date	2001 Terrorist Attacks Federal Funds Rates	S&P Index
4-Sep-01	3.67	1132.94
5-Sep-01	3.49	1131.74
6-Sep-01	3.52	1106.40
7-Sep-01	3.44	1085.78
10-Sep-01	3.50	1092.54
Markets Closed		
17-Sep-01	2.13	1038.77
18-Sep-01	1.25	1032.74
19-Sep-01	1.19	1016.1
20-Sep-01	**2.22**	**984.54***
21-Sep-01	3.11	965.8
24-Sep-01	3.31	1003.45
25-Sep-01	3.11	1012.27
26-Sep-01	2.96	1007.04
27-Sep-01	3.08	1018.61
28-Sep-01	2.75	1040.94
10-Oct-01	3.02	1038.55

*Markets were volatile. This is a reasonable estimate for an S&P 500 index trade September 19–21.

Date	S&P 500 Index	One + % Gain/Loss	Old Index	× Gain/ Loss	Equals Cumulative Index
1/1/1960 9/1/66	59 77	1 + (77 − 59/59)	1.00	1.305	1.305
2/1/67 7/1/69	86 97	1 + (97 − 86/86)	1.305	1.1279	1.4719
2/1/70 6/1/73	85 105	1 + (105 − 85/85)	1.4719	1.235	1.8182
10/1/74 12/1/78	63 94	1 + (94 − 63/63)	1.8182	1.49206	2.71286
5/1/80 11/1/80	106 127	1 + (127 − 106/106)	2.71286	1.1981	3.2503
9/1/81 10/15/87	122 298	1 + (298 − 122/122)	3.2503	2.4426	7.9401
10/20/87 10/31/89	236 340	1 + (340 − 236/236)	7.9401	1.4406	11.4391
1/1/91 7/1/98	330 1133	1 + (1133 − 330/330)	11.4391	3.4333	39.2742
9/4/98 8/1/00	973 1430	1 + (1430 − 973/973)	39.2742	1.4696	57.7293
9/20/01 10/1/02	984 815	1 − (984 − 815/984) Market Low	57.7293	0.8282	47.8041

To Lowest Point in the Market: 10/1/2002

Buy and Hold Portfolio: = 1 = (815 − 59/59) = 13.81355

Return = 42.75th root of 13.81355 = 1.06334 or **6.33%**

Trading Portfolio: Return = 42.75th root of 47.80416 = 1.09467 or **9.46%**

APPENDIX 8.1 Ten-Year Note Total Return Index, 1960–2004

Date	Expansion/Recession	Index	Date	Expansion/Recession	Index
12/31/1960	**r**	**262.9355**	**12/31/1982**	**r**	**777.3323**
12/31/1961		268.7297	12/31/1983		787.3568
12/31/1962		284.0903	12/31/1984		907.7119
12/31/1963		289.1622	12/31/1985		1200.628
12/31/1964		299.894	12/31/1986		1469.454
12/31/1965		302.695	12/31/1987		1424.907
12/31/1966		318.1967	12/31/1988		1522.404
12/31/1967		309.103	12/31/1989		1804.634
12/31/1968		316.0513	12/31/1990		1944.255
12/31/1969		298.2492	**12/31/1991**	**r**	**2320.639**
12/31/1970	**r**	**354.6713**	12/31/1992		2490.968
12/31/1971		394.532	12/31/1993		2816.402
12/31/1972		403.9418	12/31/1994		2610.121
12/31/1973		417.2524	12/31/1995		3287.272
12/31/1974	**r**	**433.9273**	12/31/1996		3291.583
12/31/1975		457.8851	12/31/1997		3687.332
12/31/1976		529.1409	12/31/1998		4220.244
12/31/1977		531.1445	12/31/1999		3903.316
12/31/1978		524.4347	12/31/2000		4575.332
12/31/1979		531.0397	**12/31/2001**	**r**	**4827.265**
12/31/1980	**r**	**517.86**	12/31/2002		5558.396
12/31/1981		538.7687	12/31/2003		5588.19

Note: Recessions are in bold type.

APPENDIX 9.1 All 30 Dow Industrial Stocks Fell on July 19, 2002

Dow = 8019
S&P = 847

Company	Symbol	18-Jul	19-Jul
3M Co.	MMM	116.65	108.88
Alcoa Inc.	AA	28.23	27
American Express Co.	AXP	33.53	31.65
AT&T Corp.	T	10.28	9.92
Boeing Co.	BA	41.29	39.92
Caterpillar Inc.	CAT	42.68	41.41
Citigroup Inc.	C	36.9	36
Coca-Cola Co.	KO	47.93	45.09
E.I. DuPont de Nemours & Co.	DD	40.11	38.3
Eastman Kodak Co.	EK	28.7	27.8
ExxonMobil Corp.	XOM	34.75	32.4
General Electric Co.	GE	27.7	26.52
General Motors Corp.	GM	44.8	42.57
Hewlett-Packard Co.	HPQ	13.23	12.8
Home Depot Inc.	HD	29.61	28.7
Honeywell International Inc.	HON	32.03	30.21
Intel Corp.	INTC	19.19	18.65
International Business Machines Corp.	IBM	72.25	72
International Paper Co.	IP	39.66	37.83
J.P. Morgan Chase & Co.	JPM	27.2	26.1
Johnson & Johnson	JNJ	49.73	41.85
McDonald's Corp.	MCD	25.11	24.17
Merck & Co. Inc.	MRK	42	41.5
Microsoft Corp.	MSFT	51.11	49.56
Philip Morris Cos. Inc.	MO	42.45	41.65
Procter & Gamble Co.	PG	80.39	74.46
SBC Communications Inc.	SBC	27.74	26.68
United Technologies Corp.	UTX	64.45	61.64
Wal-Mart Stores Inc.	WMT	47.41	46.5
Walt Disney Co.	DIS	17.66	16.64

Source: www.djindexes.com/jsp/uiComponents.

Date	S&P 500 Index	One + % Gain/Loss	Old Index	× Gain/ Loss	Equals Cumulative Index
1/1/1960 9/1/66	59 77	1 + (77 − 59/59)	1	1.305	1.305
2/1/67 7/1/69	86 97	1 + (97 − 86/86)	1.305	1.1279	1.4719
2/1/70 6/1/73	85 105	1 + (105 − 85/85)	1.4719	1.235	1.8182
10/1/74 12/1/78	63 94	1 + (94 − 63/63)	1.8182	1.49206	2.71286
5/1/80 11/1/80	106 127	1 + (127 − 106/106)	2.71286	1.1981	3.2503
9/1/81 10/15/87	122 298	1 + (298 − 122/122)	3.2503	2.4426	7.9401
10/20/87 10/31/89	236 340	1 + (340 − 236/236)	7.9401	1.4406	11.4391
1/1/91 7/1/98	330 1133	1 + (1133 − 330/330)	11.4391	3.4333	39.2742
9/4/98 8/1/00	973 1430	1 + (1430 − 973/973)	39.2742	1.4696	57.7293
7/19/02 10/1/02	847 815	1 − (847 − 815/847) Market Low	57.7293	0.9622	55.54

To Lowest Point in the Market: 10/1/2002

Buy & Hold Portfolio: = 1 = (815 − 59/59) = 13.81355

                            Return = 42.75th root of 13.81355 = 1.06334 or **6.33%**

Trading Portfolio: Return = 42.75th root of 55.54 = 1.0985 or **9.85%**

APPENDIX 16.1 Playmate of the Year, S&P 500 Index, and the Russell 2000 Index, 1960–2000

Year	Bust	Waist	Weight	S&P	Russell 2000
1960	35	20	110	58.11	N/A
1961	38	27	112	71.55	N/A
1962	38	22	122	63.1	N/A
1963	36	20	102	75.02	N/A
1964	38	22	118	84.75	N/A
1965	36	24	112	92.43	N/A
1966	36	24	117	80.33	N/A
1967	35	23	132	96.47	N/A
1968	36	21	109	103.86	N/A
1969	35	23	118	92.06	N/A
1970	35	23	115	92.15	N/A
1971	35	24	115	102.09	N/A
1972	36	23	108	118.05	N/A
1973	36	24	119	97.55	N/A
1974	34	22	103	68.56	N/A
1975	39	N/A	130	90.19	N/A
1976	36	24	125	107.46	N/A
1977	35	23	115	95.1	N/A
1978	35	24	114	96.11	N/A
1979	36	26	117	107.94	N/A
1980	36	24	123	135.76	N/A
1981	36	24	120	122.55	N/A
1982	36	25	128	140.64	N/A
1983	34	21	105	164.93	N/A
1984	35	23	105	167.24	N/A
1985	37	23	118	211.28	N/A
1986	35	24	122	242.17	N/A
1987	36	23	127	247.08	120
1988	35	24	127	277.71	147
1989	36	24	122	353.39	168
1990	36	23	112	330.21	132
1991	37	24	120	417.09	189
1992	34	22	105	435.70	221
1993	36	26	140	466.45	258
1994	38	24	120	459.27	250
1995	34	24	126	615.93	315
1996	34	24	130	740.74	362
1997	36	25	139	970.43	437
1998	34	24	125	1229.23	421
1999	36	24	117	1469.25	504
2000	32	23	112	1320.28	483

Sources: www.playboy.com and ComStock, Inc. (Yahoo.com).

APPENDIX 16.2 Monthly Playmates and the S&P 500 Index, 1982–2004

Issue	Bust	S&P	Issue	Bust	S&P
10/01/82	34	133.72	05/01/86	34	247.35
11/01/82	34	138.53	06/02/86	34	250.84
12/01/82	34	140.64	07/01/86	35	236.12
01/03/83	36	145.3	08/01/86	36	252.93
02/01/83	35	148.06	09/02/86	34	231.32
03/01/83	34	152.96	0/01/86	35	243.98
04/04/83	34	164.43	11/03/86	36	249.22
05/02/83	34	162.39	12/01/86	34	242.17
06/01/83	37	167.64	01/02/87	35	274.08
07/01/83	35	162.56	02/02/87	38	284.2
08/01/83	34	164.4	03/02/87	34	291.7
09/01/83	35	166.07	04/01/87	32	288.36
10/03/83	35	163.55	05/01/87	34	290.1
11/01/83	34	166.4	06/01/87	35	304
12/01/83	35	164.93	07/01/87	35	318.66
01/03/84	35	163.41	08/03/87	32	329.8
02/01/84	36	157.06	09/01/87	36	321.83
03/01/84	37	159.18	10/01/87	36	251.79
04/02/84	34	160.05	11/02/87	34	230.3
05/01/84	36	150.55	12/01/87	35	247.08
06/01/84	36	153.18	01/04/88	36	257.07
07/02/84	35	150.66	02/01/88	34	267.82
08/01/84	36	166.68	03/01/88	35	258.89
09/04/84	36	166.12	04/04/88	36	261.33
10/01/84	35	166.09	05/02/88	36	262.16
11/01/84	40	163.58	06/01/88	35	273.5
12/03/84	37	167.24	07/01/88	36	272.02
01/02/85	36	179.63	08/01/88	35	261.52
02/01/85	34	181.18	09/01/88	36	271.91
03/01/85	37	180.66	10/03/88	36	278.97
04/01/85	34	179.83	11/01/88	35.5	273.7
05/01/85	35	189.55	12/01/88	35	277.72
06/03/85	34	191.85	01/03/89	35	297.47
07/01/85	36	190.92	02/01/89	37	288.86
08/01/85	37	188.63	03/01/89	37	294.87
09/03/85	34	182.08	04/03/89	38	309.64
10/01/85	36	189.82	05/01/89	36	320.52
11/01/85	36	202.17	06/01/89	36	317.98
12/02/85	35	211.28	07/03/89	34	346.08
01/02/86	36	211.78	08/01/89	38	351.45
02/03/86	36	226.92	09/01/89	36.22	349.15
03/03/86	35	238.9	10/02/89	36	340.36
04/01/86	34	235.52	11/01/89	36	345.99

Sources: www.mtsu.edu/~sschmidt/methods/project2.html and ComStock, Inc. (Yahoo.com).

Issue	Bust	S&P	Issue	Bust	S&P
12/01/89	37	353.4	08/02/93	32	463.56
01/02/90	36	329.08	09/01/93	34	458.93
02/01/90	36	331.89	10/01/93	38	467.83
03/01/90	34	339.94	11/01/93	38	461.79
04/02/90	37	330.8	12/01/93	34	466.45
05/01/90	34	361.23	01/03/94	36	481.61
06/01/90	35	358.02	02/01/94	34	467.14
07/02/90	36	356.15	03/01/94	36	445.77
08/01/90	34	322.56	04/04/94	36	450.91
09/04/90	36	306.05	05/02/94	34	456.5
10/01/90	36	304	06/01/94	34	444.27
11/01/90	34	322.22	07/01/94	36	458.26
12/03/90	38	330.22	08/01/94	32	475.49
01/02/91	36	343.93	09/01/94	34	462.71
02/01/91	36	367.07	10/03/94	36	472.35
03/01/91	34	375.22	11/01/94	34	453.69
04/01/91	34	375.34	12/01/94	34	459.27
05/01/91	36	389.83	01/03/95	34	470.42
06/03/91	38	371.16	02/01/95	34	487.39
07/01/91	34	387.81	03/01/95	34	500.71
08/01/91	34	395.43	04/03/95	34	514.71
09/03/91	36	387.86	05/01/95	34	533.4
10/01/91	34	392.45	06/01/95	34	544.75
11/01/91	34	375.22	07/03/95	34	562.06
12/02/91	35	417.09	08/01/95	34.5	561.88
01/02/92	36	408.78	09/01/95	34	584.41
02/03/92	36	412.7	10/02/95	34	581.5
03/02/92	34	403.69	11/01/95	34	605.37
04/01/92	36	414.95	12/01/95	34	615.93
05/01/92	36	415.35	01/02/96	36	636.02
06/01/92	36	408.14	02/01/96	34	640.43
07/01/92	35	424.21	03/01/96	36	645.5
08/03/92	34	414.03	04/01/96	34	654.17
09/01/92	34	417.8	05/01/96	33	669.12
10/01/92	36	418.68	06/03/96	34	670.63
11/02/92	34	431.35	07/01/96	34	639.95
12/01/92	36	435.71	08/01/96	34	651.99
01/04/93	36	438.78	09/03/96	34	687.33
02/01/93	34	443.38	10/01/96	34	705.27
03/01/93	34	451.67	11/01/96	34	757.02
04/01/93	36	440.19	12/02/96	35	740.74
05/03/93	34	450.19	01/02/97	36	786.16
06/01/93	36	450.53	02/03/97	36	790.82
07/01/93	38	448.13	03/03/97	36	757.12

(continues)

Issue	Bust	S&P	Issue	Bust	S&P
04/01/97	34	801.34	12/01/00	34	1320.28
05/01/97	34	848.28	01/02/01	35	1366.01
06/02/97	34	885.14	02/01/01	34	1239.94
07/01/97	34	954.31	03/01/01	34	1160.33
08/01/97	36	899.47	04/02/01	32	1249.46
09/02/97	36	947.28	05/01/01	34	1255.82
10/01/97	36	914.62	06/01/01	36	1224.38
11/03/97	36	955.4	07/02/01	34	1211.23
12/01/97	34	970.43	08/01/01	32	1133.58
01/02/98	36	980.28	09/04/01	34	1040.94
02/02/98	34	1049.34	10/01/01	34	1059.78
03/02/98	36	1101.75	11/01/01	34	1139.45
04/01/98	34	1111.75	12/03/01	34	1148.08
05/01/98	36	1090.82	01/02/02	34	1130.2
06/01/98	34	1133.84	02/01/02	34	1106.73
07/01/98	34	1120.67	03/01/02	34	1147.39
08/03/98	34	957.28	04/01/02	34	1076.92
09/01/98	34	1017.01	05/01/02	34	1067.14
10/01/98	34	1098.67	06/03/02	32	989.82
11/02/98	36	1163.63	07/01/02	34	911.62
12/01/98	34	1229.23	08/01/02	34	916.07
01/04/99	34	1279.64	09/03/02	34	815.28
02/01/99	34	1238.33	10/01/02	34	885.76
03/01/99	34	1286.37	11/01/02	34	936.31
04/01/99	34	1335.18	12/02/02	36	879.82
05/03/99	36	1301.84	01/02/03	34	855.7
06/01/99	36	1372.71	02/03/03	34	841.15
07/01/99	34	1328.72	03/03/03	34	848.18
08/02/99	38	1320.41	04/01/03	34	916.92
09/01/99	34	1282.71	05/01/03	34	963.59
10/01/99	32	1362.93	06/02/03	34	974.5
11/01/99	34	1388.91	07/01/03	34	990.31
12/01/99	34	1469.25	08/01/03	34	1008.01
01/03/00	32	1394.46	09/02/03	34	995.97
02/01/00	35	1366.42	10/01/03	34	1050.71
03/01/00	32	1498.58	11/03/03	36	1058.2
04/03/00	35	1452.43	12/01/03	36	1111.92
05/01/00	36	1420.6	01/02/04	34	1131.13
06/01/00	34	1454.6	02/02/04	34	1144.94
07/03/00	36	1430.83	03/01/04	34	1126.21
08/01/00	34	1438.1	04/01/04	34	1107.3
09/01/00	34	1436.51	05/03/04	32	1120.68
10/02/00	36	1429.4	06/01/04	34	1140.84
11/01/00	36	1314.95	07/01/04	34	1101.72

Gross Domestic Product and War, 1800–2004

Date	Percent Change in GDP	Date	Percent Change in GDP
12/31/1800		12/31/1841	−0.84%
12/31/1801	15.03%	12/31/1842	−8.50%
12/31/1802	−7.20%	12/31/1843	−3.23%
12/31/1803	−0.41%	12/31/1844	10.97%
12/31/1804	9.43%	**12/31/1845**	**9.64%**
12/31/1805	10.86%	**12/31/1846**	**7.00%**
12/31/1806	2.87%	**12/31/1847**	**14.08%**
12/31/1807	−7.39%	**12/31/1848**	**−1.88%**
12/31/1808	−18.26%	12/31/1849	3.09%
12/31/1809	8.89%	12/31/1850	17.28%
12/31/1810	17.13%	12/31/1851	3.40%
12/31/1811	**−1.36%**	2/31/1852	7.11%
12/31/1812	**−1.90%**	12/31/1853	17.42%
12/31/1813	**9.49%**	12/31/1854	7.79%
12/31/1814	**12.52%**	12/31/1855	7.34%
12/31/1815	15.83%	12/31/1856	3.37%
12/31/1816	5.17%	12/31/1857	−1.12%
12/31/1817	−0.82%	12/31/1858	−6.56%
12/31/1818	−3.66%	12/31/1859	6.89%
12/31/1819	−7.60%	**12/31/1860**	**−3.35%**
12/31/1820	−13.00%	**12/31/1861**	**−4.22%**
12/31/1821	−7.47%	**12/31/1862**	**9.11%**
12/31/1822	15.98%	**12/31/1863**	**27.02%**
12/31/1823	−0.71%	**12/31/1864**	**27.14%**
12/31/1824	7.44%	12/31/1865	1.25%
12/31/1825	13.18%	12/31/1866	4.88%
12/31/1826	4%	12/31/1867	−0.58%
12/31/1827	−1.81%	12/31/1868	3.22%
12/31/1828	1.50%	12/31/1869	4.96%
12/31/1829	2.72%	12/31/1870	−0.81%
12/31/1830	3.09%	12/31/1871	2.72%
12/31/1831	15.01%	12/31/1872	12.85%
12/31/1832	7.64%	12/31/1873	3.17%
12/31/1833	12.38%	12/31/1874	−2.84%
12/31/1834	2.70%	12/31/1875	−3.75%
12/31/1835	22.51%	12/31/1876	−3.77%
12/31/1836	16.11%	12/31/1877	2.15%
12/31/1837	−3.48%	12/31/1878	−0.74%
12/31/1838	−3.93%	12/31/1879	9.85%
12/31/1839	9.90%	12/31/1880	19.30%
12/31/1840	−13.46%	12/31/1881	7.23%

Note: War years are in bold type.

Source: www.Globalfindata.com/gdpusad.

(continues)

Date	Percent Change in GDP	Date	Percent Change in GDP
12/31/1882	7.90%	6/30/1922	−2.80%
12/31/1883	−5.02%	9/30/1922	3.79%
12/31/1884	−5.02%	12/31/1922	10.22%
12/31/1885	−3.01%	3/31/1923	2.52%
12/31/1886	2.73%	6/30/1923	6.98%
12/31/1887	9.79%	9/30/1923	0.24%
12/31/1888	3.50%	12/31/1923	−1.20%
12/31/1889	0.64%	3/31/1924	3.78%
12/31/1890	4.80%	6/30/1924	−0.71%
12/31/1891	3.05%	9/30/1924	−4.26%
12/31/1892	5.93%	12/31/1924	2.47%
12/31/1893	−3.50%	3/31/1925	7.36%
12/31/1894	−8.70%	6/30/1925	−2.92%
12/31/1895	10.32%	9/30/1925	2.08%
12/31/1896	−4.32%	12/31/1925	6.58%
12/31/1897	**9.77%**	3/31/1926	1.91%
12/31/1898	**5.48%**	6/30/1926	−3.13%
12/31/1899	**12.99%**	9/30/1926	0%
12/31/1900	**7.47%**	12/31/1926	3.56%
12/31/1901	10.70%	3/31/1927	−2.39%
12/31/1902	4.35%	6/30/1927	−0.53%
12/31/1903	6.02%	9/30/1927	0.86%
12/31/1904	0%	12/31/1927	−0.96%
12/31/1905	9.61%	3/31/1928	6.33%
12/31/1906	14.34%	6/30/1928	−6.66%
12/31/1907	5.92%	9/30/1928	4.97%
12/31/1908	−8.88%	12/31/1928	5.66%
12/31/1909	20.58%	3/31/1929	1.56%
12/31/1910	5.69%	6/30/1929	−1.73%
12/31/1911	1.42%	9/30/1929	3.12%
12/31/1912	10.06%	12/31/1929	−1.89%
12/31/1913	0.51%	3/31/1930	−3.76%
12/31/1914	−2.53%	6/30/1930	−2.21%
12/31/1915	3.63%	9/30/1930	−5.03%
12/31/1916	**20.75%**	12/31/1930	−1.51%
12/31/1917	**25.05%**	3/31/1931	−11.51%
12/31/1918	**26.49%**	6/30/1931	−1.49%
12/31/1919	9.95%	9/30/1931	−5.53%
12/31/1920	8.93%	12/31/1931	1.86%
3/31/1921	−16.72%	3/31/1932	−15.16%
6/30/1921	−9.97%	6/30/1932	−6.32%
9/30/1921	−3.50%	9/30/1932	−11.68%
12/31/1921	−10.88%	12/31/1932	9.31%
3/31/1922	15.08%	3/31/1933	−9.37%

Date	Percent Change in GDP	Date	Percent Change in GDP
6/30/1933	6.39%	**3/31/1944**	**2.32%**
9/30/1933	4.59%	**6/30/1944**	**2.76%**
12/31/1933	−4.73%	**9/30/1944**	**2.49%**
3/31/1934	10.64%	**12/31/1944**	**2.71%**
6/30/1934	5.29%	**3/31/1945**	**−2.09%**
9/30/1934	2.28%	**6/30/1945**	**1.49%**
12/31/1934	−1.79%	**9/30/1945**	**−5.86%**
3/31/1935	2.73%	12/31/1945	8.51%
6/30/1935	2.95%	3/31/1946	−12.51%
9/30/1935	3.72%	6/30/1946	4.35%
12/31/1935	1.24%	9/30/1946	4.96%
3/31/1936	6.55%	12/31/1946	3.98%
6/30/1936	6.53%	3/31/1947	6.71%
9/30/1936	1.80%	6/30/1947	1.37%
12/31/1936	−1.06%	9/30/1947	1.70%
3/31/1937	4.30%	12/31/1947	4.02%
6/30/1937	5.84%	3/31/1948	2.35%
9/30/1937	5.08%	6/30/1948	2.67%
12/31/1937	−5.45%	9/30/1948	2.44%
3/31/1938	−11.21%	12/31/1948	0.48%
6/30/1938	−0.12%	3/31/1949	−1.88%
9/30/1938	3.07%	6/30/1949	−1.38%
12/31/1938	2.50%	9/30/1949	0.54%
3/31/1939	1.51%	12/31/1949	−0.92%
6/30/1939	1.14%	3/31/1950	3.78%
9/30/1939	3.28%	6/30/1950	3.39%
12/31/1939	0.99%	**9/30/1950**	**6.12%**
3/31/1940	5.97%	**12/31/1950**	**3.78%**
6/30/1940	0.51%	**3/31/1951**	**4.98%**
9/30/1940	2.65%	**6/30/1951**	**2.33%**
12/31/1940	0.60%	**9/30/1951**	**2.05%**
3/31/1941	10.75%	**12/31/1951**	**1.28%**
6/30/1941	7.21%	**3/31/1952**	**0.94%**
9/30/1941	7.72%	**6/30/1952**	**0.26%**
12/31/1941	**−2.31%**	**9/30/1952**	**1.81%**
3/31/1942	**10.50%**	**12/31/1952**	**3.58%**
6/30/1942	**9.43%**	**3/31/1953**	**1.88%**
9/30/1942	**8.62%**	**6/30/1953**	**0.95%**
12/31/1942	**−2.70%**	**9/30/1953**	**−0.22%**
3/31/1943	**13.90%**	12/31/1953	−1.36%
6/30/1943	**4.77%**	3/31/1954	−0.17%
9/30/1943	**1.66%**	6/30/1954	0.19%
12/31/1943	**1.12%**	9/30/1954	1.29%

(continues)

Date	Percent Change in GDP	Date	Percent Change in GDP
12/31/1954	2.27%	**12/31/1965**	**3.07%**
3/31/1955	3.38%	**3/31/1966**	**3.12%**
6/30/1955	2.06%	**6/30/1966**	**1.19%**
9/30/1955	2.09%	**9/30/1966**	**1.72%**
12/31/1955	1.56%	**12/31/1966**	**1.73%**
3/31/1956	0.54%	**3/31/1967**	**1.34%**
6/30/1956	1.37%	**6/30/1967**	**0.55%**
9/30/1956	1.17%	**9/30/1967**	**1.78%**
12/31/1956	2.02%	**12/31/1967**	**1.87%**
3/31/1957	2.03%	**3/31/1968**	**3.18%**
6/30/1957	0.43%	**6/30/1968**	**2.76%**
9/30/1957	1.58%	**9/30/1968**	**1.68%**
12/31/1957	−1.05%	**12/31/1968**	**1.84%**
3/31/1958	−1.64%	**3/31/1969**	**2.63%**
6/30/1958	0.91%	**6/30/1969**	**1.59%**
9/30/1958	2.98%	**9/30/1969**	**2.07%**
12/31/1958	2.82%	**12/31/1969**	**0.82%**
3/31/1959	2.15%	**3/31/1970**	**1.26%**
6/30/1959	2.63%	**6/30/1970**	**1.57%**
9/30/1959	0.16%	**9/30/1970**	**1.69%**
12/31/1959	0.77%	**12/31/1970**	**0.21%**
3/31/1960	2.67%	**3/31/1971**	**4.31%**
6/30/1960	−0.15%	**6/30/1971**	**1.89%**
9/30/1960	0.53%	**9/30/1971**	**1.81%**
12/31/1960	−1.01%	**12/31/1971**	**1.09%**
3/31/1961	0.82%	**3/31/1972**	**3.37%**
6/30/1961	2.10%	**6/30/1972**	**2.97%**
9/30/1961	1.94%	**9/30/1972**	**1.94%**
12/31/1961	2.39%	**12/31/1972**	**2.99%**
3/31/1962	2.40%	**3/31/1973**	**3.77%**
6/30/1962	1.25%	**6/30/1973**	**2.72%**
9/30/1962	1.16%	**9/30/1973**	**1.41%**
12/31/1962	0.56%	12/31/1973	2.95%
3/31/1963	1.54%	3/31/1974	1.03%
6/30/1963	1.45%	6/30/1974	2.65%
9/30/1963	2.09%	9/30/1974	1.94%
12/31/1963	1.53%	12/31/1974	2.59%
3/31/1964	2.55%	3/31/1975	1.07%
6/30/1964	1.42%	6/30/1975	2.27%
9/30/1964	**1.76%**	9/30/1975	3.58%
12/31/1964	**0.77%**	12/31/1975	3.09%
3/31/1965	**2.97%**	3/31/1976	3.38%
6/30/1965	**1.79%**	6/30/1976	1.82%
9/30/1965	**2.41%**	9/30/1976	1.85%

Date	Percent Change in GDP	Date	Percent Change in GDP
12/31/1976	2.55%	9/30/1987	1.66%
3/31/1977	2.87%	12/31/1987	2.48%
6/30/1977	3.44%	3/31/1988	1.34%
9/30/1977	3.03%	6/30/1988	2.24%
12/31/1977	2.17%	9/30/1988	1.66%
3/31/1978	1.82%	12/31/1988	2.08%
6/30/1978	5.84%	3/31/1989	2.16%
9/30/1978	2.66%	6/30/1989	1.62%
12/31/1978	3.46%	9/30/1989	1.43%
3/31/1979	1.96%	12/31/1989	0.95%
6/30/1979	2.57%	3/31/1990	2.36%
9/30/1979	2.89%	6/30/1990	1.42%
12/31/1979	2.30%	9/30/1990	0.89%
3/31/1980	2.43%	12/31/1990	−0.01%
6/30/1980	0.15%	**3/31/1991**	**0.67%**
9/30/1980	2.10%	6/30/1991	1.30%
12/31/1980	4.67%	9/30/1991	1.20%
3/31/1981	4.66%	12/31/1991	1.00%
6/30/1981	1.09%	3/31/1992	1.65%
9/30/1981	3.01%	6/30/1992	1.52%
12/31/1981	0.55%	9/30/1992	1.44%
3/31/1982	−0.30%	12/31/1992	1.63%
6/30/1982	1.76%	3/31/1993	0.90%
9/30/1982	1.03%	6/30/1993	1.06%
12/31/1982	1.17%	9/30/1993	0.95%
3/31/1983	2.07%	12/31/1993	1.88%
6/30/1983	2.99%	3/31/1994	1.63%
9/30/1983	3.02%	6/30/1994	1.73%
12/31/1983	2.82%	9/30/1994	1.20%
3/31/1984	3.23%	12/31/1994	1.65%
6/30/1984	2.60%	3/31/1995	0.91%
9/30/1984	1.78%	6/30/1995	0.54%
12/31/1984	1.46%	9/30/1995	1.29%
3/31/1985	2.06%	12/31/1995	1.22%
6/30/1985	1.43%	3/31/1996	1.35%
9/30/1985	1.98%	6/30/1996	2.00%
12/31/1985	1.42%	9/30/1996	1.15%
3/31/1986	1.48%	12/31/1996	1.71%
6/30/1986	0.91%	3/31/1997	1.42%
9/30/1986	1.54%	6/30/1997	1.68%
12/31/1986	1.16%	9/30/1997	1.59%
3/31/1987	1.49%	12/31/1997	1.07%
6/30/1987	1.65%	3/31/1998	1.36%

(continues)

Date	Percent Change in GDP	Date	Percent Change in GDP
6/30/1998	0.83%	12/31/2001	0.90%
9/30/1998	1.52%	3/29/2002	1.09%
12/31/1998	1.87%	6/28/2002	1.04%
3/31/1999	1.26%	9/30/2002	0.96%
6/30/1999	1.19%	12/31/2002	0.67%
9/30/1999	1.52%	**3/31/2003**	**1.20%**
12/31/1999	2.21%	**6/30/2003**	**1.30%**
3/31/2000	1.15%	**9/30/2003**	**2.14%**
6/30/2000	2.01%	**12/31/2003**	**1.39%**
9/29/2000	0.40%	**3/31/2004**	**1.79%**
12/29/2000	0.93%	**6/30/2004**	**1.61%**
3/30/2001	0.68%	**9/30/2004**	**1.25%**
6/29/2001	1.07%		
9/28/2001	0.06%		

Date	S&P	Date	S&P	Date	S&P
12/31/1800	2.7351	12/31/1844	2.6852	12/31/1888	5.14
12/31/1801	2.934	12/31/1845	2.9025	12/31/1889	5.32
12/31/1802	3.1995	**12/31/1846**	**2.4808**	12/31/1890	4.6
12/31/1803	2.8919	**12/31/1847**	**2.5111**	12/31/1891	5.41
12/31/1804	2.7688	**12/31/1848**	**2.4203**	12/31/1892	5.51
12/31/1805	2.6458	12/31/1849	2.4203	12/31/1893	4.41
12/31/1806	2.7688	12/31/1850	2.8741	12/31/1894	4.3
12/31/1807	2.8919	12/31/1851	2.7834	12/31/1895	4.32
12/31/1808	2.8919	12/31/1852	3.3279	12/31/1896	4.22
12/31/1809	2.9226	12/31/1853	2.9044	**12/31/1897**	**4.75**
12/31/1810	2.8611	12/31/1854	2.027	**12/31/1898**	**5.65**
12/31/1811	**2.6458**	12/31/1855	2.0573	**12/31/1899**	**6.02**
12/31/1812	**2.7381**	12/31/1856	2.148	**12/31/1900**	**6.87**
12/31/1813	**2.7688**	12/31/1857	1.4824	12/31/1901	7.95
12/31/1814	**2.3073**	12/31/1858	1.6942	12/31/1902	8.05
12/31/1815	2.3704	12/31/1859	1.5127	12/31/1903	6.57
12/31/1816	2.2797	12/31/1860	1.7245	12/31/1904	8.25
12/31/1817	2.5501	**12/31/1861**	**1.6942**	12/31/1905	9.54
12/31/1818	2.4679	**12/31/1862**	**2.6321**	12/31/1906	9.84
12/31/1819	2.283	**12/31/1863**	**3.6326**	12/31/1907	6.57
12/31/1820	2.391	**12/31/1864**	**3.8663**	12/31/1908	9.03
12/31/1821	2.5374	**12/31/1865**	**3.5387**	12/31/1909	10.3
12/31/1822	2.4154	12/31/1866	3.665	12/31/1910	9.05
12/31/1823	2.4154	12/31/1867	3.722	12/31/1911	9.11
12/31/1824	2.5374	12/31/1868	4.1234	12/31/1912	9.38
12/31/1825	2.391	12/31/1869	4.195	12/31/1913	8.04
12/31/1826	2.391	12/31/1870	4.4286	12/31/1914	7.35
12/31/1827	2.3178	12/31/1871	4.7498	12/31/1915	9.48
12/31/1828	2.3178	12/31/1872	5.0731	12/31/1916	9.8
12/31/1829	2.2934	12/31/1873	4.4265	**12/31/1917**	**6.8**
12/31/1830	2.4642	12/31/1874	4.5508	**12/31/1918**	**7.9176**
12/31/1831	2.5374	12/31/1875	4.3643	12/31/1919	9.0235
12/31/1832	2.6594	12/31/1876	3.581	12/29/1920	6.8118
12/31/1833	2.635	12/31/1877	3.2453	12/28/1921	7.3176
12/31/1834	2.9788	12/31/1878	3.4442	12/27/1922	8.8471
12/31/1835	3.0719	12/31/1879	4.9239	12/31/1923	8.7176
12/31/1836	2.712	12/31/1880	5.844	12/29/1924	10.3529
12/31/1837	2.4008	12/31/1881	6.0181	12/31/1925	12.76
12/31/1838	2.4388	12/31/1882	5.844	12/31/1926	13.49
12/31/1839	2.1392	12/31/1883	5.3466	12/31/1927	17.66
12/31/1840	2.2575	12/31/1884	4.3395	12/31/1928	24.35
12/31/1841	1.9579	12/31/1885	5.2	12/31/1929	21.45
12/31/1842	1.6036	12/31/1886	5.64	12/31/1930	15.34
12/31/1843	2.3256	12/31/1887	5.27	12/31/1931	8.1234

Note: War years are in bold type.

(continues)

Date	S&P	Date	S&P	Date	S&P
12/31/1932	6.8892	12/31/1956	46.6751	12/31/1981	122.55
12/30/1933	10.1008	12/31/1957	39.99	12/31/1982	140.64
12/31/1934	9.4962	12/31/1958	55.21	12/30/1983	164.93
12/31/1935	13.4383	12/31/1959	59.89	12/31/1984	167.24
12/31/1936	17.1788	12/30/1960	58.11	12/31/1985	211.28
12/31/1937	10.5416	12/29/1961	71.55	12/31/1986	242.17
12/31/1938	13.2116	12/31/1962	63.1	12/31/1987	247.08
12/30/1939	12.4937	12/31/1963	75.02	12/30/1988	277.7199
12/31/1940	10.5793	**12/31/1964**	**84.75**	12/29/1989	353.3998
12/31/1941	**8.6902**	**12/31/1965**	**92.43**	12/31/1990	330.2199
12/31/1942	**9.77**	**12/30/1966**	**80.33**	**12/31/1991**	**417.09**
12/31/1943	**11.67**	**12/29/1967**	**96.47**	12/31/1992	435.7099
12/30/1944	**13.28**	**12/31/1968**	**103.86**	12/31/1993	466.45
12/31/1945	**17.36**	**12/31/1969**	**92.06**	12/30/1994	459.27
12/31/1946	15.3023	**12/31/1970**	**92.15**	12/29/1995	615.93
12/31/1947	15.3023	**12/31/1971**	**102.09**	12/31/1996	740.74
12/31/1948	15.2015	**12/29/1972**	**118.05**	12/31/1997	970.43
12/31/1949	16.76	**12/31/1973**	**97.55**	12/31/1998	1229.23
12/30/1950	**20.41**	12/31/1974	68.56	12/31/1999	1469.25
12/31/1951	**23.77**	12/31/1975	90.19	12/29/2000	1320.28
12/31/1952	**26.578**	12/31/1976	107.46	12/31/2001	1148.08
12/31/1953	**24.814**	12/30/1977	95.1	12/31/2002	880.07
12/31/1954	35.987	12/29/1978	96.11	**12/31/2003**	**1111.07**
12/30/1955	45.4786	12/31/1979	107.94	**12/31/2004**	**1212.07**
		2/31/1980	135.76		

Source: www.globalfindata.com

APPENDIX 19.3 War in Iraq and the S&P 500 Index, 1990–1991

Date	S&P	Date	S&P	Date	S&P
1-Aug-90	355.52	11-Oct-90	295.46	21-Dec-90	331.75
2-Aug-90	**351.48**	12-Oct-90	300.03	24-Dec-90	329.9
3-Aug-90	344.86	15-Oct-90	303.23	26-Dec-90	330.85
6-Aug-90	334.43	16-Oct-90	298.92	27-Dec-90	328.29
7-Aug-90	334.83	17-Oct-90	298.76	28-Dec-90	328.72
8-Aug-90	338.35	18-Oct-90	305.74	31-Dec-90	330.22
9-Aug-90	339.94	19-Oct-90	312.47	2-Jan-91	326.45
10-Aug-90	335.52	22-Oct-90	314.76	3-Jan-91	321.91
13-Aug-90	335.73	23-Oct-90	312.36	4-Jan-91	321
14-Aug-90	339.39	24-Oct-90	312.6	7-Jan-91	315.44
15-Aug-90	340.06	25-Oct-90	310.17	8-Jan-91	314.9
16-Aug-90	332.39	26-Oct-90	304.71	9-Jan-91	311.49
17-Aug-90	327.83	29-Oct-90	301.88	10-Jan-91	314.53
20-Aug-90	328.51	30-Oct-90	304.06	11-Jan-91	315.23
21-Aug-90	321.86	31-Oct-90	304	14-Jan-91	312.49
22-Aug-90	316.55	1-Nov-90	307.02	15-Jan-91	313.73
23-Aug-90	**307.06**	2-Nov-90	311.85	16-Jan-91	316.17
24-Aug-90	311.51	5-Nov-90	314.59	17-Jan-91	327.97
27-Aug-90	321.44	6-Nov-90	311.62	18-Jan-91	332.23
28-Aug-90	321.34	7-Nov-90	306.01	21-Jan-91	331.06
29-Aug-90	324.19	8-Nov-90	307.61	22-Jan-91	328.31
30-Aug-90	318.71	9-Nov-90	313.74	23-Jan-91	330.21
31-Aug-90	322.56	12-Nov-90	319.48	24-Jan-91	334.78
4-Sep-90	323.09	13-Nov-90	317.67	25-Jan-91	336.07
5-Sep-90	324.39	14-Nov-90	320.4	28-Jan-91	336.03
6-Sep-90	320.46	15-Nov-90	317.02	29-Jan-91	335.84
7-Sep-90	323.4	16-Nov-90	317.12	30-Jan-91	340.91
10-Sep-90	321.63	19-Nov-90	319.34	31-Jan-91	343.93
11-Sep-90	321.04	20-Nov-90	315.31	1-Feb-91	343.05
12-Sep-90	322.54	21-Nov-90	316.03	4-Feb-91	348.34
13-Sep-90	318.65	23-Nov-90	315.1	5-Feb-91	351.26
14-Sep-90	316.83	26-Nov-90	316.51	6-Feb-91	358.07
17-Sep-90	317.77	27-Nov-90	318.1	7-Feb-91	356.52
18-Sep-90	318.6	28-Nov-90	317.95	8-Feb-91	359.35
19-Sep-90	316.6	29-Nov-90	316.42	11-Feb-91	368.58
20-Sep-90	311.48	30-Nov-90	322.22	12-Feb-91	365.5
21-Sep-90	311.32	23-Dec-90	324.1	13-Feb-91	369.02
24-Sep-90	304.55	4-Dec-90	326.35	14-Feb-91	364.22
25-Sep-90	308.26	5-Dec-90	329.92	15-Feb-91	369.06
26-Sep-90	305.06	6-Dec-90	329.07	19-Feb-91	369.39
27-Sep-90	300.97	7-Dec-90	327.75	20-Feb-91	365.14
28-Sep-90	306.05	10-Dec-90	328.89	21-Feb-91	364.97
1-Oct-90	314.94	11-Dec-90	326.44	22-Feb-91	365.65
2-Oct-90	315.21	12-Dec-90	330.19	25-Feb-91	367.26
3-Oct-90	311.4	13-Dec-90	329.34	26-Feb-91	362.81
4-Oct-90	312.69	14-Dec-90	326.82	27-Feb-91	367.74
5-Oct-90	311.5	17-Dec-90	326.02	28-Feb-91	367.07
8-Oct-90	313.48	18-Dec-90	330.05	1-Mar-91	370.47
9-Oct-90	305.1	19-Dec-90	330.2	**End: 4-Mar-91**	**369.33**
10-Oct-90	300.4	20-Dec-90	330.12		

Note: Dates of Kuwait invasion, troop call-up, and deployment are in bold type.

Source: ComStock, Inc. (Yahoo.com).

APPENDIX 19.4 War in Iraq and the S&P 500 Index, 2002–2003

Date	S&P	Date	S&P	Date	S&P
1-Oct-02	847.91	27-Nov-02	938.87	30-Jan-03	844.61
2-Oct-02	827.91	29-Nov-02	936.31	31-Jan-03	855.7
3-Oct-02	818.95	2-Dec-02	934.53	3-Feb-03	860.32
4-Oct-02	800.58	3-Dec-02	920.75	5-Feb-03	843.59
7-Oct-02	785.28	4-Dec-02	917.57	6-Feb-03	838.15
8-Oct-02	798.55	5-Dec-02	906.55	7-Feb-03	829.69
9-Oct-02	776.76	6-Dec-02	912.23	10-Feb-03	835.97
10-Oct-02	**803.92**	9-Dec-02	892	11-Feb-03	829.2
11-Oct-02	835.32	10-Dec-02	904.45	12-Feb-03	818.68
14-Oct-02	841.44	11-Dec-02	904.96	13-Feb-03	817.37
15-Oct-02	881.27	12-Dec-02	901.58	14-Feb-03	834.89
16-Oct-02	860.02	13-Dec-02	889.48	18-Feb-03	851.17
17-Oct-02	879.2	16-Dec-02	910.4	19-Feb-03	845.13
18-Oct-02	884.39	17-Dec-02	902.99	20-Feb-03	837.1
21-Oct-02	899.72	18-Dec-02	891.12	21-Feb-03	848.17
22-Oct-02	890.16	19-Dec-02	884.25	24-Feb-03	832.58
23-Oct-02	896.14	20-Dec-02	895.74	25-Feb-03	838.57
24-Oct-02	882.5	23-Dec-02	897.38	26-Feb-03	827.55
25-Oct-02	897.65	24-Dec-02	892.47	27-Feb-03	837.28
28-Oct-02	890.23	26-Dec-02	889.66	28-Feb-03	841.15
29-Oct-02	882.15	27-Dec-02	875.4	3-Mar-03	834.81
30-Oct-02	890.71	30-Dec-02	879.39	4-Mar-03	821.99
31-Oct-02	885.77	31-Dec-02	879.82	5-Mar-03	829.85
1-Nov-02	900.96	2-Jan-03	909.03	6-Mar-03	822.1
4-Nov-02	908.34	3-Jan-03	908.59	7-Mar-03	828.89
5-Nov-02	915.39	6-Jan-03	929.01	10-Mar-03	807.48
6-Nov-02	923.76	7-Jan-03	922.92	11-Mar-03	800.73
7-Nov-02	902.65	8-Jan-03	909.93	12-Mar-03	804.19
8-Nov-02	894.74	9-Jan-03	927.58	13-Mar-03	831.9
11-Nov-02	876.18	10-Jan-03	927.57	14-Mar-03	833.27
12-Nov-02	882.95	13-Jan-03	926.26	17-Mar-03	862.79
13-Nov-02	882.53	14-Jan-03	931.66	18-Mar-03	866.45
14-Nov-02	904.27	15-Jan-03	918.22	19-Mar-03	874.02
15-Nov-02	909.83	16-Jan-03	914.6	**20-Mar-03**	**875.84**
18-Nov-02	900.36	17-Jan-03	901.78	21-Mar-03	895.79
19-Nov-02	896.74	21-Jan-03	887.62	24-Mar-03	864.23
20-Nov-02	914.15	22-Jan-03	878.36	25-Mar-03	874.74
21-Nov-02	933.76	23-Jan-03	887.34	26-Mar-03	869.95
22-Nov-02	930.55	24-Jan-03	861.4	27-Mar-03	868.52
25-Nov-02	932.87	27-Jan-03	847.48	28-Mar-03	863.5
26-Nov-02	913.31	28-Jan-03	858.54	31-Mar-03	848.18
		29-Jan-03	864.36		

Note: Call-up and deployment dates are in bold type.

Source: ComStock, Inc. (Yahoo.com).

370

Chapter 19 Return Calculations, 1960–2002

Trade	Date	S&P	One + % Gain/Loss	Old Index	× Change	New Index
Buy	January 2, 1960	59				
Sell	September 1, 1966	77	1 + (77 – 59/59)	1	1.035	1.305
Buy	February 1, 1967	86				
Sell	July 1, 1969	97	1 + (97 – 86/86)	1.305	1.1279	1.4719
Buy	February 1, 1970	85				
Sell	June 1, 1973	105	1 + (105 – 85/85)	1.4719	1.235	1.8182
Buy	October 1, 1974	63				
Sell	December 1, 1978	94	1 + (94 – 63/63)	1.8182	1.49206	2.71286
Buy	May 1, 1980	106				
Sell	November 1, 1980	127	1 + (127 – 106/106)	2.71286	1.1981	3.2503
Buy	September 1, 1981	122				
Sell	October 15, 1987	298	1 + (298 – 122/122)	3.2503	2.4426	7.9401
Buy	October 20, 1987	236				
Sell	October 31, 1989	340	1 + (340 – 236/236)	7.9401	1.4406	11.4391
Buy	August 23, 1990	307				
Sell	July 1, 1998	1133	1 + (1133 – 307/307)	11.4391	3.6905	42.2166
Buy	September 4, 1998	973				
Sell	August 1, 2000	1430	1 + (1430 – 973/973)	42.2166	1.4696	62.04151536
Buy	July 19, 2002	847				
End	October 1, 2002	815	1 – (847 – 815/847)	62.0415	0.962	59.6975

Chapter 19 Returns   42.75th root of $61.736876 = 9.56%

To Lowest Point in the Market: 10/1/2002	Buy and Hold Trade	$13.81 $59.70	Buy and Hold Trade	**6.33%** **9.56%**

Trade	Date	S&P	One + % Gain/Loss	Old Index	× Change	New Index
Buy	January 2, 1960	59				
Sell	September 1, 1966	77	1 + (77 − 59/59)	1	1.035	1.305
Buy	February 1, 1967	86				
Sell	July 1, 1969	97	1 + (97 − 86/86)	1.305	1.1279	1.4719
Buy	February 1, 1970	85				
Sell	June 1, 1973	105	1 + (105 − 85/85)	1.4719	1.235	1.8182
Buy	October 1, 1974	63				
Sell	December 1, 1978	94	1 + (94 − 63/63)	1.8182	1.49206	2.71286
Buy	May 1, 1980	106				
Sell	November 1, 1980	127	1 + (127 − 106/106)	2.71286	1.1981	3.2503
Buy	September 1, 1981	122				
Sell	October 15, 1987	298	1 + (298 − 122/122)	3.2503	2.4426	7.9401
Buy	October 20, 1987	236				
Sell	October 31, 1989	340	1 + (340 − 236/236)	7.9401	1.4406	11.4391
Buy	August 23, 1990	307				
Sell	July 1, 1998	1133	1 + (1133 − 307/307)	11.4391	3.6905	42.2166
Buy	September 4, 1998	973				
Sell	August 1, 2000	1430	1 + (1430 − 973/973)	42.2166	1.4696	62.04151536
Buy	July 19, 2002	847				
End	January 2, 2005	1212	1 + (1212 − 847/847)	62.0415	1.4309	88.77518

| | Buy and Hold: | 45th root | $20.54 | **6.94%** |
| | Trading: | 45th root | $88.77 | **10.48%** |

Quarter	Change in Home Prices	Quarter	Change in Home Prices	Quarter	Change in Home Prices	Quarter	Change in Home Prices
1970.02	2.41	1979.01	2.97	1987.04	0.80	1996.02	0.42
1970.03	**−2.84**	1979.02	3.66	1988.01	1.83	1996.03	0.62
1970.04	1.63	1979.03	2.31	1988.02	2.25	1996.04	0.93
1971.01	1.27	1979.04	1.55	1988.03	1.16	1997.01	0.97
1971.02	4.33	1980.01	1.90	1988.04	1.12	1997.02	0.97
1971.03	**−2.81**	1980.02	2.02	1989.01	1.51	1997.03	1.56
1971.04	0.57	1980.03	2.59	1989.02	1.55	1997.04	1.38
1972.01	1.35	1980.04	0.43	1989.03	2.42	1998.01	1.53
1972.02	4.07	1981.01	0.86	1989.04	1.09	1998.02	0.81
1972.03	**−0.62**	1981.02	2.50	1990.01	0.54	1998.03	1.45
1972.04	2.00	1981.03	1.38	1990.02	0.21	1998.04	1.23
1973.01	2.63	1981.04	0.55	1990.03	0.52	1999.01	1.09
1973.02	4.31	1982.01	1.53	**1990.04**	**−0.27**	1999.02	1.44
1973.03	0.97	**1982.02**	**−0.15**	1991.01	0.90	1999.03	1.69
1973.04	1.84	**1982.03**	**−0.55**	1991.02	0.62	1999.04	1.22
1974.01	1.93	1982.04	0.46	1991.03	0.12	2000.01	2.10
1974.02	3.27	1983.01	1.88	1991.04	1.44	2000.02	1.72
1974.03	0.77	1983.02	0.95	1992.01	0.76	2000.03	1.96
1974.04	1.61	1983.03	0.70	**1992.02**	**−0.03**	2000.04	1.61
1975.01	0.09	1983.04	0.29	1992.03	1.10	2001.01	2.63
1975.02	4.22	1984.01	1.34	1992.04	0.53	2001.02	1.79
1975.03	**−0.29**	1984.02	1.61	**1993.01**	**−0.05**	2001.03	1.67
1975.04	1.63	1984.03	1.00	1993.02	0.88	2001.04	1.23
1976.01	2.61	1984.04	0.70	1993.03	0.72	2002.01	1.63
1976.02	2.87	1985.01	1.33	1993.04	0.87	2002.02	1.86
1976.03	0.95	1985.02	1.32	1994.01	0.63	2002.03	2.11
1976.04	1.47	1985.03	1.72	1994.02	0.62	2002.04	1.55
1977.01	1.94	1985.04	1.13	1994.03	0.56	2003.01	1.31
1977.02	5.08	1986.01	2.00	1994.04	0.00	2003.02	1.26
1977.03	2.87	1986.02	2.08	1995.01	0.48	2003.03	1.48
1977.04	2.87	1986.03	1.60	1995.02	1.74	2003.04	4.16
1978.01	3.60	1986.04	1.62	1995.03	1.61	2004.01	1.55
1978.02	3.92	1987.01	2.11	1995.04	0.85	2004.02	2.38
1978.03	2.91	1987.02	1.79	1996.01	1.30	2004.03	3.76
1978.04	2.76	1987.03	1.39	1996.02	0.42		

Note: Negative changes are in bold type.

Source: www.freddiemac.com.

Returns Including Treasury Bills, 1960–2004

Trade	Date	S&P	One + % Gain/Loss	× Old Index	= New Index	Cumulative Index
Buy	1/1/1960	59	1 + (77 − 59/59)	1	1.035	1.305
Sell	9/1/66	77				
Bills' return			0.021139726	1.305	1.021139726	1.33258734
Buy	2/1/67	86	1 + (97 − 86/86)	1.332587342	1.1279	1.50302526
Sell	7/1/69	97				
Bills' return			0.041917808	1.503025264	1.041917808	1.56602879
Buy	2/1/70	85	1 + (105 − 85/85)	1.566028788	1.235	1.93404555
Sell	6/1/73	105				
Bills' return			0.104005479	1.934045554	1.104005479	2.13519689
Buy	10/1/74	63	1 + (94 − 63/63)	2.135196889	1.49206	3.18584187
Sell	12/1/78	94				
Bills' return			0.150550685	3.18584187	1.150550685	3.66547255
Buy	5/1/80	106	1 + (127 − 106/106)	3.665472545	1.1981	4.39160266
Sell	11/1/80	127				
Bills' return			0.121290411	4.391602656	1.121290411	4.92426195
Buy	9/1/81	122	1 + (298 − 122/122)	4.924261947	2.4426	12.0280022
Sell	10/15/87	298				
Bills' return			0.005038356	12.02800223	1.005038356	12.0886036
Buy	10/20/87	236	1 + (340 − 236/236)	12.08860359	1.4406	17.4148423
Sell	10/31/ 89	340				
Bills' return			0.063369863	17.41484233	1.063369863	18.5184185
Buy	8/23/90	307	1 + (1133 − 307/307)	18.51841851	3.6905	68.3422235
Sell	7/1/98	1133				
Bills' return			0.00810411	68.3422235	1.00810411	68.8960764
Buy	9/2/98	973	1 + (1430 − 973/973)	68.89607637	1.4696	101.249674
Sell	8/1/00	1430				
Bills' return			0.066673973	101.2496738	1.066673973	108.000392
Buy	7/19/02	819	1 + (1212 − 847/847)	108.0003918	1.430932	**154.54**
End	**12/31/2004**	**1212**				

Buy and Hold:		**45th root of**	**20.54 =**	**6.95%**	**$20.54**
Trading:		**45th root of**	**154.54 =**	**11.85%**	**$154.54**

Source: www.federalreserve.gov/releases/h15/data.htm.

Date	Gold	Date	Gold	Date	Gold
12/31/1800	19	12/31/1842	21	12/31/1886	21
12/31/1843	21	12/31/1843	21	12/31/1887	21
12/31/1886	21	12/31/1844	21	12/31/1888	21
12/31/1801	19	12/31/1845	21	12/31/1889	21
12/31/1802	19	12/31/1846	21	12/31/1890	21
12/31/1803	19	12/31/1847	21	12/31/1891	21
12/31/1804	19	12/31/1848	21	12/31/1892	21
12/31/1805	19	12/31/1849	21	12/31/1893	21
12/31/1806	19	12/31/1850	21	12/31/1894	21
12/31/1807	19	12/31/1851	21	12/31/1895	21
12/31/1808	19	12/31/1852	21	12/31/1896	21
12/31/1809	19	12/31/1853	21	12/31/1897	21
12/31/1810	19	12/31/1854	21	12/31/1898	21
12/31/1811	19	12/31/1855	21	12/31/1899	21
12/31/1812	19	12/31/1856	21	12/31/1900	21
12/31/1813	19	12/31/1857	21	12/31/1901	21
12/31/1814	22	12/31/1858	21	12/31/1902	21
12/31/1815	22	12/31/1859	21	12/31/1903	21
12/31/1816	20	12/31/1860	21	12/31/1904	21
12/31/1817	19	12/31/1861	21	12/31/1905	21
12/31/1818	19	12/31/1862	28	12/31/1906	21
12/31/1819	19	12/31/1863	31	12/31/1907	21
12/31/1820	19	12/31/1864	46	12/31/1908	21
12/31/1821	19	12/31/1865	30	12/31/1909	21
12/31/1822	19	12/31/1866	27	12/31/1910	21
12/31/1823	19	12/31/1867	28	12/31/1911	21
12/31/1824	19	12/31/1868	28	12/31/1912	21
12/31/1825	19	12/31/1869	25	12/31/1913	21
12/31/1826	19	12/31/1870	23	12/31/1914	21
12/31/1827	19	12/31/1871	23	12/31/1915	21
12/31/1828	19	12/31/1872	23	12/31/1916	21
12/31/1829	19	12/31/1873	23	12/31/1917	21
12/31/1830	19	12/31/1874	23	12/31/1918	21
12/31/1831	19	12/31/1875	23	12/31/1919	21
12/31/1832	19	12/31/1876	22	12/31/1920	21
12/31/1833	19	12/31/1877	21	12/31/1921	21
12/31/1834	21	12/31/1878	21	12/31/1922	21
12/31/1835	21	12/31/1879	21	12/31/1923	21
12/31/1836	21	12/31/1880	21	12/31/1924	21
12/31/1837	22	12/31/1881	21	12/31/1925	21
12/31/1838	21	12/31/1882	21	12/31/1926	21
12/31/1839	21	12/31/1883	21	12/31/1927	21
12/31/1840	21	12/31/1884	21	12/31/1928	21
12/31/1841	21	12/31/1885	21	12/31/1929	21

(continues)

Date	Gold	Date	Gold	Date	Gold
12/31/1930	21	12/31/1955	35	12/31/1980	641
12/31/1931	21	12/31/1956	35	12/31/1981	431
12/31/1932	21	12/31/1957	35	12/31/1982	485
12/31/1933	32	12/31/1958	35	12/31/1983	415
12/31/1934	35	12/31/1959	35	12/31/1984	331
12/31/1935	35	12/31/1960	37	12/31/1985	354
12/31/1936	35	12/31/1961	36	12/31/1986	435
12/31/1937	35	12/31/1962	35	12/31/1987	523
12/31/1938	35	12/31/1963	35	12/31/1988	441
12/31/1939	35	12/31/1964	35	12/31/1989	433
12/31/1940	35	12/31/1965	36	12/31/1990	424
12/31/1941	36	12/31/1966	35	12/31/1991	380
12/31/1942	36	12/31/1967	36	12/31/1992	356
12/31/1943	37	12/31/1968	44	12/31/1993	419
12/31/1944	36	12/31/1969	35	12/31/1994	410
12/31/1945	37	12/31/1970	38	12/31/1995	386
12/31/1946	38	12/31/1971	44	12/31/1996	368
12/31/1947	43	12/31/1972	65	12/31/1997	289
12/31/1948	42	12/31/1973	115	12/31/1998	288
12/31/1949	41	12/31/1974	195	12/31/1999	288
12/31/1950	40	12/31/1975	151	12/31/2000	272
12/31/1951	40	12/31/1976	145	12/31/2001	279
12/31/1952	39	12/31/1977	179	12/31/2002	347
12/31/1953	36	12/31/1978	245	12/31/2003	415
12/31/1954	35	12/31/1979	579	12/31/2004	444

Source: www.globalfindata.com.

Trade	Date	S&P		Gain/Loss	Index
Buy	10/1/74	63			1
Sell	12/1/78	94	1+ (94 – 63/63)	1.49	1.492063
	Gold		1 + (490 – 194/194)	2.52	3.756994
Buy	5/1/80	106			
Sell	11/1/80	127	1 + (127 – 106/106)	1.20	4.501305
	Gold		1 + (421 – 640/640)	0.66	2.962217
Buy	9/1/81	122			
Sell	10/15/87	298	1 + (298 – 122/122)	2.44	7.235579
	Gold		1 + (464 – 466/464)	1.00	7.199913
Buy	10/20/87	236			
Sell	10/31/ 89	340	1+ (340 – 236/236)	1.44	10.37276
	Gold		1 + (412 – 375/375)	1.10	11.39815
Buy	8/23/90	307			
Sell	7/1/98	1133	1 + (1133 – 307/307)	3.69	42.06547
	Gold		1 + (285 – 296/296)	0.96	40.39306
Buy	9/2/98	973			
Sell	8/1/00	1430	1 + (1430 – 973/973)	1.47	59.36493
	Gold		1 + (322 – 277/277)	1.16	69.05236
Buy	7/19/02	847			
End	12/31/04	1212	1 + (1212 – 847/847)	1.43	98.80928

	30.25th Root of Index	
Passive:	$19.23	10.26%
Active:	$98.81	16.40%

Date		Gold Price
Buy:	12/1/78	**194.6**
Sell:	5/1/80	**490**
Buy:	11/1/80	**640.5**
Sell:	9/1/81	**421.5**
Buy:	10/15/87	**466.6**
Sell:	10/20/87	**464.3**
Buy:	10/31/89	**375.3**
Sell:	8/23/90	**412.4**
Buy:	7/1/98	**296.8**
Sell:	9/4/98	**285**
Buy:	8/1/00	**277.6**
Sell:	7/19/02	**322.9**

Source: Daily gold prices from the COMEX division of the New York Mercantile Exchange (www.normanshistoricaldata.com).

Euro Exchange Rates and U.S. Business Cycles,
1969–2004

Date	Euro/US $	Date	Euro/US $
12/31/1969	1.0193	12/31/1987	1.3034
12/31/1970	**1.0254**	12/31/1988	1.1726
12/31/1971	1.1057	12/31/1989	1.197
12/31/1972	1.1014	**12/31/1990**	**1.3633**
12/31/1973	1.1634	**12/31/1991**	**1.3409**
12/31/1974	**1.2497**	12/31/1992	1.205
12/31/1975	1.1653	12/31/1993	1.113
12/31/1976	1.1356	12/31/1994	1.226
12/31/1977	1.2464	12/31/1995	1.2795
12/31/1978	1.3779	12/31/1996	1.245
12/31/1979	1.4384	12/31/1997	1.0986
12/31/1980	**1.3096**	12/31/1998	1.1721
12/31/1981	**1.0852**	12/31/1999	1.007
12/31/1982	**0.9677**	12/31/2000	0.9422
12/31/1983	0.825	**12/31/2001**	**0.8904**
12/31/1984	0.7082	12/31/2002	1.0496
12/31/1985	0.8879	12/31/2003	1.2578
12/31/1986	1.0646	12/31/2004	1.3558

Business Cycles

Peak	Trough
December 1969	November 1970
November 1973	March 1975
January 1980	July 1980
July 1981	November 1982
July 1990	March 1991
March 2001	November 2001

Note: Recessions are in bold type.

Source: www.globalfindata.com.

APPENDIX 23.1 Gold and Nasdaq Return Calculations, 1974–2004

Date	Nasdaq	Gold	$ Change	% Change	1 + Change	Index
10/1/1974	55.48					
12/1/1978	116.19		60.71	1.0943	2.0943	2.0943
12/1/1978		194.6				
5/1/1980		490	295.4	1.5180	2.5180	5.273337
5/1/1980	139.68					
11/3/1980	193.15		53.47	0.3828	1.3828	7.291989
11/3/1980		640.5				
9/1/1981		421.5	−219	−0.3419	0.6581	4.79871
9/1/1981	195.17					
10/15/1987	422.51		227.34	1.1648	2.1648	10.38839
10/15/1987		466.6				
10/20/1987		464.3	−2.3	−0.0049	0.9951	10.33719
10/20/1987	327.79					
10/2/1989	475.19		147.4	0.4497	1.4497	14.98559
10/2/1989		366.5				
8/23/1990		412.4	45.9	0.1252	1.1252	16.86237
8/23/1990	360.22					
7/1/1998	1914.46		1554.24	4.3147	5.3147	89.6184
7/1/1998		296.8				
9/4/1998		285	−11.8	−0.0398	0.9602	86.05539
9/4/1998	1566.52					
8/1/2000	3685.51		2118.99	1.3527	2.3527	202.4597
8/1/2000		277.6				
7/18/2002		317.6	40	0.1441	1.1441	231.6325
7/18/2002	1356.95					
1/3/2005	2062		705.05	0.5196	1.5196	351.9852

30.25 root	Passive S&P	**10%**
of each index:	Passive Nasdaq	**13%**
	Active Nasdaq & Gold	**22%**
	Passive S&P	$19
	Passive Nasdaq	$37
	Active Nasdaq & Gold	$352

Sources: COMEX Closing Prices and Nasdaq Exchange.

Date	Nasdaq Composite	Date	Nasdaq Composite	Date	Nasdaq Composite
11-Oct-84	247	1-Nov-88	371.5	1-Dec-92	676.95
1-Nov-84	242.4	1-Dec-88	381.4	4-Jan-93	696.34
3-Dec-84	247.1	3-Jan-89	401.3	1-Feb-93	670.77
2-Jan-85	278.7	1-Feb-89	399.7	1-Mar-93	690.13
1-Feb-85	284.2	1-Mar-89	406.7	1-Apr-93	661.42
1-Mar-85	279.2	3-Apr-89	427.6	3-May-93	700.53
1-Apr-85	280.6	1-May-89	446.2	1-Jun-93	703.95
1-May-85	290.8	1-Jun-89	435.3	1-Jul-93	704.7
3-Jun-85	296.2	3-Jul-89	453.8	2-Aug-93	742.84
1-Jul-85	301.3	1-Aug-89	469.3	1-Sep-93	762.78
1-Aug-85	297.7	1-Sep-89	472.9	1-Oct-93	779.26
3-Sep-85	280.3	2-Oct-89	455.6	1-Nov-93	754.39
1-Oct-85	292.5	1-Nov-89	456.1	1-Dec-93	776.8
1-Nov-85	314	1-Dec-89	454.8	3-Jan-94	800.47
2-Dec-85	324.9	2-Jan-90	415.8	1-Feb-94	792.5
2-Jan-86	335.8	1-Feb-90	425.8	1-Mar-94	788.64
3-Feb-86	359.5	1-Mar-90	435.5	4-Apr-94	733.84
3-Mar-86	374.7	2-Apr-90	420.1	2-May-94	735.19
1-Apr-86	383.2	1-May-90	459	1-Jun-94	705.96
1-May-86	400.2	1-Jun-90	462.3	1-Jul-94	722.16
2-Jun-86	405.5	2-Jul-90	438.2	1-Aug-94	765.62
1-Jul-86	371.4	1-Aug-90	381.2	1-Sep-94	764.29
1-Aug-86	382.9	4-Sep-90	344.5	3-Oct-94	777.49
2-Sep-86	350.7	1-Oct-90	329.8	1-Nov-94	750.32
1-Oct-86	360.8	1-Nov-90	359.1	1-Dec-94	751.96
3-Nov-86	359.6	3-Dec-90	373.8	3-Jan-95	755.2
1-Dec-86	348.8	2-Jan-91	414.2	1-Feb-95	793.73
2-Jan-87	392.1	1-Feb-91	453.1	1-Mar-95	817.21
2-Feb-87	425	1-Mar-91	482.3	3-Apr-95	843.98
2-Mar-87	430.1	1-Apr-91	484.72	1-May-95	864.58
1-Apr-87	417.8	1-May-91	506.11	1-Jun-95	933.45
1-May-87	416.5	3-Jun-91	475.92	3-Jul-95	1001.21
1-Jun-87	424.7	1-Jul-91	502.04	1-Aug-95	1020.11
1-Jul-87	434.9	1-Aug-91	525.68	1-Sep-95	1043.54
3-Aug-87	455	3-Sep-91	526.88	2-Oct-95	1036.06
1-Sep-87	444.3	1-Oct-91	542.98	1-Nov-95	1059.2
1-Oct-87	323.3	1-Nov-91	523.9	1-Dec-95	1052.13
2-Nov-87	305.2	2-Dec-91	586.34	2-Jan-96	1059.79
1-Dec-87	330.5	2-Jan-92	620.21	1-Feb-96	1100.05
4-Jan-88	344.7	3-Feb-92	633.47	1-Mar-96	1101.4
1-Feb-88	367	2-Mar-92	603.77	1-Apr-96	1190.52
1-Mar-88	374.6	1-Apr-92	578.68	1-May-96	1243.43
4-Apr-88	379.2	1-May-92	585.31	3-Jun-96	1185.02
2-May-88	370.3	1-Jun-92	563.6	1-Jul-96	1080.59
1-Jun-88	394.7	1-Jul-92	580.83	1-Aug-96	1141.5
1-Jul-88	387.3	3-Aug-92	563.12	3-Sep-96	1226.92
1-Aug-88	376.6	1-Sep-92	583.27	1-Oct-96	1221.51
1-Sep-88	387.7	1-Oct-92	605.17	1-Nov-96	1292.61
3-Oct-88	382.5	2-Nov-92	652.73	2-Dec-96	1291.03

Date	Nasdaq Composite	Date	Nasdaq Composite	Date	Nasdaq Composite
2-Jan-97	1379.85	1-Oct-99	2966.43	1-Jul-02	1328.26
3-Feb-97	1309	1-Nov-99	3336.16	1-Aug-02	1314.85
3-Mar-97	1221.7	1-Dec-99	4069.31	3-Sep-02	1172.06
1-Apr-97	1260.76	3-Jan-00	3940.35	1-Oct-02	1329.75
1-May-97	1400.32	1-Feb-00	4696.69	1-Nov-02	1478.78
2-Jun-97	1442.07	1-Mar-00	4572.83	2-Dec-02	1335.51
1-Jul-97	1593.81	3-Apr-00	3860.66	2-Jan-03	1320.91
1-Aug-97	1587.32	1-May-00	3400.91	3-Feb-03	1337.52
2-Sep-97	1685.69	1-Jun-00	3966.11	3-Mar-03	1341.17
1-Oct-97	1593.61	3-Jul-00	3766.99	1-Apr-03	1464.31
3-Nov-97	1600.55	1-Aug-00	4206.35	1-May-03	1595.91
1-Dec-97	1570.35	1-Sep-00	3672.82	2-Jun-03	1622.8
2-Jan-98	1619.36	2-Oct-00	3369.63	1-Jul-03	1735.02
2-Feb-98	1770.51	1-Nov-00	2597.93	1-Aug-03	1810.45
2-Mar-98	1835.68	1-Dec-00	2470.52	2-Sep-03	1786.94
1-Apr-98	1868.41	2-Jan-01	2772.73	1-Oct-03	1932.21
1-May-98	1778.87	1-Feb-01	2151.83	3-Nov-03	1960.26
1-Jun-98	1894.74	1-Mar-01	1840.26	1-Dec-03	2003.37
1-Jul-98	1872.39	2-Apr-01	2116.24	2-Jan-04	2066.15
3-Aug-98	1499.25	1-May-01	2110.49	2-Feb-04	2029.82
1-Sep-98	1693.84	1-Jun-01	2160.54	1-Mar-04	1994.22
1-Oct-98	1771.39	2-Jul-01	2027.13	1-Apr-04	1920.15
2-Nov-98	1949.54	1-Aug-01	1805.43	3-May-04	1986.74
1-Dec-98	2192.69	4-Sep-01	1498.8	1-Jun-04	2047.79
4-Jan-99	2505.89	1-Oct-01	1690.2	1-Jul-04	1887.36
1-Feb-99	2288.03	1-Nov-01	1930.58	2-Aug-04	1838.1
1-Mar-99	2461.4	3-Dec-01	1950.4	1-Sep-04	1896.84
1-Apr-99	2542.86	2-Jan-02	1934.03	1-Oct-04	1974.99
3-May-99	2470.52	1-Feb-02	1731.49	1-Nov-04	2096.81
1-Jun-99	2686.12	1-Mar-02	1845.35	1-Dec-04	2175.44
1-Jul-99	2638.49	1-Apr-02	1688.23	3-Jan-05	2062.41
2-Aug-99	2739.35	1-May-02	1615.73	1-Feb-05	2082.03
1-Sep-99	2746.16	3-Jun-02	1463.21		

Source: Nasdaq Stock Exchange (Yahoo.com).

APPENDIX 24.1 Nasdaq and Centex Return Calculations, 1990–2005

Date	Nasdaq	Centex	$ Change	% Change	1 + Change	Index
8/23/1990	360.22					
7/1/1998	1914.46		1554.24	4.314697	5.314696574	
7/1/1998		14.94				
9/4/1998		14.37	–0.57	–0.03815	0.96	5.102109
9/4/1998	1566.52					
8/1/2000	3685.51		2118.99	1.352673	2.352673442	12.0036
8/1/2000		9.42				
7/18/2002		19.21	9.79	1.039278	2.039278132	24.47867
7/18/1002	1356.95					
1/3/2005	2062		705.05	0.519584	1.519584362	37.1974

	14.33 root of Index	
Passive Nasdaq	$5.72	**13%**
Active Nasdaq & Centex	$37.19	**30%**

Date	Centex	Date	Centex	Date	Centex
1-Jul-98	**14.94**	14-Aug-98	15.8	29-Sep-98	13.26
2-Jul-98	15.28	17-Aug-98	16.01	30-Sep-98	13.16
6-Jul-98	15.3	18-Aug-98	16.35	1-Oct-98	12.3
7-Jul-98	15.75	19-Aug-98	16.04	2-Oct-98	12.21
8-Jul-98	15.97	20-Aug-98	16.32	5-Oct-98	12.3
9-Jul-98	15.85	21-Aug-98	15.82	6-Oct-98	12.09
10-Jul-98	15.89	24-Aug-98	16.2	7-Oct-98	11.71
13-Jul-98	16.35	25-Aug-98	16.23	8-Oct-98	10.47
14-Jul-98	16.32	26-Aug-98	16.3	9-Oct-98	10.99
15-Jul-98	16.11	27-Aug-98	15.51	12-Oct-98	11.25
16-Jul-98	16.39	28-Aug-98	14.99	13-Oct-98	10.56
17-Jul-98	16.44	31-Aug-98	13.47	14-Oct-98	10.54
20-Jul-98	16.56	1-Sep-98	14.3	15-Oct-98	11.06
21-Jul-98	16.63	2-Sep-98	14.94	16-Oct-98	11.92
22-Jul-98	16.42	3-Sep-98	14.75	19-Oct-98	12.18
23-Jul-98	16.16	**4-Sep-98**	**14.37**	20-Oct-98	12.99
24-Jul-98	16.3	8-Sep-98	14.45	21-Oct-98	13.16
27-Jul-98	15.73	9-Sep-98	14.23	22-Oct-98	12.99
28-Jul-98	15.28	10-Sep-98	13.78	23-Oct-98	12.3
29-Jul-98	15.75	11-Sep-98	13.73	26-Oct-98	13.14
30-Jul-98	15.75	14-Sep-98	14.31	27-Oct-98	12.73
31-Jul-98	15.61	15-Sep-98	13.95	28-Oct-98	12.66
3-Aug-98	15.54	16-Sep-98	14.02	29-Oct-98	12.57
4-Aug-98	14.49	17-Sep-98	13.81	30-Oct-98	12.78
5-Aug-98	14.99	18-Sep-98	13.26	2-Nov-98	13.18
6-Aug-98	15.47	21-Sep-98	13.23	3-Nov-98	12.95
7-Aug-98	16.04	22-Sep-98	13.31	4-Nov-98	13.57
10-Aug-98	16.23	23-Sep-98	13.73	5-Nov-98	14.12
11-Aug-98	15.59	24-Sep-98	13.59	6-Nov-98	15.19
12-Aug-98	16.25	25-Sep-98	13.52	9-Nov-98	14.9
13-Aug-98	15.8	28-Sep-98	13.23	10-Nov-98	14.42

Note: Trade dates are in bold type.

Sources: Nasdaq Exchange (Yahoo.com) and ComStock, Inc. (Yahoo.com).

Date	Centex	Date	Centex	Date	Centex
11-Nov-98	14.31	1-Feb-99	17.08	20-Apr-99	15.52
12-Nov-98	14.47	2-Feb-99	16.41	21-Apr-99	15.42
13-Nov-98	14.38	3-Feb-99	16.13	22-Apr-99	14.56
16-Nov-98	14.5	4-Feb-99	16.22	23-Apr-99	14.87
17-Nov-98	14.59	5-Feb-99	15.98	26-Apr-99	14.54
18-Nov-98	14.38	8-Feb-99	16.1	27-Apr-99	15.06
19-Nov-98	14.55	9-Feb-99	16.36	28-Apr-99	15.02
20-Nov-98	14.64	10-Feb-99	16.34	29-Apr-99	14.49
23-Nov-98	14.4	11-Feb-99	16.41	30-Apr-99	14.01
24-Nov-98	14.52	12-Feb-99	16.13	3-May-99	14.18
25-Nov-98	14.74	16-Feb-99	16.17	4-May-99	13.89
27-Nov-98	14.45	17-Feb-99	16.36	5-May-99	14.18
30-Nov-98	13.62	8-Feb-99	15.5	6-May-99	14.56
1-Dec-98	13.81	19-Feb-99	14.98	7-May-99	14.99
2-Dec-98	13.88	22-Feb-99	14.98	10-May-99	15.25
3-Dec-98	13.52	23-Feb-99	14.69	11-May-99	14.75
4-Dec-98	13.54	24-Feb-99	14.53	12-May-99	14.56
7-Dec-98	14.4	25-Feb-99	13.81	13-May-99	14.82
8-Dec-98	14.38	26-Feb-99	14.07	14-May-99	14.3
9-Dec-98	14.52	1-Mar-99	14	17-May-99	14.13
10-Dec-98	14.86	2-Mar-99	14.12	18-May-99	13.53
1-Dec-98	14.74	3-Mar-99	14.1	19-May-99	13.63
14-Dec-98	15.14	4-Mar-99	13.86	20-May-99	13.87
15-Dec-98	15.31	5-Mar-99	14.03	21-May-99	13.77
16-Dec-98	15.89	8-Mar-99	13.76	24-May-99	13.94
17-Dec-98	15.65	9-Mar-99	13.64	25-May-99	13.79
18-Dec-98	15.77	10-Mar-99	13.31	26-May-99	13.58
21-Dec-98	16.7	11-Mar-99	13.14	27-May-99	13.36
22-Dec-98	16.49	12-Mar-99	13.09	28-May-99	14.2
23-Dec-98	16.77	15-Mar-99	13.2	1-Jun-99	14.32
24-Dec-98	16.53	16-Mar-99	13.36	2-Jun-99	14.2
28-Dec-98	16.92	17-Mar-99	13.36	3-Jun-99	14.27
29-Dec-98	17.35	18-Mar-99	13.51	4-Jun-99	14.46
30-Dec-98	17.16	19-Mar-99	12.86	7-Jun-99	14.61
31-Dec-98	17.22	22-Mar-99	12.53	8-Jun-99	14.58
4-Jan-99	17.3	23-Mar-99	11.92	9-Jun-99	14.3
5-Jan-99	16.82	24-Mar-99	12.14	10-Jun-99	13.6
6-Jan-99	16.99	25-Mar-99	12.72	11-Jun-99	13.3
7-Jan-99	16.65	26-Mar-99	12.84	14-Jun-99	13.49
8-Jan-99	16.1	29-Mar-99	13.1	15-Jun-99	13.54
11-Jan-99	16.06	30-Mar-99	13.29	16-Jun-99	13.99
12-Jan-99	15.46	31-Mar-99	12.79	17-Jun-99	14.3
13-Jan-99	15.08	1-Apr-99	12.45	18-Jun-99	14.16
14-Jan-99	15.24	5-Apr-99	12.6	21-Jun-99	13.94
15-Jan-99	15.39	6-Apr-99	12.57	22-Jun-99	13.9
19-Jan-99	15.67	7-Apr-99	12.62	23-Jun-99	13.78
20-Jan-99	15.77	8-Apr-99	12.26	24-Jun-99	13.32
21-Jan-99	15.31	9-Apr-99	12.24	25-Jun-99	13.39
22-Jan-99	15.29	12-Apr-99	12.24	28-Jun-99	13.51
25-Jan-99	15.53	13-Apr-99	12.14	29-Jun-99	13.75
26-Jan-99	16.22	14-Apr-99	13.51	30-Jun-99	14.42
27-Jan-99	15.96	15-Apr-99	14.15	1-Jul-99	14.38
28-Jan-99	16.06	16-Apr-99	15.28	2-Jul-99	14.35
29-Jan-99	16.51	19-Apr-99	16.07	6-Jul-99	14.4

(continues)

383

Date	Centex	Date	Centex	Date	Centex
7-Jul-99	14.64	24-Sep-99	10.73	14-Dec-99	8.96
8-Jul-99	14.64	27-Sep-99	10.76	15-Dec-99	8.69
9-Jul-99	15.03	28-Sep-99	10.16	16-Dec-99	8.79
12-Jul-99	15.1	29-Sep-99	11.53	17-Dec-99	8.81
13-Jul-99	14.93	30-Sep-99	11.38	20-Dec-99	8.86
14-Jul-99	14.74	1-Oct-99	11.02	21-Dec-99	8.96
15-Jul-99	14.52	4-Oct-99	11.12	22-Dec-99	8.86
16-Jul-99	14.28	5-Oct-99	10.78	23-Dec-99	9.01
19-Jul-99	14.14	6-Oct-99	10.64	27-Dec-99	8.84
20-Jul-99	13.75	7-Oct-99	10.61	28-Dec-99	8.96
21-Jul-99	13.66	8-Oct-99	10.59	29-Dec-99	9.13
22-Jul-99	13.18	11-Oct-99	10.47	30-Dec-99	9.51
23-Jul-99	13.34	12-Oct-99	10.21	31-Dec-99	9.54
26-Jul-99	13.13	13-Oct-99	10.21	3-Jan-00	8.98
27-Jul-99	12.89	14-Oct-99	10.06	4-Jan-00	8.77
28-Jul-99	13.11	15-Oct-99	9.96	5-Jan-00	8.93
29-Jul-99	12.79	18-Oct-99	9.82	6-Jan-00	8.84
30-Jul-99	12.94	19-Oct-99	9.63	7-Jan-00	8.98
2-Aug-99	13.32	20-Oct-99	9.72	10-Jan-00	8.81
3-Aug-99	13.06	21-Oct-99	9.34	11-Jan-00	8.55
4-Aug-99	12.75	22-Oct-99	9.36	12-Jan-00	8.67
5-Aug-99	13.06	25-Oct-99	9	13-Jan-00	9.01
6-Aug-99	12.41	26-Oct-99	9.17	14-Jan-00	9.03
9-Aug-99	11.76	27-Oct-99	9.39	18-Jan-00	9.2
10-Aug-99	11.11	28-Oct-99	10.18	19-Jan-00	9.1
11-Aug-99	11.79	29-Oct-99	10.33	20-Jan-00	8.93
12-Aug-99	11.57	1-Nov-99	10.42	21-Jan-00	8.86
13-Aug-99	11.85	2-Nov-99	10.54	24-Jan-00	8.86
16-Aug-99	11.98	3-Nov-99	10.23	25-Jan-00	8.45
17-Aug-99	11.71	4-Nov-99	9.99	26-Jan-00	8.4
18-Aug-99	11.52	5-Nov-99	10.35	27-Jan-00	8.43
19-Aug-99	11.52	8-Nov-99	10.28	28-Jan-00	8.31
20-Aug-99	11.59	9-Nov-99	10.16	31-Jan-00	8.5
23-Aug-99	11.23	10-Nov-99	10.16	1-Feb-00	8.48
24-Aug-99	11.31	11-Nov-99	10.09	2-Feb-00	8.29
25-Aug-99	11.52	12-Nov-99	10.04	3-Feb-00	8.5
26-Aug-99	11.23	15-Nov-99	10.78	4-Feb-00	8.57
27-Aug-99	11.06	16-Nov-99	11.21	7-Feb-00	8.26
30-Aug-99	10.61	17-Nov-99	10.83	8-Feb-00	8.35
31-Aug-99	10.8	18-Nov-99	10.4	9-Feb-00	8.21
1-Sep-99	10.54	19-Nov-99	10.35	10-Feb-00	8.23
2-Sep-99	10.63	22-Nov-99	10.06	11-Feb-00	8.14
3-Sep-99	10.78	23-Nov-99	9.24	14-Feb-00	7.97
7-Sep-99	10.9	24-Nov-99	9.29	15-Feb-00	8.29
8-Sep-99	10.81	26-Nov-99	9.44	16-Feb-00	7.94
9-Sep-99	10.81	29-Nov-99	9.27	17-Feb-00	8.09
10-Sep-99	10.88	30-Nov-99	9.15	18-Feb-00	7.94
13-Sep-99	10.78	1-Dec-99	9.27	22-Feb-00	7.92
14-Sep-99	10.9	2-Dec-99	9.29	23-Feb-00	7.97
15-Sep-99	10.98	3-Dec-99	9.39	24-Feb-00	7.63
16-Sep-99	11	6-Dec-99	9.24	25-Feb-00	7.51
17-Sep-99	11.24	7-Dec-99	9.32	28-Feb-00	7.54
20-Sep-99	11.38	8-Dec-99	9.15	29-Feb-00	7.61
21-Sep-99	10.98	9-Dec-99	9.1	1-Mar-00	7.54
22-Sep-99	10.76	10-Dec-99	9.12	2-Mar-00	7.51
23-Sep-99	10.83	13-Dec-99	9.15	3-Mar-00	7.44

384

Date	Centex	Date	Centex	Date	Centex
6-Mar-00	7.32	22-May-00	8.61	8-Aug-00	11.1
7-Mar-00	7.17	23-May-00	8.66	9-Aug-00	11
8-Mar-00	6.96	24-May-00	8.63	10-Aug-00	10.9
9-Mar-00	7.03	25-May-00	8.61	11-Aug-00	11.53
10-Mar-00	7	26-May-00	8.29	14-Aug-00	11.34
13-Mar-00	6.96	30-May-00	8.19	15-Aug-00	11.12
14-Mar-00	6.98	31-May-00	8.07	16-Aug-00	11.07
15-Mar-00	7.66	1-Jun-00	8.27	17-Aug-00	10.9
16-Mar-00	8.95	2-Jun-00	9.04	18-Aug-00	10.9
17-Mar-00	8.95	5-Jun-00	8.66	21-Aug-00	10.95
20-Mar-00	9.04	6-Jun-00	8.97	22-Aug-00	10.73
21-Mar-00	8.83	7-Jun-00	8.66	23-Aug-00	10.54
2-Mar-00	8.58	8-Jun-00	8.42	24-Aug-00	10.42
23-Mar-00	9	9-Jun-00	8.61	25-Aug-00	10.51
24-Mar-00	9.07	12-Jun-00	8.63	28-Aug-00	10.3
27-Mar-00	9	13-Jun-00	8.93	29-Aug-00	10.88
28-Mar-00	9.07	14-Jun-00	8.98	30-Aug-00	10.98
29-Mar-00	8.8	15-Jun-00	9.15	31-Aug-00	11.28
30-Mar-00	9	16-Jun-00	9.03	1-Sep-00	11.25
31-Mar-00	9.24	19-Jun-00	9	5-Sep-00	11.13
3-Apr-00	9.72	20-Jun-00	8.61	6-Sep-00	11.54
4-Apr-00	9.21	21-Jun-00	8.66	7-Sep-00	11.8
5-Apr-00	9.68	22-Jun-00	8.57	8-Sep-00	11.62
6-Apr-00	9.68	23-Jun-00	8.64	11-Sep-00	12.39
7-Apr-00	9.48	26-Jun-00	8.57	12-Sep-00	12.23
10-Apr-00	9.51	27-Jun-00	8.93	13-Sep-00	12.36
11-Apr-00	9.39	28-Jun-00	8.89	14-Sep-00	12.81
12-Apr-00	9.77	29-Jun-00	9.42	15-Sep-00	11.91
13-Apr-00	9.82	30-Jun-00	9.14	18-Sep-00	11.57
14-Apr-00	9.04	3-Jul-00	9.54	19-Sep-00	11.66
17-Apr-00	9.14	5-Jul-00	9.81	20-Sep-00	11.69
18-Apr-00	9.24	6-Jul-00	9.54	21-Sep-00	11.72
19-Apr-00	9.29	7-Jul-00	9.37	22-Sep-00	11.59
20-Apr-00	9.55	10-Jul-00	9.13	25-Sep-00	11.57
24-Apr-00	9.63	11-Jul-00	9.25	26-Sep-00	11.89
25-Apr-00	9.82	12-Jul-00	9.35	27-Sep-00	11.98
26-Apr-00	9.89	13-Jul-00	9.05	28-Sep-00	12.11
27-Apr-00	9.63	14-Jul-00	8.93	29-Sep-00	12.55
28-Apr-00	9.36	17-Jul-00	8.99	2-Oct-00	12.89
1-May-00	9.6	18-Jul-00	8.88	3-Oct-00	13.43
2-May-00	9.58	19-Jul-00	8.78	4-Oct-00	13.35
3-May-00	9.41	20-Jul-00	8.88	5-Oct-00	12.96
4-May-00	9.36	21-Jul-00	8.76	6-Oct-00	13.18
5-May-00	9.29	24-Jul-00	8.81	9-Oct-00	13.28
8-May-00	9.02	25-Jul-00	9.03	10-Oct-00	12.89
9-May-00	9.24	26-Jul-00	9.05	11-Oct-00	13.08
10-May-00	8.85	27-Jul-00	9.35	12-Oct-00	12.3
11-May-00	9.07	28-Jul-00	9.08	13-Oct-00	12.28
12-May-00	9.24	31-Jul-00	9.32	16-Oct-00	13.08
15-May-00	9.21	**1-Aug-00**	**9.42**	17-Oct-00	12.47
16-May-00	9.26	2-Aug-00	9.39	18-Oct-00	12.11
17-May-00	8.95	3-Aug-00	9.44	19-Oct-00	12.69
18-May-00	8.78	4-Aug-00	9.88	20-Oct-00	12.79
19-May-00	8.68	7-Aug-00	11.22	23-Oct-00	12.57

(continues)

Date	Centex	Date	Centex	Date	Centex
24-Oct-00	13.23	16-Jan-01	16.05	5-Apr-01	15.43
25-Oct-00	13.35	17-Jan-01	16.07	6-Apr-01	14.53
26-Oct-00	12.96	18-Jan-01	15.71	9-Apr-01	15.01
27-Oct-00	13.47	19-Jan-01	15.07	10-Apr-01	15.23
30-Oct-00	14.08	22-Jan-01	14.16	11-Apr-01	14.72
31-Oct-00	14.45	23-Jan-01	14.95	12-Apr-01	14.98
1-Nov-00	14.45	24-Jan-01	14.87	16-Apr-01	14.92
2-Nov-00	14.64	25-Jan-01	15.73	17-Apr-01	14.87
3-Nov-00	14.99	26-Jan-01	14.92	18-Apr-01	15.39
6-Nov-00	14.82	29-Jan-01	15.34	19-Apr-01	15.76
7-Nov-00	14.37	30-Jan-01	15.58	20-Apr-01	16.04
8-Nov-00	14.96	31-Jan-01	15.9	23-Apr-01	15.65
9-Nov-00	14.74	1-Feb-01	16.22	24-Apr-01	16.34
10-Nov-00	14.21	2-Feb-01	16.39	25-Apr-01	16.68
13-Nov-00	14.28	5-Feb-01	16.83	26-Apr-01	17.06
14-Nov-00	14.35	6-Feb-01	17.22	27-Apr-01	17.32
15-Nov-00	14.23	7-Feb-01	17.11	30-Apr-01	16.9
16-Nov-00	14.37	8-Feb-01	16.99	1-May-01	16.92
17-Nov-00	14.55	9-Feb-01	16.51	2-May-01	17.03
20-Nov-00	14.01	12-Feb-01	17.13	3-May-01	16.91
21-Nov-00	14.06	13-Feb-01	17.56	4-May-01	17.15
22-Nov-00	14.03	14-Feb-01	17.45	7-May-01	17.39
24-Nov-00	14.35	15-Feb-01	17.29	8-May-01	17.51
27-Nov-00	14.84	16-Feb-01	17.42	9-May-01	17.34
28-Nov-00	14.72	20-Feb-01	17.13	10-May-01	17.53
29-Nov-00	14.23	21-Feb-01	16.35	11-May-01	16.8
30-Nov-00	13.82	22-Feb-01	15.71	15-May-01	17.03
1-Dec-00	14.06	23-Feb-01	15.42	16-May-01	16.9
4-Dec-00	13.69	26-Feb-01	16.3	17-May-01	16.8
5-Dec-00	14.84	27-Feb-01	16.08	18-May-01	16.53
6-Dec-00	14.25	28-Feb-01	16.11	21-May-01	15.64
7-Dec-00	14.4	1-Mar-01	15.58	22-May-01	16.08
8-Dec-00	14.92	2-Mar-01	16.1	23-May-01	15.58
11-Dec-00	15.34	5-Mar-01	16.06	24-May-01	15.08
12-Dec-00	15.02	6-Mar-01	16.44	25-May-01	14.81
13-Dec-00	15.07	7-Mar-01	16.84	29-May-01	14.73
14-Dec-00	14.73	8-Mar-01	16.64	30-May-01	14.68
15-Dec-00	14.04	9-Mar-01	16.69	31-May-01	14.62
18-Dec-00	14.77	12-Mar-01	15.74	1-Jun-01	14.88
19-Dec-00	14.5	13-Mar-01	15.64	4-Jun-01	15.05
20-Dec-00	13.55	14-Mar-01	15.19	5-Jun-01	15.21
21-Dec-00	13.55	15-Mar-01	15.91	6-Jun-01	14.96
22-Dec-00	14.34	16-Mar-01	14.96	7-Jun-01	15.04
26-Dec-00	15.09	19-Mar-01	15.64	8-Jun-01	15.24
27-Dec-00	14.55	20-Mar-01	15.64	11-Jun-01	14.8
28-Dec-00	15.24	21-Mar-01	15.84	12-Jun-01	14.14
29-Dec-00	14.7	22-Mar-01	15.9	13-Jun-01	14.1
2-Jan-01	13.97	23-Mar-01	15.68	14-Jun-01	13.81
3-Jan-01	15.24	26-Mar-01	15.68	15-Jun-01	14.15
4-Jan-01	15.09	27-Mar-01	16.3	18-Jun-01	14.34
5-Jan-01	14.85	28-Mar-01	16.12	19-Jun-01	14.43
8-Jan-01	14.21	29-Mar-01	16.61	20-Jun-01	15.76
9-Jan-01	14.68	30-Mar-01	16.33	21-Jun-01	16.13
10-Jan-01	15.07	2-Apr-01	15.84	22-Jun-01	15.36
11-Jan-01	14.99	3-Apr-01	15.43	25-Jun-01	15.58
12-Jan-01	15.31	4-Apr-01	15.33	26-Jun-01	15.63

Date	Centex	Date	Centex	Date	Centex
27-Jun-01	15.98	19-Sep-01	11.81	5-Dec-01	19.95
28-Jun-01	16.11	20-Sep-01	11.48	6-Dec-01	19.67
29-Jun-01	16.01	21-Sep-01	11.84	7-Dec-01	19.73
2-Jul-01	16.6	24-Sep-01	12.42	10-Dec-01	19.58
3-Jul-01	16.36	25-Sep-01	12.7	11-Dec-01	19.94
5-Jul-01	16.25	26-Sep-01	13.07	12-Dec-01	21.53
6-Jul-01	16.12	27-Sep-01	12.83	13-Dec-01	21.54
9-Jul-01	16.1	28-Sep-01	13.28	14-Dec-01	21.06
10-Jul-01	16.31	1-Oct-01	13.02	17-Dec-01	20.99
11-Jul-01	16.25	2-Oct-01	13.23	18-Dec-01	21.84
12-Jul-01	17.17	3-Oct-01	14.47	19-Dec-01	22.08
13-Jul-01	17.12	4-Oct-01	14.33	20-Dec-01	21.82
16-Jul-01	16.66	5-Oct-01	14.09	21-Dec-01	21.51
17-Jul-01	17.09	8-Oct-01	13.86	24-Dec-01	22.3
18-Jul-01	18.35	9-Oct-01	14.07	26-Dec-01	22.94
19-Jul-01	19.5	10-Oct-01	15.24	27-Dec-01	22.65
20-Jul-01	18.76	11-Oct-01	15.91	28-Dec-01	22.94
23-Jul-01	18.82	12-Oct-01	15.43	31-Dec-01	22.51
24-Jul-01	18.37	15-Oct-01	15.23	2-Jan-02	22.07
25-Jul-01	18.31	16-Oct-01	14.76	3-Jan-02	21.96
26-Jul-01	18.19	17-Oct-01	14.21	4-Jan-02	21.9
27-Jul-01	17.64	18-Oct-01	13.79	7-Jan-02	21.59
30-Jul-01	17.7	19-Oct-01	14.07	8-Jan-02	21.46
31-Jul-01	18.48	22-Oct-01	14.14	9-Jan-02	22.28
1-Aug-01	18.42	23-Oct-01	14.3	10-Jan-02	21.47
2-Aug-01	18.47	24-Oct-01	14.48	11-Jan-02	20.77
3-Aug-01	18.2	25-Oct-01	14.98	14-Jan-02	20.78
6-Aug-01	17.01	26-Oct-01	15.53	15-Jan-02	21.17
7-Aug-01	17.1	29-Oct-01	14.88	16-Jan-02	20.7
8-Aug-01	16.8	30-Oct-01	14.25	17-Jan-02	21.13
9-Aug-01	17.35	31-Oct-01	15.06	18-Jan-02	20.93
10-Aug-01	17.33	1-Nov-01	15.71	22-Jan-02	21.17
13-Aug-01	16.38	2-Nov-01	15.46	23-Jan-02	21.22
14-Aug-01	16.49	5-Nov-01	16.13	24-Jan-02	21.71
15-Aug-01	16.36	6-Nov-01	16.3	25-Jan-02	22.42
16-Aug-01	16.84	7-Nov-01	17.03	28-Jan-02	23.07
17-Aug-01	16.22	8-Nov-01	16.61	29-Jan-02	23.06
20-Aug-01	16.15	9-Nov-01	16.3	30-Jan-02	23.58
21-Aug-01	15.81	12-Nov-01	16.81	31-Jan-02	23.45
22-Aug-01	15.71	13-Nov-01	17.54	4-Feb-02	23.3
23-Aug-01	16.25	14-Nov-01	17.47	5-Feb-02	23.19
24-Aug-01	16.66	15-Nov-01	16.58	6-Feb-02	22.67
27-Aug-01	16.36	16-Nov-01	16.9	7-Feb-02	22.08
28-Aug-01	16.23	19-Nov-01	16.57	8-Feb-02	22.08
29-Aug-01	16.55	20-Nov-01	16.14	11-Feb-02	22.06
30-Aug-01	17.04	21-Nov-01	16.24	12-Feb-02	22.57
31-Aug-01	17.21	23-Nov-01	16.46	13-Feb-02	22.48
4-Sep-01	17.37	26-Nov-01	16.39	14-Feb-02	22.57
5-Sep-01	17.25	27-Nov-01	16.12	15-Feb-02	22.16
6-Sep-01	16.41	28-Nov-01	16.15	19-Feb-02	21.78
7-Sep-01	15.69	29-Nov-01	16.49	20-Feb-02	21.37
10-Sep-01	15.09	30-Nov-01	17.79	21-Feb-02	21.37
17-Sep-01	13.44	3-Dec-01	17.71	22-Feb-02	21.02
18-Sep-01	13.11	4-Dec-01	18.51	25-Feb-02	21.86

(continues)

Date	Centex	Date	Centex	Date	Centex
26-Feb-02	22.33	16-Apr-02	20.68	4-Jun-02	19.82
27-Feb-02	22.68	17-Apr-02	20.97	5-Jun-02	20.57
28-Feb-02	23.04	18-Apr-02	20.58	6-Jun-02	21.15
1-Mar-02	23.12	19-Apr-02	20.9	7-Jun-02	21.57
4-Mar-02	24.18	22-Apr-02	21.71	10-Jun-02	21.44
5-Mar-02	23.62	23-Apr-02	23.03	11-Jun-02	21.18
6-Mar-02	24.51	24-Apr-02	22.9	12-Jun-02	21.21
7-Mar-02	23.87	25-Apr-02	22.97	13-Jun-02	20.38
8-Mar-02	23.48	26-Apr-02	22.26	14-Jun-02	20.6
11-Mar-02	23.82	29-Apr-02	22.21	17-Jun-02	21.18
12-Mar-02	24.21	30-Apr-02	22.23	18-Jun-02	21.83
13-Mar-02	23.64	1-May-02	22.81	19-Jun-02	22.33
14-Mar-02	22.98	2-May-02	22.97	20-Jun-02	22.9
15-Mar-02	22.86	3-May-02	22.9	21-Jun-02	22.91
18-Mar-02	22.17	6-May-02	21.92	24-Jun-02	22.56
19-Mar-02	22.55	7-May-02	22.21	25-Jun-02	21.78
20-Mar-02	21.23	8-May-02	21.77	26-Jun-02	22.11
21-Mar-02	20.51	9-May-02	21.91	27-Jun-02	22.4
22-Mar-02	21.89	10-May-02	20.9	28-Jun-02	22.85
25-Mar-02	20.9	3-May-02	20.53	1-Jul-02	22.97
26-Mar-02	21.51	14-May-02	22.04	2-Jul-02	21.56
27-Mar-02	20.92	15-May-02	21.27	3-Jul-02	21.8
28-Mar-02	20.5	16-May-02	20.66	5-Jul-02	22.49
1-Apr-02	19.9	17-May-02	21.28	8-Jul-02	22.05
2-Apr-02	19.4	20-May-02	21.17	9-Jul-02	21.71
3-Apr-02	19.84	21-May-02	20.67	10-Jul-02	20.83
4-Apr-02	19.71	22-May-02	20.8	11-Jul-02	20.77
5-Apr-02	19.69	23-May-02	21.32	12-Jul-02	20.54
8-Apr-02	20.88	24-May-02	21.77	15-Jul-02	20.16
9-Apr-02	21.35	28-May-02	21.42	16-Jul-02	19.26
10-Apr-02	20.77	29-May-02	21.1	17-Jul-02	19.33
11-Apr-02	20.36	30-May-02	20.8	**18-Jul-02**	**19.21**
12-Apr-02	21.02	31-May-02	21.22		
15-Apr-02	20.87	3-Jun-02	20.5		

Sources: Nasdaq Exchange (Yahoo.com) and ComStock, Inc. (Yahoo.com).

Date	Nasdaq	Placer Dome		$ Change	% Change	1 + Change	Index
8/23/1990	360.22						
7/1/1998	1914.46			1554.24	4.314696574	5.314696574	5.314697
7/1/1998		Buy	10.68				
9/4/1998		Sell	10.55	−0.13	−0.012172285	0.987827715	5.250005
9/4/1998	1566.52						
8/1/2000	3685.51			2118.99	1.352673442	2.352673442	12.35155
8/1/2000		Buy	8.28				
7/18/2002		Sell	10.28	2	0.241545894	1.241545894	15.33501
8/18/2002	1356.95						
1/3/2005	2062.00			705.05	0.519584362	1.519584362	23.30284

			14.33th root of	Equals:
Passive:	Nasdaq		$5.72	**13%**
Active:	Nasdaq &		$23.30	**25%**
	Placer Dome			

Date	PDG	Date	PDG	Date	PDG
1-Jul-98	**10.68**	6-Aug-98	9.47	11-Sep-98	11.54
2-Jul-98	10.27	7-Aug-98	9.52	14-Sep-98	11.37
6-Jul-98	10.33	10-Aug-98	9.58	15-Sep-98	11.07
7-Jul-98	10.91	11-Aug-98	9.29	16-Sep-98	10.84
8-Jul-98	10.62	12-Aug-98	9.41	17-Sep-98	11.31
9-Jul-98	10.22	13-Aug-98	9.41	18-Sep-98	11.6
10-Jul-98	10.16	14-Aug-98	9.47	21-Sep-98	11.25
13-Jul-98	10.1	17-Aug-98	9.52	22-Sep-98	11.37
14-Jul-98	10.22	18-Aug-98	9.47	23-Sep-98	12.42
15-Jul-98	9.98	19-Aug-98	9.62	24-Sep-98	13.11
16-Jul-98	10.33	20-Aug-98	10.14	25-Sep-98	13.23
17-Jul-98	10.27	21-Aug-98	9.68	28-Sep-98	13.7
20-Jul-98	10.62	24-Aug-98	9.44	29-Sep-98	12.88
21-Jul-98	10.27	25-Aug-98	9.21	30-Sep-98	12.88
22-Jul-98	10.27	26-Aug-98	9.15	1-Oct-98	13.58
23-Jul-98	9.93	27-Aug-98	8.74	2-Oct-98	14.46
24-Jul-98	9.75	28-Aug-98	8.16	5-Oct-98	13.93
27-Jul-98	9.64	31-Aug-98	7.52	6-Oct-98	14.11
28-Jul-98	9.98	1-Sep-98	7.93	7-Oct-98	15.56
29-Jul-98	9.87	2-Sep-98	8.51	8-Oct-98	15.04
30-Jul-98	9.98	3-Sep-98	9.38	9-Oct-98	13.81
31-Jul-98	9.58	**4-Sep-98**	**10.55**	12-Oct-98	13.87
3-Aug-98	9.41	8-Sep-98	10.84	13-Oct-98	13.35
4-Aug-98	9.52	9-Sep-98	10.08	14-Oct-98	12.53
5-Aug-98	9.64	10-Sep-98	11.13	15-Oct-98	13.35

Note: Trade dates are in bold type.

Sources: Nasdaq Exchange (Yahoo.com) and ComStock, Inc. (Yahoo.com).

(continues)

Date	PDG	Date	PDG	Date	PDG
16-Oct-98	13.99	29-Dec-98	10.55	12-Mar-99	11.35
19-Oct-98	13.35	30-Dec-98	10.55	15-Mar-99	10.94
20-Oct-98	13.29	31-Dec-98	10.73	16-Mar-99	11.12
21-Oct-98	12.88	4-Jan-99	10.9	17-Mar-99	11
22-Oct-98	12.53	5-Jan-99	10.78	18-Mar-99	10.82
23-Oct-98	12.18	6-Jan-99	10.96	19-Mar-99	10.94
26-Oct-98	12.24	7-Jan-99	11.83	22-Mar-99	11
27-Oct-98	13.7	8-Jan-99	12.07	23-Mar-99	10.82
28-Oct-98	13.64	11-Jan-99	12.47	24-Mar-99	11.12
29-Oct-98	14.4	12-Jan-99	11.6	25-Mar-99	10.88
30-Oct-98	14.69	13-Jan-99	11.37	26-Mar-99	10.65
2-Nov-98	14.11	14-Jan-99	11.25	29-Mar-99	10.47
3-Nov-98	14.16	15-Jan-99	11.19	30-Mar-99	9.77
4-Nov-98	15.5	19-Jan-99	11.02	31-Mar-99	10.53
5-Nov-98	16.32	20-Jan-99	10.96	1-Apr-99	10.41
6-Nov-98	15.04	21-Jan-99	10.96	5-Apr-99	10.06
9-Nov-98	15.1	22-Jan-99	10.61	6-Apr-99	10.12
10-Nov-98	14.92	25-Jan-99	10.55	7-Apr-99	10.12
11-Nov-98	14.63	26-Jan-99	10.08	8-Apr-99	9.71
12-Nov-98	15.68	27-Jan-99	10.26	9-Apr-99	10.06
13-Nov-98	15.16	28-Jan-99	10.26	12-Apr-99	10.59
16-Nov-98	14.69	29-Jan-99	10.43	13-Apr-99	10.47
17-Nov-98	14.86	1-Feb-99	11.02	14-Apr-99	10.12
18-Nov-98	15.27	2-Feb-99	11.02	15-Apr-99	10.77
19-Nov-98	15.16	3-Feb-99	10.78	16-Apr-99	11.71
20-Nov-98	14.98	4-Feb-99	11.19	19-Apr-99	12.47
23-Nov-98	15.21	5-Feb-99	11.37	20-Apr-99	12.13
24-Nov-98	14.69	8-Feb-99	11.31	21-Apr-99	11.65
25-Nov-98	14.46	9-Feb-99	10.55	22-Apr-99	12.29
27-Nov-98	14.4	10-Feb-99	10.49	23-Apr-99	12.29
30-Nov-98	13.58	11-Feb-99	10.67	26-Apr-99	11.88
1-Dec-98	13.7	12-Feb-99	11.37	27-Apr-99	12.71
2-Dec-98	13.46	16-Feb-99	10.9	28-Apr-99	13.06
3-Dec-98	12.94	17-Feb-99	10.61	29-Apr-99	13.24
4-Dec-98	13.41	18-Feb-99	10.67	30-Apr-99	13.29
7-Dec-98	13.87	19-Feb-99	10.73	3-May-99	13.77
8-Dec-98	13	22-Feb-99	10.67	4-May-99	13.29
9-Dec-98	12.88	23-Feb-99	10.61	5-May-99	13.94
10-Dec-98	13.87	24-Feb-99	10.43	6-May-99	14.71
11-Dec-98	13.11	25-Feb-99	10.38	7-May-99	12.41
14-Dec-98	11.48	26-Feb-99	10.2	10-May-99	11.53
15-Dec-98	11.6	1-Mar-99	10.32	11-May-99	11.71
16-Dec-98	11.72	2-Mar-99	10.26	12-May-99	11.47
17-Dec-98	11.02	3-Mar-99	10.47	13-May-99	11.71
18-Dec-98	11.02	4-Mar-99	10.82	14-May-99	11.53
21-Dec-98	10.73	5-Mar-99	10.82	17-May-99	11.24
22-Dec-98	10.38	8-Mar-99	11.65	18-May-99	10.94
23-Dec-98	10.61	9-Mar-99	11.65	19-May-99	11.29
24-Dec-98	10.43	10-Mar-99	11.71	20-May-99	11.12
28-Dec-98	10.2	11-Mar-99	11.77	21-May-99	10.77

Date	PDG	Date	PDG	Date	PDG
24-May-99	10.77	3-Aug-99	10	12-Oct-99	13.66
25-May-99	10.35	4-Aug-99	10	13-Oct-99	14.31
26-May-99	10.71	5-Aug-99	9.88	14-Oct-99	13.42
27-May-99	10.65	6-Aug-99	9.53	15-Oct-99	13.54
28-May-99	10.47	9-Aug-99	10.18	18-Oct-99	13.12
1-Jun-99	10.41	10-Aug-99	9.82	19-Oct-99	12.47
2-Jun-99	10.29	11-Aug-99	10.29	20-Oct-99	12.35
3-Jun-99	10.35	12-Aug-99	10.18	21-Oct-99	12.94
4-Jun-99	10.24	13-Aug-99	10.06	22-Oct-99	12.53
7-Jun-99	10.29	16-Aug-99	9.88	25-Oct-99	12.17
8-Jun-99	10.06	17-Aug-99	10.29	26-Oct-99	11.64
9-Jun-99	9.77	18-Aug-99	9.74	27-Oct-99	11.99
10-Jun-99	10.12	19-Aug-99	9.91	28-Oct-99	11.99
11-Jun-99	10.41	20-Aug-99	10.15	29-Oct-99	11.76
14-Jun-99	10	23-Aug-99	10.33	1-Nov-99	11.1
15-Jun-99	10.06	24-Aug-99	9.8	2-Nov-99	11.52
16-Jun-99	10.12	25-Aug-99	9.68	3-Nov-99	11.22
17-Jun-99	10.06	26-Aug-99	9.91	4-Nov-99	11.1
18-Jun-99	10.53	27-Aug-99	9.86	5-Nov-99	10.81
21-Jun-99	10.12	30-Aug-99	9.5	8-Nov-99	11.4
22-Jun-99	10	31-Aug-99	9.86	9-Nov-99	11.7
23-Jun-99	10.53	1-Sep-99	9.68	10-Nov-99	12.59
24-Jun-99	10.29	2-Sep-99	9.68	11-Nov-99	11.87
25-Jun-99	10.53	3-Sep-99	9.56	12-Nov-99	11.64
28-Jun-99	10.53	7-Sep-99	9.68	15-Nov-99	11.99
29-Jun-99	11.29	8-Sep-99	9.68	16-Nov-99	11.64
30-Jun-99	11.06	9-Sep-99	9.97	17-Nov-99	11.16
1-Jul-99	11.00	10-Sep-99	9.8	18-Nov-99	11.16
2-Jul-99	11.00	13-Sep-99	9.5	19-Nov-99	11.22
6-Jul-99	10.18	14-Sep-99	9.44	22-Nov-99	10.81
7-Jul-99	10.06	15-Sep-99	9.44	23-Nov-99	11.46
8-Jul-99	9.47	16-Sep-99	9.56	24-Nov-99	11.87
9-Jul-99	9.71	17-Sep-99	9.5	26-Nov-99	11.76
12-Jul-99	9.53	20-Sep-99	9.74	29-Nov-99	10.86
13-Jul-99	9.53	21-Sep-99	10.33	30-Nov-99	10.81
14-Jul-99	9.53	22-Sep-99	10.92	1-Dec-99	10.63
15-Jul-99	9.35	23-Sep-99	10.86	2-Dec-99	10.27
16-Jul-99	9.12	24-Sep-99	11.22	3-Dec-99	10.15
19-Jul-99	8.71	27-Sep-99	14.66	6-Dec-99	10.15
20-Jul-99	8.88	28-Sep-99	14.9	7-Dec-99	10.57
21-Jul-99	9.65	29-Sep-99	14.13	8-Dec-99	10.33
22-Jul-99	9.53	30-Sep-99	14.13	9-Dec-99	9.97
23-Jul-99	10.52	1-Oct-99	14.61	10-Dec-99	9.97
26-Jul-99	9.47	4-Oct-99	15.73	13-Dec-99	10.21
27-Jul-99	9.53	5-Oct-99	15.26	14-Dec-99	9.68
28-Jul-99	9.59	6-Oct-99	15.67	15-Dec-99	10.21
29-Jul-99	9.94	7-Oct-99	14.37	16-Dec-99	10.33
30-Jul-99	9.59	8-Oct-99	13.6	17-Dec-99	10.51
2-Aug-99	9.35	11-Oct-99	14.49	20-Dec-99	10.03

(continues)

391

Date	PDG	Date	PDG	Date	PDG
21-Dec-99	10.27	6-Mar-00	7.96	16-May-00	8.4
22-Dec-99	10.39	7-Mar-00	8.91	17-May-00	7.98
23-Dec-99	10.45	8-Mar-00	8.4	18-May-00	7.98
27-Dec-99	10.57	9-Mar-00	8.64	19-May-00	8.16
28-Dec-99	10.51	10-Mar-00	8.22	22-May-00	8.22
29-Dec-99	10.57	13-Mar-00	8.22	23-May-00	8.28
30-Dec-99	10.39	14-Mar-00	8.46	24-May-00	8.22
31-Dec-99	10.21	15-Mar-00	8.4	25-May-00	7.86
3-Jan-00	9.97	16-Mar-00	8.34	26-May-00	7.92
4-Jan-00	9.8	17-Mar-00	8.28	30-May-00	8.16
5-Jan-00	9.86	20-Mar-00	8.28	31-May-00	7.86
6-Jan-00	9.97	21-Mar-00	8.58	1-Jun-00	7.98
7-Jan-00	9.68	22-Mar-00	8.22	5-Jun-00	8.82
10-Jan-00	9.56	23-Mar-00	8.28	6-Jun-00	9
11-Jan-00	9.91	24-Mar-00	8.16	7-Jun-00	8.64
12-Jan-00	9.8	27-Mar-00	8.04	8-Jun-00	8.64
13-Jan-00	9.62	28-Mar-00	7.86	12-Jun-00	9
14-Jan-00	9.38	29-Mar-00	7.56	13-Jun-00	9.06
18-Jan-00	9.74	30-Mar-00	7.5	14-Jun-00	9.48
19-Jan-00	9.68	31-Mar-00	7.8	15-Jun-00	9.06
20-Jan-00	9.38	3-Apr-00	7.62	16-Jun-00	9.09
21-Jan-00	9.38	4-Apr-00	8.1	19-Jun-00	8.88
24-Jan-00	9.02	5-Apr-00	8.04	20-Jun-00	8.82
25-Jan-00	8.96	6-Apr-00	7.74	21-Jun-00	9.06
26-Jan-00	8.37	7-Apr-00	7.62	22-Jun-00	9.06
27-Jan-00	8.96	10-Apr-00	7.5	23-Jun-00	8.88
28-Jan-00	8.43	11-Apr-00	7.44	26-Jun-00	8.88
31-Jan-00	8.43	12-Apr-00	7.44	27-Jun-00	8.94
1-Feb-00	8.31	13-Apr-00	7.44	28-Jun-00	9.32
2-Feb-00	8.43	14-Apr-00	8.4	29-Jun-00	8.94
3-Feb-00	8.31	17-Apr-00	8.04	30-Jun-00	9.18
4-Feb-00	10.33	18-Apr-00	7.92	3-Jul-00	9.12
7-Feb-00	9.68	19-Apr-00	8.1	5-Jul-00	8.7
8-Feb-00	8.96	20-Apr-00	8.04	6-Jul-00	8.88
9-Feb-00	9.97	24-Apr-00	8.04	7-Jul-00	8.88
10-Feb-00	10.27	25-Apr-00	8.04	10-Jul-00	8.94
11-Feb-00	10.03	26-Apr-00	8.34	11-Jul-00	9
14-Feb-00	9.68	27-Apr-00	8.16	12-Jul-00	9.06
15-Feb-00	9.97	28-Apr-00	7.86	13-Jul-00	9
16-Feb-00	9.8	1-May-00	7.98	14-Jul-00	8.82
17-Feb-00	9.44	2-May-00	8.64	17-Jul-00	8.97
18-Feb-00	9.91	3-May-00	8.76	18-Jul-00	8.94
22-Feb-00	9.8	4-May-00	8.82	19-Jul-00	8.64
24-Feb-00	8.91	5-May-00	8.4	20-Jul-00	8.4
25-Feb-00	8.61	8-May-00	8.04	21-Jul-00	8.16
28-Feb-00	8.43	9-May-00	8.22	24-Jul-00	8.04
29-Feb-00	8.31	10-May-00	8.52	25-Jul-00	8.04
1-Mar-00	8.37	11-May-00	8.46	26-Jul-00	8.22
2-Mar-00	8.19	12-May-00	8.28	27-Jul-00	8.28
3-Mar-00	8.13	15-May-00	8.64	28-Jul-00	8.34

Date	PDG	Date	PDG	Date	PDG
31-Jul-00	8.16	11-Oct-00	7.79	20-Dec-00	10.14
1-Aug-00	**8.28**	12-Oct-00	8.21	21-Dec-00	9.96
2-Aug-00	8.4	13-Oct-00	7.97	22-Dec-00	9.66
3-Aug-00	8.04	16-Oct-00	7.85	26-Dec-00	9.6
4-Aug-00	8.22	17-Oct-00	7.79	27-Dec-00	9.6
7-Aug-00	8.28	18-Oct-00	7.85	28-Dec-00	9.42
8-Aug-00	8.22	19-Oct-00	7.67	29-Dec-00	9.3
9-Aug-00	8.04	20-Oct-00	7.61	2-Jan-01	9.42
10-Aug-00	8.1	23-Oct-00	7.54	3-Jan-01	9.11
11-Aug-00	8.52	24-Oct-00	7.3	4-Jan-01	8.81
14-Aug-00	8.46	25-Oct-00	7.36	5-Jan-01	8.57
15-Aug-00	8.34	26-Oct-00	7.54	8-Jan-01	8.81
16-Aug-00	8.99	27-Oct-00	7.79	9-Jan-01	8.81
17-Aug-00	8.69	30-Oct-00	7.97	10-Jan-01	8.69
18-Aug-00	8.69	31-Oct-00	7.85	11-Jan-01	8.45
21-Aug-00	8.57	1-Nov-00	7.73	12-Jan-01	8.51
2-Aug-00	8.39	2-Nov-00	7.79	16-Jan-01	8.45
23-Aug-00	8.33	3-Nov-00	7.85	17-Jan-01	8.39
24-Aug-00	8.51	6-Nov-00	8.09	18-Jan-01	8.33
25-Aug-00	8.81	7-Nov-00	8.21	19-Jan-01	8.39
30-Aug-00	8.57	8-Nov-00	7.97	22-Jan-01	9.17
31-Aug-00	8.59	9-Nov-00	7.79	23-Jan-01	8.75
1-Sep-00	8.81	10-Nov-00	7.73	24-Jan-01	8.21
5-Sep-00	8.81	13-Nov-00	7.67	25-Jan-01	8.33
6-Sep-00	9.3	14-Nov-00	7.54	26-Jan-01	8.39
7-Sep-00	10.14	15-Nov-00	7.48	29-Jan-01	8.19
8-Sep-00	9.96	16-Nov-00	7.91	30-Jan-01	8.49
11-Sep-00	9.42	17-Nov-00	7.73	31-Jan-01	8.53
12-Sep-00	9.48	20-Nov-00	7.79	1-Feb-01	8.73
13-Sep-00	9.3	21-Nov-00	8.51	2-Feb-01	8.52
14-Sep-00	9.17	22-Nov-00	8.63	5-Feb-01	8.57
15-Sep-00	8.93	24-Nov-00	8.45	6-Feb-01	8.26
18-Sep-00	8.87	27-Nov-00	9.17	7-Feb-01	8.17
19-Sep-00	8.81	28-Nov-00	9.05	8-Feb-01	7.83
20-Sep-00	8.51	29-Nov-00	8.69	9-Feb-01	8.06
21-Sep-00	8.81	30-Nov-00	8.75	12-Feb-01	8.01
22-Sep-00	8.87	1-Dec-00	9.11	13-Feb-01	7.8
25-Sep-00	8.93	4-Dec-00	9.48	14-Feb-01	7.75
26-Sep-00	8.93	5-Dec-00	8.75	15-Feb-01	7.73
27-Sep-00	9.3	6-Dec-00	9.36	16-Feb-01	8.06
28-Sep-00	8.99	7-Dec-00	9.48	20-Feb-01	7.96
29-Sep-00	9.11	8-Dec-00	9.48	21-Feb-01	8.13
2-Oct-00	8.87	11-Dec-00	8.93	22-Feb-01	8.39
3-Oct-00	8.87	12-Dec-00	8.93	23-Feb-01	8.86
4-Oct-00	8.81	13-Dec-00	8.57	26-Feb-01	9.23
5-Oct-00	8.39	14-Dec-00	8.63	27-Feb-01	9.41
6-Oct-00	8.09	15-Dec-00	9.11	28-Feb-01	9.1
9-Oct-00	8.27	18-Dec-00	9.05	1-Mar-01	9.36
10-Oct-00	8.27	19-Dec-00	9.6	2-Mar-01	9.09

(continues)

Date	PDG	Date	PDG	Date	PDG
5-Mar-01	9.27	15-May-01	10.7	26-Jul-01	9.89
6-Mar-01	8.98	16-May-01	11.26	27-Jul-01	10.17
7-Mar-01	9.21	17-May-01	11.36	30-Jul-01	9.83
8-Mar-01	9.89	18-May-01	11.82	31-Jul-01	9.76
9-Mar-01	9.5	21-May-01	11.75	1-Aug-01	9.65
12-Mar-01	9.88	22-May-01	11.41	2-Aug-01	9.62
13-Mar-01	9.86	23-May-01	11.2	3-Aug-01	9.71
14-Mar-01	9.63	24-May-01	10.77	6-Aug-01	9.89
15-Mar-01	9.11	25-May-01	11.28	7-Aug-01	9.77
16-Mar-01	8.69	29-May-01	10.99	8-Aug-01	9.97
19-Mar-01	8.88	30-May-01	10.51	9-Aug-01	10.62
20-Mar-01	8.75	31-May-01	10.33	10-Aug-01	10.52
21-Mar-01	8.86	1-Jun-01	10.62	13-Aug-01	10.98
22-Mar-01	8.74	4-Jun-01	10.68	14-Aug-01	10.59
23-Mar-01	8.61	5-Jun-01	10.82	15-Aug-01	10.98
26-Mar-01	8.72	6-Jun-01	10.24	16-Aug-01	11.03
27-Mar-01	8.45	7-Jun-01	10.22	17-Aug-01	10.89
28-Mar-01	8.42	8-Jun-01	10.67	20-Aug-01	10.74
29-Mar-01	8.21	11-Jun-01	10.4	21-Aug-01	10.91
30-Mar-01	8.4	12-Jun-01	10.72	22-Aug-01	10.73
2-Apr-01	8.22	13-Jun-01	10.76	23-Aug-01	10.81
3-Apr-01	8.71	14-Jun-01	11.19	24-Aug-01	10.86
4-Apr-01	9.1	15-Jun-01	10.79	27-Aug-01	10.61
5-Apr-01	9.13	18-Jun-01	10.44	28-Aug-01	10.68
6-Apr-01	9.24	19-Jun-01	10.39	29-Aug-01	10.62
9-Apr-01	9.22	20-Jun-01	10.1	30-Aug-01	10.83
10-Apr-01	9.09	21-Jun-01	9.83	31-Aug-01	10.77
11-Apr-01	9	22-Jun-01	9.82	4-Sep-01	10.5
12-Apr-01	9.32	25-Jun-01	10.1	5-Sep-01	10.88
16-Apr-01	9.41	26-Jun-01	10.42	6-Sep-01	10.57
17-Apr-01	9.2	27-Jun-01	9.97	7-Sep-01	10.58
18-Apr-01	9.45	28-Jun-01	9.55	10-Sep-01	10.82
19-Apr-01	9.46	29-Jun-01	9.51	17-Sep-01	11.44
20-Apr-01	9.26	2-Jul-01	9.37	18-Sep-01	11.8
23-Apr-01	9.25	3-Jul-01	9.46	19-Sep-01	11.92
24-Apr-01	9.34	5-Jul-01	9.49	20-Sep-01	12.68
25-Apr-01	9.08	6-Jul-01	9.48	21-Sep-01	12.99
26-Apr-01	9.68	9-Jul-01	9.48	24-Sep-01	12.4
27-Apr-01	10.02	10-Jul-01	9.76	25-Sep-01	12.39
30-Apr-01	9.82	11-Jul-01	10.1	26-Sep-01	12.68
1-May-01	10.1	12-Jul-01	9.98	27-Sep-01	12.72
2-May-01	10.17	13-Jul-01	9.9	28-Sep-01	12.47
3-May-01	9.78	16-Jul-01	9.71	1-Oct-01	12.75
4-May-01	9.73	17-Jul-01	9.92	2-Oct-01	12.81
7-May-01	10	18-Jul-01	10.36	3-Oct-01	12.25
8-May-01	10.08	19-Jul-01	10.19	4-Oct-01	12.08
9-May-01	10.71	20-Jul-01	10.45	5-Oct-01	12.67
10-May-01	10.65	23-Jul-01	10.59	8-Oct-01	12.37
11-May-01	10.73	24-Jul-01	11.26	9-Oct-01	11.9
14-May-01	10.74	25-Jul-01	10.41	10-Oct-01	11.46

Date	PDG	Date	PDG	Date	PDG
11-Oct-01	11.01	20-Dec-01	10.92	6-Mar-02	10.8
12-Oct-01	11.63	21-Dec-01	10.97	7-Mar-02	10.32
15-Oct-01	11.46	24-Dec-01	10.96	8-Mar-02	10.48
16-Oct-01	11.83	26-Dec-01	10.81	11-Mar-02	10.87
17-Oct-01	11.88	27-Dec-01	10.62	12-Mar-02	11.14
18-Oct-01	11.27	28-Dec-01	10.39	13-Mar-02	10.7
19-Oct-01	11.09	31-Dec-01	10.64	14-Mar-02	10.62
22-Oct-01	10.55	2-Jan-02	10.8	15-Mar-02	10.63
23-Oct-01	10.4	3-Jan-02	11.27	18-Mar-02	11.44
24-Oct-01	10.32	4-Jan-02	11.35	19-Mar-02	11.13
25-Oct-01	10.46	7-Jan-02	11.55	20-Mar-02	11.36
26-Oct-01	10.51	8-Jan-02	11.35	21-Mar-02	11.3
29-Oct-01	10.59	9-Jan-02	11.77	22-Mar-02	11.71
30-Oct-01	11.28	10-Jan-02	11.53	25-Mar-02	12.01
31-Oct-01	11.13	11-Jan-02	11.48	26-Mar-02	11.52
1-Nov-01	11.16	14-Jan-02	11.52	27-Mar-02	12.24
2-Nov-01	11.5	15-Jan-02	11.86	28-Mar-02	11.99
5-Nov-01	11.27	16-Jan-02	11.94	1-Apr-02	12.26
6-Nov-01	11.21	17-Jan-02	11.55	2-Apr-02	11.88
7-Nov-01	11.55	18-Jan-02	11.53	3-Apr-02	11.65
8-Nov-01	10.81	22-Jan-02	11.64	4-Apr-02	11.69
9-Nov-01	11.01	23-Jan-02	11.34	5-Apr-02	11.35
12-Nov-01	10.95	24-Jan-02	11.39	8-Apr-02	11.36
13-Nov-01	10.71	25-Jan-02	11.74	9-Apr-02	10.93
14-Nov-01	10.84	28-Jan-02	11.49	10-Apr-02	11.56
15-Nov-01	10.34	29-Jan-02	11.8	11-Apr-02	11.3
16-Nov-01	10.01	30-Jan-02	11.79	12-Apr-02	11.62
19-Nov-01	9.55	31-Jan-02	12.03	15-Apr-02	11.57
20-Nov-01	9.85	4-Feb-02	12.87	16-Apr-02	11.3
21-Nov-01	9.59	5-Feb-02	13.22	17-Apr-02	11.91
23-Nov-01	9.8	6-Feb-02	12.09	18-Apr-02	11.66
26-Nov-01	9.63	7-Feb-02	13.05	19-Apr-02	11.87
27-Nov-01	10.02	8-Feb-02	12.98	22-Apr-02	11.88
28-Nov-01	10.32	11-Feb-02	12.2	23-Apr-02	11.98
29-Nov-01	10.48	12-Feb-02	12.53	24-Apr-02	12.13
30-Nov-01	10.64	13-Feb-02	12.42	25-Apr-02	12.21
3-Dec-01	10.71	14-Feb-02	12.71	26-Apr-02	12.52
4-Dec-01	10.54	15-Feb-02	12.21	29-Apr-02	12.28
5-Dec-01	10.36	19-Feb-02	11.12	30-Apr-02	11.5
6-Dec-01	10.9	20-Feb-02	11.22	1-May-02	11.67
7-Dec-01	10.5	21-Feb-02	11.83	2-May-02	11.91
10-Dec-01	10.38	22-Feb-02	11.48	3-May-02	12.24
11-Dec-01	10.26	25-Feb-02	11.33	6-May-02	12.41
12-Dec-01	10.52	26-Feb-02	11.94	7-May-02	12.2
13-Dec-01	10.45	27-Feb-02	11.5	8-May-02	12.31
14-Dec-01	10.99	28-Feb-02	11.38	9-May-02	12.38
17-Dec-01	10.76	1-Mar-02	11.34	10-May-02	12.51
18-Dec-01	11.26	4-Mar-02	11.08	13-May-02	12.67
19-Dec-01	10.53	5-Mar-02	10.73	14-May-02	12

(continues)

Date	PDG	Date	PDG	Date	PDG
15-May-02	11.91	11-Jun-02	12.73	8-Jul-02	10.77
16-May-02	12.29	12-Jun-02	12.05	9-Jul-02	11.21
17-May-02	12.67	13-Jun-02	11.68	10-Jul-02	11.1
20-May-02	13.15	14-Jun-02	12.33	11-Jul-02	10.74
21-May-02	13.29	17-Jun-02	11.75	12-Jul-02	10.65
22-May-02	13.59	18-Jun-02	12.2	15-Jul-02	10.28
23-May-02	14.08	19-Jun-02	12.13	16-Jul-02	10.05
24-May-02	13.97	20-Jun-02	12.67	17-Jul-02	9.7
28-May-02	13.94	21-Jun-02	12.44	**18-Jul-02**	**10.28**
29-May-02	13.55	24-Jun-02	12.5	19-Jul-02	10.48
30-May-02	13.41	25-Jun-02	12.34	22-Jul-02	9.55
31-May-02	13.31	26-Jun-02	11.97	23-Jul-02	8.72
3-Jun-02	13.61	27-Jun-02	11.6	24-Jul-02	8.93
4-Jun-02	13.31	28-Jun-02	10.98	25-Jul-02	8.32
5-Jun-02	13.22	1-Jul-02	11.41	26-Jul-02	7.84
6-Jun-02	13.48	2-Jul-02	10.63	29-Jul-02	8.13
7-Jun-02	13.1	3-Jul-02	10.54	30-Jul-02	8.37
10-Jun-02	12.34	5-Jul-02	10.56	31-Jul-02	8.19

Sources: Nasdaq Exchange (Yahoo.com) and ComStock, Inc. (Yahoo.com).

Sources and Suggested Reading

Acampora, Ralph J. *The Fourth Mega Market* (New York: Hyperion, 2001).

Atlas of the World (Pleasantville: Readers Digest Association, 1987).

Bruck, Connie. *The Predators' Ball* (New York: Penguin Books, 1989).

Chancellor, Edward. *Devil Take the Hindmost* (New York: Farrar, Straus & Giroux, 1999).

Cottle, Sidney, Roger F. Murray, and Frank E. Block. *Graham and Dodd's Security Analysis*, 5th ed. (New York: McGraw-Hill, 1988).

Fama, E. F. "Stock Returns, Real Activity, Inflation, and Money." *American Economic Review* 71(4) (1981): 545–565.

Fama, E. F., and K. R. French. "Business Conditions and Expected Returns on Stock and Bonds." *Journal of Financial Economics* 25 (1989): 23–49.

Freud, Sigmund. *Group Psychology and the Analysis of the Ego* (New York: W. W. Norton & Co., 1990).

Galbraith, John Kenneth. *A Short History of Financial Euphoria* (New York: Viking Penguin, 1993).

Graham, Benjamin, and David Dodd. *Security Analysis: The Classic 1940 Edition* (New York: McGraw-Hill, 1962).

Harvey, C. R. "Forecasts of Economic Growth from the Bond and Stock Markets." *Financial Analysts Journal* 45(5) (1989): 38–45.

Homer, Sidney, and Martin L. Leibowitz. *Inside the Yield Book* (Princeton: Bloomberg Press, 2004).

Homer, Sidney, and Richard Sylla. *A History of Interest Rates* (Hoboken: Wiley, 2005).

Ibbotson, Roger G., and Rex A. Sinquefield. *Stocks, Bonds, Bills and Inflation* (Chicago: Ibbotson Associates, 2005).

Kwan, Simon. "Rising Junk Bond Yields." *Federal Reserve Bank of San Francisco Economic Letter*, No. 2001-33 (November 16, 2001). www.frbsf.org/publications/economics/letter/2001/el2001-33.html.

Mackay, Charles. *Extraordinary Popular Delusions and the Madness of Crowds*, 20th ed. (New York: Farrar, Straus & Giroux, 1972).

Meyer, Laurence H. *A Term at the Fed: An Insider's View* (New York: Harper-Collins, 2004).

Moneta, Fabio. "Does the Yield Spread Predict Recessions in the Euro Area?" ECB Working Paper No. 294 (December 2003). http://ssrn.com/abstract=487474.

Montier, James. *Beavioural Finance* (London: John Wiley & Sons Ltd., 2002).

Parker, Virginia Reynolds. *Managing Hedge Fund Risk*, 2nd ed. (London: Risk Books, 2005).

Pettijohn, T. F., II, and B. Jungeberg. "Playboy Playmate Curves: Changes in Facial and Body Feature Preferences across U. S. Social and Economic Conditions." *Personality and Social Psychology Bulletin* 30(9) (2004): 1186–1197.

Pettijohn, T. F., II, and Abraham Tesser. "An Investigation of Popularity in Environmental Content: Facial Feature Assessment of American Movie Actresses," *Media Psychology* 1 (1999): 229–247.

Pettijohn, T. F., II, and M. E. Yerkes. "Miss America Facial and Body Feature Changes Across Social and Economic Conditions." Poster presented at the 16th Annual American Psychological Society Convention, Chicago, Illinois, May 2004.

Siegel, Jeremy J. *Stocks for the Long Run*, 3rd ed. (New York: McGraw-Hill, 2002).

Woodward, Bob. *Maestro: Greenspan's Fed and the American Boom* (New York: Simon & Schuster, 2000).

WEB SITES

www.alphapatriot.com/home/archives/2004/06/16/taste_in_women_connected_to
    _the_economy.php

www.bloomberg.com

www.bloomberg.com/markets/rates/

www.bloomberg.com/markets/rates/index.html

www.cdc.gov/nchs/nvss.htm

www.census.gov/population/socdemo/hh-fam.html

www.census.gov/statab/minihs.html

www.cfainstitute.org

www.clevelandfed.org

www.clevelandfed.org/Research/index.htm; click on: Economic Trends

www.culture-of-peace.info/ppa/chapter10-28.html

www.econstats.com

www.econstats.com/BLS/blsnaa1.htm

www.econstats.com/gdp__a1.htm

www.emlab.berkeley.edu/users/bhhall/papers/BHH essidlect02.pdf

www.etfconnect.com

www.fbi.gov/ucr/ucr.htm

www.federalreserve.gov/releases/h15/data; click on: All historical data files (Zip1.5M)

www.fool.com/mutualfunds/indexfunds/table01.htm

www.globalfindata.com

www.globalfindata.com; click on: Dividend Yield

www.globalfindata.com/gdpusad

www.globalfindata.com/TRUSAGVM.csv (total return index for 10-year note)

www.golftoday.co.uk/news/yeartodate/news99/pebble

www.ibcdata.com

www.lbma.org.uk/2002dailygold.htm

www.marketscreen.com/chart/chart.asp

www.mfea.com

www.mtsu.edu/~sschmidt/methods/project2.html

www.nber.org

www.newyorkfed.org/index.html

www.ny.frb.org/markets/omo/dmm/temp.cfm

www.nytimes.com/2005/01/30/business/yourmoney/30real.html (foreign REITs)

www.papers.ssrn.com/sol3/papers.cfm?abstract_id=487474

www.pbs.org

www.pettijohn@mercyhurst.edu tpettijohn@mercyhurst.edu

www.playboy.com

www.refcopcgsimulated.com/edu/ed_papertrade_register.cgi

www.reitnet.com

www.standardandpoors.com

www.stockcharts.com

www.stockcharts.com/charts/historical/

www.stockcharts.com/charts/YieldCurve.html

www.stocksandnews.com

www.thesun.co.uk

www.treasurydirect.gov

www.vmfa.state.va.us/saralee.html

www.worldgameofeconomics.com/WorldGameNews_GoldPrices.htm

Index

Acampora, Ralph, 96, 121, 128
Advertising, corporate spending on, 184–185
American Forest & Paper Association, 271
Antwerp fair, 296
Arrogance, 109
Art collections, 194–195
Asset allocation, 231–232, 235, 244–245
Asset classes:
   buying, 246
   flow of money through, 286
   hard, 238–244
   mutual funds and, 247, 286–288
   overview of, 233–234
   paper, 235–238
   productivity of, 265
   tailoring of, 285–286
   types of, 234–235
Asset class REITs, 253–254
Averages, monthly, 16
Avon, 267

Baby boom, 172. *See also* Echo boom
Baby bust, 172–173
Background information, 268

Back-of-the-envelope forecasting model, 10–12
Banque Royale, 300–301
Barclays Bank, 260
Baseline approach to asset allocation, 231–232
Bear market:
   federal funds rate and, 351–352
   stealth, 102
Behavioral finance, 96–97
Behavioural Finance (Montier), 96
Benchmarks, 80
BigCharts.com, 122
Bill of Rights, 310–311
Birth rates, 171–174
Black Monday (1987), 45–46, 63–65, 75–76
Blunt, John, 302, 303
Body mass index, 167–168
Bogle, John, 249
Bond market:
   price, yield, and, 7
   returns and, 16–17
   U.S. Treasury and, 10
Bruges fair, 296
Business cycle:
   corporate behavior and, 196
   euro/dollar exchange rates and, 1969–2004, 378

Business cycle *(Continued)*
foreign currencies and, 270–271
industry sector funds and,
250–251
real estate and, 268–270
Business summary of stock, 268
"Buy," definition of, 11
Buy dates:
February 1, 1967, 19
February 1, 1970, 20–21
Gulf War and, 212
January 1, 2001, 29–30
January 2, 1960, 17–18
January 2, 1990, 28
January 2, 1991, 36–37
July 19, 2002, 103–104, 147–148
May 1, 1980, 24–25
November 1, 2001, 37–38
October 1, 1974, 22–23
October 20, 1987, 76
September 1, 1981, 26
September 4, 1998, 76–77
September 20, 2001, 79–80

Call options, 114, 276–277
Calvin Klein ads, 184–185
Capital markets, 313
Cash flow, 33–34
Centex Homes:
Nasdaq, return calculations, and,
1990–2005, 382–388
real estate cycle and, 269–270
Central bank. *See* Federal Reserve
CEO, leadership character traits
and vision of, 271–272
Chancellor, Edward, *Devil Take the
Hindmost*, 295
Charles, Ray, 313
Chartered Financial Analysts
Institute web site, 9
Charting, 95–96
Chicago Board Options Exchange,
108, 115

Civil War, 206–207
Clinton, Bill, 69
Clinton, Hillary, 313
Commercial paper, 33
Commodities, investment in,
239–242
Commodities pools, 278–279
Cornfeld, Bernie, 21, 306
Corporate bonds and quality
spread, 60–61
Corporate spending:
advertising, 184–185
employee benefits and, 191–193
employment rates and, 186–188
lifestyle and, 188–191
management benefits, 193–195
merchandise, outrageous, 195
overview of, 182–183
research and development, 183
Cosmo World, 307
Crash of 1987. *See* Black Monday
(1987)
Crime rates, 179–180
Crowd psychology, 111, 146
Cultural indicators. *See also*
Corporate spending; War and
rumors of war
demographics, 171–180
investment returns and, 212–215
overview of, 225–226
standards of feminine beauty,
159–168

Dark Ages, 295–296
Day trading, 308
Death rates, 174
Democracy, 310–312
Demographic data:
birth rates, 171–174
crime rates, 179–180
death rates, 174
divorce rates, 177–178
marriage rates, 174–177

Dependency ratio, 316
Deregulation, 24
Derivatives:
  call options, 276–277
  description of, 265, 275–276,
    290–291
  futures contracts, 277–278
  professional managers, 278–279
  put options, 277
Devil Take the Hindmost
  (Chancellor), 295
Distant early warning (DEW) line,
  40
Diversity of population, 316–317
Divorce rates, 177–178
Domestic ETFs, 260–261
Dow, Charles, 94, 98
Dow Jones Industrial Average:
  advancing issues in, 103–104
  components of, 98–99
  description of, 99–100
  finding, 101
  July 18–19, 2002, 355
  returns when adding, 104–106
  terrorist attacks and, 102
  usage of, 101, 147
Dow theory, 100–101

Echo boom, 173, 316
Economic forecasting:
  as art, 157–158
  Hollywood faces and, 160–162
  Miss America contest and,
    166–168
  model for, 10–12, 61–62
Economic growth:
  predictions for, 91–93
  rates, 1930–2003, 170
  yield spread and, 12
Economic Trends, 11
Economy:
  federal funds rate and, 72–73
  money supply and, 72

EconStats web site, 56
EDGAR Online web site, 269
Education, commitment to,
  314–315
Emerging economies and quality
  spread, 66–67
Employee benefits, 191–193
Employment rates:
  as cultural indicator, 186–188
  war and, 202–203
Equities:
  bottom-up selection of, 271–272
  interest rates and, 237–238
  top-down selection of, 266–271,
    285
Equity exchange-traded funds,
  260
Equity mutual funds, 249–253
ETFConnect web site, 263
Euro/dollar exchange rates and
  U.S. business cycles,
  1969–2004, 378
Exchange-traded funds (ETFs):
  equity, 260
  fixed-income, 260–261
  foreign currency, 263–264
  gold bullion, 261–262
  overview of, 259
  real estate, 261
Extraordinary Popular Delusions
  and the Madness of Crowds
  (Mackay), 297
Eyes and economic times, 161, 162,
  163

Faces, in Hollywood, 160–162
Federal funds rate:
  during bear markets, 351–352
  investing with, 74–81
  overview of, 70, 71–72
  predictions of, 72–74
  size of changes in, 75
  trading results and, 80–83

Federal National Mortgage
    Association, 270
Federal Reserve:
  back-of-the-envelope forecasting
    model, 10–12
  Black Monday (1987) and, 75–76
  as central bank, 70
  chairman of, 69
  creation and destruction of
    money by, 71
  open market operations, 70–71
  primary dealers and, 70
  Russian default on bonds and,
    76–77
  terrorist attacks and, 77–80
  web site, 16, 33
Federal Reserve Bank of
    Cleveland, 11, 15
Feminine beauty. *See* Standards of
    feminine beauty
Fidelity Nasdaq index fund
    (ONEQ), 260
Fidelity Spartan 500 Fund
    compared to Fidelity Value
    Strategies Fund, 252, 253
Fixed-income exchange-traded
    funds, 260–261
Fixed-income mutual funds,
    247–249
Fixed-income securities, 236,
    266
Fleiss, Heidi, 306
Foreign currencies:
  business cycle and, 270–271
  inflation and, 242
  security selection and, 273–275
Foreign currency ETFs, 263–264
The Fourth Mega Market
    (Acampora), 96
Freud, Sigmund, 96–97, 108
Fundamental economics:
  interest rates, 4–5
  supply and demand, 3–4

Future, investment themes for,
    318–319
Future earnings, 267
Futures contracts, 277–278

Galbraith, John Kenneth, *A Short
    History of Financial
    Euphoria*, 301
Gates, Bill, 272
GDP (gross domestic product) and
    war, 199, 201, 361–366
Genetic vigor, 316–317
Global Financial Data, Inc., 54
Gold:
  international gold funds, 256
  investment in, 239–242
  model portfolio and, 242–244,
    262
  Nasdaq return calculations and,
    1974–2004, 379
  year-end prices of, 1800–2004,
    375–376
Gold bullion ETFs, 261–262
Goldman Sachs, 260–261
Gold mining mutual funds, 254–255
Gold mining stocks, 273
Gold standard for investment
    returns, 34
Golf clubs, 193
Government securities, yield on, 5
Greenspan, Alan, 69, 91
Gross domestic product (GDP) and
    war, 199, 201, 361–366
*Group Psychology and the
    Analysis of the Ego* (Freud),
    96–97, 108
Growth, economic:
  predictions for, 91–93
  rates, 1930–2003, 170
  yield spread and, 12
Growth stocks, 252–253
Grubman, Jack, 308
Gulf War, 36–37, 211–212

Hard assets:
  gold and other commodities,
    239–244
  1960–2005, 287
  real estate, 238–239,
    272–273
Hawaii (Michener), 316
Health care benefits, 191–192
Hedge funds, 278–279
Histogram:
  description of, 132
  MACD line and, 133–134
  momentum and, 135, 136
  VIX, put/call ratio, and, 135–136,
    137
Housing prices:
  changes in, 1970–2004, 373
  inverted yield curve and,
    238–239
Hrabak, Josephine, 311–312,
    319–320
Hryb, Greg, 123

Immigration, 316, 317
Individualism, 312
Industry sector funds, 250–252
Industry sector REITs, 254
Inflation:
  acceptable, 91
  crime rates and, 179
  definition of, 204
  divorce rates and, 178
  foreign currencies and, 242
  money supply and, 72
  stagflation, 17
  war and, 204–205
Interest rates. *See also* Federal
    funds rate
  asset allocation and, 235
  competitive bidding and, 71
  economic strength and, 72
  equities and, 237–238
  importance of, 4–5

on margin accounts, 140
on Treasury bonds, 43
International ETFs, 260
International financial markets,
    46–47, 65
International mutual funds,
    255–256
International Paper, 271
International REITs, 256
Internet bubble, 47–48, 49
Investment returns:
  bond market and, 16–17
  Chapter 2 calculations, 334
  Chapter 3 calculations, 347
  Chapter 7 calculations, 353
  Chapter 9 calculations, 356
  Chapter 19 calculations, 371
  cultural indicators and, 212–215
  Dow Jones Industrial Average,
    adding, 104–106
  gold standard for, 34
  including gold, 1974–2004, 377
  including U.S. Treasury bills,
    1960–2004, 374
  money market curve and,
    38–40
  Parts One through Three, 283
  Part Three calculations, 372
  performance summary,
    228–230
  with technical analysis,
    148–150
  with yield curve, 30–31
Investment themes for future,
    318–319
Investment trusts, 304–305
Investor confidence:
  in bonds, 60–61
  in emerging economies, 66–67
Investors, behavior of, 101–102
Investor's Business Daily, 14
Investors Overseas Services, 21,
    306

Iraq, War in:
  S&P 500 index and, 369, 370
  stock market and, 215–216
IShares Dow Jones U.S. Real
    Estate ETF, 261

Japan, in 1980s, 307
Jets, private, 193–194
Junk bonds, 63, 306–307

Khosla, Vinod, 313
Knowledge workers, 313
Korean War, 209–210

Law, John, 299–301
Leadership character traits and
    vision, 271–272
Lehman Brothers, 261
Leipzig fair, 296
Leverage:
  margin debt and, 140–141,
    142–143
  market extremes and, 140
  market moves and, 141–142
  options and, 276–277
  overview of, 139, 153–155
  roaring 1920s and, 304
  short sales and, 141, 144
Life insurance companies,
    53
Lifestyle, corporate,
    188–191
Liquidity and mutual funds,
    258
Log scale, 12–13
Long-term bond and recession,
    89–90
Long-Term Capital Management,
    47, 65, 76, 141, 351
Long-term government bond
    funds, 248–249
Luxury items, 195

MACD (moving average
    convergence/divergence)
    line:
  histogram of, 133–134
  overview of, 130–133
Mackay, Charles, *Extraordinary
    Popular Delusions and the
    Madness of Crowds*, 297
Management benefits, 193–195
Managing Hedge Fund Risk
    (Reynolds), 279
Maneta, Fabio, 8–9
Mann, Catherine L., 319
Margin debt:
  description of, 140
  finding information on, 142
  movement of, 142–143
  S&P and, 155
Market bottoms, 102–103
Market breadth, 220
Market cycle, 87–88. *See also*
    Business cycle
Markets, seduction of, 85
MarketScreen.com, 122
Market Technicians Association
    web site, 96
Marriage rates, 174–177
Masonite, 270
McDonald's, 267
Medieval fairs, 296
Merchandise, outrageous, 195
Mexican-American War, 206,
    207
Michener, James, *Hawaii*, 316
Milken, Mike, 306–307
Miss America contest, 166–168
Mississippi Company, 299–301
Mob psychology, 111, 146
Model portfolio:
  gold and, 242–244, 262
  S&P or Nasdaq and gold,
    261–263, 288

three-month Treasury bills and, 236–237

yield curve and, 84–85

Momentum, 135

Money:

creation and destruction of by Federal Reserve, 71

supply of, 72

Money market curve:

investment returns and, 38–40

normalization of, 35–38

Money market mutual funds, 248

Money market securities:

commercial paper and, 32–33

U.S. Treasury bills and, 34–35

Monthly averages, 16

Montier, James, *Behavioural Finance* (Montier), 96

Moody's Investors Service BAA medium-grade quality index, 62

Mortgage loan, refinancing, 238

Mortgage rates, importance of, 4

Motorola, 102

Moving average:

finding, 122

importance of, 122

as lagging indicator, 130

overview of, 121–122, 152–153, 154

S&P graph with, 127–128

using, 122–126

volatility index with, 126–127

Moving average convergence/divergence (MACD) line:

histogram of, 133–134

overview of, 130–133

Mutual Fund Education Alliance, 247

Mutual funds:

asset classes and, 247, 286–288

equity, 249–253

fixed-income, 247–249

gold mining, 254–255

international, 255–256

limitations of, 258

in 1960s, 305–306

real estate, 253–254

S&P 500 index compared to, 108

Nanotechnology, 318

Nasdaq:

Centex return calculations and, 1990–2005, 382–388

composite, 1984–2005, 380–381

gold and return calculations, 1974–2004, 379

Placer Dome return calculations and, 1990–2005, 389–396

National Bureau of Economic Research, 171, 183

National character, 312–314

Natural resources, 317–318

Neiman Marcus Christmas catalog, 184

Newmont Mining, 273–274

New York Stock Exchange web site, 142

Oil embargo, 21, 22–23

ONEQ (Fidelity Nasdaq index fund), 260

Open market operations, 70–71

Open society, 312

Options:

call, 114, 276–277

as indicator of market sentiment, 114–115

put, 114–115, 277

Orleans, Duke of, 300, 301

Outsourcing, 319

Paper assets:
  1960–2005, 287
  yield curve analysis and, 235–238
Pebble Beach golf course, 307
Penn Central Railroad, 20–21
Pension plans, 53, 192
Performance summary, 228–230
Placer Dome:
  Nasdaq, return calculations, and,
    1990–2005, 389–396
  performance of stock in,
    273–275, 289–290
Playboy magazine standards of
    beauty, 162–166, 357–360
Population, 315–317
Portfolio guidelines, 56–57
Primary dealers, 70
Product delivery, 267
Profit margin, 267
Put/call ratio:
  critical values for, 116–117
  finding, 115–116
  histogram and, 136, 137
  options and, 114–115
  overview of, 113–114, 151–152
  record as indicator, 117–119
  volatility of, 115, 116
Put options, 114–115, 277

Quality spread:
  Black Monday (1987) and, 63–64
  emerging economies and, 66–67
  as forecasting stocks, 61–62
  in 1998, 65–66
  overview of, 60–61
  speculative bonds and, 64–65,
    348–350

Real estate. *See also* Housing
    prices
  business cycle in, 268–270
  foreign, 256
  investment in, 238–239

  in Japan, 307
  loans for, 44–46
  mortgage rates, importance of,
    4
Real estate ETFs, 261
Real estate investment trusts
    (REITs), 253–254, 256, 272–273
Recession:
  crime rates and, 179–180
  definition of, 171
  federal funds rate and, 73
  government and, 10
  long-term bond and, 89–90
  in 1980s, 16
  in 1991, 61
  ten percent return on long-term
    security and, 56
  in 2001, 37
Refco brokerage firm, 277–278
Refinancing mortgage loan, 238
REIT Growth and Income Monitor
    web site, 272
REITnet web site, 272
Religion, need for, 311
Renaissance, 296
Repurchase agreement, 77
Research and development,
    corporate spending on, 183
Return for stocks:
  long-term expected, 55–56
  portfolio benchmark, 53–55
Returns on investment:
  bond market and, 16–17
  Chapter 2 calculations, 334
  Chapter 3 calculations, 347
  Chapter 7 calculations, 353
  Chapter 9 calculations, 356
  Chapter 19 calculations, 371
  cultural indicators and, 212–215
  Dow Jones Industrial Average,
    adding, 104–106
  gold standard for, 34
  including gold, 1974–2004, 377

including U.S. Treasury bills,
    1960–2004, 374
money market curve and, 38–40
Parts One through Three, 283
Part Three calculations, 372
performance summary, 228–230
with technical analysis, 148–150
with yield curve, 30–31
Reynolds, Virginia Parker,
    Managing Hedge Fund Risk,
    279
Roaring 1920s, 304–305
Rogers, Jim, 318
Roman Republic, 294–295
Rumors of war. *See* War and
    rumors of war
Russell 2000 index, 164, 357
Russia, investment in, 46–47, 48,
    65, 76–77

Sahinoz, Earkin, 15
Sara Lee, 194–195
Schwarzenegger, Arnold, 313
Sector funds, 250–252
Security selection:
    equities, bottom-up, 271–272
    equities, top-down, 266–271, 285
    fixed-income, 266
    foreign currencies, 273–275
    hard assets, 272–273
    overview of, 265–266, 279,
        289–290
Sell dates:
    August 1, 2000, 29
    December 1, 1978, 23–24
    July 1, 1969, 19–20
    June 1, 1973, 21–22
    November 1, 1980, 25
    October 31, 1989, 27
    September 1, 1966, 18
Separation of church and state, 311
*A Short History of Financial
    Euphoria* (Galbraith), 301

Short sales:
    description of, 141
    finding information on, 142
    movement of, 144
    S&P and, 155
Short-term securities and money
    markets, 32–33
Siegel, Jeremy, *Stocks for the Long
    Run*, 55
Signing bonus, 193
Smart badges, 318–319
Smoothing returns, 279
Social Science Research Network
    web site, 9
South Sea Company, 302–303
S&P and margin debt: 1992–2004,
    224
S&P and short interest, 224
Spanish-American War, 208
S&P dividend yields: 1871–2002,
    55
Speculative bond spreads (Ba1 and
    lower rated), 1991–2003,
    348–350
S&P 500 index: 1960–2005:
    graph, 2, 229
    trades including cultural
        indicators, 214
    trades indicated by yield curve
        and technical analysis, 105,
        149
    trading with the yield curve,
        technical analysis and cultural
        indicators, 282
    trading with yield curve analysis,
        82
    with yield spread, 13
S&P 500 index funds, 249–250
S&P 500 index (SPX):
    buying, 108–109
    Civil War and, 207
    Gulf War and, 211–212
    Korean War and, 210

S&P 500 index (SPX) *(Continued)*
  monthly Playmates and,
    1982–2004, 358–360
  Playmate of the Year, Russell
    2000 index, and, 1960–2000,
    164, 357
  put/call ratio and, 114
  unemployment rates and, 187,
    189
  Vietnam War and, 211
  war and, 1800–2004, 206,
    367–368
  War in Iraq (1990–1991) and, 369
  War in Iraq (2002–2003) and, 370
  War in Iraq (2002–2005) and,
    215–216
  World War I and, 208
  World War II and, 209
  with yield curves, 1960–2004,
    322–333
S&P graph with moving averages,
    127–128
Spread. *See also* Quality spread
  economic forecasting and,
    11
  speculative bond (Ba1 and
    lower rated), 1991–2003,
    348–350
  U.S. Treasury bill, 1960–2004,
    335–346
  yield, 13–14
S&P returns for 200 years, 54
S&P with histogram:
    March–November 2002, 223
St. Germain fair, 296
Stagflation, 17
Standard & Poor's Depositary
    Receipts, 259, 260
Standard & Poor's web site, 266
Standards of feminine beauty:
  Hollywood faces and, 160–162
  measuring, 159–160
  men's ideals of, 168

Miss America contest and,
    166–168
  Playboy magazine and, 162–166,
    357–360
Stanley Works, 270
Stealth bear market, 102
Stewart, Martha, 308
StockCharts.com, 14–15, 110, 122,
    134
Stock market. *See also* Dow Jones
    Industrial Average; Nasdaq;
    S&P 500 index (SPX)
  bond quality spread and, 61–62
  Calvin Klein ads and, 185
  employment rates and, 186–188
  federal funds rate and, 74
  Playboy magazine and, 162–166
  return for, 53–56
  spread and, 11
  war and, 205–212
Stocks for the Long Run (Siegel),
    55
StreetTracks Gold Shares (GLD),
    261
Style index funds, 252–253
Supply and demand trade-off,
    3–4

Taxes and mutual funds, 258
Technical analysis:
  advancing issues in Dow and,
    103–104
  behavioral finance and, 96–97
  charting, 95–96
  overview of, 94, 146–147,
    220–225
Technology, willingness to use,
    313–314
Telecom bubble in 1990s,
    308
Ten-year note total return:
    1960–2004, 354
  for 200 years, 54

Ten-year Treasury notes:
importance of, 42–43, 48–49
ten percent return on, 51–53, 56
trading, 57–59
Terrorist attacks, 37, 77–80, 102
Theocracy, 311
Thirty-year Treasury bonds:
inversion and, 43–44
reinvestment rate for, 42–43
Three-month Treasury bills, 34,
236–237
Trade dates. *See also* Buy dates;
Sell dates; Trade dates on
graph
Part One, 85
Parts One through Three,
280–285
Part Two, 148
rationale for, 284–285
updated, 212–213
Trade dates on graph:
August 1, 2000, 29
December 1, 1978, 23–24
February 1, 1967, 19
February 1, 1970, 20–21
January 1, 2001, 29–30
January 2, 1960, 17–18
January 2, 1990, 28
January 2, 1991, 36–37
July 1, 1969, 19–20
June 1, 1973, 21–22
May 1, 1980, 24–25
November 1, 1980, 25
November 1, 2001, 37–38
October 1, 1974, 22–23
October 31, 1989, 27
September 1, 1966, 18
September 1, 1981, 26
Trades indicated by yield spread,
13–14
Trade summary, 226–228
Trading against crowd, 107
TreasuryDirect web site, 266

Trend followers, 138, 139
Tuition reimbursement, 192–193
Tulip mania, 297–299

U.S. Treasury bills:
as benchmark, 34–35
returns including, 1960–2004,
374
spreads, 1960–2004, 335–346
U.S. Treasury securities, 266
U.S. Treasury yield curve. *See*
Yield curve

VA Linux Systems, 29
Value stocks, 253
Vesco, Robert, 306
Vietnam War:
baby boom and, 173
stock market and, 210–211
Volatility index (VIX):
finding, 110
histogram and, 135–136, 137
importance of, 110
with moving averages, 126–127
overview of, 107–108, 150–151
put/call ratio compared to, 115,
116
using to trade against crowd,
110–112
when high, 110
when low, 109
Volcker, Paul, 91

Wall Street Journal, 14, 33,
142
Wall Street stories:
excessive 1980s, 306–307
go-go 1960s, 305–306
overview of, 294
roaring 1920s, 304–305
telecom bubble in 1990s, 308
twentieth-century bubbles,
304

Wal-Mart, 267
War and rumors of war. *See also specific wars*
  economy and, 198–199, 201
  employment rates and, 202–203
  gross domestic product and, 361–366
  inflation and, 204–205
  in nineteenth century, 199–200
  overview of, 197–198
  S&P 500 index and, 367–368, 369, 370
  stock market and, 205–212
  in twentieth century, 200–202
  in twenty-first century, 202
War of 1812, 205–206
Web sites:
  American Forest & Paper Association, 271
  Chartered Financial Analysts Institute, 9
  Dow Jones Industrial Average, 98–99
  EconStats, 56
  EDGAR Online, 269
  ETFConnect, 263
  exchange-traded funds, 259
  Federal Reserve, 16, 33
  Federal Reserve Bank of Cleveland, 11
  Federal Reserve Bank of New York, 70
  Global Financial Data, Inc., 54
  ibcdata.com, 248
  Market Technicians Association, 96
  Motley Fool, 250
  for moving averages, 122
  Mutual Fund Education Alliance, 247
  National Bureau of Economic Research, 183

New York Stock Exchange, 142
Refco brokerage firm, 277–278
REIT Growth and Income Monitor, 272
REITnet, 272
Social Science Research Network, 9
Standard & Poor's, 266
StockCharts.com, 14–15, 110, 122, 134
TreasuryDirect, 266
Winfrey, Oprah, 313
Work ethic, 314
World War I, 208
World War II, 208–209

Yahoo.com, 122
Yield, definition of, 5
Yield curve:
  abnormality in, 32–33
  application to model portfolio, 84–85
  average since 1952, 92
  benchmarks for, 90
  commercial paper, 33
  description of, 3, 5
  finding, 14
  flow chart with, 244–245
  forecasting ability of, 10–12
  height of, 16–17
  inverted, 7–8, 43–44
  long-term portion of, 41–50
  normal, 6–7
  predictions and, 8–9
  returns on trades using, 30–31
  shape of, 5–6
  short-term portion of, 32–40
  S&P 500 index and, 1960–2004, 322–333
  summary of, 84
Yield curve analysis, 218–220
Yield spread, 13–14

About the Author

Deborah J. Weir, CFA, is president of Wealth Strategies, a firm that does marketing for traditional money managers and hedge funds. She is a Chartered Financial Analyst and is the first woman president of the Stamford CFA Society. She holds an MBA in Finance from New York University and a BS degree in Education from Miami University in Oxford, Ohio. Prior to founding Wealth Strategies in 1986, Ms. Weir managed institutional fixed-income portfolios at Scudder Investments, now Deutsche Bank. She has almost 30 years of investment experience.

Ms. Weir contributes to *Futures* magazine and *Active Trader* and lectures at investment organizations, colleges, and universities.

You can reach her at debweir@wealthstrategies.bz, www.wealth strategies.bz, and her blog http://timingthemarketblogspot.com.